NORTHWEST
WINE
COUNTRY

WASHINGTON • OREGON • IDAHO
UPDATED PROFILES & RATINGS • MAPS & TOURISM

RONALD HOLDEN
GLENDA HOLDEN

D0048410

NORTHWEST WINE COUNTRY was first published in 1986.
This revised and updated edition, with new maps, published in 1989.

Also by Ronald and Glenda Holden:

 Touring the Wine Country of Oregon
 Touring the Wine Country of Washington

10 9 8 7 6 5 4 3 2

International Standard Book Number: 0-910571-04-X

Published and distributed by: Holden Pacific, Inc.
                               814 35th Avenue
                               Seattle, WA 98122-5206
                               Tel & Fax (206) 325-4324

Acknowledgements

  This book would not have been possible without the assistance of
hundreds of men and women working in the wineries and in the wine
country; we gratefully acknowledge their cooperation, hospitality,
and support.

Credits

Maps: May Bice
Copy editor: Miriam Bulmer
Cover concept and design: Glenn Harrington
Editorial assistants: Kathryn & Peter Conte, Lynne Hess
Production assistants: Deb Figen, Phyllis Counts
Office: Monica Mortimer-Lamb, Ambroise Guige, Janet Lyson

CONTENTS

"Wine rejoices the heart of man, and joy is the mother of virtue."
— Goethe

"With wine . . . we eavesdrop on the murmurings of the Earth and are grateful." — Matt Kramer

"Wine is the pleasantest subject in the world to discuss. . . . It brings you into friendly contact with some of the most skillful and devoted craftsmen, the most generous and entertaining hosts you will find anywhere." — Hugh Johnson

AUTHORS' FOREWORD

This guidebook, designed as a broad overview for tourists and consumers of Northwest wine alike, raises two basic questions.

First, why aren't the ratings "the same" as other writers' evaluations? Second, how can we "do this" to our friends in the industry?

The short answer: this is an independent book, not an industry handout.

Ratings first. Our judgments are based on experience (writing about wines since 1976, and about Northwest wines specifically since 1981) and personal preference (influenced, no doubt, by our travels). If we flatter ourselves into thinking we have "educated palates," they're hardly parochial; we regularly lead wine tours to France and Australia in addition to destinations around the Northwest. Still, we doubt that anyone has tasted as many Northwest wines (over 500) as carefully and analytically as we have over the past six months. Usually six wines at a time, in our home-office, always blind, devoting full attention to each wine, taking extensive notes. Privately, not at the tasting room counter of the winery, where the beaming winemaker pours Reserve wines for VIP visitors. Attentively, not like some festivals where the judges pride themselves on speeding through six flights of 10 wines in a morning.

Many wines were "donated" by the wineries. We requested samples, and many wineries complied. That's a standard practice in any industry; book reviewers get free books, too. If a major winery didn't send samples, for whatever reason, we purchased their wine. Our ratings had nothing to do with a winery's willingness to donate samples of wine, however. If we didn't have recent experience with the wines, or couldn't find them at retail in Seattle, we didn't rate them.

Why aren't our ratings substantially the same as other writers'? Shucks, they're not even the same as in our previous edition! Wines change; surely you all know that. It's a living, breathing substance. Taste the same bottle a year from now and (as long as you don't refer to your earlier notes, as long as you don't peek at the label), your opinion will be different. Taste this year's release and we guarantee it won't be the same as last year's. The weather was different, the harvest later, the winery bought grapes from a different grower, the winemaker moved, the barrels were older (or newer); a thousand things change from one year to the next. Some wineries get better, some don't; some cope well with change, others don't. We're most interested (as are most consumers) in identifying the consistently good wineries.

What about the other writers? We read what they say, but we don't copy what they write. Glenda Holden is the "front-line" palate at our tastings, and our own sensory impression is the only one we use. The ratings in this book reflect these personal judgments, not those of *The Wine Advocate, Northwest Palate,* or *The Wine Spectator.*

If we disagree with a widely read critic, consider it like the counterpoint in a piece of music. If all wines were simple, there'd be no need for reviews; there wouldn't be more than four or five flavors to review, and consumers wouldn't need guidance. Besides, the critics usually do agree on the great wines, the Best of Show and Grand Award winners.

Remember, though, that you put the wine to *your* nose and into *your* mouth. It's *your* palate that the wine must ultimately please, not the reviewer's. Beauty and pleasure are in the eye (and mouth) of the consumer.

As for **tourism**: we've always been convinced that Northwest wineries can create new customers, new markets right here at home, through effective promotion as tourist destinations. Our first guidebooks, in fact, enthusiastically promoted all wineries, without discriminating between chateaus and shacks, between the welcome of friendly winemakers and the sneers of surly staff, between wine that was nectar and wine that was noxious.

But the quality of the wine isn't always the same as the quality of the visit; we rated them on separate scales.

Most wineries answered our detailed, annual questionnaires. We didn't ask for confidential business information, but for personal and anecdotal material to make the profiles more interesting to read.

• We let winemakers and winery owners correct their profiles from previous editions.

• We asked them to contribute a short essay, called "A Word from the Winery," which we edited only for spelling.

• We asked them for labels, and for samples of their current releases.

It isn't difficult for the reader to figure out which wineries were most helpful to the project—not on the basis of their ratings, which were arrived at independently of their cooperation—but by the amount of substance in the profiles. Some hold news conferences and issue press releases; others send long letters, photocopies of clippings, or a promotional brochure; some, unfortunately, send nothing at all. If we didn't hear from a winery after several mailings and telephone calls, we figured they weren't in business anymore.

Some of our friends in the industry will be upset by their ratings. They may feel we betrayed their trust. Not so. We are journalists and winemaking is a federally regulated, public business. You can discuss industry gossip "off the record," but you can't put current releases "on background''; a spoiled bottle of Chardonnay says infinitely more than "no comment." Mature wineries (and, we hope, most readers) will recognize and appreciate this book's purpose: to tell the story of the Northwest wine industry as it moves into a new decade, as we know it, as we taste it.

Ronald & Glenda Holden
Seattle, April 15, 1989

HOW TO USE THIS BOOK

Every active, licensed winery in the three Northwest states is profiled. We've included some background on the winery, a description of a visit to the winery, an evaluation of the wines, directions to the winery, its hours of operation, and a description of special events.

In addition, each winery was asked to send us a short promotional statement. Most (but not all) wineries took advantage of this opportunity.

Maps are designed to help the reader navigate from a nearby freeway. We assume that a standard highway map will get you to the general area.

For suggestions on where to eat and where to stay, we have been highly subjective. Other guidebooks provide far more extensive listings. Our preference in restaurants is for places operated by the owners, and places with a commitment to local wines.

Bed and breakfast establishments are mushrooming in and around the wine country, and have their own guidebooks, so we haven't listed every B&B. Besides, although some people find the personal welcome at most B&Bs attractive, others find it restrictive. Sometimes you like to be pampered, sometimes left alone to hang out beside a motel pool. Sometimes you can afford luxury, sometimes inexpensive lodging hits the spot.

Based on our own experience, reports from readers, and recommendations from the local wineries, we've suggested a bit of everything.

The profiles include ratings (described more fully a bit further on) for visits and wine quality.

The ratings are relative. We have ranked nearly 150 wineries as a separate group, not in comparison to Chateau Margaux or Domaine Chandon. If you're planning a wine tour out of Portland, you want to know which wineries make the best visits in Oregon, not in Burgundy. If you're trying to decide which Northwest wine to buy in the store, you don't want ratings of 1982 Bordeaux.

Readers and winemakers may not always agree with the ratings. If we wanted to flatter our friends, we'd give everybody four-star ratings. But that would make this book into bland propaganda; instead, we hope its critical tone mirrors the bracing acidity of Northwest wine and provides a refreshing perspective.

KEY TO THE RATINGS

QUALITY OF WINE:

NR	No rating: not tasted at all or not tasted recently; no releases
★	Barely drinkable
★☆	Occasionally acceptable
★★	Uneven
★★☆	Usually good
★★★	Good
★★★☆	Usually superior
★★★★	Consistently superior

These ratings are given for a winery's overall wine production. Many wineries have occasional outstanding wines (gold medal winners, or wines that receive a high individual score from a magazine). We're looking for more: predictable, consistent results. Students can get an A on a term paper but a B for the course if they do poorly on the final exam. To carry the analogy one step further, a student has to do consistently outstanding work to merit an A+; that's the rating, ★★★★, that we reserve for the region's best wineries.

We've been following most of the wineries in this book for nearly a decade, and the blind tastings we've done for this edition were only the latest factors we took into account. Some wineries have slipped, some are better now than two or three years ago. We looked for consistently improving wines.

We also looked for value. High quality at every price point was our standard. Overpriced wines were downgraded.

It's usually easier for a winemaker to produce only one or two wines, and to make only small quantities. Some of our highest ratings went to wineries with only one wine. But a few wineries can and do make a broad range of wines very well (Hogue, Ste. Michelle), and sell them at moderate prices. If these folks can do it, everybody ought to be able to.

As a general rule, brand-new wineries didn't get ratings as high as established ones; they don't have a track record. One spectacular vintage doesn't make a four-star winery; consistency does.

We looked for "clean" wines. The occasional, fluky gold medal won't make up for flawed winemaking.

However, our ratings reflect our personal tastes, and you, our readers, may well disagree with us. It's quite likely that the wines you taste won't be the same ones we tasted; vintages change, wine evolves. That's the wonderful thing about wine.

WINERY VISITS:

NR	Not rated: tasting room not open, no visiting
★	Don't bother
★★	Moderately interesting
★★★	Worth a detour
★★★★	Worth the trip

We rated the visits on a number of factors:

• First and foremost, the quality of the welcome a visitor receives. Small, family-run wineries are almost always the best bet, simply because it's so hard to motivate tasting-room employees, to instill in them the feeling that "they are the winery" to visitors. All too often, winery staffers behave like bored sales clerks. The enthusiasm of people who own or manage the winery is infectious, and makes the wine taste better, too!

• The quality of the information provided to visitors. A hearty "Hey there, friend, how about tryin' some wine!" doesn't make sense if the person pouring the wine doesn't know anything about the product, the winery, the industry, the region. Again, owners do best.

• The winery's setting. How attractive is the scenery? How pleasant is the drive? We're trying to advise people traveling halfway across the state to visit the wine country that Winery A is in a cinderblock garage and Winery B is surrounded by hillside vineyards with a panoramic view.

• The tasting room itself. Is it a corner of the toolshed, a private living room, or a grand space? Does the winery stock a selection of wine-related souvenirs, artwork, local travel literature, wine books? Winery gift shops can bustle like busy boutiques or languish like empty department stores, depending on the skill of the tasting-room manager.

• The wines available for tasting. Are they properly handled? Are they kept fresh, or are they old and tired? Are they too cold (a common fault when wines are stored in a refrigerator between visitors)? Or too warm? Granted that state law regulates how much wine may be poured free of charge, but there's a perceptible difference between a dribble of wine and a one-ounce pour. Are spittoons or dump buckets provided? If crackers are offered, are they overly salty? Does the winery pour its better wines or only two or three of its cheapest? (And then charge up to $1 to taste the "good stuff"?) Does the winery treat the tasting room as a dumping ground for its discards, or as an opportunity to show visitors to something new. The best recent example of the latter was a "vertical" tasting at Chateau Ste. Michelle of Cabernet Sauvignon from the 1977, 1978, and 1984 vintages, introducing tens of thousands of visitors to its best red wines.

We were gratified to receive dozens of letters from readers about their visits to wineries around the Northwest. Some told of lovely visits, some told stories that would make your hair curl. We've incorporated many of these reports into our profiles

Finally, we'd like to point out that your visit may be significantly better (or worse) than our ratings. A sunny day and a pleasant attitude (yours and the winery's) can make all the difference.

RATINGS RECAP

We'll save you the trouble of leafing through the book. Here's how we rated the wineries in each category.

WASHINGTON VISITS

Wineries in Washington can be located amidst vineyards or in urban areas. No satellite tasting rooms are permitted under state law; a producer must license and bond any additional "tasting room" as a totally separate winery.

★★★★: Bainbridge Island, Chateau Ste. Michelle (Woodinville), Columbia, Columbia Crest, Kiona

★★★☆: Arbor Crest, Champs de Brionne, Covey Run (Zillah), Hogue, Latah Creek, Salishan, Snoqualmie

★★★: Bonair, Cascade Crest (Seattle), Cascade Mountain, Chateau Gallant, Chateau Ste. Michelle (Grandview), Chinook, Langguth, L'Ecole No. 41, Mercer Ranch, Mount Baker, Neuharth, Pontin Del Roza, Quilceda Creek, Staton Hills (Wapato), Stewart, Paul Thomas, Whidbeys, Woodward Canyon

★★☆: Covey Run (Kirkland), Facelli, French Creek, Gordon, Grant's, Hooper, Horizon, Hyatt, Johnson Creek, Lost Mountain, Preston, Quarry Lake, Staton Hills (Seattle), Tucker, Vierthaler, Waterbrook, Worden

★★: Blackwood, Bookwalter, Cascade Crest (Sunnyside), Coolen, Coventry Vale, Hinzerling, Hoodsport, Mont Elise, Oakwood, Yakima River, Zillah Oakes

★: Fidalgo, Foote, Hunter Hill

OREGON VISITS

Oregon wineries tend to be modest establishments located amidst vineyards. Wineries on highways or in towns are in the minority, although state law allows wineries to maintain up to two satellite tasting rooms if they want to get more exposure.

★★★★: Elk Cove, Rex Hill, St. Josef, Yamhill Valley

★★★☆: Bethel Heights, Montinore, Ponzi, Shafer, Tualatin

★★★: Alpine, Chateau Benoit, Forgeron, Girardet, Glen Creek, Henry Estate, Hinman, Hood River, Knudsen Erath, Pellier, Shallon, Siskiyou, Sokol Blosser, Veritas

★★☆: Airlie, Amity, Ankeny, Arterberry, Ashland Vineyards, Bridgeview, Broadley, Clear Creek, Cooper Mountain, Hidden Springs, HillCrest, Honeywood, Laurel Ridge, Nehalem Bay, Oak Knoll, Schwarzenberg, Serendipity, Silver Falls, Three Rivers, Tyee, Valley View, Wasson Brothers, Weisinger's

★★: Adams, Callahan Ridge, Ellendale, Eola Hills, Evesham Wood, Foris, Oak Grove, Ponderosa, Witness Tree

★: Henry Endres, Rogue River

IDAHO VISITS

★★★☆: Ste. Chapelle

★★★: Rose Creek

★★☆: Weston

★★: Pucci

WASHINGTON WINE

Ratings are based on the overall quality, value, and consistency of a winery's production.

★★★★: Chateau Ste. Michelle, Hogue, Leonetti, Quilceda Creek, Woodward Canyon

★★★☆: Barnard Griffin, Columbia, Kiona, Latah Creek, Neuharth, Snoqualmie, Paul Thomas

★★★: Arbor Crest, Bainbridge Island, Cascade Crest, Chinook, Columbia Crest, Covey Run, Facelli, Gordon, Grant's, Hoodsport, Langguth (including Saddle Mountain), Mercer Ranch, Redford, Salishan, Staton Hills, Stewart, Waterbrook, Whidbeys

★★☆: Bonair, Bookwalter, Chateau Gallant, L'Ecole No. 41, Mont Elise, Pontin Del Roza, Quarry Lake, Salmon Bay, Worden, Zillah Oakes

★★: Cascade Mountain, Champs de Brionne, Coventry Vale, French Creek, Horizon's Edge, Lost Mountain, Mount Baker, Oakwood, Preston, Tagaris, Tucker, Yakima River

★☆: Hooper, Hunter Hill, Johnson Creek, Seth Ryan

★: Fidalgo, Foote, Vierthaler

OREGON WINE

This is our rating of Oregon wineries on the basis of their overall production, including Pinot Noir. (Pinot Noir alone is considered in the next list.)

★★★★:   Adelsheim, Amity, Eyrie, Ponzi, Wasson
★★★★ (Spirits):   Clear Creek
★★★☆:   Adams, Arterberry, Cameron, Elk Cove, Knudsen Erath, Yamhill Valley
★★★:   Alpine, Bethel Heights, Girardet, Henry Estate, Montinore, Panther Creek, Rex Hill, Shafer, Siskiyou, Valley View
★★☆:   Autumn Wind, Forgeron, HillCrest, Honeywood, Laurel Ridge, Oak Knoll, St. Josef, Serendipity, Sokol Blosser, Tualatin, Tyee, Veritas
★★:   Airlie, Ankeny, Broadley, Chateau Benoit, Ellendale, Evesham Wood, Foris, Glen Creek, Hinman, Pellier, Shallon, Three Rivers
★☆:   Callahan Ridge, Eola Hills, Schwarzenberg
★:   Henry Endres, Nehalem Bay

OREGON PINOT NOIR

Oregon Pinot Noir presents a special case. Some wineries with inconsistent overall achievement excel at Pinot Noir. Here is our list of the top Pinot Noir producers in Oregon. (In the profiles, the Pinot Noir rating is reported only if it is better than the overall rating.)

★★★★:   Adelsheim, Amity, Eyrie, Knudsen Erath, Ponzi, Wasson
★★★☆:   Adams, Arterberry, Cameron, Elk Cove, Yamhill Valley
★★★:   Bethel Heights, Girardet, Henry Estate, Montinore, Oak Knoll, Panther Creek, Rex Hill, St. Josef, Shafer, Siskiyou, Veritas

IDAHO WINE

★★★:   Rose Creek, Ste. Chapelle
★★☆:   Indian Creek
★★:   Camas
★☆:   Pucci

WASHINGTON'S WINE TOURING REGIONS

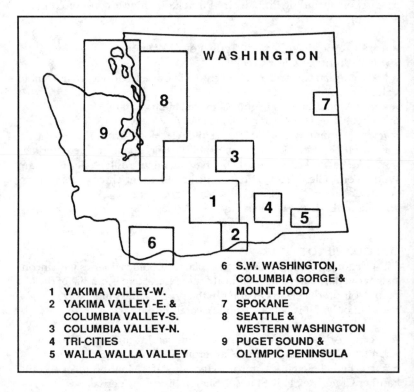

WASHINGTON

1 YAKIMA VALLEY-W.
2 YAKIMA VALLEY -E. &
   COLUMBIA VALLEY-S.
3 COLUMBIA VALLEY-N.
4 TRI-CITIES
5 WALLA WALLA VALLEY

6 S.W. WASHINGTON,
   COLUMBIA GORGE &
   MOUNT HOOD
7 SPOKANE
8 SEATTLE &
   WESTERN WASHINGTON
9 PUGET SOUND &
   OLYMPIC PENINSULA

Washington, at the northwestern tip of the United States, is divided north-to-south by the Cascade Mountains, a volcanic chain that includes the infamous Mount St. Helens. A few vineyards have been planted in western Washington, where the climate is cool, like that of Germany or southern England or even the Loire Valley in France. But most of the grapes are grown in the temperate desert of eastern Washington, where irrigation from a series of canals and from the mighty Columbia River allows growers to control with precision the irrigation of their vineyards.

Washington state grows more wine grapes (15,000 acres of vinifera in production) and makes more wine (3 million gallons in 1988) than any other state except California. The vines (which outnumber the state's pear trees) cover three distinct appellations, or federally designated growing areas: the Columbia, Yakima, and Walla Walla valleys. For those who care where a wine is grown, an appellation is an assurance of quality; for those whose interest is the selling of wine, a premium appellation (like Yakima, or Napa) can add as much as $10 to the value of the wine.

For additional information about the Washington wine industry, contact the Washington Wine Institute at 1932 First Avenue, Suite 510, Seattle, WA 98101. Phone (206) 441-1892. This is the wineries' trade association; the public is eligible for associate membership ($25). The state-sponsored Washington Wine Commission is at the same address.

YAKIMA VALLEY

The Yakima Valley bears little physical resemblance to the famous winegrowing region around California's historic town of Napa, yet it's frequently cited as the nation's "next" Napa Valley.

Mount Adams presides in the western distance. A cloudless sky arches between the low ridge of the Rattlesnake Hills, lying like a crumpled blanket to the north, and the spine of the Horse Heaven Hills to the south, a skulking, almost reptilian mass.

Between the ridges spreads the soft, green underbelly of the Yakima Valley, Washington's most fertile land, pulsating with the vitality brought by irrigation and the endeavors of man. Here, almost hidden among the pear and apple orchards, almost unseen amidst the asparagus, hops, and mint, grow over half the state's premium vinifera grapevines.

Well over a dozen wineries and a hundred vineyards have taken root in the Yakima Valley at this writing; many more are expected. No more need "wine touring" imply a trip to Europe or California. Wine country is here.

A missionary, Father Charles Pandosy, introduced irrigation and agriculture to the Indian tribe, the Eyakima ("well-fed people"), who lived here a century ago. (The Yakima Indian Nation encompasses roughly half the valley today.) The meager natural rainfall grew sagebrush and wildflowers in the desert sand, but a four-foot layer of volcanic loam and clay below the surface retained the water—drawn from irrigation ditches—and the limestone and pebbles of the prehistoric Yakima River below provided drainage.

With the promise of agricultural development unencumbered by bloody forays and vicious battles, private entrepreneurs in the last century developed a small network of irrigation canals before the federal government took over. Railroads provided access to distant markets for the abundance of fruit and produce flowing from the valley. The Yakima

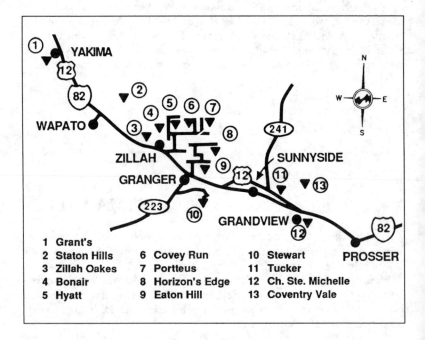

YAKIMA VALLEY (West)

1 Grant's		
2 Staton Hills	6 Covey Run	10 Stewart
3 Zillah Oakes	7 Portteus	11 Tucker
4 Bonair	8 Horizon's Edge	12 Ch. Ste. Michelle
5 Hyatt	9 Eaton Hill	13 Coventry Vale

Valley led the country in the production of apples and pears, and dominated Washington's production of apricots, peaches, sugar beets, asparagus, mint, and hops.

This was the first "appellation" in the Northwest, running roughly 50 miles between Union Gap and Kiona. About the size of Alsace, local growers are fond of pointing out. They don't mention that virtually every acre of Alsatian hillside is planted with vineyards. In the Yakima Valley, it's less than one acre in a hundred.

Anyone can admire manicured landscapes and well-kept towns, but it takes an innocent eye to appreciate the splendor of the valley, to admire its rawboned grandeur, and to ignore unsightly piles of litter and junk dotting the valley floor—the equivalent, perhaps, of urban tenements, and hardly fatal to the community's vitality.

The people don't flaunt their prosperity here. The valley's business is agriculture, which is not always pretty, charming, or quaint. You'll find few fine restaurants or fancy residences, few boutiques, no country inns.

YAKIMA VALLEY (East) & COLUMBIA VALLEY (South)

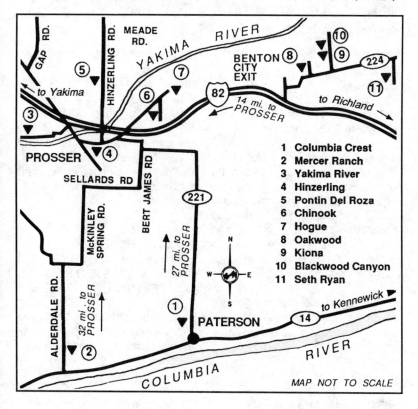

1 Columbia Crest
2 Mercer Ranch
3 Yakima River
4 Hinzerling
5 Pontin Del Roza
6 Chinook
7 Hogue
8 Oakwood
9 Kiona
10 Blackwood Canyon
11 Seth Ryan

MAP NOT TO SCALE

The boutiques and their cousins are the followers, not the precursors of tourism. Follow they surely will. For now, there is, above all, a vast sense of landscape, of distant mountains imposing themselves over the vineyards. It's beautiful country, no doubt about it. The valley's poetry transcends its topography.

Yakima, at the northwestern end of the valley, and the Tri-Cities (Richland, Pasco, Kennewick), at the southeastern end 80 miles away, are cities where you will find tourist facilities.

For more information, write to the Yakima Valley Wine Growers Association, P.O. Box 39, Grandview, WA 98930, or contact the Yakima Valley Visitor & Convention Bureau, 19 N. Eighth Street, Yakima, WA 98902. Phone (509) 575-1300.

Yakima Valley:
WINE COUNTRY MEALS & LODGING
Alphabetically by establishment

THE BARN
Wine Country Rd
P.O. Box 324
Prosser, WA 99350
(509) 786-1131 (restaurant)
(509) 786-2121 (motor inn)

The familiar restaurant next to the Prosser airport has spruced up considerably in response to wine country tourism. The menu looks better and better: Friday seafood buffet with oysters, crab legs, and scallops, for $12.95. Barbecued rib buffet for $6.50. New banquet room. All-Washington wine list.

A new motor inn with 28 moderately priced units and two suites is now ready for occupancy. Outdoor swimming pool, video arcade, cable TV, bike rentals.

BIRCHFIELD MANOR
2018 Birchfield Rd
Yakima, WA 98901
(509) 452-1960

Stately house on outskirts of town where Wil Masset serves prix fixe menu (weekends only): one seating Friday and Sunday, two on Saturday. Be on time! Truly impressive Washington wine list (62 labels) and cellar (400 choices).

Five beautifully furnished guest rooms, all with private bath, $55 to $75 per couple. Big breakfast included.

DESERT ROSE
18170 Highway 24
Moxee, WA 98936
(509) 452-2237

A country manor not far from Yakima with bed-and-breakfast accommodation. Not just for tourists, there's an office for business travelers, and a fishing pond for visitors who'd rather relax.

DYKSTRA HOUSE
114 Birch Ave
Grandview, WA 98930
(509) 882-2082

It's a National Historic Site, open daily for lunch (dinner Saturday by appointment). Yakima Valley wine list, good prices.

EL RANCHITO
1319 E. First Ave
Zillah, WA 98953
(509) 829-5880

Uncompromisingly, joyfully Mexican. Tortilla factory in the back, Mexican groceries, rosary beads, antique shop in front, along with fragrant take-out. Try the barbacoa or menudo. All day, every day.

EXTRA SPECIAL PANTRY
214 S. Sixth St
Sunnyside, WA 98944
(509) 837-5875

Popular spot for lunch (Monday through Saturday), with great sandwiches using Yakima Valley cheese. Local wines at retail plus $1 corkage.

GASPARETTI'S
1013 N. First St
Yakima, WA 98901
(509) 248-0628

Dinner house with great variations on traditional Italian dishes, fine pastas, veal, scrumptious desserts. A fine Washington wine list. Closed Sunday, Monday.

GREYSTONE
5 N. Front St
Yakima, WA 98901
(509) 248-9801

Rack of Ellensburg lamb is the specialty; always a good variety of seasonal foods. Dinner Tuesday through Saturday, with piano music in the lounge after 7 p.m. Yakima Valley bottlings.

ICHIBAN
1107 Tieton Dr
Yakima, WA 98902
(509) 248-2585

Not much choice on the wine list (Saddle Mountain only), but where else in the Yakima Valley can you get sushi?

RINEHOLD CANNERY HOMESTEAD
530 Gurley Rd
Rte 1, Box 1117
Granger, WA 98932
(509) 854-2508

B&B adjacent to Eaton Hill Winery; two bedrooms, one bath. $50 double includes full breakfast.

RIO MIRADA
1603 Terrace Heights Dr
Yakima, WA 98901
(509) 457-4444

Moderately priced motel along riverfront, just off freeway. Some kitchens. Exercise facilities.

SANTIAGO'S
111 E. Yakima Ave
Yakima, WA 98907
(509) 453-1644

"Gourmet" Mexican menu on the second floor of an old Yakima theater. Yakima Valley wines and Grant's beers.

SELAH MINING COMPANY
204 E. Naches Ave
Selah, WA 98942
(509) 697-6128

Prime rib, lobster, Alaskan salmon. Dinner nightly from 5 to 10 p.m., with eastern Washington wines.

SQUEEZE INN
613 First Ave
P.O. Box 214
Zillah, WA 98953
(509) 829-6226

Where the elite meet to eat in Zillah. Good steaks, serious interest in the community's wine producers.

TUDOR GUEST HOUSE
3111 Tieton Dr
Yakima, WA 98902
(509) 452-8112
(509) 453-6015

B&B in turn-of-the-century residence with five guest rooms sharing two baths. Grand bridal suite in old servants' quarters. Beautiful grounds, close to downtown.

VALLEY CAFE
105 W. Third
Ellensburg, WA 98926
(509) 925-3050

A happy place: great breakfasts, fine selection of pasta. Retained and enhanced its original 1930s decor. Open daily.

COLUMBIA VALLEY (North)

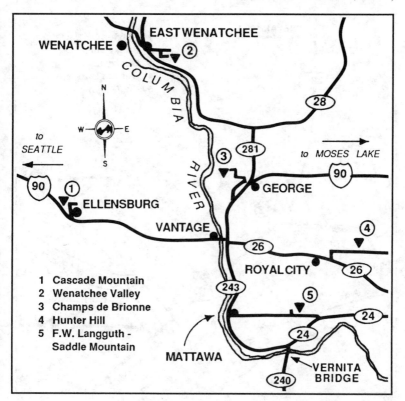

1 Cascade Mountain
2 Wenatchee Valley
3 Champs de Brionne
4 Hunter Hill
5 F.W. Langguth -
  Saddle Mountain

COLUMBIA VALLEY

This is Washington's largest appellation, encompassing both the Yakima and Walla Walla regions, as well as the huge expanse of the Wahluke Slope. Virtually all of eastern Washington's vineyards fall into this appellation, which was sponsored by Chateau Ste. Michelle.

The northern portion of the valley is known as the Wahluke Slope; see the profiles of the F.W. Langguth winery and Champs de Brionne for details on the geography.

The Tri-Cities dominate the southern part of the region, which includes a growing number of smaller wineries in addition to Columbia Crest (at Paterson) and the various Chateau Ste. Michelle vineyards. The Hanford Reservation, site of nuclear reactors and energy research, is just north of Richland; the work force is being cut back, but the region is still heavily populated with engineers and technical specialists. Tourist amenities include major and regional motel chains; the Tri-Cities area is popular for

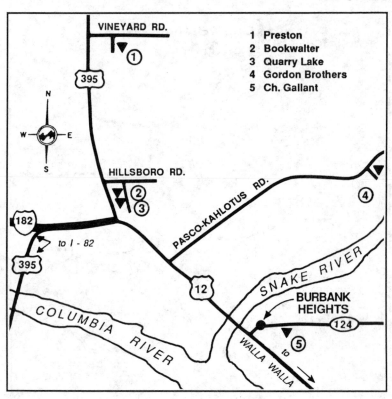

statewide conventions and conferences.

For details, contact the Tri-Cities Visitor & Convention Bureau at (509) 735-8466, or toll-free at (800) 835-0248.

Tri-Cities:
WINE COUNTRY MEALS & LODGING

Alphabetically by establishment

BLUE MOON
21 W. Canal Dr
Kennewick, WA 99336
(509) 582-6598

An ambitious new restaurant from the folks at Leo's Catering, well-known in the Tri-Cities. Five-course meal with four entree choices on Friday at 7:30 p.m. and Saturday at 7 p.m. Open Tuesday through Thursday only for groups of 10 or more. Nice linens and dishes, good Northwest wine list, a favorite with local vintners.

CAVANAUGH'S
1101 N. Columbia Center Blvd
Kennewick, WA 99336
(509) 783-0611
(800) THE-INNS (reservations)

Elegant convention complex near Columbia Center shopping mall. Recently refurbished rooms. Small pool, sauna, spa. Restaurant promotes Washington wines.

EMERALD OF SIAM
1314 Jadwin Ave
Richland, WA 99352
(509) 946-9328

EMERALD OF SIAM II
8300 Gage Boulevard
Kennewick, WA 99336
(509) 783-6214

Authentic Thai food provides a note of originality on the Tri-Cities culi-nary landscape. Ravadi Quinn is a gracious hostess. Washington wines, with Kiona highlighted.

GIACCI'S
94 Lee Blvd
Richland, WA 99352
(509) 946-4855

Friendly, hardworking couple offer a variety of homemade Italian specialties. Not a pizza joint. Lunch menu served weekdays till 7 p.m.

HOLIDAY INN
1515 George Washington Wy
Richland, WA 99352
(509) 946-4121

Refurbished property with indoor pool and sauna (great in colder months). Washer and dryer, tennis courts, nonsmoking rooms, moderate prices. Standup comedy acts (often hilarious) in the lounge nightly, free for guests.

MISTY'S
Red Lion Motor Inn
2525 N. 20th
Pasco, WA 99301
(509) 547-0701

Upscale dinners with the best "dining atmosphere" in the Tri-Cities, good choice of Northwest wines.

WALLA WALLA VALLEY

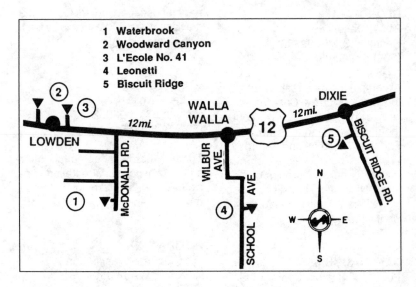

Walla Walla itself is a quiet city with many fine old homes on tree-lined streets and pleasant parks for urban picnics. The Whitman College campus, close to downtown, is a fine place for a stroll. There's a good deli in town (Merchant's, Ltd.), and a fine restaurant a short drive away (Patit Creek, in Dayton).

The Walla Walla Valley was first associated with the Lewis and Clark passage westward, then with medical missionary Marcus Whitman, who was massacred in an Indian raid in 1847. Today the mission is a National Historic Site, with trails and a visitor center. Locally grown Walla Walla onions are sweet enough to eat like apples.

But it's the grape-growing climate that's turning Walla Walla into a center for wine touring. Darcey Fugman-Small, a county land-use planner married to Woodward Canyon Winery's Rick Small, helped draw up a petition to the Bureau of Alcohol, Tobacco, and Firearms that designated the Walla Walla Valley as a separate wine-growing appellation.

Walla Walla Valley:
WINE COUNTRY MEALS & LODGING
Alphabetically by establishment

MERCHANT'S LTD.
21 E. Main St
Walla Walla, WA 99362
(509) 525-0900

Breakfast daily (brunch on Sunday), lunch Monday through Saturday, dinner Wednesday through Saturday. Also a wine shop and deli.

PATIT CREEK RESTAURANT
725 E. Dayton Ave
Dayton, WA 99328
(509) 382-2625

Best French restaurant in eastern Washington prospers in this tiny community half an hour outside Walla Walla. Bruce Hiebert cooks like a man possessed (a good sign). Nineteen-forties art deco atmosphere. Heather Hiebert does desserts. Twelve-page wine list. Open for lunch and dinner, Tuesday through Saturday (except Saturday lunch). Prices moderate by big city standards.

REES MANSION
260 E. Birch St
Walla Walla, WA 99362
(509) 529-7845

Georgian colonial B&B with two guest rooms. $65 includes large breakfast.

Restaurant seats 52 in living room, dining room and library; lunch and dinner served Tuesday through Saturday. All-Washington wine list.

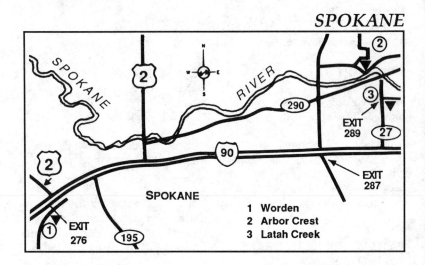

The city of Spokane isn't a viticultural area at all; it's too cold in winter. But four wineries have chosen to locate their facilities here, so visitors to the Lilac City are in for a treat.

Spokane, Washington's second largest city, is the hub of a region called the Inland Empire, a land of lumber, fishing, and mining, whose commercial strength is based on Idaho's silver mines, high-country wheat fields, and the financial, retail, and medical community that has grown up around this economy.

The leisure attractions of Spokane today include dozens of lakes and rivers suitable for boating, rolling hills for hunters and hikers, steep slopes for skiers. Spokane is an Indian word meaning "children of the sun," and the city receives twice as much sunshine, it's said, as does Seattle.

Riverfront Park, the site of Expo '74, is as pleasant an urban space as one could hope for, with 100 acres of undulating meadows, a turn-of-the-century carousel, and the splendid splash of Spokane Falls. Manito Park, with its rose gardens, overlooks the city from the South Hills. A Lilac Festival is held every May, kicking off with a footrace called the Bloomsday Run, with as many as 40,000 participants.

Downtown shopping in Spokane is a treat, with 10 blocks of the central business district linked by the nation's second-largest system of glass-enclosed skywalks. There's a shiny new convention center, and many older buildings have been restored to a high level of elegance. It's clearly a town where tradition matters. There are occasional moments, where a street curves past a Victorian building, with the Spokane River in the background, when the place looks downright European.

For more information about Spokane, write to the Spokane Regional Convention & Visitor Bureau at W. 301 Main, Spokane, WA 99201, or call (509) 624-1341.

Spokane:
WINE COUNTRY MEALS & LODGING
Alphabetically by establishment

AMLETO'S
W. 259 Spokane Falls Blvd
Spokane, WA 99201
(509) 456-7410

Carefully presented Italian specialties, muted decor, in a strategic location opposite the convention center. Large selection from Spokane
wineries. Parking available next door
(no mean trick).

CAVANAUGH'S INN AT THE PARK
W. 303 North River Dr
Spokane, WA 99201
(509) 326-8000

CAVANAUGH'S RIVER INN
N. 700 Division
Spokane, WA 99202
(509) 326-5577
(800) THE-INNS (reservations)

Two fine hotels, centrally located.
The Inn at the Park is newer and
spiffier, the River Inn more moderately priced.

THE COEUR D'ALENE RESORT
Coeur d'Alene, ID 83814
(208) 765-4000

Developer Duane Hagadone's version of Disneyland-on-the-lake.
Glitzy, luxurious resort tower on
Lake Coeur d'Alene, an hour's drive
east of Spokane. Booked months
ahead with conventions, tours.

Beverly's restaurant probably has
the best wine list between Seattle
and Chicago.

FOTHERINGHAM HOUSE
W. 2128 Second Ave
Spokane, WA 99204
(509) 838-4363

Sue Holter opened Spokane's first
B&B with this 100-year-old, antique-
filled house five years ago. Three
rooms, one with private bath, in a
quiet neighborhood of grand old
homes. (The original Fotheringham
was the contractor for Patsy Clark's
mansion across the street.) Prices,
including breakfast, range from $37
to $50.

FOUR SEASONS COFFEE
N. 222 Howard St
Spokane, WA 99201
(509) 747-2315

Luncheon entree changes daily. Northwest wine by the glass. Open 9 to 6, Monday through Saturday.

HOWARD STREET CAFE
N. 221 Howard St.
Spokane, WA 99201
(509) 624-6003

At last! A Northwest wine bar in Spokane. Close to 20 Northwest wines by the glass, more in bottles. Soups prepared from scratch, foccaccio and other breads baked on the premises. Open 11 to 8 Monday through Saturday, with white cloth service at dinner Friday and Saturday.

PATSY CLARK'S
W. 2208 Second St
Spokane, WA 99204
(509) 838-8300

Fine restaurant in a grand old mansion (Patsy Clark was a mining baron) refurbished to Victorian splendor. Setting outclasses the cuisine, but the wine list has many treasures; listen to the sommelier.

RIDPATH HOTEL & MOTOR INN
W. 515 Sprague Ave
Spokane, WA 99204
(509) 838-2711

Older downtown hotel with view restaurant (Ankeny's) on top floor.

COLUMBIA GORGE & SOUTHWEST WASHINGTON; MOUNT HOOD

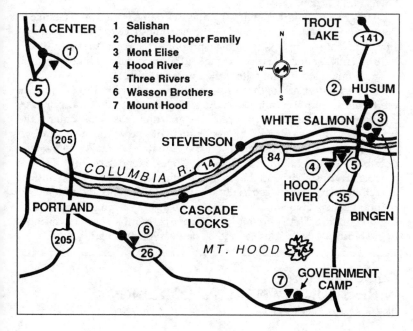

The Columbia ranks fourth among North America's great rivers, behind the Mississippi, the St. Lawrence, and the Mackenzie. It drains a basin that extends from the Rockies to the Pacific Ocean, an area of nearly a quarter-million square miles that reaches into Oregon, Washington, Idaho, and British Columbia. The river has twice the flow of the Nile; 10 times as much water courses through its gorge as the Colorado River sends through the Grand Canyon.

From its headwaters deep in the Canadian Rockies, the Columbia gathers momentum as it winds though the coulees of eastern Washington's dry tableland, its power harnessed by a series of hydroelectric dams.

As it makes its final westward surge from the desert toward the sea, the Columbia carves its way through a basalt chasm known as the Columbia River Gorge. This 60-mile-long canyon, created 15 million years ago by cataclysmic upheavals in the earth's crust, forms a political boundary today that divides Oregon and Washington.

Along the Columbia's upper reaches among sand hills and pines, the plateau Indians flourished in past centuries. Downstream, in the forests of Douglas fir, coastal Indians developed their culture. Both tribes depended on the bountiful Pacific salmon. They would meet at Celilo Falls, an ancient fishing ground at the east end of the Columbia Gorge, to trade:

the hides and baskets made by Indians of the interior for shells and woven bark produced by the coastal tribes. This was the Columbia discovered by Lewis and Clark in 1804.

The great river is tamed now by massive dams from Grand Coulee to Bonneville, its waters monitored by the Northwest River Basins Commission. A bi-state commission has been proposed to protect the Gorge itself. Railroad tracks and a freeway line the southern shoreline, a highway (and, at one point, a log flume) follow the northern shore.

At the western end of the Columbia, between Portland and the ocean, the fertile Columbia Valley permits a variety of agricultural pursuits, from dairy farming to viticulture. Salishan Vineyards at LaCenter is the first winery in this splendid microclimate, with new vineyards nearby.

Upstream, in the Gorge itself, the climate also makes viticulture possible. In the hills above Bingen, Chuck Henderson and Charles Hooper have established vineyards that complement the region's tourist attractions of recreation (especially windsurfing), wildlife, and unmatched natural beauty. Two wineries with vineyards in Washington operate on the Oregon side. The Columbia Gorge is one of the most spectacular sights in the Northwest, and deserves to be on everyone's itinerary.

Columbia Gorge:
WINE COUNTRY MEALS & LODGING
Alphabetically by establishment

COLUMBIA GORGE COUNTRY INNS & BED-AND-BREAKFAST ASSOCIATION
P.O. Box 797
Bingen, WA 98605

Information and brochure about wineries and B&Bs in Hood River, Bingen, The Dalles.

COLUMBIA GORGE HOTEL
4000 Westcliff Dr
Hood River, OR 97031
(503) 386-5566
(800) 826-4027 (in Oregon)
(800) 345-1921 (nationwide)

Expensive lodgings, popular for trysts and getaways, overlooking the Columbia River.

Restaurant menu highlights salmon and sturgeon from the Columbia, plus venison, wild duck, pheasant. Admirable commitment to local wines among the 500 selections. Four-course country breakfast (featuring "honey from the sky") draws crowds but can be overwhelming.

FLYING L RANCH
Rt 2, Box 28
Glenwood, WA 98619
(509) 364-3488

No wine here, but a rustic, peaceful setting on 160 acres with views of Mount Adams. Some of the dozen bedrooms in the lodge share baths. Housekeeping cabins, nature trails. Huckleberry pancakes for breakfast.

INN OF THE WHITE SALMON
172 W. Jewett
White Salmon, WA 98672
(509) 493-2335

Delightful 21-room inn (all private baths) with reasonable prices ($60 double) and views of Mount Hood. Evening "dessert hour" and hot tub for guests. Famed breakfasts ($10 on weekends, $7.50 weekdays).

THE LOGS
Hwy 141 at BZ Corner
White Salmon, WA 98672
(206) 493-1402

Old-fashioned crossroads tavern featuring deep-fried chicken and jo-jos. Close to Hooper winery in Husum.

MOUNT ADAMS CHAMBER OF COMMERCE
P.O. Box 449
White Salmon, WA 98672
(509) 493-3630

Informative brochures about B&Bs in Hood River, Bingen, The Dalles, and Trout Lake.

OLE'S SUPPER CLUB
2620 W. Second St
The Dalles, OR 97508
(503) 296-6708

Obscure but worth seeking out, with superb prime rib and its own wine shop.

SCANDIAN MOTOR LODGE
Columbia Gorge Center
(I-84 Exit 44)
Cascade Locks, OR 97014
(503) 374-8417

Inexpensive, spotless 30-room motel.

STONEHEDGE INN
3405 Cascade Dr
Hood River, OR 97031
(503) 386-3940

Good, plain food served in a romantic turn-of-the-century home. Regional wines.

Additional tourism in Oregon Wine Country section.

SEATTLE & WESTERN WASHINGTON

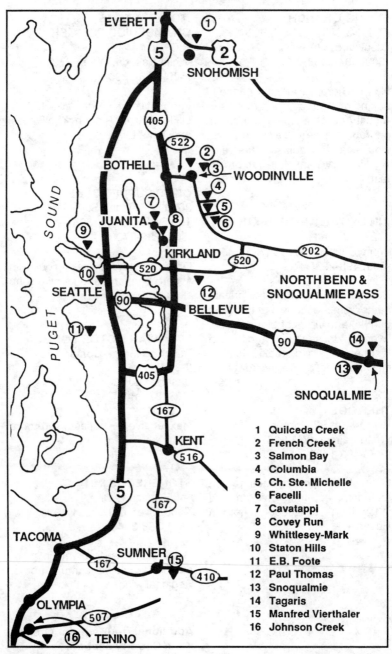

1 Quilceda Creek
2 French Creek
3 Salmon Bay
4 Columbia
5 Ch. Ste. Michelle
6 Facelli
7 Cavatappi
8 Covey Run
9 Whittlesey-Mark
10 Staton Hills
11 E.B. Foote
12 Paul Thomas
13 Snoqualmie
14 Tagaris
15 Manfred Vierthaler
16 Johnson Creek

SEATTLE & WESTERN WASHINGTON

A city, not a winegrowing region, greater Seattle is nonetheless home to quite a few wineries, including the headquarters of Chateau Ste. Michelle, the largest winery in the Northwest.

The old image of wineries as country estates, as half-timbered manor houses surrounded by vineyards and orchards, is romantic but not absolutely accurate. Wineries are essentially factories; grapes are the raw material. (And winemakers are basically factory production managers, but don't tell them.) The glamor of winemaking doesn't disappear in an urban setting, even when the wine is made in an industrial park. After all, the independent vineyards of Burgundy where the grapes are grown may be graced with stone mansions and handsome farmyards, but the famous wines are made by the negociants, who blend and ship the wine from nondescript buildings.

Thus, while Seattle is well over 100 miles from Washington's nearest large-scale vineyards, it's the center of the Northwest's wine industry. The reasons are complex but understandable. Some small-scale winemakers hold other jobs in the area. Some recognize that "farming" isn't their strong suit. Several large wineries prefer proximity to their biggest market rather than to their vineyards. With modern transportation, after all, it's sometimes easier to ship grapes (or freshly pressed must) from the vineyards once a year during harvest than to ship heavy bottles throughout the year.

For more information about visitor facilities in Seattle, contact the Seattle-King County Convention & Visitor Bureau at 1815 Seventh Avenue, Seattle, WA 98101. Or telephone (206) 447-4200.

Tourism listings follow for Seattle and the greater Seattle area.

Seattle:
WINE COUNTRY MEALS & LODGING
Alphabetically by establishment

ALEXIS HOTEL
1007 First Ave
Seattle, WA 98104
(206) 624-4844

A well-heeled, thickly padded, intimate hotel with opulent service.

The Cafe Alexis on the main floor (624-3646) offers excellent light meals, many Northwest wines.

CAFE SPORT
2020 Western Ave
Seattle, WA 98121
(206) 443-6000

Refined, tasty dishes; classic arrangements yet unpretentious. Wine list on computer, regular updates, broad variety.

CHINOOK'S
Fisherman's Terminal
1735 W. Thurman
Seattle, WA 98199
(206) 283-4665

High-energy eatery fronts a sheltered port of swaying masts. Come on Monday night for unlimited tempura-battered fish and chips; drink the Champs de Brionne Brut or the Chinook Sauvignon Blanc.

CUTTERS BAYHOUSE
2001 Western Ave
Seattle, WA 98121
(206) 448-4884

Lively and successful food combinations, bustling crowds, friendly service, terrific view. Good wine list.

ENOTECA
414 Olive Way
Seattle, WA 98101
(206) 624-9108

Only $2 corkage on any retail bottle of wine. Tiny kitchen turns out remarkably good fare. Tapas at the bar.

FOUR SEASONS OLYMPIC HOTEL
411 University St
Seattle, WA 98101
(206) 621-1700

Grand public spaces in this fine old Seattle building. Sumptuous guest rooms, health club, pool.

Choice of restaurants: Garden Court for informal lunch and afternoon tea; Shuckers for seafood; Georgian Room for elegant dining, power breakfasts. This is where Larry Stone worked when he won the title of world's best sommelier in French wines and spirits.

FULLERS
Seattle Sheraton Hotel
1400 Sixth Ave
Seattle, WA 98101
(206) 447-5544

A showcase of Northwest delights: Pilchuck glass, tapestries, paintings by top regional artists, and, not least of all, imaginative food and the best local wines. Smooth PR operation keeps publicity spotlight on the chef (currently Caprial Pence, formerly Kathy Casey).

INN AT THE MARKET
86 Pine St
Seattle, WA 98101
(206) 443-3600

Ideal location at the Pike Place Market; best (and priciest) rooms overlook Puget Sound. Order a room service breakfast, or duck out to the market and buy a croissant and a grand creme.

Campagne restaurant in the Inn's courtyard (728-2800).

KENNEDY HOTEL
1100 Fifth Ave
Seattle, WA 98101

Inexpensive, perfectly adequate lodgings in a prime downtown location. Free breakfast and newspaper, valet parking. Popular with business travelers who don't have expense accounts.

LE TASTEVIN
19 W. Harrison St
Seattle, WA 98109
(206) 283-0991

Seattle's flagship French restaurant, winner of the Wine Spectator's Grand Award for its wine list. Unforgettable dish: Alaskan black cod with pomegranate beurre blanc. Gentle service.

THE OTHER PLACE
96 Union St
Seattle, WA 98101
(206) 623-7340

Robert Rosellini's restaurant survives wrecking ball by changing locations, responding to preference for lighter, less pretentious, and less pricey fare. Vigilant owners, long-time staff, sound suppliers, knowledgeable wine list.

RAY'S (DOWNTOWN)
950 Second Ave
Seattle, WA 98104
(206) 623-7999

Impeccable local seafood . One of the best wine lists in the Northwest. Ray's Boathouse (6049 Seaview N.W., 789-3770) offers similar wines, great waterfront view.

SORRENTO HOTEL
900 Madison St
Seattle, WA 98104
(206) 622-6400

Seattle's most intimate small hotel; hilltop views, mahogany-paneled lobby with fireplace for tea and drinks. Hunt Club restaurant under the vital leadership of Barbara Figueroa. Quality service, very Old Seattle.

Greater Seattle Area:
Alphabetically by establishment

ANTHONY'S HOMEPORT
Moss Bay Marina
Kirkland, WA 98033
(206) 822-0225

Popular group of waterfront restaurants with fresh seafood menu, solid local wine list, marina views. Also in Des Moines, Seattle (Shilshole Bay), Edmonds.

CAFE JUANITA
9702 N.E. 120th Pl
Kirkland, WA 98033
(206) 823-1505

Perennially good Italian food. Caniglio (rabbit) is wonderful with Peter Dow's own Nebbiolo.

THE HERBFARM
32804 Issaquah-Fall City Rd
Fall City, WA 98024
(206) 784-2222

High-end fixed price lunches ($30 plus tax, tip; wine $7 extra) weekends from May through Christmas are booked weeks ahead. Remote country setting with superb garden for pre- or post-prandial amble. Mouthwatering use of fresh garden pickings!

KIRKLAND ROASTER & ALE HOUSE
111 Central Wy
Kirkland, WA 98033
(206) 827-4400

Spit-roasted meats to accompany red wines (Covey Run's Lemberger from next door, for instance). Superb location in strollable waterfront community.

NEW JAKE'S
401 Bellevue Square
Bellevue, WA 98004
(206) 455-5559

Trendy update of "Original Jake O'Shaugh-
nessey's" at Seattle Center, upscale and
honest. Simple but impeccable seafood.
Beverage list highlights local microbreweries and Northwest wineries.

PACIFICA
14450 Woodinville-Redmond Rd
Woodinville, WA 98072
(206) 487-1530

On a grand scale yet informal, this new
"wine country restaurant" gets it right. John
Jorgenson commands the large, open
kitchen, whipping up crustless seafood
quiche and homemade sausages; his sister Kristi manages the front of the house
with precision and warmth. The wine list is
truly "local": Columbia, Chateau Ste. Michelle, Facelli, French Creek, Paul Thomas. No small ambition, no small success.
Bravo!

THE SALISH LODGE
37807 S.E. Fall City-Snoqualmie Rd
Snoqualmie, WA 98065
(206) 888-2556

Expensive lodgings and restaurant adjacent to spectacular Snoqualmie Falls.
Location draws too many gawking tourists
for seekers of privacy, but restaurant wine
list (by Phil deVito of Oregon's Salishan
Lodge) is extensive.

PUGET SOUND & OLYMPIC PENINSULA

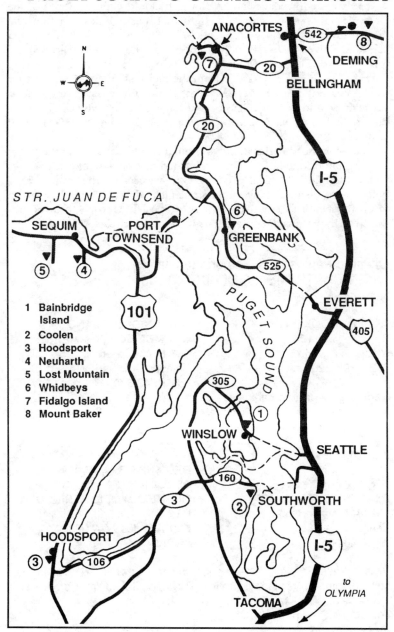

ANACORTES

542

8

DEMING

20

BELLINGHAM

20

I-5

STR. JUAN DE FUCA

SEQUIM

PORT TOWNSEND

6

GREENBANK

525

5   4

EVERETT

405

101

1   Bainbridge Island
2   Coolen
3   Hoodsport
4   Neuharth
5   Lost Mountain
6   Whidbeys
7   Fidalgo Island
8   Mount Baker

7

P U G E T   S O U N D

305

1

WINSLOW

SEATTLE

160

3

2   SOUTHWORTH

HOODSPORT

3   106

I-5

to OLYMPIA

TACOMA

Streams with poetic Indian names trickle down the slopes of the Olympic National Forest toward Highway 101 as it circles the peninsula: the Dosewallips, Humptulips, Quinault, Hoh, Soleduck, and Hamma Hamma. Towns have names like Forks, Sappho, Queets, and Sequim (pronounced "Skwim"). Mount Olympus itself, shrouded in the mists of the rain forest, is rarely visible from the highway; you can get a better feeling for this impressive, 8,000-foot mountain mass during a clear sunset in Seattle. But the full impact doesn't come until you climb the 20-mile road from Port Angeles to the spectacular viewpoint ★★★★ at Hurricane Ridge.

Three of the wineries in this section grow at least some of their own grapes. Bainbridge Island Winery, located just outside of Seattle, does well with Muller Thurgau. Hoodsport Winery uses a variety called Island Belle from a historic vineyard on Stretch Island, and Neuharth grows a few rows of Labrusca (native American grapes). But most of the wine produced on the peninsula comes from grapes grown in eastern Washington.

Olympic Peninsula & Bainbridge Island: WINE COUNTRY MEALS & LODGING

Alphabetically by establishment

ALDERBROOK INN
E. 1701 Hwy 106
Union, WA 98592
(206) 898-2200

Rambling lodge and cabins at water's edge, popular for business seminars and weekend getaways. Restaurant wine list emphasizes Washington wines.

ALICE'S RESTAURANT
19248 Johnson Creek Rd
Tenino, WA 98589
(206) 264-2887

Visit Johnson Creek Winery and stay for dinner, Thursday through Sunday; a grilled rainbow trout is served with every meal. Or come for Sunday brunch.

BAINBRIDGE ISLAND CHAMBER OF COMMERCE
153 Madrone Ln N.
Bainbridge Island, WA 98110
(206) 842-3700

Information on the five B&Bs on Bainbridge Island.

BED AND BREAKFAST ASSOCIATION OF THE OLYMPIC PENINSULA
P.O. Box 1741
Port Angeles, WA 98362
(800) 942-4042

Over a dozen B&Bs in Port Townsend, Sequim, Port Angeles, Forks.

C'EST SI BON
4 mi east of Port Angeles
on Hwy 101
Port Angeles, WA 98362
(206) 452-8888

French classical favorites prepared
and presented by a wonderful couple.
Rose garden.

THE FOUNTAIN CAFE
920 Washington St
Port Townsend, WA 98368
(206) 385-1364

A favorite with the locals but only
two of 20 wines are from the Northwest. Lunch and dinner daily.

LAKE CRESCENT LODGE
On Hwy 101
20 mi west of Port Angeles
HC 62, Box 11 (mail)
Port Angeles, WA 98362
(206) 928-3211

Open May to mid-November, this
nicely maintained lodge offers
marvelous outdoor enticements.
Restaurant.

LITTLE ITALY WEST
Winslow Way at Madison
Bainbridge Island, WA 98110
(206) 842-0517

Great picnic fare to go from this tiny
cafe: pick anything on the menu,
from calzone to veal dishes. Open
daily from 5 to 9:30.

MANOR FARM INN
26069 Big Valley Rd N.E.
Poulsbo, WA 98370
(206) 779-4628

A rural inn of great charm. Six elegant suites (two more share a bath);
two cottages. Dinner (available by
reservation for nonresidents, too)
begins nightly with sherry in the
paneled drawing room at 6:30, and
a two-course meal served at 7 in
the dining room; more lavish dinners Thursday through Sunday.
Gracious English hosts. Comfortable, pretty, to be recommended.

THE OAK TABLE
Third and Bell
Sequim, WA 98382
(206) 683-2179

Apple pancakes, crepes, espresso:
everybody's favorite breakfast
hangout on the peninsula. No wine!

PLEASANT BEACH GRILL &
OYSTER HOUSE
4738 Lynwood Center Rd
Bainbridge Island, WA 98110
(206) 842-4347

Successfully converted island home.
International Evening on Wednesday. You can enjoy your oysters
with Arbor Crest Sauvignon Blanc
or Paul Thomas Dry Riesling here.

SALAL CAFE
634 Water St
Port Townsend, WA 98368
(206) 385-6532

Traditionally famous for breakfast and lunch, now open for dinner on weekends. Features Waterbrook and Tualatin wines.

SALTWATER CAFE
403 Madison St S.
Bainbridge Island, WA 98110
(206) 842-8339

The essence of Bainbridge in summer: ferries, boats, view. Lunch (daily special sheet) and dinner every day, along with Bainbridge Island Winery's Muller Thurgau and other Northwest wines.

STREAMLINER DINER
397 Winslow Way
Winslow, WA 98110
(206) 842-8595

Consistently good down-home food in a funky '50s atmosphere. Saturday-night coffee house with entertainment. Bainbridge Island wines.

THREE CRABS
101 Three Crabs Rd
Sequim, WA 98382
(206) 683-4264

A modest restaurant with a cheery fireplace and a stunning view over the Strait of Juan de Fuca and the Dungeness Spit. Eat fresh cracked crab (what else?) if it's in season, and drink a wine from Neuharth, just up the road.

Bellingham-Whidbey Island:
Alphabetically by establishment

CAPTAIN WHIDBEY INN
2070 W. Captain Whidbey Inn Rd
Coupeville, WA 98239
(206) 678-4097

Romantic, 80-year-old inn made from madrona logs on beachfront overlooking Penn Cove. Cozy interior, stone fireplace, library. Rooms in the lodge share baths; cabins and newer rooms (overlooking quiet lagoon) are self-contained. Popular for small retreats, weekend getaways. Innkeeper John Stone is a genial host. Meals and full bar available; decent selection of Northwest wines.

CHUCKANUT MANOR
302 Chuckanut Dr
Bow, WA 98232
(206) 766-6191

Restaurant with good selection of Northwest wines, plus two-bedroom B&B suites for three or four people ($65 to $80), overlooking Samish Bay and the San Juan Islands.

IL FIASCO
1309 Commercial St
Bellingham, WA 98225
(206) 676-9136

Popular Italian restaurant winning design awards after its recent move to this location. Weekday lunch, nightly dinner. Wine list rotates four Washington labels, also includes Italian and California selections. Lounge, banquet room.

THE INN AT SEMIAHMOO
9565 Semiahmoo Parkway
Blaine, WA 98230
(206) 371-2000

Classy resort on the water, with condos, golf, fine dining.

M'SIEUR'S RESTAURANT
130 E. Champion St
Bellingham, WA 98225
(206) 671-7955

Menu could be described as French-Northwest or Northwest-French. Yummy desserts. Good Washington wine list.

NORTH GARDEN INN
1014 N. Garden St
Bellingham, WA 98225
(206) 671-7828
(800) 922-6414 (inside Washington)

Victorian B&B with 10 guest rooms overlooking Bellingham Bay and the islands. Full breakfast with fresh-ground coffee. Rose garden. Welcoming hosts.

OYSTER CREEK INN
190 Chuckanut Dr
Bow, WA 98232
(206) 766-6179

Unique Northwest wine list with many vintages represented. Impeccably fresh seafood. Same lunch/dinner menu from noon till 9. Prioprietors Mick and Cheryl August used to own the Oyster Bar; Doug Charles is the knowledgeable sommelier.

Also, a lovely guest cottage (rent through the restaurant): $75 per night for two includes champagne and breakfast makings.

RHODODENDRON CAFE
535 Chuckanut Dr
Bow, WA 98232
(206) 766-6667

Fresh seafood, local produce and wines. Lunch on Friday, Saturday; brunch Sunday. Dinners Wednesday through Sunday begin at 4 p.m. Seats 35 indoors, 15 more on deck in summer. Reservations only for groups of five and up.

SCHNAUZER CROSSING
4421 Lakeway Dr
Bellingham, WA 98226
(206) 734-2808
(206) 733-0055

Luxury destination B&B with hot tub, tennis, canoeing. Homegrown blueberries and raspberries with the full breakfasts. Fresh flowers year-round.

WHIDBEY ISLAND
BED AND BREAKFAST ASSOCIATION
PO Box 259
Langley, WA 98260
(206) 321-6272 or
(206) 321-5325

The island is peppered with two dozen unique, high-quality B&Bs. About half are registered with the association.

COLUMBIA VALLEY
SAUVIGNON BLANC
1987

ARBOR CREST

N. 4705 Fruithill Road
Spokane, WA 99207
(509) 927-9463

Owners: David & Harold Mielke
Winemaker: Scott Harris
Year established: 1982
Production capacity: 100,000 gal.
Vineyards: 80 acres
Touring region: Spokane [p. 24]

A bit of background. Dave and Harold Mielke, whose family has owned orchards in the Spokane area almost since the turn of the century, did the Northwest a favor by getting into the wine business. They showed the vision, supplied the capital, and demonstrated the enthusiasm it takes to get a premium winery off the ground: they have made a lot of exceptionally good wine, and managed to get the wine distributed nationwide.

It doesn't detract from the Mielkes' accomplishments to single out the talents of their winemaker, Scott Harris, who was hired after graduating from the fermentation science program at the University of California at Davis. Harris, a tall, sandy-haired, aw-shucks sort of fellow, wasn't awed by the responsibility of running a winery. His first job: to install the equipment from a bankrupt California winery in a former pie-cherry plant on Spokane's outskirts and get the operation running . . . in under six weeks!

Five years later, when the original winery was bulging at the seams with tanks and barrels, Dave Mielke purchased the Riblet Mansion, a historic landmark on a 475-foot cliff overlooking the Spokane River east of town. A new, 100,000-gallon winery is under construction on the bluff behind the house, ready for the 1989 crush, while the imposing, 14-room mansion (renamed the Cliff House) is being renovated and furnished with French antiques as a guest center for people in the wine trade.

Visiting the winery ★★★☆. The only way to get here, when the mansion was built 50 years ago by business magnate Royal Riblet, was by an electric tramway of his own design that wouldn't pass the most rudimentary safety inspection by current standards. Fortunately, there's now a paved road leading up from the banks of the Spokane River. An impressive, panoramic view ★★★★ of the Spokane Valley greets visitors. A pergola (the original tramway landing) and patio make terrific viewpoints. (Riblet, by the way, was a tireless inventor; he filled his house with so many gadgets—such as the region's first electric garage door opener—that he had the highest electric bill in Spokane.) The tasting room, where most visitors are welcomed, has a window to the west, so it makes a particularly nice stop at sunset.

Tasting the wines ★★★. Arbor Crest's reputation was made with Sauvignon Blanc. The first one they made was finished a little sweet, which proved a very palatable foil to the grape's natural herbaceousness. The current vintage (1987) does not have the balance and delicate juniper character of the 1986 (double gold in San Francisco) or the 1985, though. The 1987 Chardonnay smells lightly of vanillin and apple, has good balance, soft texture, and a light, toasty apple finish. The two reds currently available, the 1985 Cabernet Sauvignon and the 1987 Merlot, are black-red wines which suggest an intensity of fruit and flavor that are not fulfilled in the mouth. Perhaps some bottle aging will bring the fruit to life.

From the beginning, all the Arbor Crest wines have been released in distinctly premium packages (long corks, purple ribbons, and embossed labels) that make them very popular in restaurants, where the wine's appearance on the table is an important selling factor. And in competitions, where the package makes no difference, Arbor Crest wins at least as many medals as any Washington winery. Why? Scott Harris is very, very good. And the Mielkes, an old-line Spokane family, have the capital to finance a first-class operation.

Getting there. Take Exit 287 from I-90 and proceed north on Argonne, across the Spokane River, and turn right on Upriver Dr. In 0.5 mi, turn up Fruithill Rd.

Open daily from noon to 5. Visitors under 21 are discouraged due to the hazardous nature of the area surrounding the Cliff House.

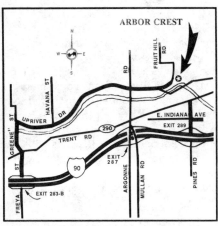

A word from the winery. *"From the beginning, Arbor Crest has had a global view of the wine industry and a determination to make Washington an internationally acclaimed wine region. After establishing a network of distributors throughout the United States, we concentrated our efforts on the expansion of the international marketplace. Because we have exported our wines to Europe, including such famous wine-producing regions as France and Italy, as well as to Pacific Rim countries and others, Arbor Crest was named by the S.B.A. as "1988 Exporter of the Year" for the state of Washington. Our aggressive attitude stems from our belief that Washington's grapes are the finest in the world. We invite you to visit us at the Cliff House and to look for our wines in the best restaurants and wine shops at home and abroad."*

THE COMRADESHIP OF WINE

Spokane's Arbor Crest winery has taken advantage of *perestroika* by importing two popular wines from the Soviet Union.

The wines come from valleys of the Caucasus Mountains in the Republic of Georgia. Lying between the Black and Caspian seas, this region produces the bulk of the Soviet Union's wine.

The Soviet Union, by the way, is the world's third-largest wine-producing nation (after Italy and France). The fertile region north of Tbilisi (capital of the Georgian republic) has a 9,000-year history of cultivating grapes. Indeed the word "wine" is thought to be of Georgian origin.

Most of the grape varieties in the Soviet wines are unfamiliar in the west, and the wines have what Arbor Crest delicately describes as "traditional regional flavors." The Tsinandali is a dry white wine made from Rkatsitei and Mtsvane grapes with three years of oak aging; it reminded us of a barrel-fermented Chardonnay gone wrong. The Mukuzani is a full-bodied, oak-aged (and sour) red made from a variety called Saperavi ($5).

Reaction so far has been mixed. The volatile, oxidized nose and heavy, madeirized flavors of these wines are a far cry from the clean and crisp varieties grown in the Northwest. Some tasters appreciate this style, however; the newly landed Tsinandali and Mukuzani will be the featured house wines at the tony Russian Tea Room in New York.

The difficulty for many consumers is not so much in unfamiliar grape varieties as in the Soviets' antiquated cooperage and winemaking technology. "We'd like to get them to ship the younger, fresher wines," says Arbor Crest's sales manager Joe Algeo. "We're selling them more modern equipment and hope the wines will continue to improve."

Meantime, for its success in selling its own wines overseas, Arbor Crest was named Exporter of the Year by the Small Business Administration; the fine Arbor Crest Sauvignon Blanc is a hit in London and Paris.

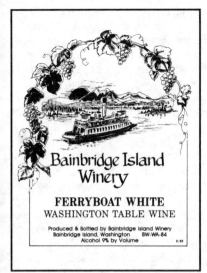

Bainbridge Island Winery

FERRYBOAT WHITE
WASHINGTON TABLE WINE

Produced & Bottled by Bainbridge Island Winery
Bainbridge Island, Washington   BW-WA-84
Alcohol 9% by Volume

BAINBRIDGE ISLAND WINERY

682 State Highway 305 N.E.
Bainbridge Island, WA 98110
(206) 842-9463

Owners: JoAnn & Gerard Bentryn
Winemaker: Gerard Bentryn
Year established: 1982
Production capacity: 6,000 gallons
Vineyards: 5 acres
Touring region: Seattle [p. 30]

A bit of background. A planner with the National Park Service in Seattle, Gerard Bentryn turned down a promotion that would have meant leaving the area; he had planted viticultural roots on Bainbridge Island and wasn't about to leave. To stay, he had to quit his job, and his family hobby became his livelihood.

Gerard's fascination with wine began when he and JoAnn were first married, while he was stationed in Germany with the U.S. Army. His interest became a passion that he pursued with the discipline of his professional training as a climatologist. Posted to Seattle, Gerard discovered on Bainbridge Island the attributes suited to growing the grapes that make German-style wines. Already his vanity license plates read WINE, and he foresees a time when the island becomes as well known for its vineyards as it once was for its strawberries. His own vineyard is planted with Muller Thurgau, Madeleine Sylvaner, Madeleine Angevine, and Siegerrebe. "Every climate is best for something," Gerard says, reminding visitors that the island's climate is almost identical to the Loire Valley and very similar to Germany's Moselle Valley. He is producing German-style wines from locally grown grapes: low alcohol, off-dry, luscious, complex. "We are in a 'cool-climate' growing region, and our style shows a lot of flavor and fragrance in the wine," Gerard says. In fact, one of the judges at the Western Washington State Fair once told Gerard that his wines had too much varietal character!

Visiting the winery ★★★★. Could you imagine a more romantic approach to a winery than on a ferry? Board the boat at the ferry terminal in Seattle, spend half an hour aboard ★★★★ and see the sights: the Seattle skyline recedes, Mount Rainier rises above the cranes on Harbor Island, the snowcapped Olympics guard the western distance, gulls swoop overhead. From the ferry dock in Winslow, it's a 10-minute walk to

Bainbridge Island Winery, perhaps the ultimate cottage winery in Washington, where two acres of grape vines slope gently toward a blue barn under whose gambrel roof you'll find not only a working winery but also a museum of wine artifacts, glassware, and antique bottles. There's a picnic area, too, complete with a fragrance garden, a pet goose named Pâté, and two lovable German Shepherds named Bacchus and Chardonnay. The Bentryns live in a house on the upper end of the vineyards, and a newly built windmill overlooks the entire property. (Even so, it's not a playground!) "We want to be *the* western Washington winery," they say. They're succeeding admirably.

The Bentryns now devote full time to winemaking (the crush has gone from 3,000 gallons in 1982 to 5,000 gallons), and they're proud of the fact that they sell virtually all their wine (except for a few restaurant accounts) only at retail, right at the winery.

Tasting the wines ★★★. The popular Ferryboat White and the estate-bottled Muller Thurgau are two of the winery's most popular products, with beguiling notes of tropical fruit in the nose and flavor. Chardonnay is available in several styles; a wonderful Late Harvest Chardonnay was made one year as a dessert wine. Riesling is available, but the marvelous Siegerrebe won't be (the October rains weren't kind to it). Two unusual wines will be available only in very limited quantities: Washington's first Scheurebe, and a botrytis-affected Late Harvest Pinot Noir, both grown east of the mountains by a friend of the Bentryns. Gerard himself has had good color from Pinot grown on the island and will be planting a couple of acres.

Finally, there's the first strawberry wine produced from the famous Bainbridge Island strawberries, rationed to customers in early December. Because the Bentryns have no distributor markups, Bainbridge Island wines are remarkably good values.

The wines are dry to off-dry, retaining natural sugar. "Sugar's got a bad name, used when there's no taste or bad taste. But it's fine if the wine can carry it, if there's enough fruit and acid, and not as an excuse to cover defects," Bentryn points out. "You can buy acid, you can buy sugar, but you can't buy flavor."

Getting there. From the Winslow ferry terminal, walk or drive 0.25 mi along Hwy 305 to the winery.

Open from noon to 5, Wednesday through Sunday. Tour groups are welcome without charge, but require an appointment.

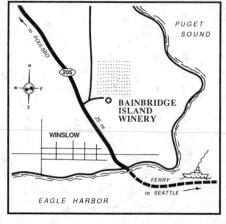

Special events. The winery celebrates its anniversary with an open house every summer on the Sunday nearest August 7. A troop of morris dancers (traditional English folk dancers) performs in the fragrance garden occasionally during the first week in September and at Oktoberfest.

A word from the winery. *"From the mouth of Puget Sound to the headwaters of the rivers flowing into it, Bainbridge Island Vineyard and Winery is the only winery providing Puget Sound residents with locally grown vinifera wines sold only at the winery. As in the small towns of Europe, where one tastes the food and wine grown in the surrounding countryside, our wines provide you with a sense of place—the essence of Puget Sound culture and climate. Our five acres of vineyards can supply only a fraction of the wine consumed in the Seattle area, but, steadily, more people are sharing with us the belief that our locally grown wines are an essential element of Puget Sound living. Grown in daily temperatures virtually identical to those of the Loire Valley of France, our wines are distinctly different from those of hotter regions such as eastern Washington or California. Our local climate produces wines with lower alcohol levels, crisp acidity, and intense varietal character that give our wines their distinctive Puget Sound country flavor. You are welcome to visit us and taste our locally grown wines."*

WESTERN WASHINGTON VITICULTURE

The acreage devoted to wine grapes west of the Washington Cascades is tiny compared to eastern Washington. But the cooler climate also mandates different varieties, cool-climate varieties such as Muller Thurgau, Madeleine Angevine, and Madeleine Sylvaner, that require sunlight (as opposed to direct sunshine) and less heat to reach maturity. Three people have devoted a lot of energy to viticulture in the Puget Sound region: Gerard Bentryn of Bainbridge Island Winery, Al Stratton of Mount Baker Vineyards, and Dr. Robert Norton of the Western Washington Agricultural Research Station in Mount Vernon. Mount Baker has put its emphasis on Madeleine Angevine while Bainbridge Island has led the drive to plant Muller Thurgau. "MT," as it's usually called, was long thought to be a century-old cross between Riesling and Sylvaner, developed by a German viticulturist named Müller. (More recent research indicates it was most likely a cross between two clones of Riesling.) At any rate, it's the most widely planted variety in Germany, forming the basis for many popular wines. In 1981, the German wine industry proudly celebrated the 100th anniversary of the variety by inviting winemakers from around the world to bring their MT to the institute at Geisenheim where MT was developed; it was Gerard Bentryn and Bainbridge Island's Muller Thurgau that represented the United States. Bentryn's latest idea: Pinot Noir from Puget Sound. He's made wine from a few experimental vines and likes the results well enough to plant two acres of Pinot on his Bainbridge Island vineyard.

Washington State
Fumé Blanc
(Dry Sauvignon Blanc)
Barrel Fermented
1984
PRODUCED & BOTTLED BY BARNARD GRIFFIN WINERY
KENNEWICK, WASHINGTON ALCOHOL 12.4% BY VOLUME

BARNARD GRIFFIN
1707 W. Eighth Place
Kennewick, WA 99336
(509) 586-6987

Owners: Deborah Barnard &
    Rob Griffin
Winemaker: Rob Griffin
Year established: 1983
Production capacity: 2,000 gallons
Vineyards: None

A bit of background. Deborah Barnard, a hospital adminstrator, is married to Rob Griffin, the talented general manager of The Hogue Cellars. "On the side," so to speak, he makes his own wine: small amounts of Chardonnay and Fume Blanc fermented in French oak barrels and left on the yeast to develop more intense flavors. (Most winemakers, less confident or careful, will rack and filter their wine frequently to avoid the possibility of its developing off-flavors.) "Minimal appropriate technology" is how Rob describes it. It's a handcrafted winemaking style not suited to large-scale commercial winemaking, which is fine with both Rob and his employers at Hogue.

In addition to a tiny and not very menacing griffin, the Barnard Griffin label shows a colorful array of yellow and red tulips. They were picked in the front yard of the Griffin home in Kennewick

Visiting the winery (NR). Not open to the public. Barnard Griffin wines were first made at Caroway Vineyards in Kennewick; now Griffin leases the "original" winery used by The Hogue Cellars: an old mint still on the Hogue ranch outside of Prosser. Plans for expansion and a separate tourist facility are unsettled, given Griffin's responsibilities for Hogue. ("I don't have any free time or weekends as it is," Griffin explained.)

Tasting the wines ★★★☆. Barnard Griffin makes limited quantities of a few varieties (Cabernet Sauvignon, Fume Blanc, Chardonnay, Riesling), but has no winery of its own and no tasting room.

In theory, barrel fermenting Fume Blanc is a good way to tame Washington's distinctive Sauvignon Blanc grapes, but the 1987 bottling we tasted recently had little varietal character, smelling more like pears and bananas; its finish was curiously bitter.

Barnard Griffin wines are occasionally available at premium wine shops and in some restaurants; they sell out quickly. It's a very personal brand, whose prestige may sometimes exceed the quality in the bottle. But if Rob Griffin can make Washington's best wines for The Hogue Cellars, we'll forgive anything he wants to fool around with on his own time.

BISCUIT RIDGE

Route 1, Box 132
Waitsburg, WA 99361
(509) 529-4986

Owners: Jack & Helen Durham
Winemaker: Jack Durham
Year established: 1986
Production capacity: 2,200 gallons
Vineyards: 5 acres
Touring region: WallaWalla [p.22]

A bit of background. "Like everyone else who deals in wine, I'm a romantic," Jack Durham told us a few years back. It's been a quarter century now since he retired from the Navy. He spent the intervening years as a commercial fisherman and big-game guide in Alaska, also fitting in work as a real estate broker and cattle rancher.

Travel in Europe had triggered his interest in wine (his favorite: a German Lemberger) and he'd made wine at home; eventually, he moved to Walla Walla and started planting a Gewurztraminer vineyard (with Pinot Noir on tap next season). A spot of bad health and a devastating frost delayed but didn't daunt his plans.

Visiting the winery (NR). Driving along the southern fringes of the Palouse, you might miss the town of Dixie if you blinked; it's become a bedroom community for Walla Walla. And Biscuit Ridge winery won't overwhelm you, either; the whole set-up includes only two upright tanks and an open fermenter. But the welcome is genuine, and the owners' ambitions modest. "We'll add a couple of tanks later this year, and expand our storage space, and put in a new tasting room when we get the money," says Jack Durham.

Progress comes slowly. The 1988 crush was 1,400 gallons, up from 750 in 1987. Ultimately, Jack says, he'd like to make perhaps 2,000 gallons of three varieties; for the time being, he just has the Gewurztraminer.

One thing's for sure: Jack isn't blind to reality; he describes his current position as "owner, winemaker . . . and weed puller."

Tasting the wine (NR). Biscuit Ridge 1987 Gewurztraminer, at $8 per bottle, is the only release to date. The 1988 vintage will be ready by summer. You can sample it at the winery, or at two local restaurants: the Patit Creek Inn in Dayton and the Three-Mile Restaurant in Asotin.

Getting there. From Walla Walla, go 11 mi east on Hwy 12 to Dixie. Turn right at the schoolhouse and proceed 0.9 mi south on Biscuit Ridge Rd to the winery.

Open daily from 10 to 5. Special opening over the weekend of the Walla Walla Balloon Stampede.

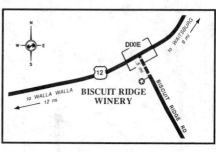

A word from the winery. *"Uniquely situated at 1,700 feet above sea level in the foothills of the Blue Mountains, Biscuit Ridge Winery and Vineyard enjoy the best of both worlds; the warm sunshine of the valley during the day and the cool mountain air at night, a perfect combination to bring the Gewurztraminer and Pinot Noir grapes to a well-rounded ripeness required to make a noble wine. Visitors are always welcome to the winery and tasting room on the estate. We are open nearly every day of the year except major holidays. Our annual releases are scheduled for the Fourth of July weekend holiday, and we participate in the annual Balloon Day celebration at Walla Walla. Drop by and see our progress."*

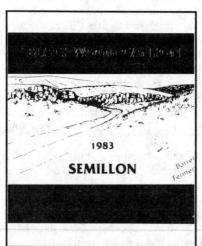

1983

SEMILLON

BLACKWOOD CANYON VINTNERS

Sunset Road
Route 2, Box 2169 H
Benton City, WA 99320
(509) 588-6249

Owners: M. Taylor Moore, Eunice S. Moore, W. T. Moore, Dr. Ernest O. Svenson
Winemaker: Mike Moore
Year established: 1983
Production capacity: 55,000 gallons
Vineyards: 51 acres
Touring region: Yakima Valley [p.15]

A bit of background. The night of October 1, 1985, was a nightmare for Mike Moore. In the middle of crush, a fire broke out in his hand-built, cedar-sided winery overlooking the Yakima Valley from the slopes of Red Mountain; Blackwood Canyon burned to the ground. A million dollars' worth of capital equipment was destroyed, and barrels holding thousands of gallons of wine went up in flames. By next morning, it seemed, Blackwood Canyon was ruined. What made the disaster all the more poignant was Moore's recent success; after several years of awkward winemaking, he had begun to achieve a measure of respect and recognition with a bold Semillon and an assertive "Ultra Late Harvest."

Mike Moore didn't take time to feel sorry for himself. He finished his crush at Kiona Vineyards, just down the hill, made arrangements for fermentation at nearby Preston, salvaged what he could from the ashes, and settled his insurance claims. By summer he was rebuilding.

Moore's early career was spent as a wildlife biologist in Idaho. He is also a graduate of the University of California at Davis and learned winemaking at Martini, Ventana, and Domaine Chandon. He then studied business administration at the University of Washington (and consulted for Haviland Vintners) before moving back across the mountains to follow his interest in wine. He was the manager of Ciel du Cheval Vineyard, a major supplier of premium grapes located on the slopes of Red Mountain (a massive outcropping at the eastern end of the Yakima Valley). His own property covers 180 acres above Kiona Vineyards, where he has begun planting Chardonnay, Cabernet Sauvignon, and Merlot grapes.

Visiting the winery ★★. Blackwood Canyon's new winery stands on the sagebrush-covered slope overlooking the last great loop of the Yakima River before it joins the Columbia, at the southeastern end of the Yakima Valley. The hillside setting, surrounded by vineyards, is dramatic ★★★ and the view up the valley on a clear day, toward Mount Adams, is magnificent. The approach to the winery through sagebrush and newly planted vineyards is also lovely.

Production levels keep rising, so something is always under construction. The last few times we've been here, we've missed seeing Mike, so we can't give a reliable report on his hospitality.

Tasting the wines (NR). Blackwood Canyon aims to produce serious, highly personal wines. The danger of such a venture is that the wines are not going to be to everyone's taste. We've been very impressed with the Semillon (high alcohol, oak-fermented, with bold flavors of green peppers) and the "Ultra," a late-harvest wine probably made from Gewurztraminer and Chardonnay (Moore doesn't say).

We haven't tasted the Chardonnay lately (but didn't care for the one we tried some time ago), or the newly released Cabernet from Portteus Vineyard grapes. Meantime, production is switching to estate-grown wines, which we look forward to sampling; there's also a second label of lower-priced wines called Windy River.

Getting there. From Hwy 224 (between West Richland and Benton City) turn north on Sunset Rd. Blackwood Canyon is 1 mi past Kiona Vineyards. [Map: Kiona]

Open weekends 10 to 6; by appointment during the week. $1 per person charge for buses.

A word from the winery. *"Basically, my winemaking beliefs are simple. Start with the best grapes. Use knowledge, attention to detail, and T.L.C. when making the wine. Bend yourself to the wine, not the wine to you. Have patience, as all truly great wines must be allowed to develop and this always takes time.*

"Blackwood Canyon was founded to produce the best Chardonnay, Cabernet Sauvignon, and late harvest wines possible. This is not, and was not expected to be, an overnight adventure."

BONAIR WINERY

500 S. Bonair Road
Route 1, Box 1669
Zillah, WA 98953
(509) 829-6027

Owners: Gail & Shirley Puryear
Winemaker: Gail Puryear
Year established: 1986
Production capacity: 6,000 gallons
Vineyards: 5 acres
Touring region: Yakima Valley [p.14]

A bit of background. Gail Puryear, the principal at the Kirkwood-Mount Adams schools in Toppenish, grew up in the Yakima Valley, as did his wife, Shirley, a social worker. They lived in California in the early stages of his career in education, and fell in love with the wines of the Napa Valley. By 1969 they had returned to eastern Washington, where Gail taught wine appreciation classes, served a term as president of the Yakima chapter of the Enological Society, and made wine at home.

In retrospect, the main reason the Puryears moved back to eastern Washington was to grow grapes and eventually establish a winery. They bought a five-acre plot of alfalfa, cleared away the morning glory vines, and began planting test plots of grapes. (Chardonnay seemed to do best, and that variety remains the winery's specialty.) Gail began reading every technical magazine he could find, and the Puryears' family enterprise, Bonair Winery, finally began to take shape in the summer of 1985. "Writing checks for all the expensive equipment we needed" was the hardest part, says Gail.

The Puryears' teenage children, Natasha and Joseph, share the workload of this family winery. During the summer they spend half days tending the vineyards (it's their summer job), in fall they help with the harvest, and in winter and spring they help with bottling and labeling. It helps, no doubt, that their mother is the winery's general manager. "I love it," says this one-time Los Angeles social worker who currently directs a night-school program for migrant workers. "I wouldn't trade it for anything."

Visiting the winery ★★★. A classic example of a "family" winery, something you're more likely to see in Oregon's Willamette Valley than in eastern Washington. The grandeur of the Yakima Valley provides the setting: a five-acre vineyard, planted mostly with Chardonnay vines, straddles the end of Bonair Road; the winery itself sits near the imposing, half-timbered Puryear family home ("Chateau Puryear," they call it). The recently enlarged tasting room features maps of the United States and the world, densely studded with pushpins as visitors indicate their hometown.

"Meeting the interesting people from all over is the most fun part of the business," marvels Shirley Puryear. Her friendly welcome makes even a brief stop enjoyable, while Gail is delighted to show off his winemaking equipment. You'll find a large, grassy lawn and picnic tables outside the winery, and a frisky puppy named Filter Pad (Paddy for short).

Tasting the wines ★★☆. Mike Januik acted as consultant for the first crush, and Gail Puryear seems to have made a successful transition from home winemaker to commercial vintner. (The winery has doubled in size since it opened.) Three barrel-aged Chardonnays are now on the market: from Outlook Vineyards (down the road), a Chateau Puryear bottling, and a Reserve. There's also a decent Riesling and a not-too-sweet blush. The newest wine, which we haven't tasted, is a red called Nouveau Rouge, made from Cabernet Sauvignon.

Getting there. Take Exit 52 from I-82. In Zillah, turn left at Cheyne Rd and proceed 2 mi to Highland. Left 1 mi to Bonair Rd, left once more to the winery. [**Map**: Covey Run]

Open daily from 10 to 5. In winter, Saturday, Sunday, Monday only.

Special events. Anniversary party, mid-August. Tour groups are welcome; no fee.

A word from the winery. *"We invite you to come and see what happens when a little hobby gets out of hand! Wander through our vineyard, marvel at our newly enlarged winery (twice as big as last year), enjoy the peaceful country setting of our picnic area, and, most important, let us share with you our passion for making and enjoying excellent wines."*

1984
WASHINGTON STATE
Chardonnay

Balcom & Moe Vineyards
PRODUCED AND BOTTLED BY BOOKWALTER WINERY
PASCO WASHINGTON USA BW WA 104 ALCOHOL 13% BY VOLUME

BOOKWALTER WINERY

2708 Commercial Avenue
Pasco, WA 99301
(509) 547-8571

Owner & winemaker:
   Jerrold Bookwalter
Year established: 1984
Production capacity: 10,000 gallons
Vineyards: None
Touring region: Tri-Cities [p.20]

A bit of background. From 1976 to 1983, Jerry Bookwalter was the general manager of Sagemoor Farms—the largest group of vineyards in the Northwest. It could be argued that the ready availability of good grapes from Sagemoor became the backbone of Washington's emerging wine industry, and that Bookwalter was Washington's most respected grower. The Seattle-based partnership that owns Sagemoor relied on Bookwalter not only to manage the vineyards but also to negotiate sales contracts with the various winemakers. His flexibility and fairness were highly respected in the industry, and when he left Sagemoor he had little trouble starting his own consulting and brokerage firm, Agricultural Marketing & Management Services. He also served as vice-president of the Washington Association of Wine Grape Growers, urging that organization to pay more attention to the need for marketing their fruit. Still, he doesn't believe that growers should run out and buy wine tanks: that's trading the grape marketing problem for another, far more complex issue (marketing wine), and the tuition could be expensive.

Bookwalter travels some 40,000 miles a year visiting Washington's 7,500 acres of producing vineyards, looking for what he calls "pockets of greatness" in the vineyards of the Columbia Basin: vineyards with a southwestern exposure, five to 10 degrees of slope, and a microclimate close to the river where the temperatures are kept relatively stable by the water.

Visiting the winery ★★. You drive along Commercial Avenue past tractor sales yards, past the building that housed both the Bookwalter and Quarry Lake wineries in their infancy, to the much larger industrial building Bookwalter has now. Lots of room for a short-lived increase in production capacity (part of a no-longer-active deal to process grapes for a New Jersey manufacturer of sulfite-free wines).

Tasting the wines ★★☆. Among the early releases from Bookwalter, the best was a 1983 Chardonnay that had a lovely whiff of seacoast air, evoking visions of oysters and fresh cracked crab. The 1986 Chardonnay is a balanced wine with good fruit and oak components. The 1987 will be released in late spring of 1989.

Much of the 1986 Riesling can be tasted as a nonvintage sparkling wine. (It was sent to California for its secondary fermentation in the bulk Charmat method, and cannot legally be vintage dated.) The Late Harvest Riesling—a good value at $5.50 per half bottle—is a charmer: apricot, floral nose, and a mouth-watering finish.

Bookwalter didn't make a Cabernet Sauvignon in 1985, but the 1986 release will coincide with the publication of this book in May 1989.

Early consultants here included Bill Broich and Kay Simon; various other wine professionals continue to assist Bookwalter.

Getting there. Take Hwy 395 out of Pasco northbound; turn right on Hillsboro Ave and immediately turn right again on Commercial Ave. Continue along Commercial for about 1 mi to the winery, which is on the left. [Map: Quarry Lake]

Open weekdays from 10 to 5, weekends from noon to 5. Groups of 20 or more need an appointment, but there is no charge for tasting.

Special events. "Catch the Crush" in early October.

A word from the winery. *"When you're in the Tri-Cities, you're most cordially invited to visit our winery and tasting room."*

CAROWAY VINEYARDS

P.O. Box 6273
Kennewick, WA 99336
(509) 582-7041

Owners: Wayne & Carol Miller
Year established: 1983
Production capacity: 2,500 gallons
Vineyards: 40 acres
Touring region: Tri-Cities [p. 20]

A bit of background. Carol Miller, with a degree in botany and a fascination with grape growing, runs this 40-acre vineyard. Her husband, Wayne, handles the paperwork with the ease of a professional accountant (he is, in fact, a C.P.A.). Caroway Vineyards grows Riesling, Chardonnay, Chenin Blanc, Cabernet Sauvignon, Semillon, Pinot Noir, and Lemberger, and for a time had its own wines on the market. Now almost all its grapes are spoken for by outside winemakers; whatever's left over gets vinified at the little Caroway Vineyards winery outside Kennewick and is sold in bulk. If you see a supermarket special with the bonded winery designation BW WA 101, it's Caroway's.

Open by appointment only.

CASCADE CREST ESTATES
WINERY

Sauvignon Blanc

Yakima Valley
1987

ALCOHOL 13% BY VOLUME

CASCADE CREST ESTATES

111 E. Lincoln Avenue
Sunnyside, WA 98944
(503) 839-9463

1210 Valley Street
Seattle, WA 98109
(206) 624-5310

Owners: Rolla "Toby" Halbert,
Stanley Zeitz, Robert Fay,
William Pierson
Winemaker: Christopher Smith
Year established: 1988
Production capacity: 250,000 gal.
Vineyards: None
Touring regions:
Yakima Valley [p. 14]
Seattle [p. 30]

A bit of background. Toby Halbert holds degrees in engineering and business administration from the University of Washington and spent two decades at Boeing, where he worked his way up the corporate ladder to a position as corporate assistant secretary. In 1977 he took charge of Chateau Ste. Michelle vineyard and winery operations, where he directed the purchase of the vast River Ridge vineyards, and six years later was named vice-president of administration and finance.

Two of his partners in this ambitious venture are investors: Dr. William Pierson is a pediatrician, Dr. Stanley Zeitz has a practice in Seattle. The third partner is Bob Fay, one of Washington's most respected grape growers; Fay manages the Sunnyside Land Group, a 15-year-old, 250-acre vineyard.

The winery they've created has one eye on Sunnyside Land Group's enormous supply of raw material, the other on a barely tapped international market for Washington wine. No mom-and-pop winery could realize that potential, Halbert figures; Halbert's business plan has Cascade Crest starting out as the state's fourth-largest winery.

Visiting the winery (Sunnyside) ★★. From the front, all you see is a low brick office building, but there are 40,000 square feet of space in this old dairy, which was built (and abandoned) by Carnation before Cascade Crest took it over. The best pieces of Haviland Winery's old equipment found a home here, and there's a lot of new tanks and barrels, but the spaces are so vast it looks almost empty. A recent remodeling project created a tasting room that overlooks the cellar floor.

Visiting the winery (Seattle) ★★★. The same fondness for scale is evident here. A three-story, 5,000-square-foot building at the south end of Lake Union, formerly used for offices and storage by a distributor of office equipment, is being transformed into an urban winery, warehouse, and visitor center. Cavernous space in back for case goods, a token winemaking operation (but big enough to qualify as a legal winery), generously proportioned offices, and an attractive tasting room furnished with original art and antiques. From the roof, you look out over the lake; tables will be put out in good weather.

The staff at both locations are cheerful and welcoming. The only disquieting note might be the leftover Haviland wine for sale, but these are actually the 1985 Cabernet and 1986 Chardonnay that Lou Facelli bottled for Haviland, and Facelli's skill is unquestioned.

Tasting the wines ★★★. No one would blame you for being skeptical of a winery that starts out at the 180,000-gallon level. But the 1987 wines were custom-crushed by the talented Mike Januik at Langguth, and Wayne Marcil had a hand in finishing the first releases (as he bounced from Covey Run to Preston and on to his own consulting business). The 1988 crush took place at Langguth and at the new winery, with Marcil in charge; the new permanent winemaker at Cascade Crest is Christopher Smith, a lanky Californian who moved up from Jordan Vineyard, where he had been assistant winemaker.

Our favorite Cascade Crest Estates wine so far was the 1987 Muscat Canelli, with a cheerful nose of orange blossoms and passion fruit. The 1987 Sauvignon was wild and grassy, with underlying fruit. The 1987 Semillon Blanc may have had a bit too much oak, but the oak treatment of the 1987 Chardonnay gave it a warm, buttery flavor.

A full dozen wines are available, all of them clean and sound.

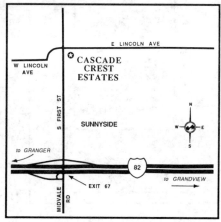

Getting there (Sunnyside). Take Exit 67 from I-5 and go north 0.5 mi on First St toward Sunnyside to Lincoln Ave (the first traffic signal). The winery is on the southeast corner.

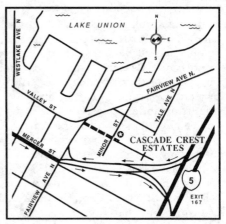

Getting there (Seattle). From I-5, take Exit 167 (Mercer St), turn right onto Fairview, right again on Valley.

Open 11 to 6 Tuesday through Sunday in Sunnyside, 10 to 6 in Seattle.

A word from the winery. *"Cascade Crest Estates winery will make and market superpremium Washington state wines on an international basis. We will have facilities in both Sunnyside and Seattle where visitors and tastings will be encouraged. The winery in Sunnyside will have picnic facilities as well and will be the principal production facility. We look forward to having visitors come to our winery and try our wines."*

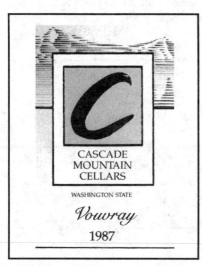

CASCADE MOUNTAIN CELLARS
606 W. Third
Ellensburg, WA 98926
(509) 925-2998

Owners: Jürgen & Julie Grieb
Winemaker: Jürgen Grieb
Year established: 1987
Production capacity: 10,000 gallons
Vineyards: None
Touring: Columbia Valley N.[p.19]

A bit of background. Jürgen Grieb grew up in Germany's famous Mosel region and studied winemaking at the Enology Institute in Trier. After working for several German wineries, he joined the giant firm of F.W. Langguth Erben as a winemaker and was sent to the U.S. in the early

1980s to help start Langguth's new winery in Washington state. Romance blossomed in this remote outpost: Jürgen married Julie, the office manager; Jacques Sipp, the Alsatian-born cellarmaster, married Laura Stroup, the lab technician. In 1985 the Griebs were house hunting and came across the old Burlington Northern depot in Ellensburg; they hadn't planned to start their winery right away but felt they couldn't pass up the extraordinary location.

Visiting the winery ★★★. The freeway bypasses Ellensburg's fine old downtown, whose Historic District encompasses many noteworthy buildings but stops short of the railroad station. Saved from the wrecking ball by the efforts of the local historical society, the 1910-vintage depot today gleams with pride: polished oak paneling, buffed terrazo floors, Tiffany tile wainscoting, bright nickel trim. But it took the Griebs months of backbreaking work and a ton of resolve to accomplish this task, to keep going despite escalating costs and unforeseen setbacks (vandals broke in and painted graffiti on the walls).

Visitors are received in the high-ceilinged waiting room, where antiques are for sale and wines are poured from the ticket window. The winery itself is on the lower level, where horse-drawn carriages used to drive in. There's lots of space in the depot; a coffee shop is already installed, and more merchants could easily fit in.

Tasting the wines ★★. Wines currently available are a 1986 Chardonnay, 1987 Vouvray, 1987 Sunset Blush, 1987 Muller Thurgau (at the winery only), a Merlot, and some 1987-vintage sparkling wines. The Vouvray (Chenin Blanc) is fine and clean; its nose is rather faint but the taste is distinctly varietal. We found the Chardonnay rather austere and slightly oxidized.

On tap for 1989 are some reds, Merlot, and Lemberger. We haven't tasted the sparkling wines.

Getting there. From I-5 Exit 109, follow Canyon Rd and Main St into Ellensburg. Turn west on Third Ave and go four blocks to the train station.

Open Monday through Saturday from 11 to 5, Sunday from noon to 4. There's a $2 charge for tasting the sparkling wine.

Special events. A gift shop, Das Kringle Haus, opens for the Christmas holiday season.

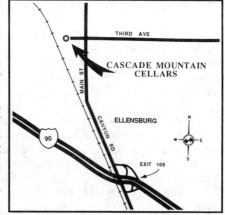

A word from the winery. "*You will get a glimpse of the old while tasting the new in this elaborate setting dating back to the early 1900s at Cascade Mountain Cellars. Still vividly preserved are the original train ticket booth and*

the beautifully detailed 18-foot ceilings. We offer visitors a rare look into the past while savoring some of the region's finest handcrafted wines and champagnes. Jürgen Grieb, our winemaker, arrived from Germany just a few short years ago to start handcrafting his wines in the tradition that was honored by his forefathers. You will see the oak barrels and hand equipment used for our quality product, blending in to become part of Ellensburg's rustic charm."

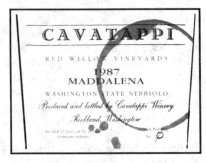

CAVATAPPI

9702 N.E. 120th Place
Kirkland, WA 98034
(206) 823-6533

Owner & winemaker: Peter Dow
Year established: 1984
Production capacity: 2,000 gallons
Vineyards: None
Touring region: Seattle [p. 30]

A bit of background. Cavatappi ("corkscrew" in Italian) is one of the first restaurant wineries on the West Coast and Peter Dow is one of Seattle's most popular restaurateurs; his Cafe Juanita is justly celebrated for the consistently high quality of its Northern Italian cuisine. Now, having overcome various licensing hurdles, he has begun offering true "house" wines, as many restaurants in Italy have done for generations, so that he has more control over the type of wine served with his meals. Not that he really needs another wine; his list already features over 250 Italian selections!

Visiting the winery (NR). The restaurant occupies a ranch-style house of white brick, overlooking woods and a stream; its spacious dining room is enhanced by natural wood and colorful napery. In this cheerful setting, half a dozen choices per night are listed on a blackboard. Specialties include chicken in a creamy sauce of pistachio nuts, and rabbit.

The Cavatappi winery was expanded to 1,000 square feet in the roomy basement in 1987. Production is up sharply, too, because of the new varieties Dow is making.

Tasting the wines (NR). Dow's original output was confined to Sauvignon Blanc (available only at Cafe Juanita, where it sells for $12.50). Washington's first Nebbiolo, from Dow's own vineyard in the Yakima Valley, is now available; there's also a Cabernet Sauvignon.

Getting there. From I-405, take Exit 18 (Kirkland) and go west through downtown Kirk-land. Turn right on Market and proceed north 2 mi to the community of Juanita. Turn left on 97th, right a block later on 120th. [**Map:** Covey Run at Moss Bay]

Open by appointment only.

A word from the winery. *"Nothing really to promote other than we are part of Cafe Juanita."* (Peter Dow is modest to a fault.)

Washington
CHARDONNAY RESERVE
1983

CHAMPS DE BRIONNE
98 Road W N.W.
Quincy, WA 98848
(509) 785-6685

Owners: Vince & Carol Bryan
Winemaker: Cameron Fries
Year established: 1983
Production capacity: 140,000
Vineyards: 110 acres
Touring: Columbia Valley N. [p.19]

A bit of background. Champs de Brionne is based on a concept that seems almost old-fashioned in the modern American wine industry: the preeminent importance of soil. Vince and Carol Bryan first sensed this when they lived in Europe; after returning to the Seattle area, where Vince established a practice in neurosurgery, they spent a year poring over the reports of soil samples taken around the state during the Depression by the U.S. Geological Survey. What they were looking for was not the unique Jory loam of the Red Hills of Dundee, not the Willakenzie soil of the Willamette Valley, not even the irrigable desert of the Yakima Valley. Instead, they wanted the almost infertile wasteland which produces the great wines of Bordeaux, combined with the mild, frost-free climate of Burgundy.

The Bryans found their ideal site on a 900-foot basalt cliff overlooking the Columbia River five miles west of the town of George. In 1980 they bought a 700-acre parcel and began planting a vineyard, which they named Champs de Brionne (which translates, roughly, as "Bryan's Fields"). The vines planted in this microclimate, in sandy loam and gravel, seem to be flourishing and suggest that the Bryans have discovered another viticultural area for Washington.

Visiting the winery ★★★☆. The setting is one of the most magnificent in the state; it overlooks a jagged, snakelike gorge carved by the Columbia through its prehistoric channel. "It's like having the Grand Canyon in your back yard," Vince Bryan suggests.

Adjoining the cellar is an expansive, glassed-in tasting room with a barrel-vaulted ceiling, tiled floors, Oriental carpets. On the lawn outside stand several picnic tables. By following an easy trail through the vineyard, visitors can reach an observation point above the bluff, just above the property's most stunning achievement, an amphitheater hewn out of the cliff. You can see nearly 50 miles upriver from this remote, awe-inspiring site ★★★★. Migrating elk come down off Colockum Pass and browse on a sandbar.

Champs de Brionne's large building is full of first-class machinery and French oak barrels, far more than needed to make just Champs wine. The winery is putting its excess production capacity to good use, custom-crushing tens of thousands of gallons of wine for outside clients. In fact, Champs intends to double its capacity again, to 300,000 gallons.

One advantage of the site is that the estate-grown grapes don't mature until a week or two after those from the warmer Yakima Valley; as a result, Champs can ferment, filter, and process grapes for its "custom-crush" clients before it makes wines from its own grapes.

Tasting the wines ★★. The winemaker, Cameron Fries, trained in Switzerland and worked at Worden's in Spokane before signing on here. "A Swiss winemaker," he says "would consider it an offense not to ferment to dry. I always do that. Many winemakers ferment only to 0.5 percent alcohol." That half percent in many commercial wines (even in supposedly dry wines like Chardonnay) gives them just a hint of sweet-ness to balance bitterness or other undesirable characteristics. In most cases, though not with the 1987 Riesling or Chenin Blanc, Fries induces a malolactic fermentation.

In recent blind tastings, Champs wines haven't fared particularly well. The 1987 Semillon had a tired nose of old apples, very soft-textured in the mouth, with a bitter finish. The estate-bottled, barrel-fermented 1987 Chardonnay was mistaken for dry Chenin Blanc because of its green-tomato nose. The 1986 Pinot Noir shows clear varietal character but lacks the fruit and texture one looks for in this grape. Best was the 1987 Riesling, which had a pretty bouquet and balanced flavors.

Fries also makes a small amount of his own wines here under the White Heron label.

Getting there. From I-90 eastbound, take Exit 143 and follow Champs de Brionne Rd. A series of signs leads 11 mi to the intersection of Baseline and Rd W; the winery and vine-yards are 0.75 mi to the north, overlooking the river.

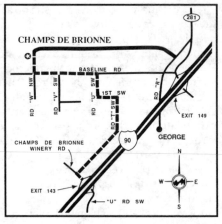

Westbound, take Exit 149 at George; follow Beverly Burke Rd off Hwy 281 to Baseline Rd and continue west.

Open daily from 11 to 5, March through December. Weekends only, January and February.

Special events. Champs Summer Music Theater has a monthly concert schedule from Memorial Day through mid-September. Top name musicians perform in the amphitheater; Bob Dylan drew 18,000 fans in the summer of 1988—more people than had ever assembled before in Grant County. Tickets available through Ticketmaster outlets in major cities.

A word from the winery. *"We invite you to visit our beautiful winery, located on a bench above the Columbia River. It provides breathtaking vistas and the perfect setting for a leisurely picnic or a stroll down to our renowned, 15,000-seat amphitheater. Our friendly staff looks forward to touring the facility with you and talking with you about our fine wines.*

"We know that you have to make a special trip to see us. We work hard to make sure that the trip is truly worthwhile. We hope to see you soon!"

CHATEAU GALLANT
S. 1355 Gallant Road
Pasco, WA 99301
(509) 545-9570

Owners: Bart Gallant,
  Theresa Gallant
Winemaker: Mike Wallace
Year established: 1987
Production capacity: 5,000 gallons
Vineyards: 25 acres
Touring region: Tri-Cities [p.20]

A bit of background. David and Mary Gallant own 155 acres of eastern Washington farmland (potatoes, wheat, corn) and have interests in an insurance and accounting business, a real estate agency, cattle. A busy, active, prosperous couple. For the last 10 years, as they've been withdrawing from day-to-day involvement in their various commercial and agricultural activities, they've traveled extensively to the wine regions of the world. So it's only logical that the culmination of their retirement is a new winery that they've established in the names of their children, Bart and Theresa. David retains the title of controller.

Visiting the winery ★★★. From this verdant vantage on the banks of the Burbank sloughs, you can often watch migrating waterfowl (swans, white geese, Canada geese, ducks) on their trips north or south; the property is adjacent to an extensive wildlife refuge. The south-facing vineyard, on the slope above the winery, is planted mostly with Riesling and Chardonnay. A patio and lawn outside the winery offer an inviting spot for picnics. Inside, the tasting room is large, airy, and inviting.

Tasting the wines ★★☆. Chateau Gallant's first releases, purchased in bulk from Langguth, were made by Max Zellweger. The 1986 Chardonnay showed good varietal character with an appealing, flinty quality to the nose along with a hint of flowers and pears. It was enhanced and nicely balanced by its oak treatment. In our blind tasting, the 1986 Sauvignon Blanc was mistaken for a Semillon because of its dusty, light bell pepper nose, but it had the nice bright acid of a Sauvignon Blanc and good breadth of flavors. A nicely controlled example of this variety. The 1986 Riesling, on the other hand, had unhealthy chemical notes to the nose, tasted overly sugared, and lacked the acid to support its sweetness; it didn't taste like Riesling at all. Wines from estate-grown grapes, made with the assistance of Mike Wallace, will be released shortly.

Getting there. From Pasco, go 4 mi toward Walla Walla on Hwy 395, turn left toward Ice Harbor Dam on Hwy 124 (Waitsburg Rd), turn right on Gallant Rd east of Burbank; the winery is at the end of the road.

Open Monday through Saturday from noon to 5. Tour groups are welcome.

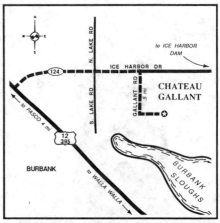

A word from the winery. *"Chateau Gallant winery is situated on the southern border of our farm adjoining the Burbank U.S. Fish and Wildlife Refuge, which is a resting and feeding stop for migratory birds. There is a patio and ample lawn for picnicking. The vineyard is on a slope above the winery.*

"The surrounding land is either refuge or farmland. The winery is the only building at the end of Gallant Road; you can't miss it!"

CHATEAU STE. MICHELLE

One Stimson Lane
(1411 NE 145th Street)
P.O. Box 1976
Woodinville, WA 98072
(206) 488-1133

Owners: Stimson Lane
 Wine & Spirits, Ltd.
Winemaker: Cheryl Barber
**Vice-President, Winemaking
 Operations:** Peter Bachman
Year established: 1934
Production capacity: 750,000 gal..
Vineyards: 3,000 acres
Touring region: Seattle [p. 30]

also at:
205 W. Fifth Avenue
(Fifth and Avenue B)
Grandview, WA 98930
(509) 882-3928

Production capacity: 240,000 gal.
Touring region: Yakima Valley
 [p.15]

A bit of background. Chateau Ste. Michelle is a classic example of success in the business world. Granted, they were in on the ground floor, when all the wineries in Washington were making fortified fruit wines and the state legislature passed a law that reduced their favorable tax treatment. Competition from California and Europe reduced the number of Washington wineries within a year to two, Associated Vintners (now Columbia) and American Wine Growers, whose two brands—Pomerelle and Nawico—exemplified the Skid Road product of the day. But American Wine Growers had a visionary founder, Victor Allison, who recognized the Yakima Valley's potential for growing vinifera grapes; he created Ste. Michelle Vintners and hired the dean of American winemakers, Andre Tchelistcheff, as a consultant.

At this point, the fledgling winery had some good vineyard sites and the expertise to make fine wine, but it needed what so many small wineries lack even today: financial development and public visibility. In a one-two punch, they got both. A group of savvy investors, led by whiz-kid Wally Opdycke, took over in the late 1960s. They built a showplace winery in Woodinville, then sold the winery to the United States Tobacco Company. Now Ste. Michelle had access to unheard-of amounts of capital, and, above all, to management experience in areas as diverse (and necessary) as personnel, financial planning, construction, operations, and marketing.

Sure, big companies screw up. (Ford botched the Edsel, after all.) Size alone is no guarantee of success, but talented and motivated people sure improve the odds. And U.S. Tobacco (a producer of snuff and chewing tobaccos like Copenhagen) was never as big as the jealous winemakers of the Northwest imagined. Today, in fact, the wine side of the business, consolidated as Stimson Lane Wine & Spirits, Ltd., has become the dominant side of the overall holding company, UST. The former money-losing subsidiary has turned into a profitable, freestanding operation, and it's thanks to corporate vision, corporate financing, corporate planning, corporate winemaking, corporate marketing.

By corporate, we don't mean anonymous but collective, collaborative. In so many instances, the owner of a winery does (or tries to do) everything, from driving the tractor to pulling hoses in the winery, from designing the label to corking the bottles to hauling cases to the warehouse, from greeting visitors in the tasting room to meeting distributors in far-flung markets, from filling out BATF reports to writing promotional copy. "Winemaking" (let alone grape growing) has become a *minor* aspect of the owner's responsibilities. Of course, it's charming to visit these overworked people (as we urge you to do), and easy to complain if they're not in the tasting room when you drive by on a weekend (as we've frequently done). Some will tell you they wouldn't have it any other way, others regret the impulse that ever got them started down this road. The realistic ones know that to make a profit from the business of winemaking, you've either got to be so tiny that you don't bother with the time-consuming stuff, or you have to be big enough to hire specialists.

Look at the successful wineries who maintain their quality and independence: tiny operations such as Wasson, Eyrie, Woodward Canyon, Neuharth, Bainbridge Island, Leonetti; and sophisticated commercial enterprises like The Hogue Cellars and Chateau Ste. Michelle.

It's no accident that Ste. Michelle's current president, Allen Shoup, came up through the marketing ranks. Wine is above all a selling business.

In its effort to become a national winery, Stimson Lane hired a nationwide sales force (nearly 50 people) and has developed or acquired an increasing variety of products to sell: the Chateau Ste. Michelle line; Columbia Crest; Whidbeys liqueur, Port, and loganberry wine; two Napa Valley wineries (Conn Creek and Villa Mt. Eden); and assorted imports. The result is that you're as likely to find Chateau Ste. Michelle or Columbia Crest in Belleville, Kansas, as in Bellevue, Washington.

What makes Ste. Michelle's business so remarkable is the overall quality of its products. The credit goes above all to winemaker Cheryl

Barber, who started in the lab under Kay Simon.

But it's a team effort, and that's probably the difference. At any given stage in a wine's evolution (from grapes to bottle), the winemaker has a range of choices that depend on his or her sensory evaluation of the wine. Consider a small winery, with a single winemaker and limited resources. If the winemaker is competent and experienced, the wines may have a certain deliberate style. If the winemaker is less competent, or if the right equipment is lacking, the wines will suffer. Now, consider a corporate winery like Stimson Lane. Half a dozen winemakers tasting together, often, reaching a consensus on the potential and direction for each wine, with all the equipment needed to produced the desired result. And the sales force to sell it.

Fortunately, we're not talking about some schlock producer of jug wine. Chateau Ste. Michelle is the only Northwest winery that's truly national; the fact that it's producing excellent wine is fortunate indeed. Chateau Ste. Michelle's outstanding quality helps every small and medium-sized Northwest winery that's trying to get a foot in a distributor's door between Anaheim and Zurich.

Visiting the winery (Woodinville) ★★★★. Contemplate for a moment the dilemma of a big winery: on the one hand, it needs to attract a large public following; on the other hand, the demands of high-volume production threaten to ruin the romance of winemaking and disillusion visitors. Gallo (and many other wineries) solve the problem neatly: they admit no visitors, period. Many of the larger Canadian wineries carefully control their visitors' access to the production areas.

Chateau Ste. Michelle has taken a diametrically opposite tack. Their showcase winery, built around a 1977-vintage "chateau" on an 87-acre campus outside of Seattle, is one of the most attractive facilities in the Northwest. Tours are enthusiastic and peppy, led by well-trained guides, and go poking into every area of the winery's operations. Even the waiting area is adorned with educational displays about viticulture and enology. You can buy your favorite wine from the gift shop (frequently at bargain prices); picnics on the lawn are encouraged.

Visiting the winery (Grandview) ★★★. This is actually the oldest winemaking facility currently in use as a winery in the state of Washington. Chateau Ste. Michelle kept its existence quiet and its doors closed to the public for many years, but later opened it to the public, due to the increasing interest in wine touring, when it joined the Yakima Valley Winegrowers Association in the early 1980s.

"This can't be the way to one of Chateau Ste. Michelle's wineries," you tell yourself as you bump across the railroad tracks south of "downtown" Grandview, heading toward a clumsy complex of fruit packers and tomato processors in their corrugated iron sheds. You're wrong, of course: this is as much "wine country" as the wide-open vineyards on the nearby hillsides. The grand old facility is used only for red wine. It can turn out a quarter-million gallons a year if the vineyards produce enough grapes and there's sufficient demand.

Still, the Grandview winery will surprise you by its relatively small scale; it's like visiting the Petit Trianon once you've been to Versailles. The tasting room has a cozy "country store" atmosphere, stocked with well-chosen accessories related to wine and food; it's a pleasant place to browse until it's time for your visit to start (to go "out back" as the staff calls it). Your tour passes great upright redwood tanks, where wines are aged. You gaze down into the open concrete vats where the red wines are fermented: they're like swimming pools.

Tasting the wines ★★★★. Within the past six months, Chateau Ste. Michelle has received the kind of honors normally reserved for tiny craft wineries, as well as major awards. Most important is probably the designation as "Best American Winery" by *Wine Country* magazine, which ranked 400 wineries according to the quality, consistency, and value of their offerings. The 1983 Cabernet Sauvignon was named best in the country by *Wine & Spirits* magazine, the same honor won five years earlier by Leonetti Cellar. And Tasters Guild, a new national wine society, named Chateau Ste. Michelle as its first Winery of the Year for 1989.

Our own conclusion, after tasting the wines several times a year with our tour groups at Chateau Ste. Michelle, and after a number of blind tastings that included Ste. Michelle wines, confirms this status. Across the board, these wines are consistently at the top.

Is there anything of Ste. Michelle's we don't like? The Chenin Blanc and Gewurztraminer don't do much for us, and the Riesling Blush could be retired; it's an obvious copy of the Staton Hills Pink Riesling. (The Cabernet Blush, on the other hand, has all the taste of Cabernet Sauvignon for people who don't like dry, tannic red wines.) But even the wines we would not, perhaps, choose personally are varietal, clean, and balanced. They're almost always good value, too.

Sometimes we run into people who say Chateau Ste. Michelle wines are too expensive. Not compared to other Northwest wines, certainly, although the superb Chateau Ste. Michelle Blanc de Noir sparkling wine was overpriced in the $20 range. (It's now repackaged as "Domaine Ste. Michelle" and sells for a third less.) We also run into people who say they used to drink the Ste. Michelle Riesling "before the winery started making it so sweet." It's their taste that's changed, not the winery's style.

The 1987 edition of the bright green-gold Johannisberg Riesling (the wine that put Washington on the viticultural map) shows the classic Riesling nose, light spritz, and good honeyed lime flavors. The current release of Fume Blanc is the 1985 vintage, and it's maturing beautifully, with lots of menthol and juniper in the nose and a fresh, citric palate. The "regular" 1986 Semillon is grassy and oaky, the remarkable 1983 Reserve has the variety's dusty, Anaheim pepper characteristics but has developed an astonishing raspberry nose, an unexpected facet of the fruit.

Single-vineyard bottlings of Chardonnay and Cabernet Sauvignon are in the works, in addition to the previous line of Chateau Reserve wines.

The 1986 Cold Creek Vineyard Chardonnay suggests that these wines will not take extreme stylistic positions but will offer more depth than the regular bottlings; it had a hint of pineapple and anise in its floral nose, with a touch of perceptible oak to round out the palate.

Ste. Michelle is one of the few Northwest wineries that doesn't shovel its wines onto the market as soon as possible; the 1983 Merlot was still for sale in 1989. It was very restrained in the nose and taste. But the 1983 Chateau Reserve Merlot had matured beautifully, with a ripe nose of cherries and raspberries, balanced by herbal and floral notes. In the mouth, it had luscious flavors, with moderate tannins remaining.

And Cabernet Sauvignon! After the superb 1983, would the 1984 suffer by comparison? A bit; it had a chalky-minty nose, very recognizable as Chateau Ste. Michelle's, with good flavors and a spicy, cedar-accented finish. Even better is what's coming up: the 1985 Cabernet (we snuck a pre-release bottle into a blind tasting), with black currants and berries in the nose, fine, balanced fruit flavors with a hint of green pepper, and a long finish. And at a barrel tasting recently, we had the chance to try the 1988 Cabernet: terrific, sweet berry flavors en route to a year or more of oak aging.

Getting there (Woodinville). From I-405, take Hwy 522 eastbound toward Monroe and exit almost immediately onto 131st N.E., which leads into "downtown" Woodinville. Turn right on N.E. 175th, then sharp left onto Hwy 202 (the Woodinville-Redmond Rd); proceed south to the winery.

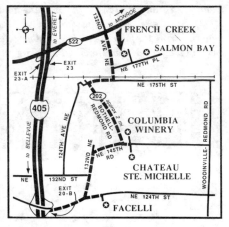

Alternatively, take Exit 20B from I-405 and go east on N.E. 124th. Turn left on 132nd N.E. (Slater Rd), go up the hill, and continue almost until its very end, then turn right, down N.E. 143rd, which intersects with the Woodinville-Redmond Rd at the winery.

Getting there (Grandview). Take Exit 73 or Exit 75 from I-82 to downtown Grandview. Proceed south on W. Fifth to Ave A, turn left, and continue one block to Ave B.

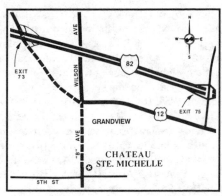

Open (both wineries) daily from 10 to 4:30. Groups are welcome; there is no charge for the tour and tasting.

Special events. A calendar of events (and there are many—concerts, art shows, historic tours, and so on) is available by calling the winery. For the past several years, Chateau Ste. Michelle has sponsored a Grape Stomp at a shopping mall in Woodinville in mid-September, in conjunction with the annual Woodinville Festival.

A word from the winery. *"Chateau Ste. Michelle deserves a few hours on your itinerary while you're in the Seattle area. The knowledgeable staff, beautiful facility and grounds, along with the award-winning wines, are well worth a visit.*

"If you like red wine, you should visit Chateau Ste. Michelle's Grandview winery during the fall crush. The oldest working winery in the state, Grandview has an Old World, traditional winemaking atmosphere."

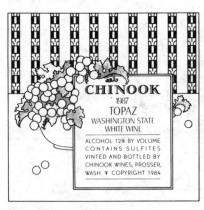

CHINOOK
Wittkopf at Wine Country Road
P.O. Box 387
Prosser, WA 99350
(509) 786-2725

Owners: Kay Simon &
    Clay Mackey
Winemaker: Kay Simon
Year established: 1984
Production capacity: 4,000 gall.
Vineyards: None
Touring: Yakima Valley [p. 15]

A bit of background. Kay Simon—one of the wine industry's most gracious and savvy women—graduated from the University of California at Davis and began her career as a lab technician for United Vintners in California. She joined Chateau Ste. Michelle in Woodinville as assistant to Joel Klein in 1977 and took over winemaking duties at the Paterson winery when it opened in 1981. By 1983 she had set off on her own, opening a freelance consulting laboratory in Prosser and starting a winery with her partner (now her husband, too), Clay Mackey. Along the way she helped many wineries around the state solve a variety of enological crises, and served a term on the board of directors of the Washington Wine Institute.

Mackey's parents owned a vineyard in the Napa Valley; he managed vineyards for Freemark Abbey and Rutherford Hill after graduating from Davis. In 1979 he joined the Chateau Ste. Michelle staff and managed their eastern Washington vineyards before becoming a consultant to independent growers.

Today, Kay and Clay have cut back their consulting; both work at Chinook virtually full-time, tending to winemaking chores and delivering their wine to a list of prestigious restaurants around the state during the week, and personally greeting visitors to the winery on weekends.

Chinook, by the way, is an Indian name; it's one of the major species of salmon, as well as the name for a warm, moist southwest wind. Simon and Mackey decided early on that they didn't want to put their own names on the label and didn't want anything in French or Spanish. They narrowed their criteria to geographical and place names that were easy to pronounce. Camas and Quamish (names for lilies) were among the early contenders. "We want to be recognized for producing good wines," said Mackey, "not to see our own names on the bottle."

Visiting the winery ★★★. The little white farmhouse stands in a seven-acre orchard of peach and cherry trees: a reminder, you think, of traditional agriculture in a valley transformed by enormous new packing plants. Blue chicory flowers bloom in profusion alongside the road. (In the industrial park across the tracks, you see neatly painted stripes on the asphalt.) A handsome red barn houses newly installed fermenting tanks, while the property's garage serves as a warehouse. A frisky golden retriever, tethered outside the winery, sports the name "Chief Chinook."

Come in and sit down; there's no tasting counter. Ask a technical question about winemaking or grape growing and you'll get a thorough answer: Kay and Clay, after all, used to teach commercial winemakers and grape growers how to do it, or fix it when it went wrong. ("She makes house calls," the saying went.) Have a bit of bread and cheese with your wine: it's Gouda from a cheesemaker in Sunnyside, and the bread is from Kay's oven.

Tasting the wine ★★★. Chinook buys its grapes from four vineyards in the Yakima Valley. Its best-known wine, Topaz, is a blend of Semillon and Sauvignon Blanc in the style of a white Bordeaux; several restaurants promote it as an accompaniment to oysters. The recent Sauvignon Blanc has a grassy quality, tempered by American oak, which also gives the wine a soft mouth feel. Not that all Chinook wines are entirely successful, however. We've found the pleasant harmony of fruit and French oak in the Chardonnay marred, sad to say, by its lingering, bitter finish. Chinook also makes small amounts of Merlot and sparkling Riesling.

Getting there. Take Exit 82 from I-82 at Prosser, proceed one block west on Wine Country Rd (formerly Hwy 12) to Wittkopf Rd. The winery is on the right. [**Map:** The Hogue Cellars]

Open Friday through Sunday from noon to 5; closed in January.

Special events: Merlot released on Memorial Day weekend.

A word from the winery. *"We invite you to visit the friendly home of Chinook Wines to sample our uniquely styled wines and enjoy a wine country picnic in the adjoining garden. Our specially selected lots of Chardonnay, Sauvignon Blanc, Semillon and Merlot grapes are carefully crafted into wines that are an ideal companion to regional foods."*

COLUMBIA CREST

Columbia Crest Drive
Highway 221
P.O. Box 231
Paterson, WA 99345
(509) 875-2061

Owners: Stimson Lane
    Wine & Spirits, Ltd.
Winemaker: Doug Gore
Year established: 1982
Production capacity: 2,000,000 gal.
Vineyards: over 2,000 acres
Touring: Columbia Valley S. [p15]

A bit of background. Columbia Crest is the biggest and most technologically advanced winery in the Pacific Northwest as well as one of the area's most attractive for tourists. The winery evolved from a need by Chateau Ste. Michelle to crush the grapes closer to the eastern Washington vineyards where they were grown and harvested, and to provide additional production and storage facilities for Chateau Ste. Michelle's rapid expansion in the early 1980s. The company had purchased (from Amfac, a Hawaii-based agribusiness concern) an enormous piece of property overlooking the Columbia River. Most of the land had been planted in 300-acre circles of corn, irrigated through center pivots with wheeled, quarter-mile-long sprinklers. Ste. Michelle converted some of the cornfields to vineyards, replaced the pivots with conventional sprinklers, spent over $25 million to build a magnificent new winery on the property, and named it River Ridge. At the facility's dedication in the summer of 1983, dignitaries spoke admiringly of Ste. Michelle's commitment to the future of Washington winemaking. Surveying the 2,000 acres of vineyards, wine historian Leon Adams called it "a viticultural miracle."

A year later, Ste. Michelle created a new label, Columbia Crest, to showcase wines made from Columbia Valley grapes. The first releases were blends (a white and a blush) of Riesling, Gewurztraminer, and Muscat; handsomely packaged and extensively advertised, the brand took hold. By 1987, the entire Columbia Crest concept was spun off as a separate winery. The River Ridge complex was rechristened Columbia Crest, and a full line of Columbia Crest varietal wines, no longer a "second label," began showing up on shelves and restaurant wine lists across the country.

Visiting the winery ★★★★. The road across the Horse Heaven Hills climbs 2,000 feet above the Yakima River, with magnificent views ★★★★ up and down its fertile valley, then deposits you on a vast plateau stretching as far as the eye can see. This isn't Washington, you think, it's Kansas! On and on you go, up and down the softly undulating roads bordered with Russian thistle; occasional grain towers break the skyline. You might even see a family of giant combines crossing the wheat fields like a futuristic army. After half an hour, you begin to see vineyards, stretching into the distance like wheat fields. At last the winery itself comes into view, built on a ridge overlooking the Columbia.

At the receiving dock outside, stainless steel dejuicing tanks stand tall, like shiny grain silos, with scales and crushers at their feet. The rest of the winery—acres and acres worth—is bunkered into the hillside to keep out the heat of the sun. The public side of the facility is on the grand scale of farmhouse estates in the wine country of France: solid stone walls, enormous wooden gates, and an inner courtyard big enough for wagons to deliver loads of grapes, and for freight trucks to pick up cases of finished wine. Vines are planted right up to the doors of the redwood-paneled tasting room, tapestries adorn the walls of the lobby, and there's a patio overlooking the river that is set up for picnics.

Tasting the wines ★★★. Columbia Crest's mission, if you will, was to use up the vast tonnages of grapes from newly matured vines. Selling enough Columbia Crest wine to justify the investment required good marketing as well as good winemaking; fortunately, both these talents were available. Under guidance from Ted Baseler and Bob Betz, the marketing consultants produced some of the most attractive packages seen on Northwest wines; they also put Columbia Crest advertising on national television, a first for Northwest wine. Meantime, Doug Gore, who had been making red wines for Chateau Ste. Michelle, was named overall winemaker for the new "sister" winery. He has avoided competing for regular Ste. Michelle customers by offering slightly different styles (at significantly lower prices) while maintaining the company's reputation for high quality.

Indeed, many Columbia Crest wines are superb. The 1987 Chardonnay, for instance, impressed us with its lovely vanilla, oak and fruit bouquet, and a pleasing, lemony taste. Even better was the 1986 Sauvignon Blanc, with a distinctly figgy nose and herbaceous flavors; many restaurants in Seattle sell it for about $10, providing one of the best values to be had among local wines.

Getting there. From Yakima, take Exit 82 off I-82 at Prosser and proceed across the Horse Heaven Hills on Hwy 221. The winery is north of Paterson, 26 mi from Prosser.

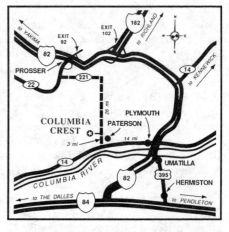

From the Tri-Cities, take I-82 south toward Umatilla; exit at Plymouth and proceed westbound for 14 mi to Paterson. Take Hwy 221 up the hill 3 mi to the winery.

Open daily from 10 to 4:30. Tour groups are welcome; there is no charge for visiting or tasting.

A word from the winery. "*In its first year, Columbia Crest varietal wines won an award at every competition in which they were entered. Taste these wines at the state-of-the-art winery, which is located in the center of its vineyards overlooking the Columbia River.*"

WHAT THE RATINGS MEAN FOR QUALITY OF WINE:

NR	No rating: not tasted at all or not tasted recently; no releases
★	Barely drinkable
★☆	Occasionally acceptable
★★	Uneven
★★☆	Usually good
★★★	Good
★★★☆	Usually superior
★★★★	Consistently superior

COLUMBIA WINERY

14030 N.E. 145th
P.O. Box 1248
Woodinville, WA 98070
(206) 488-2776

Owners: Private corporation
Winemaker: David Lake, M.W.
Winery operations manager:
 Max Zellweger
Year established: 1962
Production capacity: 240,000 gall.
Vineyards: None
Touring region: Seattle [p. 30]

A bit of background. It's been three decades since Lloyd Woodburne, the retired dean of the University of Washington's College of Arts and Sciences, began making wine in his Laurelhurst garage. By 1961, Woodburne and a coterie of academics and businessmen, all enthusiastic amateur winemakers, formalized their relationship as "Associated Vintners" and bought a small vineyard of their own in the Yakima Valley to assure a steady supply of premium wine grapes, Woodburne recalls.

In 1967, A.V. leased a warehouse in Kirkland and went commercial. When the first wines were released in 1969, Stan Reed wrote admiringly in the Seattle *Post Intelligencer* that "a revolutionary industry" had been born in Washington. A.V. grew rapidly along with the industry it helped spawn. Many of its wines won major awards, and its Gewurztraminer became a regional favorite. When they couldn't find A.V. wines in local stores, wine drinkers would line up outside the winery and buy out entire releases in a weekend. Three times the winery outgrew its facilities.

By 1980, A.V. was producing 25,000 gallons of wine a year, but further development was hampered by high interest rates and increasingly capable competition. The original vineyards were sold off in order to finance additional production capacity, and new investors signed on. Most significant of all the changes, a new winemaker, David Lake, was hired to take over from Lloyd Woodburne and the "tasting committee" that still controlled the winemaking. With Lake on the scene, the winery's designation as an "association of vintners" was no longer accurate, and the name was changed to Columbia Winery. (Another important Washington state producer, Columbia Crest, has nothing to do with Columbia Winery; Columbia Crest began in 1984 as an offshoot of Chateau Ste. Michelle. See the previous entry.)

Lake, a soft-spoken and unassuming Canadian, spent 10 years in the English wine trade, where he earned the coveted title of Master of Wine.

He left the genteel world of London's wine merchants to attend the University of California at Davis, then migrated to the vineyards of Oregon for hands-on experience. Today, he's the only one of about a hundred M.W.'s working as a winemaker in the U.S. His manner is quietly probing, searching. He spends at least one week a month in the vineyards with his contract growers. At the winery, whether he's tasting tank samples, barrel samples, or bottled wine, his routine is the same: he cocks his head slightly, poises one nostril above the glass, and repeatedly sniffs. Long after everyone else has finished talking about the wine, he will continue to sniff, swirl, and taste, seeking one last nuance, one last element of the wine's structure. He seems to approach every wine as a new opportunity for discovery.

Lake pulled off a great coup a couple of years ago, selling 1,000 cases of Columbia's 1984 Chardonnay to the prestigious London Sunday Times Wine Club. It was the largest export shipment of a varietal wine from the Northwest in history, a full container of Washington state Chardonnay; the reorder, a year later, was another 800 cases!

As Lake became more involved with the vineyards and the winery's marketing efforts, and spent less time at the winery, it became clear that Columbia needed a strong second-in-command (not just an assistant winemaker or cellar master). Again, a coup of sorts: Columbia hired Max Zellweger, the award-winning winemaker at Langguth. It's not at all common for two men of such caliber to work side-by-side. But there's only one winemaker, says Zellweger, and it's Lake.

Almost every survey of Northwest wineries recognizes Columbia as one of the region's outstanding producers. One of the most prestigious is the Critics' Choice award, for overall winery achievement, from the New York Wine Experience (an offshoot of *The Wine Spectator*); about 50 wineries in the world are chosen. Every year since the award was established in 1985, two winners have been from the Northwest: Chateau Ste. Michelle and Columbia.

Visiting the winery ★★★★. Columbia's old winery, a warehouse in Bellevue, was clearly too small, bursting with tanks, barrels, wine aging in bottles, and wine ready for shipment. Operations were divided between Bellevue and Coventry Vale in the Yakima Valley. Columbia's community profile was low and its visitor facilities minimal, yet the winery had grown to 100,000 cases with distribution into 40 states and seven foreign countries. Clearly an untenable situation.

Winery executives had spent many anxious months searching without success for a new facility near Seattle until the bankruptcy of Haviland Winery in Woodinville made its almost-new winery available. The Victorian mansion has 10,000 square feet of space for visitors and offices: a tasting room, a well-merchandised sales room, a big lobby for tours to assemble in, a spacious banquet room, private meeting rooms along with offices upstairs, stained glass windows, and broad verandas. Not to mention 30,000 square feet of winery space in back of the mansion, enough for close to half a million gallons of production capacity.

The new winery, welcomed with open arms (and some relief, no doubt, given Haviland's ups and downs) by top brass at Chateau Ste. Michelle, gives Woodinville two world-class wineries across the street from each other. The guided tour here becomes more interesting each month as equipment is moved over from the Bellevue warehouse, and the tastings usually provide an opportunity to try some of Columbia's older vintages.

Haviland had established quite a clientele for special events (such as weddings) in the banquet rooms; Columbia encourages members of the surrounding community to use those facilities.

Tasting the wines ★★★☆. Columbia has exclusive contracts with two of Washington's best growers (the Otis and Red Willow vineyards) and buys from several other highly regarded vineyards, including Wyckoff, Sagemoor, and Graves. Special lots of outstanding grapes receive vineyard designations and are embraced by the title "David Lake Signature Series".

There are several bottlings of Cabernet Sauvignon, ranging from an inexpensive vintage made from Columbia Valley grapes to three vineyard-designated wines (the Red Willow Cabernet won the Governor's Trophy for Washington's best red wine in 1985) to an illustrious 1979 Cab that's being sold under the name "Millennium" to encourage people to put it down until the year 2000. Our current favorite is the 1982 Otis Vineyard Cabernet, which gives off a heady bouquet of black currants and violets and shows uncommon richness on the palate. One or two of these older bottlings are usually available for tasting at the winery. The 1985 Columbia Valley Cabernet Sauvignon is now available; it has good body, well supported by its fruit.

Columbia's Merlots are distinctive, as are the Chardonnays, especially the barrel-fermented Wyckoff Vineyards bottling. Lake is particulatly fond of his Semillon, which he calls the undiscovered secret of the Northwest; see if you enjoy its assertive, bell pepper character. His philosophy: "Young wines are remarkably like young people, benefiting from a stable environment (sound cellar treatment) but allowed the freedom to develop their talents; they will often rebel if they are forced by winemakers into stylistic straitjackets."

A couple of years ago we concluded that Columbia produced some of the best wines in the Northwest; today we'd have to say that the honor belongs to The Hogue Cellars. We don't quibble with the bland "house" wines blended by Columbia for the restaurant trade; it's a good way for any winery to sell off less-than-first-quality juice, and the high end wines are invariably good. But in the course of blind tastings, we've encountered Semillon with a finish too bitter, a Chenin Blanc with insufficient varietal character, Rieslings lacking acid. Wines that lack the distinction and harmony that characterized Columbia for us in the past. But you must try them for yourself.

Getting there. Follow the directions (and **map**) to Chateau Ste. Michelle in Woodinville; Columbia is across the street.

Open daily from 10 to 5. There's no charge for tour groups. The winery's banquet and meeting facilities are available for rent.

Special events. "Crush weekends" take place during October, offering visitors a taste of the grapes, the crushed grape juice, and a sample of the wine made last year from the juice. An open house in December features Columbia wines with a variety of holiday foods from Bellevue caterer Penny Rawson.

A word from the winery. *"Our aim is to make distinctive Washington wines, not copies of wines from other classic wine regions. Comparisons are illuminating, but preoccupation with them can stifle the development of characteristic wine styles in promising new regions. We buy European vinifera grapes from areas of Washington state best suited to each variety, supervising all aspects of growing and picking, and select winemaking techniques suited to the unique qualities of each variety. Art as well as science plays a role in production, yielding wines of delicacy that age slowly and gracefully. Columbia wines are designed to be enjoyed with food and to appeal to America's maturing wine palate."*

"COLUMBIA GORGE"
A Marketing Primer

For two days in January, hundreds of people crowded into the "ballroom" of Columbia Winery's new manor in Woodinville, sampling a cornucopia of cakes, cheeses, mustards, relishes, breads, dried fruit, and smoked salmon. They tasted wine, they nibbled samples of sausage. They bought jars of pepper jellies, shortbread mix, and chili spices from three dozen local specialty food producers.

The public had been invited to discover the wealth of fine foods produced by the specialty purveyors in a wildly successful promotion the winery called "Columbia Gorge." Attracted by lots of publicity, posters, and advertising, some 2,000 people attended the event, four times the number expected, and generated some $25,000 in revenues for the winery.

Now, if 2,000 people turn out for a football game, the stadium looks empty. Even if 2,000 people attend a food event like Bite of Seattle, it's a failure. For Chateau Ste. Michelle, across the street from Columbia, 2,000 people is a slow weekend. But for many wineries, 2,000 visitors over a Friday and Saturday is an almost unheard of number.

That's because most wineries don't have a background in events management, in promotion, in tourism marketing. A few wineries sponsor concerts (Chateau Ste. Michelle and Champs de Brionne in Washington, Ste. Chapelle in Idaho, Oak Knoll in Oregon come to mind), but most wineries simply make wine, open the doors to the tasting room, and hope that people will drop by. At many wineries, tasting room staff get so bored that they almost pounce on the occasional hapless visitor.

Yet it's clear that aggressive marketing for visitor traffic can sell a good deal of wine. Anna Murch, who runs visitor operations at Snoqualmie and Langguth wineries, maintains that a medium-size winery can sell up to 30 percent of its production from a well-run tasting room. Tiny Bainbridge Island winery sells all of its 5,000 cases a year right out of the tasting room. Even Chateau Ste. Michelle, the largest winery in the Northwest, is believed to sell 10 percent of its wine at its four production facilities.

Enter Columbia Winery, a respected, 100,000-case winery which had operated from a serviceable but scarcely elegant warehouse in Bellevue.

In October 1988, Columbia moved into a much grander—and highly visible—facility built by the now-defunct Haviland Winery before its bankruptcy. Haviland's founder figured that the location alone, across the street from Chateau Ste. Michelle's popular winery and tourist attraction in Woodinville, would bring lots of overflow traffic and retail wine sales. Haviland was wrong; the wines were too uneven. So Columbia left its warehouse and took over the facility with its 10,000 square-foot visitor center.

By early December, winery operations manager Max Zellweger asked Columbia's head of retail sales, Sarah Carlton, to come up with a promotion that would increase traffic at the new location.

Carlton had come up with the catchy name, "Columbia Gorge," back in July; now she added the idea of involving members of a small trade organization called Northwest Specialty Food Producers. She sent letters of invitation in late December and by New Year's had some three dozen replies.

Columbia's barrel master, Alan Moen, happened to be a trained artist (with an MFA degree from Central Washington University) and freelance graphics designer before he joined the winery staff. He had sketched the concept for the humorous "Columbia Gorge" poster earlier in the year but had three days' notice to execute the final drawings.

A silk screen process was used to print 300 posters, and a Seattle company, Keep Posted, was commissioned to deliver (and post) copies in local stores and restaurants. Cost of the poster promotion was slightly more than $1,000. This included $350 to the artist, $500 to the printer, and about $200 for distribution. Left-over posters were sold at the event for $10. (Carlton had developed an understanding of the poster business during a stint as manager of Elliott Bay Graphics in Pioneer Square.)

Advertising was limited to *The Seattle Weekly,* an outlay Carlton now believes was unnecessary, given the response to her news releases.

A two-page release describing the event and listing the participants went out in early January to about 100 local writers and editors. "The media embraced the concept," Carlton recalled. KING-TV's *Tracy & Company* scheduled live television coverage. Carlton was interviewed by several local radio stations; the event received mention by *Seattle Times* columnists Carole Beers and Alf Collins and was prominently featured as a weekend "Best Bet." The *Journal American* put it on the front page of its weekend section, as did papers as far afield as Bremerton and Everett.

Carlton cites three reasons for the publicity success:

First, it was a "dead" time of year in terms of winery promotions. Second, it was an event involving people from the entire region, in a positive way. And, not least, "The media seemed to enjoy the humor in the name."

Columbia's president, Tacoma investor Dan Baty, said he enjoyed the "down home" feeling of the event. "We want the little guys, the small producers, the mom-and-pops, and we want the connection between wine and food." And unlike the big winery across the road, Baty said Columbia doesn't do events like car shows. "You don't sell wine to car shows."

The numbers are impressive: 2,000 people came. The first 500 were charged $5 admission and got a souvenir wineglass. When the wine-glasses ran out, the fee went down to $3 (although 300 paid the full price and got vouchers for a glass, which means that they'll be returning to the winery). A hundred or so autographed posters were sold at $10 each.

Carlton purchased inventory from the producers on consignment, expecting 500 people. The producers, for their part, brought samples for 500. Instead, four times that number came, stretching the "sample" budgets. Even so, the producers averaged between $200 and $500 apiece. At retail, the total was $11,500. Add to that some $4,500 worth of wine sold.

Additional costs to the winery: extra staff to set up, tear down, pour wine, and back up the producers (including a couple of teenagers hired just to run errands), and the cost of extra wine.

Gross revenues for the weekend approached $25,000, not a bad return on an out-of-pocket investment of about $2,000 for advertising, publicity, and materials. Still, as Carlton points out, "*Nothing* pays for a $6 million facility."

The real benefit, she concludes, is that everybody "won." The visiting specialty food people not only sold some product but got exposure to new customers. The winery generated new traffic and sold about 100 cases of wine. Best of all, Carlton believes, Columbia Winery's name was "every-where" in a very positive context.

"What we're learning," Carlton says, "is that Columbia is no longer just in the wine business, as we were in Bellevue. Here in Woodinville, we've got to be in the entertainment business."

COOLEN WINE CELLAR

5759 Banner Road S.E.
Port Orchard, WA 98366
P.O. Box 4031
South Colby, WA 98384
(206) 871-0567

Owners: Dick & Linda Coolen
Winemaker: Dick Coolen
Year established: 1986
Production capacity: 1,000 gallons
Vineyards: 0.5 acre
Touring: Olympic Peninsula [p. 36]

A bit of background. Masonry contractor Dick Coolen made wine as a hobby for five years before getting a commercial license. A jack-of-all-trades (farmer, musician), Coolen tasted the fruity wines of Germany and resolved to "give others that experience." He visited a number of small wineries in California and Washington to get an idea of where he wanted to go in his winemaking. Gerard Bentryn at Bainbridge Island Winery became a mentor.

Visiting the winery ★★. An ambitious construction project is in the works: a 40-by-80-foot winery with a cellar and a second floor to be used for entertainment. Dick Coolen envisions brick arches forming a portico around the new building. Until that's finished, visitors to the wooded, 10-acre site will use a tasting room in the barn. No picnic facilities are currently available at the winery itself, but Manchester State Park is only three miles away, and there's a park at the marina in downtown Port Orchard. Fishing is good at Long Lake, half a mile away.

Port Orchard, the Kitsap County seat, has a reputation as an antique-shopper's heaven. Should you sail your boat into Port Orchard, give the Coolens a call; they'll pick you up and show you the winery.

Tasting the wines (NR). Coolen currently uses California grapes (Valespina, Carignane) and Washington Merlot to make three red wines: a dry Banner Red, an off-dry Port Orchard Red, and a fruity Port Orchard Rose. They're finished without sulfites and are available only at the winery.

Plans call for a sparkling white wine to be produced from estate-grown Madeline Angevine and Siegerrebe grapes.

Getting there. Seven mi southeast of Port Orchard. From the Southworth ferry terminal, head west on Sedgewick Rd for 2.5 mi and turn left on Banner Rd. The winery is 0.3 mi south. From Hwy 16 (which runs from Tacoma toward Bremerton) take the Sedgewick turnoff, and go east about 5 mi to Banner Rd.

Open Saturday from noon to 5.

Special events. "Fathoms of Fun" celebrated at the end of June.

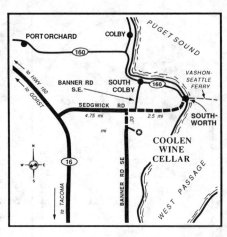

A word from the winery. *"A unique personal experience to visit a small winery that gives you individual attention. Located on 10 acres among the tall evergreen trees, Coolen Wine Cellar has just that warm touch for a weekend trip that gets you away and into the country atmosphere, and gives you a lift and refreshes the spirit. The wine is premium, free-run with no sulfites added. Give yourself a chance to taste wine that cannot be purchased in any store. The future release of Cremont will be an experience to share. Come and find out what Cremont is all about!"*

COVENTRY VALE
Wilgus Road at Evans Road
P. O. Box 249
Grandview, WA 98930
(509) 882-4100

Owners: David Wyckoff & Donald Toci
Winery manager: Bill Bagge
Production capacity: 1.3 million gallons
Vineyards: 650 acres
Year established: 1983
Touring: Yakima Valley [p. 15]

A bit of background. Coventry Vale is the Yakima Valley's largest premium winery, crushing over a million gallons a year, much of it for other wineries. David Wyckoff, a former Seattle attorney who returned to the valley to manage his family's farming interests, decided that he would invest in production facilities rather than a marketing organization; he's been joined within the past year by Donald Toci, who moved the tanks he'd put in at Yakima River Winery over to Coventry. Together, they've got a winery second only to Columbia Crest in terms of production capacity.

The actual business of making wine (crushing the grapes and fermenting the juice) is very capital intensive: it requires a large investment in expensive machinery and tanks. Coventry Vale makes it possible for at least three types of customers to produce wine without having to build their own facilities: grape growers who figure they can strike a better deal selling bulk wine than perishable fruit, winemakers who can't afford to build their own facility, and winemakers who need a temporary increase in production capacity.

Coventry Vale offers equipment that's as good as (or better than) other premium wineries (no "bulk" presses here) and rents its facilities for a fee that might depend on such factors as tonnage of grapes crushed, volume of wine made, or length of time it's being stored. In charge of operations here is Bill Bagge, who helped run Sonoma Vineyards before moving to Washington.

Visiting the winery ★★. Coventry Vale occupies a 25,000-square-foot building at the intersection of Wilgus and Evans roads amidst the fields and orchards outside Grandview; it looks like any other farm outbuilding, except that there's now a little lawn out front. The inside is filled to capacity with a dense array of tanks, barrels, hoses, bottling equipment, and a sophisticated lab; the crushing pad out back is crowded with more equipment, including a 22-ton Bucher press. It's a very busy place, with clients in and out all the time to check on their wines, and a very sophisticated lab to run the tests.

Tasting the wines ★★. The Coventry Vale line of sparkling wines is made by the traditional méthode champenoise, and is affordably priced. We think the best is the Brut. Another brand, Washington Discovery, doesn't have Coventry's name on it. Samples we've tried lately haven't been particularly distinguished, but they're quite palatable and certainly not expensive.

A number of other labels are or have been Coventry products: private bottlings for distributors or restaurants; out-of-state wines such as Houston Vineyards in Oregon, and the early Rose Creek wines in Idaho; the first Snoqualmie wines (in fact, David Wyckoff was the original owner of Snoqualmie); a lot of Columbia's wines have been made here, too. You can spot them by checking the Bonded Winery number; look for the designation BW WA 99.

Getting there. From I-82, take Exit 72 (Grandview) and go north on County Line Rd to Hawks Rd. Turn right, go 3 mi to Wilgus, then left to Evans.

Open by appointment only.

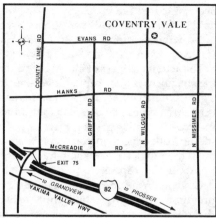

A word from the winery. *"Coventry Vale strives to bring you the very best in premium varietal wines. Look for our Washington Discovery label featuring Johannisberg Riesling, Chenin Blanc, Muscat Canelli, and Chardonnay. For those special occasions, try our Coventry Vale methode champenoise premium champagnes in Brut, Extra Dry, Extra Dry Rose and Demi Sec."*

COVEY RUN
Route 2, Box 2287
Zillah, WA 98953
(509) 829-6235

COVEY RUN AT MOSS BAY
107 Central Way
Kirkland, WA 98033
(206) 828-3848

Owners: Quail Run Vintners
Winemaker & general manager: Dave Crippen
Year established: 1982
Production capacity: 100,000 gal.
Vineyards: 180 acres
Touring regions:
  Yakima Valley [p. 14]
  Seattle [p. 30]

A bit of background. The origins of this winery are in the land, in two slopes overlooking the Yakima Valley—the 100-acre Whiskey Canyon Vineyard and the 80-acre Willard Farms. Planted with premium grapes in 1980, these vineyards formed the basis for a partnership that evolved into one of Washington's foremost wineries.

You cannot drive past any orchard or town in the valley without seeing the name Holtzinger on a fruit tote or processing plant, and it is this same Holtzinger family, Charles and Felicia, who spearheaded the investment: developing the vineyards, hiring the key people, building a winery big enough to make plenty of wine and attractive enough to draw plenty of tourists.

Winemaker David Crippen, who holds a master's degree in enology from U.C.-Davis, has recently taken on additional duties as general manager. The position was held since the winery's founding by the energetic Stan Clarke, who remains on the board of Quail Run Vintners and will continue to do part-time promotional work for Covey Run; Clarke will spend most of his time consulting on vineyard management and winemaking for other wineries, notably Hyatt.

Visiting the winery (Zillah) ★★★☆. As much as anything, it's the view ★★★★ from Covey Run that explains what wine touring is all about: green vineyards and lush orchards in the foreground, the deep purple spine of the Horse Heaven Hills reclining across the fertile valley floor. The winery, built of concrete and cedar, is dug into a hillside in the foothills of the Rattlesnake Mountains, adjacent to the Roza Canal, the irrigation project that makes it possible for the valley to flourish. The tasting room, on the mezzanine level overlooking the production area, is filled with antiques, quilts, and Oriental rugs. The conference room/private dining room doubles as an art gallery. Outside, a wide patio and lawn have been set with tables, providing the perfect spot for a picnic.

The advent of Covey Run—a beautiful winery with fine, clean wine, an easy half-hour's drive from Yakima—probably did more for wine touring in Washington than a decade of competitions and medals and advertising. "The advent of the wine industry has literally changed the faces of the people of the valley," in Stan Clarke's opinion. "People are saying, 'We've really got something to offer,' rather than just 'I farm here.'"

Visiting the winery (Kirkland) ★★☆. Kirkland's bustling waterfront, a marina and Moss Bay Park, are surrounded by upscale boutiques, seafood restaurants . . . and the western Washington outpost of Covey Run. Washington law requires these satellites to be functioning wineries (unlike Oregon, where any winery is permitted to have a couple of extra tasting rooms), and the function here is the production of champagne and the barrel aging of some Merlot. Neither requires any particular attention, so the law is satisfied while the winery sales room gets a few visitors.

Covey Run's operation in the refurbished building occupied by the Kirkland Roaster, is flanked by a microbrewery, Hale's Ales. There's a big window, so visitors can watch the brewmasters at work; there's also a tasting counter and a full line of Covey Run wines for sale.

Tasting the wines ★★★. Covey Run's Johannisberg Riesling provided its first big success; to many people, this luscious, off-dry Riesling, with its distinctive nose of apricots, was the epitome of Washington wine.

Covey Run's best current release is a superb sweet Riesling from the Mahre Vineyards that smells like apples, apricots, and linalool (the unique character a Riesling acquires with successful bottle-aging); it has an unctuous, silky mouth feel and matches beautifully with fruit desserts.

The winery's original Chardonnay captured some of the most significant awards in the state, including "Washington Wine of the Year" in 1986. More recently, however, Covey Run Chardonnays have been uneven; our recent tastings found that the 1986 Chardonnay lacked the depth and elegance of earlier vintages. Other whites worth noting are a "poor cousin" of Chardonnay called Aligote, which can make a decent wine in its better years. The 1988 Fume Blanc has none of the variety's pleasing grassiness; it's austere and bitter. Covey Run's La Caille de Fume, which used to contain Sauvignon Blanc, will be mostly Semillon when it's released later in 1989.

Among the reds, there's a fruity, "nouveau"-style Lemberger, a potent and spicy Merlot, and an intense Cabernet Sauvignon.

Getting there (Zillah winery). From I-82, take Exit 52 (westbound) or Exit 54 (eastbound) into the town of Zillah. The winery is on Morris Rd, 5 mi northeast of town.

Getting there (Kirkland winery). From I-405, take Exit 18 and head west toward Kirkland's shopping district. From Hwy 520, take the Kirkland exit and go north. The winery is next to the Kirkland Roaster restaurant and Hale's brewery.

Open daily from 10 to 5; Sunday from noon. (Winters from 11 to 4:30.) Tour groups are welcome, but should make an appointment; there is no charge for the visit or tasting.

Special events. The winery's annual anniversary weekend gives rise to a three-day celebration at the beginning of April. There's also a "Longest Day Evening" picnic toward the end of June.

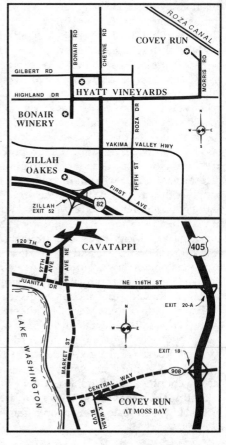

A word from the winery. *"From the first vintage in 1982, Covey Run wines have received tremendous consumer and critical acclaim. The winery was built just above the vineyards to take advantage of the panoramic view stretching across the Yakima Valley to snowy Mount Adams in the distance. The outside deck and lawn are available for picnics."*

EATON HILL WINERY

530 Gurley Road
Granger, WA 98932
(509) 854-2508

Owners: Edwin & JoAnn Stear
Winemaker: To be named
Year established: 1987
Production capacity: 3,000 gallons
Vineyards: 7 acres
Touring: Yakima Valley [p. 14]

A bit of background. Ed Stear holds a Ph.D. from UCLA in electrical engineering. He's been a teacher on two of the University of California campuses, done a lot of consulting for private industry and the space program, and, since 1983, he's been executive director of the Washington Technology Center on the University of Washington campus. The center, established by the state legislature, channels money to the state's research universities to support projects whose commercial applications will strengthen and diversify the state's economy.

How then does this paragon of the scientific establishment get the wild idea to restore an old homestead in the middle of the Yakima Valley? Ed's father made wine (using an old press that will be displayed at Eaton Hill), and the Stears have traveled extensively in Europe. And though he's had no formal enological training, Ed Stear has given the subject of winemaking extensive study. "We wanted to start a winery years ago, when we lived in Santa Barbara," he told us. Now the project is taking life at last.

Visiting the winery (NR). Not far from the freeway stands the turn-of-the-century Rinehold Cannery Homestead. Floyd Rinehold, who started the cannery, was a builder of homes and commercial structures in the valley in the early 1900s. He married Emma Eaton, and the family formed the nucleus of the canning operation, which processed local produce for several decades under the "Yakima Farmer" label. Today, the cannery homestead is a bed-and-breakfast inn operated by Gary and Arlene Rogers, with a couple of beautifully furnished bedrooms and a big dining room that can serve 15. (For reservations, call the number listed for the winery.)

Adjacent to the homestead stands the cannery itself, which Ed Stear is turning into a winery. It's a large building, 12,000 square feet, with lots of space for the winery's operations and expansion. But its size has slowed the winery's opening; Stear decided to restore it and that meant, among other things, replacing 800 window panes and the entire roof. "It's slower going than I expected," Stear told us. He'll end up with a winery big enough to produce 50,000 gallons a year.

Tasting the wines. Riesling and Semillon will be produced from the first crush. Eventually, Stear hopes to make the whole gamut of white and red wines.

Getting there. Take Exit 58 from I-82 at Granger and follow the Yakima Valley Hwy (Old Hwy 12) along the north side of the freeway. At the Punkin Corner intersection, turn onto Gurley Rd. The winery is 0.5 mi from Punkin Corner. [Map: Horizon's Edge]

Hours: Eaton Hill did not have a schedule at press time. Picnic facilities will be available. No charge for tour groups.

A word from the winery. *"Eaton Hill Winery, offering its first wines in 1989, is a large gray-block building on the south side of Gurley Road near Highway 12. Visitors may stay at the Rinehold Cannery Homestead, the adjacent bed-and-breakfast inn, convenient for touring the several fine wineries in the immediate vicinity. Development of Eaton Hill Winery is continuing, with the tasting room, gift shop featuring homemade items, and picnic areas moving from the planning stage to completion in 1989. Stop by and encourage us in this family project, which we plan to build into a premier winery."*

WHAT THE RATINGS MEAN FOR QUALITY OF WINE:

NR	No rating: not tasted at all or not tasted recently; no releases
★	Barely drinkable
★☆	Occasionally acceptable
★★	Uneven
★★☆	Usually good
★★★	Good
★★★☆	Usually superior
★★★★	Consistently superior

FACELLI WINERY

12335 134th Court N.E.
Suite 100
Redmond, WA 98052
(206) 823-9466

Owner: Louis & Sandy Facelli
Winemaker: Lou Facelli
Year established: 1988
Production capacity: 6,000 gallons
Vineyards: None
Touring region: Seattle [p. 30]

A bit of background. Lou Facelli is back! This news will hearten his many fans, who fondly remember the winery he built in Wilder, Idaho, and lost to the very people he thought had saved him. Boiling down a complex story: to finance expansion of his vineyards, Lou had sold a two-thirds interest in the original Facelli Winery to the Batt brothers. A syndicate headed by Boise financier and winemaker Bill Broich—in a venture that was briefly known as Petros Winery—was looking for a winemaking facility. The Batts sold it their majority interest in Facelli, effectively getting rid of Lou. Petros is now defunct, but it's small consolation to Lou Facelli. He moved his family to Seattle, found short-term assignments with Salmon Bay and Haviland, and worked diligently to start his own winery again. Fortunately, his enthusiasm didn't dim.

It's going to be a craft winery, Lou promises. He's starting with less than 3,500 gallons, will double that in 1989, and peak at 12,000 to 15,000. He intends to distribute the wines himself.

"I enjoy the entire business of wine," Lou says. "It's my life."

Visiting the winery (NR). The opening in a modest industrial space in the Totem Lake area, was scheduled for April 1989. The sign that hung over the entrance to the old Idaho winery will become the tasting room counter in the new space. Salute!

Tasting the wines ★★★. First releases include a 1988 Riesling, almost dry, with flavors of apricot, grapefruit, and pineapple. Also a 1988 Semillon, which we tasted just two weeks after bottling; the wine had spent a month in new Nevers oak and was still "coming together," but has a fine, crisp balance.

Additional releases in the course of 1989 will include Chardonnay and Sauvignon Blanc, with Merlot to follow in a year or so.

Getting there. From I-405, take Exit 20; follow N.E. 124th to 134th Ct N.E. in the Willows Ridge Technical Center, opposite Graham Steel. [Map: Chateau Ste. Michelle]

Open Friday and Saturday from noon to 4.

Special events will be announced as additional wines are released.

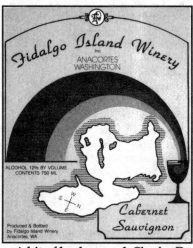

FIDALGO ISLAND WINERY

5303 Doon Way
Anacortes, WA 98221
(206) 293-4342

Owner & winemaker:
  Charles C. Dawsey
Year established: 1986
Production capacity: 8,400 gallons
Vineyards: None
Touring: Western Washington
  [p.30]

A bit of background. Charles Dawsey, with a background in law and life insurance, started making wine in the late 1950s. He soon found that wine gave him headaches and breathing problems. The problem, he determined, was the sulfur compounds in wine, which gave him asthma. Most people would give up their hobby, but not Dawsey: he discovered a way to make wine without sulfites. It doesn't taste like conventional wine, he admits, but he's catering to the market for sulfite-free wine, not the festival judges. "I'll put my wine into competitions when the judges are asthmatics," he says.

Dawsey apparently became discouraged by unexpected malolactic fermentations in his wines after bottling (which made the wines cloudy) and withdrew the products from the market early in 1989. Unable to afford a membrane filter or floating-top tanks, and unwilling to decant the wines lest they be exposed to oxygen, he had to carefully siphon the wines into new bottles. Slow going: four or five cases a day. "But I don't want the concept [of sulfite-free wines] to die," he told us.

Visiting the winery ★. The winery is located in Charles Dawsey's garage. There's no tasting room. (Dawsey wanted to buy the Mount Baker Vineyards winery in 1988 and tried unsuccessfully to raise about half a million dollars to finance the deal.) He's still hoping to move out of his garage soon.

Tasting the wines ★. The Bureau of Alcohol, Tobacco and Firearms has certified that the wine contains no "free" sulfur dioxide, but doesn't make any judgment that it's palatable. The Fidalgo Island Chardonnay we tasted was dark, oxidized, and didn't taste like Chardonnay. ("Horrible" was one of the nicer terms on the tasting sheets.) The Cabernet Sauvignon, described by one Seattle wine writer as "a gem" and "soft and drinkable," tasted like sweet nail polish to us.

Some of the flavor in Fidalgo Island wines comes from small amounts of "oak tea" that Dawsey brews with oak chips. (He says he invented the use of oak chips in 1960.) And regardless of what we say, his wines get high marks from asthmatics who can't drink regular wine.

Getting there. Head through Anacortes toward the ferry terminal. Follow the side streets indicated on the map to reach the winery.

Open weekends by appointment only.

A word from the winery. "*I have been especially gratified at the response of people who are allergic to sulfur dioxide. Hopefully we will be able to make our wines available to more people in the near future after our expansion.*"

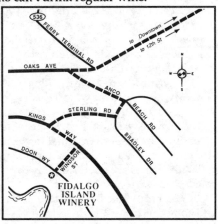

E. B. FOOTE WINERY

9354 Fourth Avenue S.
Seattle, WA 98108
(206) 763-9928

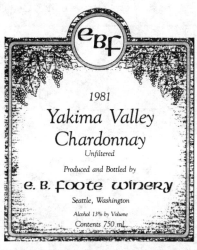

1981
Yakima Valley Chardonnay
Unfiltered

Produced and Bottled by

e. B. foote winery

Seattle, Washington

Alcohol 13% by Volume
Contents 750 mL

Owners: Eugene B. & Jeanie Foote
Winemaker: Eugene B. Foote
Year established: 1978
Production capacity: 12,000 gallons
Vineyards: None
Touring region: Seattle [p. 30]

A bit of background. Gene Foote, who runs this little winery in a patch of farmland in South Park, grew up in the Yakima Valley but has made his professional career as a senior engineer with Boeing. An active person who didn't foresee gardening or travel as ideal retirement activities, Gene told us, "I needed something to keep me busy." He was an amateur winemaker for 15 years before turning his avocation into a commercial operation; the grapes for his wines come from vineyards owned by Mary Foote's family in the Grandview area of the Yakima Valley. "Trying to grow grapes in western Washington," Foote told us once, "is like butting your head against a wall."

Visiting the winery ★. Gene Foote outgrew his first winery by 1983 and moved into an older farmhouse property amidst the truck farms of the rapidly changing South Park neighborhood, where row crops are regularly gobbled up by industrial buildings. On a clear day, you can see the Space Needle and the Seattle skyline from his loading dock.

Gene Foote is doubtless not alone when he says (as he did to us), "If I had known how expensive the wine business is, I wouldn't have done it." Similarly, anyone in the wine industry will tell you that it's not hard to sell wine, just hard to make money at it.

Tasting the wines ★. E. B. Foote wines are all made without recourse to many of the modern winemaking techniques, such as filtering, or even stopping fermentation by means of chemicals or centrifuging. The result is that the wines are all remarkably dry—often too dry even for sophisticated palates.

"If I had my choice," Gene told us, "my wines wouldn't be displayed and compared with Northwest wines—that's provincial." For example, he maintains that his Gewurztraminer should be compared to the wines of Alsatian producer Hubert Trimbach. The trouble is that many Americans don't know what classical wines are supposed to taste like, Gene laments.

Getting there. From I-5 northbound, take Exit 156 (West Marginal Wy), proceed about 5 miles to the Des Moines Wy exit. Turn onto 96th Ave S., continue north onto Fourth Ave S. At the second house, turn right onto the dirt road; the winery is half a block farther on the right.

From I-5 southbound, take Exit 162 (Michigan-Corson St) to East Marginal Wy S., turn south and cross the 16th Ave S. Bridge into South Park. Turn right on 96th Ave S., continue north onto Fourth Ave S., and turn right onto the dirt road at the second house.

From Hwy 509, take the Cloverdale exit; turn right on Fifth Ave S., right again on S. Henderson, left on Fourth Ave S., left again onto the dirt road.

Open Tuesday and Thursday evenings from 6:30 to 9:30; Saturday from 9:30 to 3:30.

Special events. Foote has a Harvest Festival in October. And local craftspeople show their wares at his Christmas Arts and Crafts Fair over two weekends in early December, at which he also releases his new wines.

**1985
Washington State
Merlot**

Produced and Bottled by French Creek Cellars BWC-WA-97
Woodinville, Washington Alcohol 14.4% by Volume
CONTAINS SULFITES

FRENCH CREEK CELLARS

17721 132nd Avenue N.E.
Woodinville, WA 98072
(206) 486-1900

Owners: Bill Mundy,
   Hans &   Trudel Doerr,
   Wendell Clifford,
   Nancy Clifford & Maurice
   Hooks, Fred Mundy
Winemaker: Richard Winter
Year established: 1983
Production capacity: 15,000 gallons
Vineyards: None
Touring region: Seattle [p.30]

A bit of background. A winery in search of itself. Founded by two families, psychiatrist Hans Doerr and his wife, Trudy, and bassonist Arthur Grossman and his wife, Leah, French Creek Cellars was founded with the premise of producing only the best Cabernet Sauvignon. The first wines weren't Cabernet but uncompromising versions of Muscat Morio, Gewurztraminer, and Riesling, made by the partners themselves. French Creek survived an early trauma when the Grossmans gave up, Arthur to pursue his career with the Soni Venturum quintet, Leah to devote more time to the Boulangerie bakery. Fred Mundy, a longstanding amateur winemaking companion, stepped in, along with his brother and a few others, to keep French Creek alive. A full-time cellarmaster helped a lot, as did a new label, a move to Woodinville, and an award-winning marketing campaign (by the Solkover Group). What the winery still lacks, for want of better terms, is artistic direction and technical authority.

Visiting the winery ★★☆. French Creek's move from Redmond to Woodinville has made it easier to find and has boosted tourist traffic. The new setting doesn't aspire to the grand scale of Chateau Ste. Michelle or Columbia; we find the change of pace refreshing. A couple of picnic tables stand on the bank above Little Bear Creek, a stream where salmon still spawn at harvest season.

A large, paneled tasting room overlooks the picnic area. A picture of the real French Creek hangs on the wall, showing a silver streak of water swirling across the dark stones in the deep woods of the North Cascades. The tasting room staff is generous with samples, and prices are more than fair.

Tasting the wines ★★. French Creek's advertising agency has devised an admirable communications program to keep its customers and the general public informed of special events. We get more mail from French

Creek than any other winery in the state, but the winery is still trying to develop an identity that merges the partners' vision of "handmade" wine with the realities of the marketplace. Winemaking styles swing widely from one vintage to the next, many of the wines are so tannic and alcoholic they need extensive aging, and too many of them develop unacceptable faults by the time they're released. This is unfortunate, because most French Creek wines we've tasted have shown promise in the early stages; they don't seem to recover from the insult of being barrel-aged and bottled.

Recent blind tastings of French Creek wines haven't improved our assessment. The 1987 Chardonnay, to name just one wine, was quite alcoholic (14.5 degrees) and lacked the acid to show off its underlying fruit. The most disappointing French Creek wine we've tasted lately was a deep violet 1986 Reserve Merlot, which offered a hint of cherries and wood violets in the nose; but the fruit was so overwhelmed with almost gagging levels of tannin and alcohol that its varietal character was destroyed. At our blind tasting, we couldn't imagine anyone actually drinking this wine with anything and enjoying it.

A sample of the 1988 Merlot, on the other hand, was young and flavorful, clean and moderately tannic; it was on its way into barrels, though, so we can't predict its fate.

We liked the 1984 Reserve Cabernet Sauvignon, which had pleasant flavors of licorice, berries, and flowers. (The grapes came from Otis Vineyards, where yields in 1984 were about half a ton to the acre.) The 1988 White Lemberger had a candylike nose of cherries, oranges, and melon; its low alcohol was in balance with the modest character of the wine. We were also quite taken with the 1986 French Creek Ice Wine at a consumer panel in the Tri-Cities a couple of years back; it had a wonderful nose of apricots and tasted like nectar. The current Late Harvest wine was made from Semillon in 1987; it has a clean aroma of new-mown hay, light flavors, and an almost syrupy texture.

Getting there. From I-405, take Exit 23-A (Hwy 522) toward Monroe and turn off at the Woodinville exit. Go one block toward Woodinville on 132nd Ave N.E.; turn left (before the railroad overpass) onto N.E. 177th Pl and left again to French Creek Cellars. [**Map:** Chateau Ste. Michelle]

Open daily from noon to 5.

Special events. An enjoyable bottle-your-own event for "cellar rats" takes place in May. July is anniversary month. There's a Fall Red Sale in September, and a holiday food and wine open house in November.

A word from the winery. *"French Creek is a small premium winery, family-owned, located in Woodinville, the wine capital of the Northwest, at the beginning of the 'winery route.'*

"Many of our wines have received national and international acclaim. Please join us at the winery for regular tastings and enjoy a picnic next to Little Bear Creek. Visit our gift shop, tour the winery, and include your name on our mailing list, which announces many special events during the year."

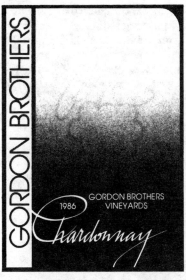

GORDON BROTHERS CELLARS

531 Levey Road
Pasco, WA 99301
(509) 547-6224

Owners: Jeff & Bill Gordon
Winemaker: Jeff Gordon
Year established: 1983
Production capacity: 8,000 gallons
Vineyards: 80 acres
Touring region: Tri-Cities [p. 20]

A bit of background. Jeff and Bill Gordon grew up in Whitman County and have been farming since 1977. Originally, they grew potatoes on their property outside of Pasco; they began planting wine grapes in 1980. When their first commercial crop was ready in 1983, the Gordons found that grape prices in Washington state had plummeted after a bumper harvest from a crop that many were saying had been drastically overplanted. (The market price for some premium varieties dropped below $200 a ton for grapes that had sold for $750 a ton the year before; some 2,000 tons of grapes simply remained unharvested.) So Jeff Gordon, a grower's grower, bonded a winery to find a home for his own grapes.

Visiting the winery ★★☆. There are only eight inches of rainfall per year out here on the edge of this dryland wheat country (known as the Palouse); the Gordon property encompasses 160 acres, half of it vineyards, half a mixture of cherries, walnuts, and pears. The vineyards, first planted in 1981, contain Chardonnay, Sauvignon Blanc, Merlot, and Cabernet.

Jeff Gordon's home stands high on a hillside, with a terrific view ★★★ over the lush vineyards and an idyllic park on the shore, below, of a narrow strip of water called Lake Sacajawea, formed by damming the Snake River. Atop this bluff, beside the house, stand the two structures that currently make up Gordon Brothers Cellars: a wooden shed filled with tanks and a tasting counter, and a 45-foot "reefer" trailer without its undercarriage where the case goods are stored. A gas pump reminds you of the remoteness of the location.

Tasting the wines ★★★. Six varieties are now available, with the reds (Cabernet Sauvignon and Merlot) showing enormous promise. In fact, the splendid 1986 Merlot won the Grand Prize at the 1988 Enological

Society festival in Seattle. The off-dry Riesling and Chenin Blanc are very nicely balanced. The 1986 Chardonnay, produced along classical lines, showed the serious, almost flinty character of a fine Chablis. Some of the Gordons' Chardonnay grapes also find their way into Woodward Canyon wines, by the way. Meantime, in a show of confidence that his magnificent site can "grow some of the best red grapes in the state," Jeff Gordon has replaced his 16-acre block of Chenin Blanc with Merlot and Cabernet Sauvignon.

Getting there. Two mi out of Pasco along Hwy 12, heading toward Walla Walla, turn northeast onto the Pasco-Kahlotus Rd; proceed for 12 mi to Levey Park. Turn right and continue 0.5 mi on Levey Park Rd, then left onto Levey Rd.

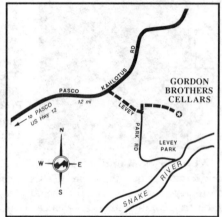

Open weekends from 11 to 5, June through August.

Special events. Anniversary celebration, first weekend in July. Vineyard tours and special tastings are available by appointment.

A word from the winery. *"The vineyard of Gordon Brothers is rapidly developing as one producing fruit of the highest quality. The quality comes through in our wines. This is proven by the 30-plus awards our wines have received in our short history. Our vineyards and winery overlook the Snake River at Levey Park, two miles above Ice Harbor Dam in Franklin County. Please join us and enjoy an incredible view and taste our outstanding wines."*

RATING THE WINERY VISITS:

NR	Not rated: tasting room not open, no visiting
★	Don't bother
★★	Moderately interesting
★★★	Worth a detour
★★★★	Worth the trip

See the introduction (page 8) for additional information on the criteria used to rate winery visits.

GRANT'S

(Yakima Brewing & Malting Co.)
25 N. Front Street
Yakima, WA 98901
(509) 575-1900
(509) 575-2922 (brewpub)

Owner & winemaker: Bert Grant
Year established: 1983
Production capacity: 4,500 gallons
Vineyards: None
Touring region: Yakima Valley [p14]

A bit of background. Why is Yakima Brewing in a directory of wineries? Because it makes a hard cider. And the government, in its wisdom, requires a winemaking license for cider production. (After all, it's "wine" from apples.) That's how H.L. (Bert) Grant, probably the foremost brewer in Washington, ends up in this book. Or starts out. He's also been a home winemaker for years, and still hints that he just might crush enough Cabernet Sauvignon one of these days to produce a commercial release.

Canadian-born and trained as an analytical chemist, Grant is the technical consultant for S.S. Steiner, a Yakima-based producer of hops, the aromatic and bitter flavoring agent for beers everywhere. Grant travels the world on behalf of his employer, advising Steiner's clients on the best use of their hops. Their very best use is probably back in Yakima, where Grant set up a tiny brewery after his friends insisted that the small batches of ale he used to brew at home tasted better than anything on the market. Even the English concurred. Grant's Scottish Ale and Imperial Stout have been dispensed at the Great British Beer Festival in Brighton for several years now, to great acclaim.

Visiting ★★☆. The brewery and ciderworks are housed in one of Yakima's oldest buildings, a storefront that used to be an opera house, then a cold storage vault for the storage of furs. The brewery's tall, conical brewing kettle is visible from the street; the fermenting tanks are tucked away in the vault where the furs were kept.

Next door, Grant has built a British-style pub, complete with dart games (but no smoking), where all his products can be sampled: the various brews and the cider. Tours are sometimes conducted by the staff of the pub, who seem reluctant to take time away from the serving counter. Tastes of the various ales are handed out in tiny cups. They'll let you taste a few, but you get the feeling they'd rather have you buy a schooner.

Tours of the brewery don't have the spontaneity and welcome we've come to expect from wineries; the staff isn't geared up for visitors. But the brewpub makes an interesting stop after a day of wine touring.

Tasting ★★★. Well, there's no wine as such, and only one variety of hard cider. It's on the tart side, faintly prickling on the tongue, and bears about as much resemblance to the sweet, sticky apple juice of childhood as a Ramos Fizz does to a milkshake. You can sample it at the brewpub and buy it in bottles from specialty shops statewide.

Grant's ales hold a lot of interest for adventurous wine drinkers: copper-colored Scottish Ale; dark, fragrant Imperial Stout; a light wheat beer in the German style, named White Bear, brewed for summer drinking; a special ale brewed for winter; a highly hopped India Pale Ale. And sometimes more, depending on the season.

Compare the two kinds of Scottish Ale, the "regular" filtered product and the unfiltered "cask-conditioned" version. You'll understand why the British call the cask-conditioned stuff "real ale."

We encourage wine drinkers to become acquainted with the diversity of ales and lagers from Northwest microbreweries. They're no more like "industrial" beer than jug wine resembles Chateau Margaux; they offer unique rewards to the palate and the spirit.

Getting there. Take the downtown Yakima exit from I-82 (Exit 33) and head west on Yakima Ave. Turn right on Front St.

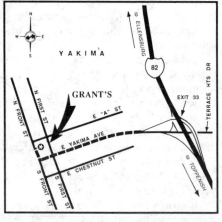

The brewpub is **open** Monday through Saturday from 11:30 to 11. The brewery itself, running flat-out to fill the demand for Grant's products, operates from 6 a.m. to 10 at night. Visitors are welcome, and there's no charge for tour groups.

Special events. An anniversary street party in early July.

A word from the winery. *"End your wine tour with a visit to Bert Grant's unique brewery and pub! Taste our fine, clean cider and our many prize-winning ales—Scottish Ale, Imperial Stout, India Pale Ale, Celtic Ale, and Weiz Beer. All unique and true to their traditional styles."*

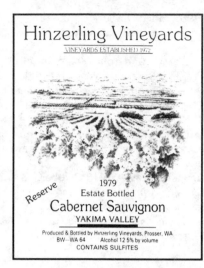

Hinzerling Vineyards

VINEYARDS ESTABLISHED 1972

Reserve
1979
Estate Bottled
Cabernet Sauvignon
YAKIMA VALLEY

Produced & Bottled by Hinzerling Vineyards, Prosser, WA
BW—WA 64   Alcohol 12.5% by volume
CONTAINS SULFITES

HINZERLING VINEYARDS

1520 Sheridan Avenue
Prosser, WA 99350
(509) 786-2163

Owners: Mike & Jerry Wallace families
Winemaker: Mike Wallace
Year established: 1976
Production capacity: 10,000 gallons
Vineyards: None
Touring region: Yakima Valley [p.14]

A bit of background. Mike Wallace, the Yakima Valley's longest-established winemaker, started growing grapes on Hinzerling Road near Prosser in 1972. Originally a medical technician at the University of Washington, Wallace studied at the University of California at Davis and worked as a research assistant for Dr. Walter Clore (Washington's "Mr. Grape"). He bonded Hinzerling (the name of a pioneer Prosser family) in 1976. After a decade of winemaking and politics (he was the Washington Wine Institute's first president), Mike sold the winery to Don Allen and started a consulting business.

Allen and his brother-in-law Bill Broich (founder and former winemaker at Ste. Chapelle) were in the process of changing Hinzerling's emphasis from older reds to younger whites, building a picnic area and hillbilly bandstand, and injecting a Western theme into the winery's marketing ... when (for reasons that may never be known) everything fell apart.

By March of 1989, Wallace had taken over the winery again. At press time he was in the process of selling off the vineyards and reasserting his control over the wines.

Visiting the winery ★★. From the outside, Hinzerling itself is one of Washington's least imposing wineries: a modest cinderblock garage. Visitors admitted beyond the tasting room into the barrel-storage area, however, will be charmed by Mike Wallace's generosity, by his earnest and intelligent discussion of winemaking techniques, by his enthusiastic tank- and barrel-sampling. But the tasting room itself is quite tiny.

Tasting the wines (NR). Cabernet Sauvignon, from vintages between 1979 and 1983, is the highlight here; Mike Wallace has usually done well with older reds. There's also a 1985 Merlot. We've found Hinzerling Chardonnays more than a trifle oaky; the 1986 vintage is in current release. A

Select Cluster Gewurztraminer from 1985, called Die Sonne ("the sun") is still available; it's a fine example of dessert wine that's not made from Riesling.

Getting there. Take Exit 80 from I-82 eastbound, follow Gap Rd (also called Wine Country Rd) across the Yakima River into Prosser; turn left on Sherman, which curves past the winery. From I-82 westbound, take Exit 82 and follow Wine Country Rd back toward Prosser to the winery. [**Map**: Yakima River Winery]

Open Monday through Saturday from 10 to 5 (with an hour off for lunch). The winery is also open Sundays from noon to 3. Group tours are admitted without charge, but by appointment only.

Special events. Hinzerling sponsors a harvest party in October.

A word from the winery. "*The Wallace family invites visitors into the wine cellar to taste wines and observe winemaking close up. One of the family is usually on hand to conduct tastings and answer questions. Please ask about receiving our newsletter to learn about special events and tastings.*"

RATING THE WINERY VISITS:

NR	Not rated: tasting room not open, no visiting
★	Don't bother
★★	Moderately interesting
★★★	Worth a detour
★★★★	Worth the trip

See the introduction (page 8) for additional information on the criteria used to rate winery visits.

THE HOGUE CELLARS

Lee and Meade Avenues
Route 2, Box 2898
Prosser, WA 99350
(509) 786-4557

Owner: Michael Hogue
General manager: Rob Griffin
Winemaker: David Forsyth
Year established: 1982
Production capacity: 250,000 gal.
Vineyards: 220 acres
Touring region: Yakima Valley [p.15]

A bit of background. The Hogue Ranches constitute the largest contiguous landholding in the Yakima Valley, some 1,200 acres of grazing land for cattle, plus fields of hops, spearmint, potatoes, and asparagus, and vineyards of Concord and wine grapes. For many years, patriarch Wayne Hogue (currently serving as mayor of Prosser) and his sons Mike and Gary were content to sell their crops to processors like Wrigley's or Welch's. Now, with wine grapes, they have moved from strictly agricultural commodities into a product for consumers to enjoy.

Using their agricultural expertise, not to mention family pride, the Hogues set about establishing a premium winery on the scale of Preston Wine Cellars or Columbia Winery. (The same concept, more or less, was used at the same time by the Holtzinger family to start Quail Run Vintners.) Young Mike Hogue began by striking a deal with Mike Conway, a talented winemaker who had just left the Worden winery in Spokane: Hogue would help finance a winery for Conway, and Conway would contribute his expertise to start up The Hogue Cellars.

The first results, a zingy Chenin Blanc and two bright Rieslings, were spectacular: award-winning sell-outs. Now, it's one thing to make a few thousand gallons, another to maintain that quality in a period of dizzying expansion, at the same time achieving lower prices. Yet Hogue, the overnight star of Washington's wine industry, currently produces 100,000 cases a year and wins awards for virtually every wine, from tiny batches of reserve wine to humble bottlings of blush.

After Conway left to start his own winery in Spokane (Latah Creek), Hogue signed up Rob Griffin as winemaker. Griffin, then in his early 30s, is an honors graduate in enology from the University of California at Davis who won a cascade of awards for Preston Wine Cellars between 1977 and 1983. Superlatives and gold medals just keep coming, including a gold medal sweep at the Enological Society festival in 1988, the first time a single winery had ever won three golds for all three wines entered. A couple of additional notes. As Washington's wine industry evolves and its vineyards mature, some growers wind up with more grapes than they need; the Hogue Cellars, ever creative, has found a lucrative market for Washington grapes in, of all places, Japan! And a twin testament to the respect the industry has for the people who have been responsible for Hogue's remarkable success: Mike Hogue was appointed by the Governor as co-chairman of the Washington State Wine Commission, and Rob Griffin was elected president of the wineries' trade association, the Washington Wine Institute.

Visiting the winery ★★★☆. The Hogue Cellars' very first winery, a tiny shed on the family ranch, next to the mint still, was long ago supplanted by a functional facility in the Prosser Industrial Park. Its stark metal siding has been softened with a coat of burgundy paint; there's some stonework, too, around the doors and windows of the tasting room. The tasting room is a large and attractive space, with a gift shop to one side and a separate gallery for art shows or group functions. Several picnic tables stand on the manicured lawn between parking lot and winery.

A tour of the facility shows off an ever-increasing number of stainless steel fermenting tanks and oak barrels. In the tasting room, Hogue markets a very popular line of non-wine products: pickled vegetables from the family ranch. The asparagus is harvested between April and June; each spear is hand-cut and pickled within five hours.

Just before press time, the Hogue Cellars announced that a new winery, down the street from the current facility, would be operational by midsummer. It will consolidate all winemaking activity and storage under one roof, and will be surrounded by a new Chardonnay vineyard.

Tasting the wines ★★★★. The best of the excellent wines here, we feel, is the wonderful Fume Blanc, a lovely dry wine with a touch of oak and a dose of Semillon that exhibits a floral and juniper berry nose and tastes incredibly good with seafood. Hogue's Reserve Chardonnay, too, stands out in the crowded field of Washington Chardonnays for its true, clean bouquet and flavors of apples, lime, and butterscotch. The Hogue Semillon, with the classic Anaheim pepper nose balanced by French oak, is not only a textbook example of this variety, it's a great bargain, too.

Among the off-dry and sweeter whites, the Chenin Blanc, Johannisberg Riesling, and Late Harvest Riesling all taste bright, floral, and distinctive.

Of the red wines we'd recommend the reserve Cabernets and Merlots. Griffin's got a sure touch with these wines, and the winery has the resources to wait three or four years before putting them on the market.

Though not the whole story, consistent medal-winning (by Hogue, by Arbor Crest, by Chateau Ste. Michelle, and a few others) bespeaks an understanding of how to make and care for wine; ultimately, this is how the Northwest's reputation will be made. It's a source of great pleasure (not to mention pride in the Northwest) to taste almost any wine produced by The Hogue Cellars.

Getting there. Take Exit 82 from I-82 and proceed east on Wine Country Rd to the Prosser Industrial Park.

Open from 10 to 5 daily. Group tours are welcome by appointment, without charge.

Special events. The Yakima Valley's annual barrel tasting in late April; an Oktoberfest in late October.

A particularly interesting visit can be arranged to tour the Hogue Ranches, for $1 per person, by calling (509) 973-2338.

A word from the winery. *"Come visit The Hogue Cellars and taste our award-winning wines. Sample our pickled asparagus and beans, which have also gained quite a following. While sampling, you may wander through our gift shop and art gallery. If you're interested, you may take a tour of our cellars and learn about the winemaking process. Afterwards you can picnic on our neatly manicured lawn, where several picnic tables are provided."*

WHAT THE RATINGS MEAN FOR QUALITY OF WINE:

NR	No rating: not tasted at all or not tasted recently; no releases
★	Barely drinkable
★☆	Occasionally acceptable
★★	Uneven
★★☆	Usually good
★★★	Good
★★★☆	Usually superior
★★★★	Consistently superior

1986
*Washington
Gewurztraminer*
Select Premium Washington State Wines
Produced and bottled by Hoodsport Winery, Inc.
Hoodsport, Washington. Alcohol 12% by vol.

HOODSPORT WINERY

N. 23501 Highway 101
Hoodsport, WA 98548
(206) 877-9894 or 877-9508

Principal owners:
Richard & Peggy Patterson
CEO: Peggy Patterson
Winemaker: Richard Patterson
Year established: 1980
Production capacity: 40,000 gallons
Vineyards: 8 acres
Touring: Olympic Peninsula [p.36]

A bit of background. Fruit wineries, as a rule, don't seem to succeed unless they make "serious" wine (from vinifera grapes) as well. Unfortunately, most don't know how. Hoodsport Winery, a family winery that got started making fruit wines, has succeeded.

Winemaker Dick Patterson, a counselor and teacher at Tacoma Community College, believes that fruit wines have a bum rap: the memory of loganberry wine and high school dates, or the vision of cheap fortified wines consumed from paper bags by down-and-outers. The way he counters those memories is by creating new ones: gold medal bottlings of Loganberry and Raspberry.

Hoodsport is branching out, with several vinifera varieties and a labrusca-vinifera cross called Island Belle. "It would be a shame if wine drinkers were to lose the regional tastes and products that add so much interest to our industry," Dick told a reporter not long ago. The Island Belle grapes are grown on Stretch Island, a "sun belt" in the middle of Puget Sound. (Stretch Island was the site of Washington's first post-Repeal bonded winery, the defunct St. Charles Winery, now a museum.) The grape is descended from a native American variety identified in New York as Campbell's Early; it acquired its more romantic name after it became more widely planted in the Puget Sound area.

Hoodsport Winery's growth (production has doubled within the past three years) is due in large measure to Peggy Patterson's acumen and energy: a new label, expanded distribution, overseas marketing, and a new consultant (Brian Carter) to "finish" the wines.

Visiting the winery ★★. A tour around the Olympic Peninsula ★★★★ is an absolute must for visitors to Washington. Highway 101 circles the entire promontory, winding through spectacular scenery. As it begins its loop from Olympia northward, it hugs the shoreline between dark evergreens and the placid waters of Hood Canal. Hoodsport Winery, just south of the fishing village of Hoodsport proper, occupies a Bavarian-style building with a tasting room and gift shop out front; the recently expanded winemaking facilities extend toward the green hills out back. Plans have been drawn up for additional remodeling during 1989, with a new winery set for construction in 1990.

For fanciers of fresh seafood, especially Hood Canal shrimp, there's a little fish shop, Skipper John's, right across the highway. And you can enjoy your fare on the waterfront at Potlatch State Park, two miles down the road.

Tasting the wines ★★★. Consultant Brian Carter, whose brilliant work for Paul Thomas established him as one of Washington's top winemakers, will be starting from a strong base on the fruit wine side: a wonderful Raspberry, a delicious Loganberry. Grape wines include Riesling, Chenin Blanc, Gewurztraminer, Chardonnay, Merlot (with grapes from the prized Chalet Vineyards near Tri-Cities), Island Belle, even a Lemberger(!).

The 1987 Chardonnay had a bouquet and flavor of pears, with good acidity and a hint of residual sweetness. The 1987 Gewurztraminer came through with spice, rose petals, and peaches in the nose, with luscious flavors of apricots. Our two disappointments with Hoodsport wines have been the 1987 Merlot, released too young (its immature cherry character not standing up yet to the alcohol); and a sappy nonvintage Chenin Blanc whose peanut-like oxidation suggested that it was probably a single bad bottle.

Overall, Hoodsport's progress is remarkable. We congratulate them.

Getting there. Hwy 101 is the main loop around the Olympic Peninsula; the winery is on the west side of the highway, just south of the town of Hoodsport.

Open daily from 10 to 6. Group tours by appointment, without charge.

Special events. There's an annual grape picking with appropriate celebration the second weekend in October at the Branch Vineyard on Stretch Island; contact the winery for an invitation. An open house

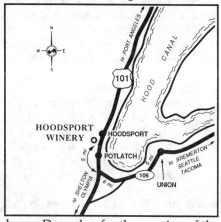

is held at the winery in November or December for the opening of the shrimp season.

A word from the winery. *"Come visit our tasting room on Washington's scenic Hood Canal and sample our award-winning wines. We make eight premium varietals and four nationally acclaimed fruit wines. Be sure to sample our famous raspberry wine truffle."*

Charles Hooper
family winery

WASHINGTON STATE

PINOT NOIR BLANC

1987

Produced and bottled by
Charles Hooper Family Winery
Husum, Washington   BW-WA-117
Alcohol content 12% by volume
Contains sulfites

CHARLES HOOPER FAMILY WINERY

196 Spring Creek Road
P.O. Box 215
Husum, WA 98623
(509) 493-2324

Owners: Charles & Beverlee Hooper
Winemaker: Charles Hooper
Year established: 1985
Production capacity: 2,500 gallons
Vineyards: 6 acres
Touring region: Columbia Gorge
[p.27]

A bit of background. Charles Hooper, a slight, bearded, twinkling-eyed man who grew up in Southern California, once served as an administrator for school systems operated by the military overseas. After assignments in England, France, and Germany, he settled in the Northwest to grow grapes and make a little wine. We had the pleasure of tasting his homemade 1982 Riesling and liked it very much. The Hoopers had already begun planting their 33-acre property with Riesling; it was only a matter of time until they "went commercial."

The time has come. For now, the winery is still in the basement garage of their rural home, with the tanks standing on the porch outside, but they have begun construction on a separate building with the capacity to produce 10,000 gallons.

Visiting the winery ★★☆. The road out of Bingen toward Husum starts by climbing to the quaint village of White Salmon. The view from here is breathtaking ★★★★: the Columbia Gorge is one of nature's most magnificent phenomena; the river snakes along the canyon floor like a silver ribbon bordered by soft gray hills. Then you head toward the lava caves near Trout Lake, with Mount Adams straight ahead. Husum lies snuggled in the hills some nine miles from Bingen; the winery is farther along, up a narrow road that winds through the woods northwest of Husum, and it has a terrific view of Mount Hood.

Ironically, the Washington State Department of Agriculture inadvertently left the Hooper winery out of its brochure, which in turn meant that it was left off at least one magazine's "complete" listing of Northwest wineries. "But we're open, and we'd sure like people to visit!" insists Beverlee Hooper.

Tasting the wine ★☆. The Hoopers made 500 gallons of wine in their first year, a modest start, but a start all the same. We've sampled and enjoyed the 1985 Riesling—the first commercial wine Hooper made—but were disappointed by a seriously oxidized bottle of 1987 Chardonnay.

The 1987 Gewurztraminer was quite pleasant though not particularly varietal, with floral aromas and a taste of apples.

Fortunately, the quality of the 1988 crush (described as "exceptional" by the Hoopers) suggests that better things lie ahead.

Getting there. Husum is on Rte 141, about 9 mi north of Bingen, on the way to Trout Lake. The winery is on the north fork of Spring Creek Rd, at milepost 2. [**Map:** Mont Elise]

Open weekends April through October from 10 to 6, and weekdays in summer (call to confirm). No charge for visits, but the road is impassable for tour buses.

A word from the winery. "`What a spectacular view!' and `There really is a winery up here!' are the two most common exclamations of the first-time visitor to our winery. We invite you to share our view of Mount Hood and the Husum Valley, to enjoy our picnic area, to walk in the vineyard, and to taste our wines. Our Riesling is a crisp wine, very pleasant as a sipping and dinner wine; the Gewurztraminer is a delicate, spicy dinner wine; our Chardonnay is lean, appley, lightly oaked; and our Pinot Noir Blanc is light and fruity, a pleasant blush wine. Members of the family will take you on a tour of the vines and grapes, explain our winemaking process, and pour you a taste of the wines. And we hope you will think our wines are as great as our view!"*

CHARDONNAY
Yakima Valley
1986
ALCOHOL CONTENT 13.3% BY VOLUME

HORIZON'S EDGE WINERY

4530 E. Zillah Drive
Zillah, WA 98953
(509) 829-6401

Owners:
 Tom Campbell & Hemlata Shah
Winemaker: Tom Campbell
Year established: 1985
Production capacity: 7,000 gallons
Vineyards: 20 acres
Touring region: Yakima Valley [p14]

A bit of background. Winemaker Tom Campbell is a friendly, energetic red-haired fellow whose accomplishments to date include boat building, forestry, research chemistry, and a degree in zoology from the University of Montana. An article in *Time* magazine about Joe Heitz sent him off to the University of California at Davis, where he took every course they offered in enology and viticulture. By 1980, he was assistant winemaker at Jekel Vineyards; the following year he moved to Grandview as Chateau Ste. Michelle's cellarmaster. He helped Mike Moore get Blackwood Canyon started while working simultaneously as winemaker for both Tucker Cellars and Stewart Vineyards. Campbell went on to open two wineries of his own, Horizon's Edge in Zillah and Mission Mountain in Montana.

Visiting the winery ★★☆. If you think the view from Covey Run (across the vineyards and along the entire Yakima Valley) merits a visit, wait until you get to Horizon's Edge, just down the road! From its ridge-top setting (at an elevation of 1,200 feet), this winery commands a view ★★★★ encompassing both Mount Adams and Mount Rainier. These two majestic mountains have mystical significance to the Native Americans, who farmed here long before white missionaries brought their concepts of religion and civilization to the region.

A 20-acre vineyard surrounds the property, growing Chardonnay, Muscat Canelli, and Pinot Noir. Shaded picnic tables are set out in the garden, with additional landscaping planned for the 1989 tourist season.

For a time, Horizon's Edge also maintained a satellite winery and tasting room in Seattle's Pike Place Market; the facility closed in 1988.

Tasting the wines ★★. The first wines produced by Horizon's Edge were crushed in 1984. The Chardonnay won a silver medal at the Atlanta competition; we liked it better than the 1985 vintage. By 1987, there were three Chardonnays, none really harmonious or finely tuned. A Cabernet

Sauvignon, released in the fall of 1986, tasted like simple Beaujolais Nouveau.

Wines currently available include Chardonnay, Cabernet Sauvignon, and Muscat.

Getting there. Take Exit 54 from I-82; go north on Hwy 12 for 0.7 mi, then east on E. Zillah Dr 2.5 mi to the winery. From Covey Run, follow Highland Dr eastbound to Lucy, which leads to E. Zillah.

Open daily from 10 to 5.

Special events. There's an anniversary celebration the first weekend in August, when the winery breaks out the bubbly (the 1985 Blanc de Blancs) for visitors.

HUNTER HILL VINEYARDS
2752 W. McMannaman Road
Othello, WA 99344
(509) 346-2607

Principal owner: Arthur Byron
Year established: 1984
Production capacity: 13,500 gallons
Vineyards: 28 acres
Touring: Columbia Valley N. [p.19]

A bit of background. Airline captain Art Byron, a 25-year veteran with Western Airlines who maintains a residence in Bellevue, has been an amateur winemaker since 1967. He also operates a construction business (Byron Construction), a salmon troller (the *Kathleen Two*), and a 233-acre ranch near Othello (the Flying W). In 1982, Byron began planting grapes on the ranch and launched Hunter Hill Vineyards. Busy man!

It's the first winery in Adams County, on the southeastern slope of Royal Ridge, and it commands a splendid view ★★★ of the Columbia

National Wildlife Refuge and nearby recreational land. Byron is enthusiastic about the quality of his own grapes and about Washington wines in general.

Visiting the winery ★★. Some 26 acres of the 250-acre property, 900 feet above the river, are planted with grapes (Riesling, Merlot, Gewurztraminer), in a microclimate that Byron says is ideally suited to vineyards. The winery's location, just above the Columbia National Wildlife Refuge, is in the heart of some of Washington's best hunting (ducks, geese, quail, pheasant) and fishing (particularly bass). The tasting room itself is modest, but there are plans for expansion; meantime, it's only 100 yards from the winery to a private hunting and fishing club.

Tasting the wines ★☆. Winemaking at Hunter Hill has had a checkered start. The first wines (including a bright Riesling and an assertive Semillon) were made at the nearby Langguth winery, but custom winemaking arrangements in 1987 fell through; Hunter Hill scrambled to build its own winery in the six weeks before crush. Gary Graves (who started Pacific Crest Cellars) acted as winemaker for the 1988 crush, with Joel Klein serving for a time as chief executive officer. Dale Garza, a local construction worker and home winemaker, is currently the on-site manager, pending Art Byron's expected retirement from the flying business later in 1989.

The current wines, which aren't in wide distribution, include two styles of Riesling and a 1986 Petit Rouge (Riesling, Chenin, Cabernet).

Getting there. From Othello, go west on Hwy 26 to D Rd S.E., turn right to Royal Camp and right again on McMannaman Rd, which runs straight into Hunter Hill Vineyards. From I-90, take Exit 164 and head south 13.5 mi on Dodson Rd. Turn left (east) on Rd 12 S.W. and continue 12 mi to the east end of the Royal Slope.

Open daily from 10 to 5 (Sunday from 1 p.m.).

A word from the winery. "*As a visitor you are welcomed into a comfortable and cozy tasting room totally different from the usual commercial wine facilities. The feeling you get is that of coming home to the farm, and indeed the tasting room was part of the original farmhouse. It is an opportunity to enjoy the breathtaking natural panorama that surrounds Hunter Hill while enjoying the experience of sampling our fine wines.*"

HYATT VINEYARDS WINERY

2020 Gilbert Road
Zillah, WA 98953
(509) 829-6333

Owners: Leland & Linda Hyatt
Winemaker: Stan Clarke
Year established: 1987
Production capacity: 30,000 gallons
Vineyards: 72 acres
Touring region: Yakima Valley [p14]

A bit of background. The Hyatts are longtime Yakima Valley grape growers (mostly Concords) with a large vineyard; a few years ago they started planting vinifera varieties, and decided to give the winemaking business a try. Their respected viticultural consultant, Wade Wolfe, once managed Chateau Ste. Michelle's vast vineyards; their winemaker is Stan Clarke, who until earlier in 1989 was the general manager at Covey Run. Hyatt offers them an opportunity to deploy their skills on a smaller scale.

Visiting the winery (NR). The setting here resembles nearby Bonair Winery: vineyards with a broad vista over the valley to the snowcapped mountains. Until recently, the Hyatts devoted most of their attentions to a land-leveling business they operate. Stan Clarke's arrival early in 1989 suggests that more energy will be devoted to tourism.

Tasting the wines (NR). Several varieties of estate-grown whites (Chardonnay, Sauvignon Blanc, Chenin Blanc, Riesling) from the 1987 vintage have been released but are not widely available. The 1987 Merlot is expected in late 1989. Future releases will include Late Harvest Riesling and Sauvignon Blanc.

The Thurston-Wolfe label will be used by Wade Wolfe for his own Black Muscat dessert wines, made in a style similar to California's Qady Winery.

Getting there. Take Exit 52 (Zillah) from I-82 and go 3 mi out Cheyne Rd. Turn left on Gilbert Rd and go 0.5 mi to the winery. [Map: Covey Run]

Open weekends from 1 to 5.

A word from the winery. *"Please come and visit one of the newest wineries in the Yakima Valley. We are on a hill overlooking the valley, with a beautiful view of Mount Rainier and Mount Adams. Enjoy our wines and our outside facilities. We are new at this game but we are enjoying meeting all the interesting people. We have had visitors from South Africa and Indonesia. It is exciting and very rewarding when people compliment you on your efforts, so come and visit us and enjoy our fine wines with a view. We have one of the finest winemakers in the state, Stan Clarke. He is looking forward to visiting with you."*

JOHNSON CREEK WINERY
19248 Johnson Creek Road S.E.
Tenino, WA 98589
(206) 264-2100

Owners: Vince & Ann de Bellis
Winemaker: Vince de Bellis
Year established: 1984
Production capacity: 6,000 gallons
Vineyards: 3 acres
Touring region:
    Western Washington [p. 30]

A bit of background. Vince de Bellis, who comes from a big Italian family in San Francisco, grew up in what he describes as "the good old days of 1934 to 1964." His subsequent interest in wine led him to a year of formal studies in viticulture at the University of California at Davis. In 1974, he won the national home winemaking championship, held in San Francisco. (The Johnson Creek tasting room currently displays the three silver champagne buckets he won for the first-place awards.) After Vince's retirement as a broker and partner with Better Homes Realty in fashionable Walnut Creek, he and Ann moved to the Northwest and bought Alice's Restaurant with the intention of adding a winery.

He started out in 1984 with 1,500 gallons, buying grapes from small growers in the Yakima Valley, crushing and stemming in the vineyards, then transporting the must back to Johnson Creek for pressing and fermentation. He's quadrupled his production since then, selling every drop right at the winery and in shops between Chehalis and Tacoma. By 1990, his own vineyard will produce a Muller Thurgau.

What it's like to visit ★★☆. Coming from Olympia, Mount Rainier is in the foreground as you travel first past fields of farmland, barns, and paddocks, then through corridors of tall firs. The gravel road follows a rushing creek for miles and miles, before depositing you in a remarkable oasis: a Little Red Riding Hood of a 50-year-old farmhouse (that's Alice's Restaurant) with a manicured lawn and gazebo out front, a spanking new winery in back, and a three-acre vineyard planted with Muller Thurgau grapes behind the parking lot. (To reach the restaurant from the parking lot, you cross a little footbridge over Johnson Creek; migrating salmon travel up the shallow creek to their spawning grounds.) Altogether, the property covers 33 acres, complete with a waterfall and trails; the de Bellis's modern house sits on a promontory overlooking the idyllic scene.

There's another lovely reason to visit this spot, quite apart from the scenic drive and the handsome, wood-finished winery. That's the recognized high quality of the welcome and the six-course dinners at Alice's Restaurant. Typical menu: relish tray, cream of peanut soup with homemade bread, tossed salad, rainbow trout (served with every dinner!), stuffed pork chop, assorted vegetables, and dessert. Open for dinner Wednesday through Sunday; reserve a table by calling (206) 264-2887.

Tasting the wines ★☆. The winery's first releases of Riesling, Chardonnay, and Muller Thurgau have been supplemented with Chenin Blanc and Pink Riesling (colored with Pinot Noir). We thought that the 1986 Chardonnay had a nice butterscotch nose but nonvarietal flavors. Among the reds, Johnson Creek has Merlot, Pinot Noir, and Cabernet Sauvignon. The 1985 Merlot has quite a few fans ("A smashing Merlot at an affordable price," according to Bev Andrews at Green Frog Vintners in Olympia), and it took a bronze medal at the Enological Society festival in Seattle; we found it spritzy, overly tannic, and oxidized at a tasting in early 1989. Vince de Bellis maintains that he's making notable improvements in winemaking every year.

Getting there. For the scenic approach, take Exit 109 (Lacey) from southbound I-5. Turn left on College St and go 15 mi to the town of Rainier. Turn right on Hwy 507, go 2 mi; just past the second highway bridge, turn left onto Johnson Creek Rd. The restaurant and winery are 5.5 mi down this gravel-topped road. (Drive slowly!)

From northbound I-5, take Exit 88A to Tenino, then go 5 miles further on Hwy 507 to Johnson Creek Rd.

For access along paved roads, take Exit 81 at Centralia and go north on Hwy 507 toward Tenino; turn right on Rd 184 to the winery.

Open Wednesday through Saturday from 5 to 7, and Sunday from 3 to 5. Groups and other hours by appointment.

Charming picnic facilities are available: a gazebo on the lawn adjoining Johnson Creek, and a deck overlooking a trout pond. Both spots have picnic tables and chairs.

A word from the winery. *"Vince and Ann de Bellis wish to offer our warmest greetings to you all and invite you to taste our wines and dine with us at Alice's Restaurant."*

1986
WASHINGTON
Columbia Valley
LEMBERGER

KIONA VINEYARDS

Sunset Road
Route 2, Rox 2169 E
Benton City, WA 99320
(509) 588-6716

Owners: Jim & Pat Holmes,
John & Ann Williams
Winemaker: Jim Holmes
Manager: Scott Williams
First wine released: 1980
Production capacity: 32,000 gallons
Vineyards: 30 acres
Touring region: Yakima Valley [p15]

A bit of background. Kiona Vineyards ("brown hills" in the local Indian language, and pronounced Keye-OWN-ah) started over a decade ago with an 80-acre parcel of sagebrush on the eastern edge of the Yakima Valley. Looked good for a vineyard, thought Jim Holmes, a research manager for Westinghouse at the Hanford complex and an amateur winemaker who grew up near Calilfornia's Napa Valley: chalky soil, plenty of heat. But there were disadvantages, too: the property was just outside the Roza Irrigation District, and there was no road access.

No matter. Holmes and his partner, John Williams, bought the property from Ann Williams' father; then they set to work clearing away the tumbleweeds, planting 26 acres of vineyards (Chenin Blanc, Chardonnay, Cabernet Sauvignon, and a little-known red variety called Lemberger), installing an irrigation system, putting in a road. In the early years, Kiona sold grapes to Quilceda Creek Vintners, Amity Vineyards, and Yakima River Winery while the partners made a little wine for themselves in Jim Holmes' garage in West Richland. (Jim Holmes modestly describes himself as a "middle manager" for Westinghouse; in fact, he's published over 200 scientific articles, and is in charge of a research and development group working on materials for magnetic fusion power plants.) The garage is still in use, filled with fermenting tanks, but the rest of the operation has been moved to the vineyard itself.

Among the most recent honors bestowed on Kiona: Washington Winery of the Year, at the Grand National Wine Competition in Snowbird, Utah, after winning best-of-class gold medals for its Dry White Riesling, Chenin Blanc, and Merlot Rose.

Visiting the winery ★★★★. The wines are outstanding, but the real pleasure is visiting the winery itself. By 1983, the Williams family had built a new home on the edge of the vineyard, with views toward Mount Adams in the west and toward Red Mountain due north. Barrels were rolled into the basement and amenities for visitors completed. Now there's a spacious lawn with shade trees, plenty of room for picnics and a playground set, and a broad patio outside the tasting room where the vintages can be sampled at leisure.

Scott Williams (John and Ann's son) has moved from his own vineyard consulting business to managing Kiona; he's often on hand to take visitors into the vineyards, where he demonstrates the subtle yet essential differences between various trellising systems, or to draw barrel samples in the cool cellar behind the tasting room. On weekends, when he's available for tasting room duty, Jim Holmes talks with great clarity and skill about any part of the viticultural or enological process, such as the makeup of soil strata. John Williams looks like a lovable circus bear as he hands wineglasses to visitors as they step off the bus. Altogether, these people make winemaking interesting and fun. Group tours can also arrange to see a slide show on the history of the winery, in the Williams' living room upstairs. It's as close as a winery can come to an open-armed welcome.

Tasting the wines ★★★☆. We've enjoyed every recent sample, both at the winery and in blind tastings: the 1987 Estate-Bottled Chardonnay (with a beguiling nose of vanilla and butterscotch); a delicious dry 1987 Riesling (its citrus overtones went beautifully with turbot); the newly bottled 1988 Riesling; luscious Late Harvest wines (Riesling, Gewurztraminer, Muscat Canelli); a rich Cabernet Sauvignon (deep oaky flavors); not to mention the acclaimed Chenin Blanc and Kiona's two best-known wines, Lemberger and Merlot Rose (which won the Governor's Trophy at the Central Washington State Fair in 1983 for the best red wine in the state). Coming soon: a full-bodied Merlot with minty, oaky flavors, altogether amazing.

All the wines are exceptionally good values; the Merlot Rose is about $5, the Lemberger under $9, for instance.

The little-known Lemberger turned out to be the most promising of Kiona's experimental varieties, producing a dark, rich wine; today, despite the wine's "difficult" name, it's the first wine to sell out. Covey Run's Lemberger is made more like a Beaujolais, fresh and fruity; Kiona's is matured in oak for an extra year, adding a lovely dimension of color and complexity. The Kiona Lemberger regularly wins silver medals but is still something of an oddball for the judgings; it doesn't fit handily into any category except "Open Red," where it has to compete with all the proprietary blends.

Getting there. From I-82, take the Benton City exit. Turn right just before the bridge onto Hwy 224, and proceed toward West Richland to Sunset Rd. The winery is 1 mi down Sunset Rd.

From the Tri-Cities, take Hwy 240 toward Richland. Turn left onto Hwy 224, go through West Richland, and continue to Sunset Rd.

Open daily from noon to 5; closed on major holidays.

Special events. A Lemberger Gala in June.

A word from the winery. *"Kiona loves visitors. We would like to extend a personal invitation to visit our vineyard and winery and try firsthand the large variety of Kiona wines. In addition to our widely distributed products, personal and professional interest in experimenting with new ideas has produced some outstanding but very limited wines available only in our tasting room. We work very hard at what we do and are proud of the finished product. Hope to see you soon."*

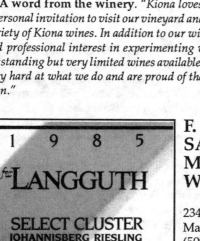

F. W. LANGGUTH - SADDLE MOUNTAIN WINERY

2340 S.W. Winery Road
Mattawa, WA 99344
(509) 932-4943

Principal owner:
   Snoqualmie Falls Holding Co.
Winemaker: Mike Januik
Year established: 1982
Production capacity: 800,000 gallons
Vineyards: None
Touring: Columbia Valley [p.19]

A bit of background. Observers of the Washington wine industry, hoping for some indication that they were right about the state's strategic location and its importance as one of the world's best (or potentially best) growing regions, received their validation from an unexpected source: a

German wine producer called F.W. Langguth, one of the largest suppliers of wine to the supermarkets of Europe. Its president, Wolfgang Langguth, the seventh generation of the Langguth family to head the firm, wanted to expand its operations to the United States.

On the Wahluke Slope, overlooking the Columbia River, Langguth found what he needed. An ideal climate for grapes of the highest quality. Local capital to participate in a vineyard. He even found a German-speaking winemaker, Max Zellweger, working in Oregon.

The local capital for the vineyard came from a group of investors led by Alex Bayless and Win Wright, whose earlier projects included Sagemoor Farms. They planted a 265-acre vineyard called Weinbau (which means "vineyard" in German) on a 320-acre section of the Wahluke Slope, overlooking the Columbia River and the Hanford Reservation.; Langguth originally held a 10 percent share of the vineyard.

Things didn't work out as planned, however. Discouraged by a series of unsuccessful marketing efforts, Wolfgang Langguth sold a controlling interest in his winery to Joel Klein, founder of Snoqualmie Winery. The story took another unfortunate turn: to finance the purchase of Langguth, Klein raised money from local sources, only to find himself replaced within a year as winemaker and head of the company. The legal battles aren't over yet (see the Snoqualmie Winery entry for details).

Snoqualmie, Saddle Mountain, and Langguth wines are all made here, using the winery's extensive production capacity; a few small, independent producers also custom-crush here. The Langguth label is used now only for sweeter Rieslings; Saddle Mountain is a lower-priced (but high quality) label which gets wide distribution in restaurants. Both have seen definite improvements under the gifted Mike Januik, who took over after the collapse of the short-lived Petros operation in Idaho.

Visiting the winery ★★★. The winery stands east of Mattawa on the Wahluke Slope, a region that's going to produce more and more of Washington's grapes. The Hanford Reservation lies just across the Columbia River, with the purple-tinged Rattlesnake Hills beyond; Mount Rainier's snowcapped peak can be seen to the west, while the Saddle Mountains form the slope's northern boundary like a crumpled brown blanket. Quarter-mile-long sprinklers move slowly through circles of alfalfa like giant Tinker-Toys. Beneath the vast sky, the 35,000-square-foot winery looks no bigger than a farmer's shack.

Inside, there's state-of-the-art equipment on an enormous scale: the biggest Bucher press in Washington, enormous roto-vats to ferment red wines, a roomful of filters and centrifuges, a vast forest of stainless steel tanks, a warehouse the size of a soccer field, a lab that could be a magazine test kitchen. Everything is spotless and computer controlled, a virtually ideal winemaking environment.

The staff has done a good job of making the stark, mammoth facility welcoming. Tours are conducted with enthusiasm and are loaded with information; tastings are extensive. You'll find many of the same touches (and merchandise) in the tasting room that make Snoqualmie Winery an appealing visit.

Tasting the wines ★★★. Until recently, most of the production capacity at this near-million-gallon facility was dedicated to processing grapes for other wineries; only 15,000 cases or so of Langguth and Saddle Mountain wines were produced. That's changing now, with upsurge in production for all three labels.

The best Langguth wines have always been Late Harvest Rieslings, including an unforgettable 1983 "Select Harvest Special Release" that won the Grand Prize at the Seattle Enological Society Festival. Some older vintages of the Langguth line haven't survived well, but the 1985 Select Cluster, in particular, has matured nicely.

Most of the effort goes into the Saddle Mountain label, which is seen regularly on "by-the-glass" wine lists. The Sauvignon Blanc resembles the excellent Snoqualmie version, and Chardonnay, produced with only moderate oak aging, is very agreeable. There's also a blush, and red and white table wines. The quality of this brand will continue to improve as Januik's wines reach the shelves.

Getting there. From I-90, take Exit 137 (Othello-Vernita). Proceed on Hwy 243 toward Vernita for 15 mi, turn left at Mattawa, and continue for 13 mi on Road 24 to Winery Rd. Turn left to reach the winery.

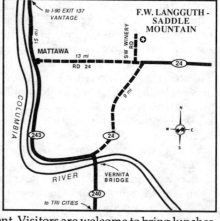

From the Tri-Cities, take Hwy 240 to the Vernita Bridge. Cross the bridge and turn right on Hwy 24. After 9 mi, turn left onto Rd 24, then right on Winery Rd.

Open daily from 10 to 4:30. Groups are welcome without fee; call ahead for an appointment. Visitors are welcome to bring lunches.

Special events. There's an annual open house with a barbecue and bluegrass music, held over a two-day period in late July.

A word from the winery. *"Come visit our state of the art facility, taste the fine wines, and enjoy the picturesque view of the southern slopes of the Saddle Mountain Range."*

LATAH CREEK WINE CELLARS

E. 13030 Indiana Avenue
Spokane, WA 99216
(509) 926-0164

Owners: Mike & Elena Conway
Winemaker: Mike Conway
Year established: 1982
Production capacity: 35,000 gallons
Vineyards: None
Touring region: Spokane [p. 24]

A bit of background. Rich Chardonnays, complex Pinot Noirs, and tannic Cabernet Sauvignons all have their place, but wine competitions (and wine writers) tend to focus too narrowly on these "serious" wines, while the wine-drinking public buys most of its wines to be enjoyed. Fortunately, many of the Northwest's best wines fall into the "enjoyable" category, wines that have the charm and allure of dance music: familiar, skillfully put together, popular. The master of this art is Mike Conway, winemaker at Latah Creek (named for a real creek in Spokane, and pronounced LAY-tah).

Conway began his career as a microbiologist for two giant California wineries, Gallo and Franzia, then learned about winemaking at Parducci. He came to Washington as winemaker for Worden's, where his Rieslings won acclaim. After a stint at The Hogue Cellars, he returned to Spokane to start his own winery.

Conway's view of his winemaking colleagues is a generous one: "We're all working together to improve the industry. It only takes one bad winery to spoil our image." He's shown the Northwest winemaking community that popular, drinkable wines can also win international medals.

Each year, Latah Creek commissions a new painting from Floyd Broadbent, a wildlife artist from Yakima, for the label. The first was a wood duck, the second a Chinese ringneck pheasant, the third a mourning dove, and so on.

Visiting the winery ★★★☆. Latah Creek is located in a new, Spanish-style stucco building along I-90 east of Spokane. It's a very picturesque winery, with tile walkways leading to an arched entrance. Inside, there's a large tasting room, well-stocked gift shop, and an art gallery, as well as modern fermenting and processing equipment and oak cooperage. It's one of the very few smaller wineries in the Northwest that was built as a winery from the ground up, and perhaps the only one of such character on a site that's remote from any vineyards.

Finally, the picnic tables on the patio make this a most inviting place. Tourists as well as local residents make the winery a regular stop; Conway sells a quarter of his production in the tasting room, and he's usually around to help visitors make a selection. A most worthwhile visit.

Wines to taste ★★★☆. Mike Conway is one of Washington's most honored winemakers, with gold medals and best-of-show awards for his Chenin Blanc, Riesling, Chardonnay, Muscat Canelli, and Merlot. In 1986, his Chardonnay won one of only 10 gold medals awarded by *Vintage* magazine in a nationwide Grand Prix tasting. *Wine Country* magazine gave his 1986 Riesling its top rating in a field of 90 wines. Current vintages continue to reward tasters with true varietal aromas and clean, balanced flavors.

The 1987 Merlot, with deep, black cherry fruit and big tannins, could be considered overwhelming if you're not expecting its massive flavors. There's lots of bright fruit (and cedar) in the Cabernet Sauvignon, too.

Best bets: the wonderful Chenin Blanc, with its aroma of honeysuckle and melon; two delightful Rieslings; a fine Semillon; the Chardonnay; and a flowery Muscat Canelli. Conway also makes a Maywine, which he calls "springtime in a bottle"; it's a blend of premium white wines (mostly Riesling) with woodruff, herbs, and strawberries. And there's a wine called "Spokane Blush" made from Merlot. Some of the wines are available only at the winery.

Conway's preference has always been to make light, fruity wines; his technique is to bottle them very cold, under pressure, which causes the wines to retain a slight amount of carbon dioxide. As a result, the wines are ever so slightly spritzy when drunk, enhancing the natural acidity and refreshing quality of the wine. Now, without cutting back on the whites, he's started making more reds. Five times as much in 1988 as 1987.

Getting there. Go north on Pines Rd (Exit 289 from I-90) to Indiana Rd, then west to the winery. [**Map:** Arbor Crest]

Open Monday through Saturday from 10 to 4, Sunday from noon to 4 (5 in summer). Write or phone for group or evening tours, which are offered without charge.

Special events. A Maifest in mid-May; an anniversary party in mid-July; an Oktoberfest at the end of September.

A word from the winery. "*Architecturally Spanish Mission style, Latah Creek's facility provides a specifically designed tasting room full of charm and warmth. The intention of our staff here is to provide an atmosphere of affable encouragement to wine newcomers, as well as in-depth information for the more experienced and serious wine collectors. A cloistered patio provides a beautiful seating area, ideal for that summertime picnic. A cheery welcome and multiple-award-winning wines await every visitor.*"

L'ECOLE No. 41

Lowden Schoolhouse Corp.
41 Lowden School Road
P.O. Box 111
Lowden, WA 99360
(509) 525-0940

Owners: Baker & Jean Ferguson
Winemaker: Jean Ferguson
Year established: 1983
Production capacity: 6,000 gallons
Vineyards: None
Touring region: Walla Walla [p.22]

A bit of background. "The measure of a society's civilization," Baker Ferguson tells his visitors over lunch, "is proportional to its consumption of garlic." This imposing, white-maned gentleman is clearly not going to release any namby-pamby wines.

L'Ecole No. 41's parent company, Lowden Schoolhouse Corporation, has been licensed as a winery since 1983 in the building that once housed School District 41, but it didn't open to the public or release any wine until 1985. The reason lay with its (garlic-loving) owners: they did things their own way, in their own time, and not because some banker told them it was time to open the doors or to sell wine. Baker Ferguson himself, you see, *is* the banker, the retired president of the oldest bank in Washington, the Baker Boyer National Bank in Walla Walla, founded by his great-grandfather. Today he handles the planning and administration of the winery. Jean, with the kind of beauty you find on cameos, draws on her background as a teacher of chemistry to handle the winemaking—and on her poise and good nature to handle the vicissitudes of the business, we might add.

Baker, a history buff, points out that the Lowden area has traditionally been called Frenchtown (it was the home of French-Canadians employed in the 1820s by the Hudson Bay Company's post, Fort Nez Perce). By 1825, residents of the village were engaged in small-scale irrigated agriculture, including the cultivation of grapes, so the Fergusons decided to call the winery L'Ecole No. 41 to salute pioneer viticulture east of the Cascades.

Baker and Jean Ferguson have begun establishing a permanent collection of children's art to brighten the schoolhouse walls in the style of the Christmas mural that they discovered painted on the basement walls of the schoolhouse when the winery equipment was being installed—a mural now hidden behind the stainless steel fermenting tanks. (One of the schoolchildren who participated in those long-ago Christmas pageants was Rick Small, who now manages his family's grain elevators across the road and also owns Woodward Canyon Winery next door to the schoolhouse.) They ran a contest among their relatives for the best label design, with third-grader Ryan Campbell turning in the winning design, a whimsical drawing of the Walla Walla Balloon Stampede.

The time is drawing near for the Fergusons to retire again. Major changes are in store here.

Visiting the winery ★★★. The schoolhouse is an imposing, cream-and-tan, turn-of-the-century wooden structure that commands the eastern approach to Lowden; it's the only building of note in town except for the million-bushel grain elevators across the highway. The Fergusons make their home on the third level, having raised the roof, installed modern conveniences, and put out flower boxes. The middle level has been converted into a handsome office and elegant salon, which doubles as a tasting room and visitor facility; a caterer's kitchen adjoins the living room. The lowest level, where Baker had to lower the floor by almost a foot, contains the winery itself.

Tasting the wines ★★☆. A rich, assertive, high-alcohol Semillon was the first wine released by L'Ecole No. 41. It was followed, in 1986, by a Merlot of astounding proportions, perhaps the "biggest" Merlot released commercially in Washington, and good enough to win a gold medal at the Seattle Enological Society Festival; the announcement brought huge cheers for Jean Ferguson's success.

We tasted a number of L'Ecole's wines recently. We couldn't find any varietal character in the oaky and alcoholic Semillons, but the reds are faring very well. Our favorite was the 1985 Merlot, with a serious and satisfying bouquet of oak and wild blackberry; tobacco and cherry flavors came to life in the glass. (It won't be released until the winter of 1990.) The 1983 also showed well, with massive amounts of green pepper in the nose, and strong, extracted fruit flavors; for all that, it was perfectly balanced.

Getting there. Lowden is 12 miles west of Walla Walla on Hwy 12.

Open by appointment. A caterer is available on the premises for group functions.

LEONETTI CELLAR

1321 School Avenue
Walla Walla, WA 99362
(509) 525-1428

Owners: Gary & Nancy Figgins
Winemaker: Gary Figgins
Year established: 1977
Production capacity: 5,000 gallons
Vineyards: 1 acre
Touring region: Walla Walla [p.22]

A bit of background. Gary Figgins, a modest but uncompromising man who worked full-time as a machinist for Continental Can Company in Walla Walla while building up Leonetti Cellar, has a legion of devoted followers who believe he produces Washington's best red wines. His wines have received numerous accolades but are not without some controversy.

In 1983, for example, a fragrant Leonetti Merlot was voted the favorite red wine of the Tri-Cities Northwest Wine Festival by a panel of consumers, as well as by the winemakers in attendance. But the Merlot got no better than a bronze from the festival judges; one of them, a California retailer, described it as "an example of flawed winemaking" and gave it his lowest score. (Imagine some contemporary critic saying that the Sistine Chapel is just so much graffiti!)

Two years later, at the same festival, another Leonetti Merlot received a gold medal and best-of-show honors!

Merlot was the second Leonetti variety to achieve prominence. *Winestate Wine Buying Guide* named Leonetti's 1978 Cabernet Sauvignon as "best in the country" after a taste-off of award-winning wines; and the Washington Wine Writers named the 1982 Cabernet "Washington Wine of the Year" in 1985.

Gary Figgins began making wine when he and Nancy were first married, producing a wine (from an abundant crop of Concord grapes) that he recalls as "cloudy and undrinkable." Then he was bitten by the Cabernet bug. That meant no more hunting (it conflicts with crush), no more fishing (it takes too much time), no more sports cars or motorcycles (too expensive).

Visiting the winery (NR). The Figgins family owns a smart little house southeast of Walla Walla with a 300-square-foot shed in back where Gary used to store his barrels, wine press, fermenting tanks, and bottles. A small vineyard of Merlot, which Gary prunes personally and fastidiously, adjoins the house. Says his colleague and friend Rick Small (of Woodward Canyon Winery), "It's the best-tended vineyard in the state."

In the beginning, the wines were aged in the cellar of the house, in new barrels of French, Yugoslavian, and American oak. Figgins has now finished building a new winery in the back yard; it's natural basalt stone in classic European architecture, with cellars below. Will the "big" winery spoil him? Gary says no. "Our philosophy remains the same: stay small and select the best grapes from the best vineyards, exercise meticulous care throughout the creation, and always use new cooperage." Expensive, but worth it.

Tasting the wine★★★★. It's all Cabernet Sauvignon and Merlot at Leonetti (his mother's maiden name) Cellar. Some tasters find the volatile acidity in the wines overwhelming; others find, if they notice it at all, that it heightens the fruit and oak. The flavors are massive, yet the wines are smooth and balanced even in the presence of intense tannin.

The 1986 Merlot had a magnificent nose of cedar, black currants, coffee, licorice, and green peppers. It made a lovely accompaniment to a dinner of broiled lamb cutlets. The 1985 Cabernet was distinguished by a deep fruitiness that made it an excellent accompaniment to food, yet with the potential to last a decade or more. (In fact, the 1982 Cabernet Sauvignon was named "Washington Wine of the Year" in 1985 by the Washington Wine Writers as the best red wine to complement food.) And the 1985 "Seven Hills Vineyard" Cabernet had even more rich, dark color, berry nose, and cedar character.

Getting there. Take the Wilbur St exit from Hwy 12; head south, turn left on Pleasant St, then right on School Ave. After the street crosses a little creek, turn left; the Leonetti residence and winery are at the end of the driveway.

Open by appointment. Leonetti releases its wines on the weekend after Labor Day and holds a second open house in mid-May (coinciding with the Walla Walla Balloon Stampede); call or write for an invitation.

A word from the winery "Leonetti Cellar began operations in 1978 as the first winery in the Walla Walla Valley. In its 10-year history, Leonetti has won numerous medals and acclaim from critics across the U.S. Specializing in Cabernet Sauvignon and Merlot only, our uncompromising approach to winemaking has established its reputation in its time-honored bottlings. Leonetti is a small family winery owned and operated by Gary and Nancy Figgins. In 1985 construction was completed on an underground cellar to facilitate the cool aging of our fine red wines. In 1987 construction was started on the upper portion of the winery, which will accommodate the production and storage. The walls of this building will be of native stone collected personally by Gary from our Blue Mountains in the Walla Walla Valley."

LOST MOUNTAIN WINERY

730 Lost Mountain Road
Sequim, WA 98382
(206) 683-5229

Owner & winemaker: Romeo Conca
Year established: 1981
Production capacity: 1,300 gallons
Vineyards: None
Touring: Olympic Peninsula [p.36]

A bit of background We know winemakers throughout the Northwest who have built wineries with their own hands, but only one who makes his own bacon, sausage, and prosciutto as well. He is Romeo Conca, a gentleman of dignity and exquisite manners, vital and talented, a retired research chemist who has turned his passion for hearty wines and Italian food into a second career.

Romeo Conca grew up in New Haven, Connecticut, where his father, Matteo—a renowned Italian chef—worked at the Taft Hotel. Young Romeo attended Yale, just across the Commons, and stayed in town long enough to earn a doctorate in organic chemistry. He then went to work as a research chemist, spending 30 years with ITT Rayonier, and ended up in Shelton. As a youngster, he had always helped his father make wine; now, in his retirement, he lives in his hand-built cabin in the mountains, with a spotless, tiny winery burrowed in the basement like a snug, furry animal. It is a venture that springs from his soul.

Visiting the winery★★☆. Romeo Conca owns 47 acres of this hillside forestland, high in the foothills of the Olympic Mountains west of Sequim. From the patch he cleared to plant an experimental vineyard, you can see the nearby peaks of Blue Mountain, Tyler Peak, and Graywolf Ridge. The vineyard project has been abandoned, however, a victim of browsing deer and an uncertain climate. "It was a nice idea, but we just don't have enough heat units up here at 1,500 feet for the grapes to ripen," Romeo points out, citing frosts as late as mid-June.

We once brought a tour group to Lost Mountain to visit Romeo and savor an Italian country lunch that he had personally prepared: prosciutto with melon, turkey tonnato with garlic mayonnaise, homemade breads, with fresh peaches in Muscat for dessert. Wine touring at its best! We sat around the living room drinking Lost Mountain Red and listened to Romeo tell stories about his travels and winemaking. He still maintains a busy consulting practice, and said of a 10-day sojourn in Moscow, "Russian wine isn't too exciting, but I could easily get hooked on caviar!"

Wines to taste★★. Romeo Conca says, "As people learn to enjoy wine with food, I suspect there will be a trend toward more full-bodied wines."

The wines made from Washington grapes include a light 1986 Merlot (despite its 13.9 percent alcohol!), and a 1985 Cabernet Sauvignon that we liked for current drinking, though the floral nose in our sample wasn't particularly varietal. There's also an intensely colored 1987 Pinot Noir from Oregon grapes, which has a full-blown varietal nose but lacks the structure and balance to be a satisfying food wine. The best value is the vintage-dated "Red," a blend of California-grown Zinfandel, Petite Syrah, and Muscat with an intriguing fruitiness.

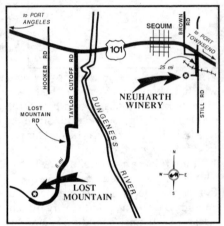

Getting there. From Hwy 101 west of Sequim, just past the bridge across the Dungeness River, take the Taylor Cutoff and head 2.5 mi south to Lost Mountain Rd. Turn right and follow Lost Mountain Rd to number 730. The winery is a total of 6 mi from Hwy 101.

Open by appointment.

Special events Annual Release and Open Winery, last week of June and first week of July.

A word from the winery "*Lost Mountain is an intimate, accessible winery. You can talk to the winemaker, see how the wines are made, and, if you come at the right time, you can help! Currently the wines are all reds, ranging from a delightfully quaffable Pinot Noir to a robust, distinguished Dago Red. In between there's a marvelous Merlot, a classic Cabernet, and a `Zinsyr' blend of Zinfandel and Petite Syrah. The Poetry Series sports a newly designed label by Rebecca Wild and will henceforth carry the name Poesia (Italian for poetry), with a new poem each year. This year's edition features a charming poem, `Burning Aged Fir' by Susan E. Hamilton. The wine, a blend of Merlot and Cabernet Sauvignon, has a wonderful intensity of flavor—the whole is truly greater than the sum of its parts! I hope you'll find Lost Mountain.—Sincerely, Romeo Conca.*"

McCREA CELLARS
12707 18th Street S.E.
Lake Stevens, WA 98258
(206) 334-5248

Owners: Douglas & Susan McCrea
Winemaker: Doug McCrea
Year established: 1988
Production capacity: 1,200 gallons
Vineyards: None

A bit of background This may be the smallest winery in Washington (for this edition), with barely 500 gallons produced, and no great hurry to release it. "Our top priority will always be style and quality," says co-owner Doug McCrea, who spent 10 years teaching music to high school and junior college students, and working as a professional musician on a variety of woodwind instruments. His wife, Susan, has a degree in music performance from Stanford, held positions in administration and computer programming in Palo Alto, and currently manages part of Hewlett-Packard's operation in Lake Stevens. Doug, also an alum of Hewlett-Packard, is the office manager for French Creek Cellars.

Visiting the winery (NR) The McCreas plan to build a rural "destination winery" for eastern Snohomish County, offering visitors the opportunity to spend the day in one of Puget Sound's most beautiful recreational areas.

Tasting the wines (NR) Most of the wine produced so far is Chardonnay, about 400 gallons made from grapes grown in the Yakima Valley on the Portteus Vineyard. At last report, it was still on the lees, in barrels, and not available for tasting.

Plans for the future include Cabernet Sauvignon (they made 150 gallons of Cab from Mercer Ranch). And if they reach their goals, within eight to 10 years, the McCreas will move the winery from their home to a (projected 6,000-gallon) facility in south Snohomish County.

Having been performing musicians, the McCreas recognize that the art of winemaking also requires technical expertise, discipline, and aesthetic sensitivity. They've made a wise move in getting Brian Carter to work with them; his guidance and experience will be valuable in the early years.

A word from the winery "*McCrea Cellars is a small family winery specializing in barrel-fermented Chardonnays of high quality and distinctive style. We strive for elegance, rich flavor, and balance, achieved through gentle handling of the finest grapes and classical winemaking techniques.*

"*We are honored to be a part of the Washington state wine industry and hope that our wines will help elevate the growing recognition of Washington as a leading world viticultural region.*"

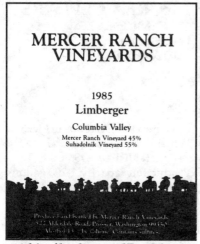

MERCER RANCH
VINEYARDS

1985
Limberger

Columbia Valley
Mercer Ranch Vineyard 45%
Suhadolnik Vineyard 55%

Produced and bottled by Mercer Ranch Vineyards
522 Alderdale Road, Prosser, Washington 99350
Alcohol 13% by volume. Contains sulfites.

MERCER RANCH VINEYARDS

522 Alderdale Road
Prosser, WA 99350
(509) 894-4741

Owners: Don & Linda Mercer
Winemaker: Don Mercer
Year established: 1985
Production capacity: 5,000 gallons
Vineyards: 131 acres
Touring: Columbia Valley S. [p15]

A bit of background Don Mercer once spent four years as an architect's apprentice, but for the last 20 years he has been a farmer and grape grower. His wife, Linda, is a fourth-generation farm wife (from Waitsburg); his children have been active in Future Farmers of America. Their land, part of a 30,000-acre family holding put together by Don's father, Milt, overlooks the Columbia River on the southern side of the Horse Heaven Hills, in the far eastern corner of Klickitat County.

The 130-acre vineyard was first planted with seven acres of Cabernet Sauvignon in 1972; the fine, sandy soil and warm eastern slopes proved successful, and additional blocks of Cabernet, Riesling, Chenin Blanc, Chardonnay, and Lemberger were added after 1979. Don has 20 acres in apples and another 2,500 acres devoted to dryland wheat, and rents most of the rest as pasture land to his brother Rick for cattle, but he has kept the best slopes—another couple hundred acres—for eventual expansion of the vineyards when the children grow up and join the family business.

In 1975, Don's Cabernet Sauvignon grapes went to Hinzerling Vineyards; four years later, Ste. Chapelle began using them, too. Now Mercer Ranch Vineyards has become a label of its own.

Visiting the winery★★★. There's less than seven inches of annual rainfall in these desert hills, so irrigation is necessary in the vineyards and orchards. When Milt sold his sheep and turned to cattle in the 1960s, he also planned a private irrigation project to bring Columbia River water to thousands of acres. The Carma Irrigation Project transformed the ranch: today, it grows crops from hay to potatoes, carrots to wine grapes, apples to cattle. It supports some 30 full-time owners and employees (and much more seasonal help), and is home to 15 families, three farming-and-ranching corporations, and several small farms. The irrigation is by center-pivot, a central source of water connected to quarter-mile-long sprinklers that rotate through 130-acre circles like slow, stalking spiders.

Visitors can see the winery from a mile away, across the hillside vineyards, and approach on a road that curves between circles of manicured vines of Riesling and Muscat Canelli, past the Cabernet Sauvignon, to the two-story building. Picnic tables stand on a lawn, surrounded by flowers and aromatic shrubs; it's a wonderful place to picnic.

Don Mercer enjoys showing his visitors through the vineyards, and his enthusiasm is a delight to watch, as he climbs onto a flatbed trailer, glass in hand, to talk about viticulture. His "vineyard experience" is a real treat, especially for tour groups.

Tasting the wines★★★. Mercer Ranch first used the winemaking services of Steve Redford; now Don himself has taken over as winemaker, and plans to specialize in Lemberger (or Limberger). Limberger is the name of a grape variety hardy enough to withstand eastern Washington's relatively cold winters, and it makes a wine that lends itself well to barrel aging. It goes particularly well with foods like roast lamb and game (and has nothing whatsoever to do with a cheese called Limburger).

Some of the best Cabernet grapes in the state grow on this property; Mercer keeps some for himself and sells the rest. The fine Mercer Ranch 1985 Cabernet Sauvignon received a silver medal at the Central Washington State Fair. There's also a delightful blush wine called "Sadie Louise," named after a pet lamb hand-raised by Carma Mercer some 50 years ago. A sparkling wine is in the works, too.

Getting there. Mercer Ranch lies 35 miles southwest of Prosser. (There's a 2,200-foot airstrip, but watch out for sheep on the runway!) From Prosser, take Hwy 221 south for 3.8 mi; turn right onto Bert James Rd, go 4.3 mi; right onto Sellards Rd, go 7 mi; fork left to McKinley Springs Rd (name changes to Smith Rd), go 11 mi; left onto Alderdale Rd, go 7.7 mi to the winery.

From Paterson, go west approximately 19 mi on Hwy 14, turn right on Alderdale Rd at milepost 149, and proceed 5 mi to the winery.

From Mabton, go 8 mi south on Bickleton Rd, then left on Alderdale Rd for 20.2 mi to the winery.

Open Monday through Saturday from 9 to 5:30; Sundays, noon to 5:30. Tour groups should make appointments.

Special events A "Lamburger/Limberger" festival on the third weekend in April features wildflower tours, kite flying, golf chipping contest, and grilled lamb burgers.

A word from the winery:*"The Mercer family welcomes visitors to their vineyard and winery operation. The winery is set among well-tended lawn and garden in the midst of the much recognized Mercer Ranch Vineyards. A family member is always on hand to greet and talk with the winery visitor, assuring that the drive to the winery will be remembered as a friendly and worthwhile experience. We are proud to be part of the agricultural heritage of Washington state and enjoy sharing our past and present history with our visitors. Quality grapes make quality wines, making the vineyard an intrinsic part of winemaking."*

1987 WASHINGTON
GAMAY BEAUJOLAIS
MONT ELISE VINEYARDS

PRODUCED AND BOTTLED BY MONT ELISE VINEYARDS, BINGEN, WA. ALC. 12.0% BY VOL.

MONT ELISE VINEYARDS

315 W. Steuben
P.O. Box 28
Bingen, WA 98905
(509) 493-3001

Owners: Charles Henderson family
Winemaker: Chuck Henderson, Jr.
Year established: 1975
Production capacity: 18,000 gallons
Vineyards: 40 acres
Touring: Columbia Gorge [p.27]

A bit of background On a sunny morning a few years back, we found Chuck Henderson, Sr., maneuvering an orange Kubota tractor through his vineyard, 1,700 feet above White Salmon. The Columbia River was snaking through the Gorge below, and you could see the peak of Mount Hood in the distance; Mount Adams was hiding beyond a rise to the north. "This used to be a cherry orchard," he gestured. "Sixty-five acres of the wrong variety of cherries! Candy for gophers!" In frustration, some two decades earlier, Henderson had approached the agricultural research station at Prosser, where viticultural consultant Dr. Walter Clore suggested wine grapes.

The Columbia Gorge provides remarkable growing conditions: the warm, dry desert air of eastern Washington's Columbia Valley encounters the cool maritime air of Oregon's Willamette Valley, and the convergence creates a microclimate almost ideally suited to viticulture. With guidance from Clore, Henderson concentrated on varieties that showed the most potential; today, his Mont Elise Vineyards have replaced 40 acres of the cherry orchard with grapes: Gewurztraminer, Gamay, Pinot Noir. The Hendersons named their vineyard Mont Elise, after their daughter Elise.

More recently, the Hendersons commissioned artist Sebastian Titus to design a new label that depicts the deep chasm of the Columbia Gorge. And Chuck Sr., who came west from Wisconsin because he loved farming, can spend more time on his tractor now that his son Chuck Jr. has graduated from the enology program at U.C.-Davis and has taken over as the Mont Elise winemaker.

Visiting the winery★★. There's a breathtaking view ★★★★, from halfway across the toll bridge between Hood River and Bingen, of the majestic, windswept Columbia rolling downstream through the canyon walls of the Columbia Gorge. (The high winds that blow through the Gorge have turned Hood River into a windsurfing destination second only to Hawaii; international tournaments are held on the Columbia, bringing thousands of enthusiasts to the region.) Then you encounter mock Bavarian storefronts that the town of Bingen has put on for visitors. Somebody thought it could make the place look more like Germany's Bingen-am-Rhein (which most local folks pronounce BIN-JEN).

Mont Elise Winery, with a squat, gabled tower and southern German half-timbering, fits into the game. The building is part of a former apple and pear warehouse, whose cool cellars provide the right conditions for fermenting and aging wine. The small and chilly tasting room, on the main level, has a large window overlooking the barrels and tanks. A deli has been added to the retail complex adjacent to the tasting room.

Interesting as the old building is, with its enormous timbers and cavernous spaces, we think the visitor facility should be in those beautiful vineyards, five miles up the hillside along back roads!

Tasting the wine★★☆. Mont Elise is one of the very few consistent Gewurztraminer producers in the Northwest. Classic sensory notes of cinnamon, grapefruit, and rose petals, without the overt bitterness that so frequently troubles this wine.

The Pinot Noir grape is still recognizable in the Pinot Noir Blanc. So often this style of wine takes on vague, unidentifiable candy-like aromas; this one is off-dry, zesty, interesting. The Gamay Beaujolais is a fine, light, everyday red wine. There's also a methode champenoise sparkling wine, made from Pinot Noir and Chardonnay.

Getting there. From Oregon, take Exit 63 from I-84, cross the Columbia on the toll bridge, and turn east on Hwy 14; the winery is in downtown Bingen.

Open from noon to 5, daily in summer; and noon to 5 on Thursday, Friday, and Saturday only in winter.

Special events. Mont Elise participates in Bingen's Mayfest, held on the third Saturday in May. It also sponsors its own Huckleberry Fest in late August, as well as a pre-Christmas sale in early December.

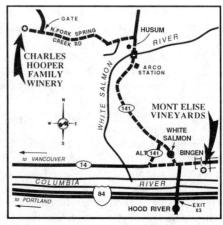

Washington State Sparkling Brut

MOUNTAIN DOME WINERY

Temple Road
Route 2, Box 199M
Spokane, WA 99207
(509) 922-7408

Owners & winemakers:
  Michael & Patricia Manz
Year established: 1986
Production capacity: 4,200 gallons
Vineyards: 1.5 acres
Touring region: Spokane [p. 24]

A bit of background His ambitious colleagues in medical school wanted to be cardiovascular surgeons, but Michael Manz didn't want to deal with patients when they're asleep. He did his residency in pediatrics instead. Today, a patient, bearded man, given to wearing plaid shirts, knit ties, tweedy jackets and corduroy trousers, Manz projects the image of a trustworthy confidant. Indeed, he has spent 15 years as a child psychiatrist, maintaining a private practice (and a position as chief of the child and adolescent psychiatry unit at Sacred Heart Hospital), dealing with child abuse and other devastating problems. His wife and partner, Patricia Manz, is a preschool teacher at the Woodland Montessori School. They needed something to mitigate the emotional toll of their professional lives, and had found a partial retreat in a domed hideaway Michael built in the hills behind Spokane.

Something else was needed, and Manz found it after spending a season (one day a week) at Worden's Washington Winery, working alongside Rollin Soles. "I've always enjoyed wine, and toiling in the vineyards seems honorable," Manz reports. The development of Mountain Dome also provides a project that Michael and Patricia can share during the limited time they have together.

Visiting the winery (NR) The Manz property, at an altitude of 2,800 feet with southern exposure, covers 40 acres, including a vegetable garden, dense woods, and a vineyard that could eventually grow to 20 acres of Chardonnay and Pinot Noir.

After a cautious beginning in the dome's basement, Manz has begun a program of expansion. There's now a pressing station equipped with a Willmes tank press outside the dome; the juice flows downhill, through pipes, to an enormous winery Manz built in the trees below. Classical music fills the air; Manz designed and constructed the speakers himself. The tanks in the temperature-controlled barrel room and nearby winemaking apparatus have been given the names of famous figures in psychology, education, and music (Freud, Mahler, Montessori, Rorschach). Manz has constructed a three-story tower on the building which will one day house a tasting room.

The grand design includes more tanks, more oak, 200-foot caves for bottle storage. It's not a tourist attraction, though. "I didn't move to the country to have the world come to me," Michael explains.

Tasting the wine (NR) No wine has been released yet, but more and more base wine for the champagne is in the works. Six tons were crushed in 1987, 16 tons in 1988, with plans for 24 tons in 1989, and ultimately 200 tons a year. Enough production, no doubt, to justify a 5,000-square-foot winery, but a far cry from relying on "lots of friends and lots of homemade beer" at crush and at bottling. And there may be some brandy, eventually. We've tasted barrel samples of as-yet-unblended Pinot Noir and Chardonnay, and find them very intriguing.

"Our only interest is a superior product," Manz says. By 1991 or 1992, with some 7,000 bottles of champagne ready for release, the public will find out how successful that ambition is.

Getting there. The Manz residence is on Temple Road, 2 mi north of the town of Foothills, on the way to Mount Spokane.

Open by appointment.

A word from the winery *"We are the smallest sparkling winery that uses only Washington state grapes. Our family-run operation is dedicated to producing the finest French-style sparkling wine possible. The wine is fermented in French oak barrels and aged four years on the yeast. Our winery is nestled in the foothills of Mount Spokane."*

PRODUCED AND BOTTLED BY MOUNT BAKER VINEYARDS'
B.W.#88 EVERSON, WASHINGTON, ALCOHOL 10% BY VOLUME

MOUNT BAKER VINEYARDS

4298 Mount Baker Highway
Everson, WA 98247
(206) 592-2300

Owners: Dr. Albert & Marjorie
Stratton, James Hildt
Winemaker: Kurt Larsen
Year established: 1981
Production capacity: 25,000 gallons
Vineyards: 25 acres
Touring: Puget Sound [p. 30]

A bit of background Al Stratton, a career military surgeon, grew up within a few miles of what is now Mount Baker Vineyards. His family bought him a home winemaking kit when he retired, and within a short time Stratton became preoccupied with viticulture. He started spending time at the Western Washington Research Station in nearby Mount Vernon, where Dr. Robert Norton was growing and evaluating dozens of grape varieties. Before long, Stratton took over the station's winemaking chores, learning about the unique character of cool-weather grapes.

By 1979, the Stratton family had begun planting their own vineyards, eventually putting in 25 acres of Muller Thurgau (Germany's most widely planted variety), Madeleine Angevine (a fruity variety bred in the Loire Valley as a table grape), and Madeleine Sylvaner (a fast-ripening variety, ready for harvest by early September).

From the beginning, Marjorie Stratton has been responsible for much of the vineyard work while Al has applied his military discipline and scientific curiosity to the development of appropriate winemaking techniques.

Jim Hildt, with a background in both contracting and orchard management, is general manager in charge of sales; he's slowly buying out the Strattons' interest in the winery, leaving Al and Marjorie to manage the vineyards.

Mount Baker was recently the target of a takeover attempt by Fidalgo Island Winery of Anacortes. It's difficult to say what prompted the early sense of harmony among the principals, or what motivated the alarm and acrimony that followed, but in the end the deal didn't come off. "It put us in an unfortunate situation and cost us a ton of grief, plus attorneys' fees," says Hildt. "But it's over."

Visiting the winery★★★. The early stretches of the Mount Baker Highway still have a perspective on the Cascades; you're not swallowed up by them. Snowcapped Mount Baker, Black Butte, the Sisters, and Mount Shuksan all come into view between Bellingham and the head of the Nooksack Valley. The valley, in fact, drains away the cold mountain air and provides a nearly perfect pocket of warmth between Deming and Nugent's Corner.

The winery itself, located at the edge of the smaller of two vineyards owned by Mount Baker Vineyards, stands on the site of an old mill and dairy homestead. It was built with visitors in mind: a bright and airy tasting room, plenty of parking, pretty vineyards (and an orchard of plum trees), a playground for youngsters, a picnic area for anyone who would like to stay awhile, and views of Mount Baker and the Twin Sisters. Another picnic area, fronting on the river, is accessible from Mount Baker's big vineyard a mile or so west of the winery; ask for directions at the tasting room.

Tasting the wine★★. Western Washington bottlings include Madeline Angevine, Muller Thurgau, and a variety known as Okanagan Riesling (which isn't a German Riesling at all but a Hungarian variety given its name by Canadians). Also available are Gewurztraminer, Chardonnay, and two proprietary wines, Crystal Rain and Island Classic, blended from French and German varieties. In addition, there's the popular (and relatively pricey) nonvintage plum wine, a not-to-be-missed treat even for vinifera fans; it smells exactly like plum jam gently simmering on the back burner of grandmother's stove. It's made from fruit grown in the orchard adjacent to the winery. More than 100 wild plum trees in Whatcom County were evaluated to find the right sugar/acid balance and hardiness, then grafted onto existing rootstocks. We've been meaning to try it in a sauce to accompany duck.

Wines like Okanagan Riesling or Madeline Angevine don't fall into any easy category in festivals (as there would be for Riesling or Chardonnay). Lumped unceremoniously into "Open Whites," they have a harder time impressing the judges. For all that, Mount Baker wines have acquitted themselves well in competition, winning a gold or top rating for every wine, somewhere, sometime.

The most interesting of the Mount Baker wines is the 1987 Muller Thurgau. It was the subject of long debate before being unveiled at our blind tasting: it smelled like a classic Chenin Blanc from Vouvray but lacked the expected acidity. It was spritzy, too, as were the 1987 Madeline Angevine and the 1986 Island Classic. The Island Select (a blend of Riesling, Gewurztraminer and Muscat) had a surprising (and not unpleasant) taste of raspberries. Unequivocally, however, Mount Baker's best wine is its Plum Nectar from the trees beside the tasting room.

Getting there North of Bellingham, take I-5 Exit 255 (Sunset Dr). Follow Hwy 542 toward Mount Baker for 11.1 mi; turn left on Hilliard Rd.

Open Wednesday through Sunday, 11 to 5 (weekends only, January through March). Group tours, $1 per person, refundable with a purchase.

Special events Picnics for case buyers and new releases over the first weekends in May and September. In July, there's

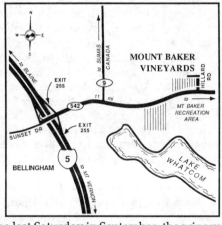

a summer music festival. On the last Saturday in September, the winery sponsors a Grape Stomp competition and barrel tasting of new wines; specialty food producers from the Nooksack Valley feed the spectators.

A word from the winery *"The microclimates of the Nooksack Valley in the northwest corner of Washington provide a long and mild 240-day growing season, comparable to select regions of Germany and France. These favorable conditions provide the classic Chardonnay, Gewurztraminer, and Pinot Noir grapes for winemaking. Working in conjunction with Washington State University, Mount Baker Vineyards has experimented with nearly 100 varieties and numerous unique grapes. Some, like Muller Thurgau and Madeleine Angevine, have become keynotes of Mount Baker Vineyards' crisp and floral styles, which capture the intense flavor of the Nooksack region."*

NEUHARTH
148 Still Road
Sequim, WA 98382
(206) 683-9652

Owners: Eugene & Maria Neuharth
Winemaker: Eugene Neuharth
Year established: 1979
Production capacity: 4,000 gallons
Vineyards: 0.5 acre
Touring: Olympic Peninsula [p.36]

A bit of background When Gene Neuharth left behind his grape-growing business in California's Lodi Valley and "retired" to Sequim, he was happy to give up 10-hour days in 100-degree heat, driving a tractor early in the morning, staying up till midnight to dust the crops. He and Maria had no intention of becoming commercial winemakers, but they got involved with a group of local people who made wine as a hobby, and before long they succumbed to the romantic notion that, as Gene put it, "Every little town should have its own winery."

He buys his grapes from Sagemoor Vineyards in eastern Washington, trucks them straight to the winery, and crushes the next day. Gene has also planted three dozen Labrusca varieties in a nearby half-acre vineyard for experimental purposes. In the tiniest of quantities, he blends them with his proprietary Dungeness wines to give them a distinctive, faintly perfumed flavor.

Visiting the winery★★★. It could be an alpine meadow, this hillside with snowcapped peaks in the distance and cows grazing amid the wildflowers. But the dark brown dairy barn, decorated with wood carvings, houses a winery, and the courtyard where milk wagons once loaded up is now the crushing pad. From a window in the stucco-covered tasting room, you look into the winemaking cellar, where massive cedar poles support the roof, high enough to provide year-round natural insulation for the stainless steel tanks and golden barrels on the winery floor.

Gene and Maria Neuharth shun many modern winery shortcuts; they hand-cork every bottle, and until recently did their own distributing as well. Gene doesn't use any pumps in his winery; he's afraid (certain, actually) that a pump seal will break down eventually, contaminating the wine. Besides, he reminds us, pumps stir up the wine, bruising it needlessly. So he uses a forklift to pick up his tanks and barrels, allowing the wine to flow by gravity to its next destination. More work, of course, but worth it.

Tasting the wines★★★☆. The three current reds include a black-red 1986 Cabernet Sauvignon, with berries and oak in the nose and balanced flavors; it's an exercise in restrained winemaking: not over-extracted or overly tannic, and a pleasure to drink now, though it will be even better in a year. The 1986 Merlot shows the varietal green pepper nose with judicious and satisfying use of oak, not upstaging the fruit. Surprisingly, it's more tannic and acidic than the Cabernet, but with opulent flavors. (We'll be putting a few into our cellar.) The nonvintage Dungeness Red is like a Beaujolais in the nose and pleasingly balanced.

Chardonnay is truly the queen of Neuharth's whites. The 1987 vintage doesn't yet reveal the rich complexity of some earlier Neuharth Chardonnays (the 1982 won the Governor's Trophy for the best white wine in the state), but it is, like all his wines, clean and balanced. There's a citrus-like character to the Riesling that makes it zesty while remaining true to its varietal character. The dominant grape in the Dungeness White is also Riesling, and it shows.

Getting there. Just east of "downtown" Sequim, turn south from Hwy 101 onto Still Rd; the winery is about 0.25 mi up the hill, across the railroad tracks, on the right. [**Map:** Lost Mountain]

Open daily, summers (mid-May to early October) from 9:30 to 5:30, winters from noon to 5. Small groups are welcome with advance notice. Picnic areas are available on the other side of the highway at Carrie Blake Park or at Sequim Bay State Park four miles west.

A word from the winery. *"Come visit and enjoy our fine dinner wines. Our tasting room wants to make you feel as though you are in an elegant wine cellar and lets you view the `real cellar' too. The old (vintage 1933) cedar pole barn has been restored and remodeled to accommodate the winery and it is interesting in itself. The small, handmade stainless steel vats and oak barrels (American and European) lend credence to the handmade wines produced here."*

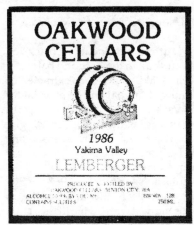

OAKWOOD CELLARS
1986
Yakima Valley
LEMBERGER

PRODUCED & BOTTLED BY
OAKWOOD CELLARS BENTON CITY WA
ALCOHOL 12.9% BY VOLUME   BW WA 128
CONTAINS SULFITES   750 ML

OAKWOOD CELLARS

2321 Demoss Road
Benton City, WA 99320
(509) 588-5332

Owners:
Bob Skelton & Evelyn McLain
Winemaker: Bob Skelton
Year established: 1986
Production capacity: 5,000 gallons
Vineyards: 3 acres
Touring region: Yakima Valley [p.15]

A bit of background Bob Skelton, an engineering manager for Boeing at Hanford, has lived outside the United States a great deal: nine years in Europe, five in Asia. It's the lifestyle of wine that he finds appealing. His early training as a chemical engineer helped, of course, when he took up winemaking as a hobby, then started taking courses in commercial winemaking and enology at U.C.-Davis.

Visiting the winery★★. Skelton's home sits on a bluff overlooking the Yakima River, lower down on the same slope of Red Mountain as Blackwood Canyon and Kiona; the winery, tasting room, and gift shop occupy the lower level of the house. Three acres of Riesling have been planted on the property, with five picnic tables under the trees out back.

Skelton plans to double the size of Oakwood Cellars in the near future, which would mean building a separate winery.

Tasting the wines★★. We've only tasted wines from the first vintage, but Skelton is more enthusiastic about recent production. "Best wine we've tasted in years," he says of the 1988 vintage.

For the moment, the wines available include barrel-fermented 1986 and 1987 Chardonnays, 1987 Semillon, Merlot aged in French and American oak, and Cabernet. Skelton is particularly proud of the Cabernet, which he promises "will be a world-class wine."

Getting there. Take Exit 96 (Benton City) from I-82. Turn right onto Hwy 224 (toward West Richland); after 0.5 mi, turn left and go 1 mi on Demoss Rd to the winery. [Map: Kiona]

Open weekends from noon to 6. Wednesday, Thursday, and Friday, the winery is open evenings, from 6 to 8. Groups should call ahead.

Special events. There's a Volksmarch at Oakwood Cellars in June, and a bicycle team race in early July.

A word from the winery *"Oakwood Cellars wines are limited to high-quality premium Washington varietal wines. Although few in number, all are medal-winners in high-level wine competitions. If you get one you don't like, bring it back. . . . We'll drink it!"*

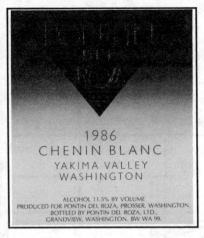

1986
CHENIN BLANC
YAKIMA VALLEY
WASHINGTON

ALCOHOL 11.5% BY VOLUME
PRODUCED FOR PONTIN DEL ROZA, PROSSER, WASHINGTON.
BOTTLED BY PONTIN DEL ROZA, LTD.,
GRANDVIEW, WASHINGTON. BW WA 99.

PONTIN DEL ROZA

Hinzerling Road
Route 4, Box 4735
Prosser, WA 99350
(509) 786-4449

Owners: Pontin family
Winemaker: Scott Pontin
Year established: 1984
Production capacity: 25,000 gallons
Vineyards: 15 acres
Touring region: Yakima Valley [p.15]

A bit of background Nesto Pontin's father, Angelo, began farming west of Yakima in the 1920s, planting local grapes on terraces as his family had done in Italy. By the mid-1950s, Nesto and his wife, Delores, had a place of their own north of Prosser; they worked hard, raised a fine family, and in 1975 made a trip to the Old Country. There, in the hills of provincial Italy, they visited the original family vineyards. When they returned to the Yakima Valley, they began planting a vinifera vineyard of their own, which they named, logically enough, after themselves and their location on the "Roza."

The Roza Irrigation District has helped transform the Yakima Valley from a dusty brown desert into the fruitbowl of the Northwest. Irrigation of the valley began in the late 1800s with private financing, then fell to the Bureau of Reclamation. The best grape-growing sites—the south-facing slopes on the north side of the river—had to wait until the mid-1930s for a system of canals to divert water from the dams of the Cascade Mountains. Today, some 77,000 acres of the valley fall within the boundaries of the Roza district.

Visiting the winery★★★. The Pontin estate covers 300 acres of grain, alfalfa, potatoes, and vines. Most of the grapes are Concords, sold for juice, but 15 acres are given over to Riesling. For the first two years of the winery's existence, the wines were custom-crushed at Coventry Vale, using purchased grapes as well as the Pontin's Riesling crop, with consultant Kay Simon helping Nesto's son Scott make the wine.

Even before the first bottles were released, Pontin's unusual red and silver label, executed by Seattle designer Tim Girvin, won a gold medal for excellence in packaging from the Seattle Design Association.

A winery and tasting room have now gone up behind the Pontin family home on Hinzerling Road. Scott and his sister Colleen (who runs the tasting room) are as delightful and friendly a duo as you'll ever meet; their enthusiasm alone could make tap water taste like nectar.

Tasting the wine★★☆. The best wine so far, an off-dry 1986 Riesling, has lovely apricot flavors. The 1986 Chenin Blanc shows good varietal character; the 1986 Roza Sunset is a simple, sweetish blush wine. There's a Chardonnay, too, and very limited production of a Cabernet Sauvignon.

Getting there. From Prosser, go 3.5 mi north along Hinzerling Rd; the Pontin winery is on the left.

Open daily from 10 to 5. Annual open house at the end of May. Spring barrel tasting the last weekend in April.

A word from the winery *"We invite you to visit our winery in the Yakima Valley of Washington state, experience the farmlands and vineyards around our winery, and taste our elegant premium varietal wines grown on our farm. Come and enjoy the sunshine on our picnic grounds, and the quiet of the surrounding farmland."*

PORTTEUS VINEYARDS

P.O. Box 1444
Zillah, WA 98953
(509) 829-6970

Owners: Paul Portteus Sr. &
   Paul Portteus Jr.
Winemaker: Paul Portteus Jr.
Year established: 1987
Production capacity: 26,000 gallons
Vineyards: 36 acres
Touring region: Yakima Valley [p15]

A bit of background You're in Cabernet Country here, high in the hills above Zillah. Mercer Island businessman Paul Portteus, a lifelong lover of good wine, and his son (also named Paul) started planting the 47-acre property overlooking the Yakima Valley with Cabernet Sauvignon,

Chardonnay, and Semillon in 1982. For several years, the vineyard has had a very high reputation among winemakers (like Mike Moore at Blackwood Canyon) who make wines with lots of punch and eagerly purchased the small crop.

Visiting the winery (NR) A tasting room was planned for the Yakima Valley barrel tasting in April 1989, but was behind schedule at last report.

Tasting the wines (NR) First wines to be released are 1986 and 1987 vintages of Cabernet Sauvignon and Chardonnay, and a 1987 Semillon. Independent reports suggest that the 1986 Cabernet, especially, is worth watching. (Not tasted.)

Getting there. From Zillah, head north on Cheyne, Roza, or Lucy Rd, go right on Highland Dr to the corner of Highland and Houghton, then left 0.25 mi.

Open Friday and Saturday from 10 to 5, Sunday 1 to 5. (Monday to Thursday by appointment or chance.)

A word from the winery *"When you visit our vineyard and winery the first thing you will notice is the view of the Yakima Valley with Mount Adams and Mount Rainier dominating the background. When you leave, we hope you will remember the unique wines produced on one of the highest vineyards in the state at just under 1400 feet in elevation.*

"Most of our production is split between barrel-fermented Chardonnay and oak-aged Cabernet. The heavy loam soil and high heat units at this site produce rich, complex ripe fruit. The wines show the characteristics well with deep color, balance, and intense flavors. These wines are not for the faint of heart."

1982
CABERNET
SAUVIGNON
WASHINGTON STATE

PRESTON WINE CELLARS

502 E. Vineyard Drive
Pasco, WA 99301
(509) 545-1990

Owners:
  S.W. ("Bill") & Joann Preston
Year established: 1976
Production capacity: 200,000 gallons
Vineyards: 181 acres
Touring region: Tri-Cities [p. 20]

A bit of background Bill Preston, a gregarious, generous man who doesn't mind making fun of himself, once told us, only half in jest, that he started his vineyard because he wanted an investment for his children's college education and that the premiums on an annuity were too expensive. The land he bought—on a dry plateau outside of Pasco—has been transformed into a lush, 200-acre vineyard planted with 16 varieties of grapes. Back in 1972, Bill Preston believed in the future of viticulture in the Tri-Cities and built Preston Wine Cellars into what was then the largest family-owned winery in the Northwest, with an annual production of some 150,000 gallons.

Rob Griffin served as Preston's winemaker for several vintages; during his tenure, Preston released a string of brilliant wines. Since Griffin left to join The Hogue Cellars, quality has suffered and sales have declined. Preston still gets some awards, but often for wines that Griffin crushed. Two more winemakers have come and gone; the post was vacant at press time.

For all his winery's successes, and they have been many, Bill Preston has no ambitions to be an enologist himself. Instead, he and Joann, their son, Brent (now vineyard and operations manager), and daughter, Cathy (public relations director), are promoters, enthusiasts in the cause of Washington wine. Before the Prestons started the winery, Bill earned his living selling farm and irrigation equipment; his sprinklers helped turn the dry desert into the ideal climate for viticulture. "The Columbia Basin is going to be the wine capital of the world," he told an interviewer 10 years ago. Today, as the winery's reputation begins to fade, Bill Preston's original vision deserves to be remembered.

Visiting the winery★★☆. You can't miss the huge WINE sign on the roof of the warehouse as you drive past the vineyards. There's an amphitheater and picnic area filled with assorted Tri-Cities memorabilia as you approach the two-story winery. A ramp leads up to the tasting room, which is surrounded by wide verandas overlooking the vineyards. Inside, dark wooden furniture and a handcrafted bar (as elaborate as a Byzantine altar) face picture windows. An informative self-guided tour takes visitors along catwalks safely above the winery floor, then back to the high-ceilinged tasting room and gift shop.

Unfortunately, our own observations, confirmed by reports from readers, suggest that the staff can be less than welcoming; the glasses too tiny to taste properly; and the wines poured for visitors oxidized. "In perspective to all the other visits I made, Preston was the most awful experience I have ever made in Washington state," a wine consultant from Sweden wrote to us.

Tasting the wines★★. The 1982-vintage Cabernet Sauvignon gets good marks (a gold medal and best-buy recommendation at the *International Wine Review* competition in New York), but one wonders what's going on in the warehouse if the 1982 Cab is Preston's current release. Another good wine is the luscious "ISBA" White Riesling, made from individually selected, botrytis-affected berries; the 1982 vintage won the Governor's Trophy for the best white wine at the Central Washington State Fair in 1986.

A generation of Washington wine drinkers probably got its start on Preston's Desert Gold, Washington's original blush wine. An early Sauvignon Blanc was hailed by a British friend as comparable to any Pouilly Fume or Sancerre he'd ever tasted. And an early Chardonnay won the very first Grand Prize at the Enological Society festival in Seattle.

That was then, this is now. We're comfortable recommending the most recent Chardonnays. But skip the nonvintage "Cuvee du Chardonnay," oxidized every time we've tried it, and avoid the heavy, overpriced red called Decade, blended from every vintage between 1976 and 1986.

Getting there. Cross the Columbia on either the Blue Bridge (Hwy 14) or the new I-182 bridge, turn toward Spokane on Hwy 395, and go north 5 mi. Preston Wine Cellars is on the right side of the highway.

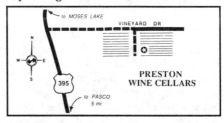

Open daily from 10 to 5:30.

Special events. A kite festival in early May, an open house toward mid-June, and a Holiday Gift Pack Preview in early December.

A word from the winery *"Visitors may sip four wines of the 14 award-winning wines on the tasting bar daily, either inside or outside on the overhanging deck, while enjoying a panoramic view of the vineyards and surrounding countryside. You may wish to go on a self-guided tour, or spend a few minutes admiring the hundreds of unique wine-oriented gifts, including our showcases of grape-related antiques and collectibles. Time permitting, you can enjoy an* *afternoon picnic and a bottle of wine in our `conversation piece' park, which includes our newly built amphitheater and cooking facilities."*

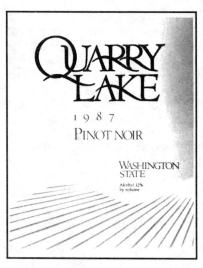

QUARRY LAKE VINTNERS

2520 Commercial Avenue
Pasco, WA 99301
(509) 547-7307

Owners: Balcom & Moe, Inc.
Winemaker & general manager:
Maury Balcom, Jr.
Cellarmaster: Richard Pfister
Production capacity: 50,000 gallons
Vineyards: 110 acres
Year established: 1986
Touring region: Tri-Cities [p. 20]

A bit of background No boutique winery here, no second-career start-up, no haphazard farm; the people behind Quarry Lake are firmly rooted in the land, in agricultural production and marketing. The parent company goes back half a century or so, when Eric Moe grew potatoes near Ellensburg and Maury Balcom marketed potatoes. The business they started together, Balcom & Moe, Inc., has grown into one of the state's most influential and diversified agricultural enterprises. (When the Wendy's chain began offering stuffed baked potatoes, they chose Balcom & Moe Farms as their supplier.) The company owns 3,500 acres, growing and shipping potatoes, fruit, wheat, and wine grapes.

Balcom & Moe began planting wine grapes in a big way, second only to Sagemoor Farms, in 1971, after Balcom's son Maury Jr. graduated from the University of California at Fresno with a degree in viticulture and enology. Maury Jr. spent 15 years as general manager of Balcom & Moe, providing the grapes for many of Washington's award-winning wines before the company started its own winery.

One reason for Quarry Lake's success is Maury's background in viticulture. Like, say, David Adelsheim in Oregon, Maury is both a theoretician and a practical experimenter who uses the latest technology to challenge conventional wisdom. For example, Maury points out that neutron probes now allow him to measure the moisture content of the soil five feet down, reducing irrigation costs and keeping the vines at a threshold level of stress. (Plentiful irrigation used to be an article of faith.) The vine senses the lack of water and literally struggles for life, growing better grapes in an effort to reproduce.

Maury also serves on the Washington Wine Commission and the Tri-Cities Economic Development Commission, contributing to both the promotion of wine and to the revitalization of eastern Washington's economic future. Among the projects Tri-Dec is working on: finding investors for new crops (a better popcorn is one project) and new agricultural processes (turning the waste from potato processing into high-grade cattle feed, for example), as well as increasing opportunities for tourism (with wineries, natch).

No description of Quarry Lake would be complete without a word about Maury's wife, Kathy, who is responsible for public relations. Well known for her promotional work on behalf of the Tri-Cities Northwest Wine Festival, Kathy must be one of the brightest, most amiable people in the wine business. You can't quite get over the feeling that she's barely out of high school, let alone a woman of considerable accomplishment (general manager of the biggest AM/FM radio stations in the Tri-Cities, founder of the Tri-Cities wine tour). She dresses like a teenager and probably gets asked for I.D. by bartenders, but she's one of the real movers and shakers of the eastern Washington wine community: it's impossible not to like her, and she gets things done.

Visiting the winery★★☆. An ambitious winery and visitor center will eventually be built across the highway from Preston Wine Cellars five miles to the north, at a reservoir (called Quarry Lake) for the Lower Columbia Irrigation District. Cellarmaster Richard Pfister says candidly, "Potatoes will drive [construction of] the winery." Meantime, Quarry Lake's wines are being made at Coventry Vale, and aged in an industrial facility just outside of Pasco.

It's a serviceable building, with several offices and a tasting room in front, barrels galore in the warehouse out back. There's twice as much space here as in the first location (just across the street), but you quickly get the feeling that the "real" winery is yet to come.

Tasting the wines★★☆. Clean wines with an occasional winner.

The much-applauded 1986 Chardonnay (double gold in San Francisco, gold in Tri-Cities) is all gone now; its successor is a bright, balanced wine with less intense flavor than the 1986. The 1987 Sauvignon Blanc has seen some new American oak, which adds complexity and balances the fruit well. There's a tasty, tannic 1986 Merlot waiting in the wings for a timely release. The 1985 Cabernet Sauvignon was unctuous in the mouth with a long finish.

Less successful are Quarry Lake's Riesling and Chenin Blanc, which lack the distinctive character of these varieties. Quarry Lake also markets two proprietary blush wines, Rainshadow and Sunburn (a blend of Riesling, Gewurztraminer and Muscat).

Getting there. From Pasco, take Hwy 395 toward Spokane, turn right on Hillsboro Rd, right again on Commercial Ave. Quarry Lake is about 0.75 mi down the road, on the right.

Open weekends from noon to 5 and by appointment.

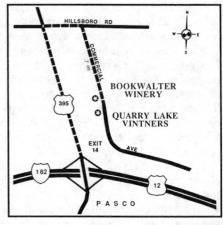

A word from the winery *"Tradition. In a word, that's what Quarry Lake is all about. In 1971, Balcom & Moe planted some of Washington's first vineyards. With meticulous agricultural practices and a demand for quality, this partnership developed into one of Washington's largest producers of world-class wine grapes…and now award-winning wines. The second generation of Balcom & Moe is now carrying on the tradition of excellence with Quarry Lake wines, using only the finest fruit from the 110-acre vineyard. The wines of Quarry Lake reflect the maturity of a vineyard in its prime."*

WHAT THE RATINGS MEAN FOR QUALITY OF WINE:

NR	No rating: not tasted at all or not tasted recently; no releases
★	Barely drinkable
★☆	Occasionally acceptable
★★	Uneven
★★☆	Usually good
★★★	Good
★★★☆	Usually superior
★★★★	Consistently superior

QUILCEDA CREEK VINTNERS

5226 Machias Road
Snohomish, WA 98290
(206) 568-2389

Owners: Alex & Jeannette Golitzin, Don Kotzerke
Winemaker: Alex Golitzin
Year established: 1978
Production capacity: 3,000 gallons
Vineyards: None
Touring region: Seattle [p. 30]

A bit of background The vanity license plate on Alex Golitzin's Oldsmobile, parked under a stand of alder at the top of his gravel driveway, expresses the family's magnificent passion: CLARET. Claret is what the British call the wines of Bordeaux; it is the only wine that Alex Golitzin has made for the past decade, and the only wine he ever intends to make. He is a French-born chemical engineer who works full-time at the Scott Paper Company in nearby Everett; his wife, Jeannette, is a teacher's aide, and partner Don Kotzerke is a colleague from work.

We first encountered Alex's wines on a wintery morning late in 1982 in the living room of the Golitzen home overlooking the Pilchuck River, and tasted his 1974, 1975, and 1976 vintages, made for home consumption. They were stunningly good, full of finesse, balance, complexity, and deep, rich blackberry character. We eagerly awaited the commercial release of his 1979 vintage, whose bottles were stacked up behind chicken wire in the garage.

The 1979 Quilceda Creek Cabernet Sauvignon was entered in only one competition, the Seattle Enological Society festival, and it won the Grand Prize, which requires the unanimous vote of the judges and had been awarded only once before. Frank Prial of the *New York Times* was one of the judges, and he wrote a column about it. Alex took a day off work, unplugged the phone, and raised the price of the wine from an unbelievably low $10 a bottle to $25; overnight, Alex Golitzen's Quilceda Creek became the standard by which Washington Cabernet Sauvignon is measured.

It shouldn't detract one whit from Alex Golitzin's skill as a winemaker to mention that his uncle is the world-famous winemaker Andre Tchelistcheff, who guided Alex's home winemaking efforts and inspired him to begin making wine commercially.

Visiting the winery★★★. Visits, by appointment only, are a treat. The winery is in two sections. The first part is the original winery; more recently, handsome redwood buildings have been added in back of the home for winemaking equipment, barrel storage, and bottle aging.

Tasting the wines ★★★★. Cabernet and more Cabernet! In our opinion, and we're not alone, this is the best Cab produced in Washington. Ah, one might argue, it's easy when you're only producing a few thousand bottles a year. Well, it's never easy, but it's undoubtedly less complicated if you stick to one variety, as Alex has. And if you have a full-time, outside job to finance your expensive passion. But at a time when almost every other winery in the Northwest is trying to be all things to all wine drinkers, Quilceda Creek is making its reputation producing only one wine.

What's the secret to Quilceda's success? Certainly part of it is Alex's scientific background, which has instilled in him an appreciation for the importance of rigorous quality control, discipline (and cost accounting). The winemaking process itself shows that there's no substitute for good grapes, time, and quality: fruit from Kiona and Mercer Ranch, malolactic fermentation, 22 months of barrel aging in French Nevers and American oak, two years of bottle aging. More touches: Alex uses a hand-held eggbeater to whip the eggwhites he uses to fine the wines; the bottles are filled three at a time and hand-corked.

Only once has a Quilceda Creek wine failed to win a gold medal (the 1981, which got a silver). The 1982, when we had it late last year, was going through a dumb phase; it wasn't particularly seductive or interesting. The 1983, which took second place in a "shoot-out" of Washington state Cabernets and 1983 Classified Bordeaux, turned up in a blind tasting just the other day; we found it very appealing, with a cedary, blackberry nose, and great purity and depth of flavor. It's still a very young wine, with lots of potential to get even better. The 1984 is on the market now, and the 1985 will be released at mid-year.

Getting there. From I-5 Exit 194 in Everett, take Hwy 2 eastbound (toward Stevens Pass) to Hwy 9. Go north one block and turn east on New Bunk Foss Rd (also called 52nd St S.E.), which ends after 1.2 mi on Old Machias Rd; the Golitzin home and winery are at the end of the first driveway on the left.

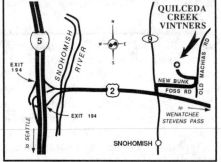

If you are already in Snohomish to visit the old homes or antique stores, go north on Maple. The name changes to Machias Rd and passes under the highway to Stevens Pass; 3 mi out of Snohomish, after passing the model-airplane airport, double back onto Old Machias Rd.

Open by appointment only.

A word from the winery. *"Quilceda Creek Vintners is dedicated exclusively to the production of world-class Washington state Cabernet Sauvignon wines. Utilizing the finest grapes available, we use a blend of traditional Bordeaux vinification techniques and current state-of-the-art knowledge to consistently produce elegant wines that are approachable when released and yet have excellent aging potential.*

"Nestled on a hill overlooking the Cascade Mountains, Quilceda Creek is located just north of the historic town of Snohomish, approximately 25 miles north of Seattle. We are open for tours and tastings by appointment and would like to cordially invite you to visit our winery."

COLUMBIA VALLEY
CABERNET SAUVIGNON
1985

PRODUCED & BOTTLED BY REDFORD CELLARS, PROSSER, WASH.
13.8% Alcohol/Volume   Contains Sulfites
100% Cabernet Sauvignon – Morrison & Mercer Vineyards

REDFORD CELLARS
4035 Eighth Avenue N.E.
Seattle, WA 98105
(206) 633-2249

Owner & winemaker
  Stephen Redford
First vintage: 1978
Vineyards: None
Production capacity: None

A bit of background For three years in the late 1960s, Stephen Redford owned the Blue Moon Tavern in Seattle's University District, when it was famous as the center of a hippie lifestyle. A decade later, he joined his older brother Myron as cellarmaster and assistant winemaker at Amity Vineyards in Oregon. Starting with the 1978 crush, while Myron concentrated on white wines and Pinot Noir, Steve made some wines at Amity under the Redford Cellars label, using Cabernet Sauvignon and Merlot grapes.

Steve's wines met with considerable success, but production at Amity was always limited. So in 1983 he began the difficult business of putting together a 10,000-gallon winery of his own. He spent a year as winemaker at Mercer Ranch Vineyards, and since early 1988 has been looking for a new location and funding for a winery in the Seattle area.

Tasting the wines★★★. Cabernet and Merlot are the two varieties of Redford Cellars that are available, especially in a blended version. They are robust wines with deep fruit character and fine balance. There's a good supply of 1985 wine available; as 100 percent Cabernet and in a Cabernet-Merlot blend. The 1986 vintage hadn't been bottled at press time; there was no crush in 1988.

A word from the winery *"Redford Cellars wines are unique blends of Cabernet and Merlot grapes designed to give the highest complexity of aromas and flavors from each vintage. The Cabernet-Merlot is especially smooth now and will only gain in complexity. The very powerful 100 percent Cabernet is only for serious people as it requires patience and age. Enjoy!!"*

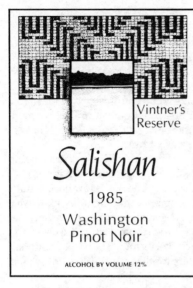

SALISHAN VINEYARDS
Route 2, Box 8
LaCenter, WA 98629
(206) 263-2713

Owners: Joan & Lincoln Wolverton
Winemaker: Joan Wolverton
Year established: 1982
Production capacity: 10,000 gallons
Vineyards: 12 acres
Touring region:
 Southwest Washington [p. 27]

A bit of background A young Seattle couple, both professionals and intellectually inclined, Joan and Lincoln Wolverton had a wild notion, long before it became fashionable, to own a small vineyard and winery. So in the early 1970s, Joan (then a reporter for *The Seattle Times*) and Linc (then an economist for Boeing) spent virtually every weekend planting and nurturing a 12-acre vineyard three hours south of Seattle, a vineyard they named Salishan in honor of the Salish Indians who once roamed the entire coastal region.

By 1976, Linc had found a job in Portland, and Joan, a tall, outgoing woman with boundless energy and a sharp sense of humor, was devoting all her time to the vineyard's management. Two years later, they started producing wine (first at Hinzerling, then at Ponzi), and in 1982 bonded their own facility. Today Linc has his own consulting business (East Fork Economics, named for the river below), and Joan directs the winery's operations.

Visiting the winery★★★☆. LaCenter is a bucolic place halfway between Portland and Mount St. Helens; the geography and climate here are closer to Oregon's Willamette Valley 40 miles to the south (moderate "maritime" temperatures, long daylight hours) than to eastern Washington's warm and sun-drenched vineyards. It's more difficult for grapes to ripen here than in the Yakima Valley, but the long growing season intensifies the fruit flavors in the grapes. The Wolvertons pioneered the planting of vinifera grapes in Clark County, and have been followed by many others. Their next-door neighbor started a 40-acre vineyard under black plastic less than five years ago (a technique that retains the ground's natural heat, keeps out weeds, and allows bare-root cuttings to be poked directly into the ground) and now sells his Pinot Noir and Chardonnay crop to Columbia Winery.

From Salishan's winery, on the hillside above LaCenter, you can see Mount Hood and the Oregon Cascades. Behind you is Mount St. Helens, whose eruption in 1980 covered the vineyard with ash but proved less harmful than the annual swarms of robins. The real treat here is to walk through the vineyards with Joan. Like her "counterpart" in Oregon, Nancy Ponzi, she's a great communicator—intelligent, humorous, down-to-earth, unpretentious. She makes the hard work and long hours of viticulture and winemaking sound like great fun.

Tasting the wines★★★. A fine line of wines: dry Riesling, dry Chenin Blanc, oak-aged Chardonnay, Pinot Noir, and Cabernet Sauvignon.

First things first. The 1986 Chardonnay was one of the few harmonious Chardonnays we tasted from the growing area that includes southwest Washington and the Willamette Valley. It displays the regional character of Chardonnay fruit (pineapples, fermenting tropical fruit) in a clean and exciting form, complemented by French oak fermentation (for about half the wine) and oak aging. The flavors were toothsome, the texture viscous, and the finish bright with acid.

The 1985 Pinot Noir is still available. At first in the glass it showed strawberries and sweet raw beef, but gradually added notes of tobacco and plums. Nice balance in the mouth with bracing acidity. Two versions of 1986 Pinot will be marketed. Lot 1 shows strawberry and leather in the nose, Lot 2 strawberry and white pepper. Both are delicate but penetrating in flavor and proved very accommodating with food.

The 1987 Chenin Blanc—hardly a bad wine—has a tought act to follow, after the star-studded 1986 vintage. It has the honeyed, green tomato nose and flavors that mark its variety, and a flinty characteristic that is like some Loire Valley Chenin Blanc.

Getting there. Take Exit 16 (LaCenter) from I-5. At the entrance to town, follow Main St up the hill and proceed 1 mi along North Fork Rd.

Open from 1 to 5 on weekends, May through December. Other times by appointment.

A word from the winery *"We are different, but we win about as many medals per gallon as anybody. Our wines are more like western Oregon's than eastern Washington's. We have green hillsides, gorgeous weeds, and a terrific view of Mount Hood—when the rain stops. We grow all our own grapes and make them into wine on the premises—with the help of a few good friends, part-time workers, and low-tech tools.*

"We are so small we can offer a genuine, hands-on experience: where else will you be asked to help fix the tractor, lift a hose, or walk up to the house if no one is at the tasting room when you come?"

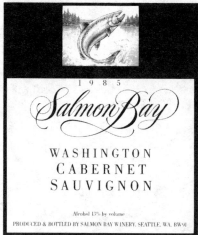

1 9 8 5

Salmon Bay

WASHINGTON
CABERNET
SAUVIGNON

Alcohol 13% by volume

PRODUCED & BOTTLED BY SALMON BAY WINERY, SEATTLE, WA. BW91

SALMON BAY
13416 N.E. 177th Place
Woodinville, WA 98072
(206) 483-9463

Owners: Bruce Crabtree, Kenneth Rogstad, Bobby Capps
Winemaker: To be named
Year established: 1982
Vineyards: None
Production capacity: 12,000 gallons
Touring region: Seattle [p. 30]

A bit of history Bruce Crabtree, formerly the sommelier at the posh Rosellini's Four-10 restaurant, has a winning manner with people and a talented hand with wines. Four years ago he started his own winery, named Vernier after the patron saint of wine; a couple of years later the name was changed to Salmon Bay.

Visiting the winery (NR) Salmon Bay's original space in an industrial park next to E.B. Foote served the purpose of making wine but not meeting the public, which Crabtree does best. It wasn't until early 1989 that he finally managed to pull off a move to Woodinville; his grand opening there is expected to coincide with the publication of this book. There's no picnic area at the new winery, but room for a large gift shop.

Tasting the wines ★★☆. It's hard to run a 12,000-gallon winery without a full-time winemaker; Crabtree recognizes this and hopes to remedy the situation soon. (Lou Facelli worked here briefly, finishing up some of the wines.) For now, Salmon Bay has a bit of everything for a variety of tastes.

Starting with the bad news: the nonvintage Oyster Shell White, made entirely from Semillon. The winery's technical data says it has a finish of anise and figs, and recommends it be served very chilled with shellfish or chicken. We found it madeirized, with unpleasant aromas of burned apples, licorice, and soft cheese; the finish was bitter. The nose on the 1986 Sauvignon Blanc was pleasantly varietal, but the flavors were unbalanced and bitter. The 1987 Chardonnay from Outlook Vineyard was clean but undistinguished.

Now for the good news. First, two reds with a little age showing at the temples. The 1983 Cabernet Sauvignon is a "user-friendly" wine, redolent of black currants and green pepper (it's 14 percent Merlot), with an earthy complexity. It's bright and generous in the mouth with mild tannin and good balance; a delight. Its younger brother, the 1984 Merlot (12 percent Cabernet) is a more austere and reticent wine with higher tannin but an enticing nose of green pepper and mushroom; balanced and satisfying!

Of the two Salmon Bay Rieslings, our favorite is the 1985 Select White Riesling. Gorgeous, classic stone fruit nose, a hint of the petrol-like chemical taste one expects in a fine Reisling with a few winters behind it, and a lingering, clean-as-a-whistle finish.

Getting there. Follow the directions to French Creek Cellars in Woodinville, but go another two blocks on 177th Pl.

Open noon to 5 daily.

Special events. Open house in spring and fall.

SETH RYAN WINERY

681 S. 40th
West Richland, WA 99352
(509) 967-9204 or 375-0486

Owners: Jo & Ron Brodzinski, Khris Olsen, Robert Olsen
Winemaker: Khris Olsen
Year established: 1986
Production capacity: 1,000 gallons
Vineyards: 20 acres
Touring region: Tri-Cities [p. 20]

A bit of background This tiny winery fits into the garage at Khris Olsen's house in suburban West Richland. Khris, a chemist for Batelle, works with Ron Brodzinski; Ron's wife, Jo, runs a theater program and has a flair for the dramatic. (Robert Olsen, Khris's father, lives on the East Coast and is a silent partner in this venture.) At one early tasting Ron turned up dressed as Abraham Lincoln; the owners frequently turn out in evening dress to pour their wines.

Visiting the winery(NR). A suburban garage says it all. The vineyard property owned by the two families covers 20 acres on Red Mountain, but planting still awaits a source of water for irrigation. There's no tasting room.

Tasting the wines★☆. Riesling in varying degrees of sweetness and oak aging, as well as some Chardonnay and Gewurztraminer. What we've seen so far might best be described as experimental rather than commercial winemaking.

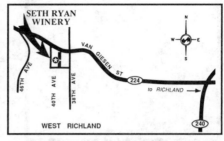

Getting there. To reach the Olsen residence from the Tri-Cities, take Exit 4 from I-182 and follow Hwy 240 to the West Richland turnoff (Hwy 224). Cross the bridge into West Richland, turn south on 38th, right one block later on Grant, and right again on 40th.

Open by appointment.

Special events. Special barrel tasting, winter tastings, and a grand opening when appropriate.

A word from the winery *"Seth Ryan Winery, one of the newest Washington wineries, is in its infancy. We are just starting to crawl and are pleased to share with you, by appointment, the plans and dreams for our wines. We are growing and learning and want your input, as our main goal is to make quality wines with character and style that are great to drink. We feel wines can be pleasant from the minute you pull the cork, and we will pull corks anytime our customers want to learn about us. We'll do private tastings at your place as well as ours and look forward to meeting our friends, the customers. We want to give you the personal touch, so when you pull the cork, you'll know the wine as well as we do. So give us a call and let us share our new family additions with you. We want you to watch our baby grow."*

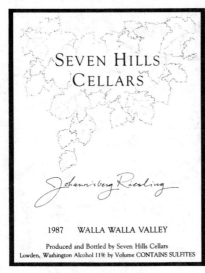

SEVEN HILLS
CELLARS

Johannisberg Riesling

1987   WALLA WALLA VALLEY

Produced and Bottled by Seven Hills Cellars
Lowden, Washington Alcohol 11% by Volume CONTAINS SULFITES

SEVEN HILLS WINERY

1450 Brookshire Drive
Walla Walla, WA 99362
(509) 529-3331

Owners: Herbert Hendricks &
    James McClellan families
Winemaker: Casey McClellan
Year established: 1987
Production capacity: 5,000 gallons
Vineyards: 30 acres
Touring region: Walla Walla [p. 22]

A bit of background The greatest French wines come from relatively tiny patches of ground where weather and soil conditions combine to grow specific varieties with the highest quality. Cabernet Sauvignon, for example, grows with more or less success in vineyards around the world, at its best in the gravelly soils around Bordeaux, and with superlative quality only on a few acres in the Medoc.

It's appropriate, then, that Dr. Herb Hendricks of Milton Freewater, who enjoyed the wines of Bordeaux, decided to plant Cabernet Sauvignon grapes when he started planting a vineyard on his property out toward Umapine. (Mind you, this is on the Oregon side of the Walla Walla Valley.) A fellow doctor, Jim McClellan of Walla Walla, soon joined him in the venture, as did their wives and children. Today, Scott Hendricks oversees the vineyard (which covers 30 acres, half of it Cabernet and Merlot), and Casey McClellan is the winemaker.

It didn't take the local winemakers long to recognize the remarkable quality of these grapes; Leonetti Cellars won the national Cabernet championship with Seven Hills grapes in its bottles, and Woodward Canyon is a regular customer.

Vineyard owners often become wine producers, especially when a member of the family has the proper training. Casey earned his stripes in the family vineyard while earning a degree in pharmacy at the University of Washington. He went on to a master's degree at the University of California at Davis, winning a couple of prestigious fellowships and publishing some scholarly papers along the way, and has spent time working in the cellars of Spain and Portugal.

Seven Hills Winery (a business separate from the vineyard) doesn't have its own facility yet; Eric Rindal made the 1987-vintage wines at

Waterbrook, with Casey taking over in 1988.

Visiting the winery (NR). Seven Hills plans a winery close to the vineyard, on the Oregon side of the Walla Walla Valley, within a year or so. "We plan to have an atmosphere hospitable to visitors and would enjoy contact with the public," says Casey.

Tasting the wines (NR) None available at the Waterbrook winery, and only small quantities of Sauvignon Blanc, Riesling, and a proprietary white called Overture have been released to local restaurants and retailers. (Not tasted.)

A word from the winery:*"The goal of Seven Hills is to produce premium quality wines of the Walla Walla Valley appellation. Through careful viticultural and winemaking techniques, we will strive to create wines which reflect the best of European and American winemaking traditions, adapted to the unique wine grapes of the Walla Walla Valley. We invite you to taste and enjoy these wines, made with care and pride."*

SILVER LAKE

17616 15th Avenue N.E.
Unit 106-B
Bothell, WA 98012
(206) 485-2437

Owner: Washington Wine &
        Beverage Company
Winemaker: Brian Carter
General manager: David Adair
Year established: 1989
Production capacity: 15,000 gallons
Vineyards: None
Touring region: Seattle [p. 30]

A bit of background: Reunion time! Brian Carter (a consulting winemaker with a fistful of consulting contracts around Washington, including his former full-time employer, Paul Thomas) and David Adair (a manager at Paul Thomas, Columbia, Haviland) are together again. And all because of fermented apple cider.

The unlikely turn of events began when an enterprising group of investors began importing cider from Canada, bottling it in Bothell (a suburb north of Seattle), and selling it under the Spire Mountain label. Last year, they sold 9,000 cases of the imported cider.

The company's president, Sal Leone, thought he might do even better if he could make cider from domestic apples, and hired Brian Carter to help. Leone is also an avid amateur winemaker, so the conversation naturally got around to wine. Just as we were going to press, we learned that Leone had given Carter carte blanche to start a winery right away: money for juice, for grapes, for equipment, for barrels. Silver Lake (the name of a nearby body of water) will have an "elegant, understated" package, Adair says. The plan is to sell high-quality wines in the niche between $8 and $12 a bottle, a hole, according to Adair, that no Northwest winery currently fills.

The cider production will go forward, too, with Washington state apples; the only difference will be that the permit for Spire Mountain's facility will change from "licensed bottling house" to "bonded winery."

Visiting the winery (NR) Silver Lake is in a pocket-size industrial park about three miles north of Bothell, in a facility that will be big enough if the owners adhere to their plan of limited production. The bottling machine is designed to handle both cider and wine.

Tasting the wines (NR) The 1988 wines will be bottled from juice purchased on the open market. Silver Lake intends to start (and stick) with the four major varieties: Cabernet Sauvignon, Merlot, Chardonnay, Fume Blanc. "Plus maybe a little Riesling for the tasting room," adds Adair. The crush in 1989 is expected to produce about 15,000 gallons.

Getting there. Take Exit 26 (Canyon Creek) from I-405 and head north on the Bothell-Everett Hwy to the winery.

Open five days a week by June 1989. Call the winery for hours.

JOEL KLEIN

Joel Klein, tall, bearded, unfailingly polite, a truly towering figure in Washington's wine industry, came to enology after early training as a chemical engineer. He spent eight years at Chateau Ste. Michelle, where he made many of the wines that put Washington on the map of world viticulture, then left to start his own winery. "It must be masochism," he said at the time, half kidding. "Although winemaking is a craft, not a science, and a craftsman is supposedly free to do what he wants, you're never quite your own boss as a winemaker."

As he found out all too soon.

The winery he dreamed of creating became Snoqualmie Winery. For a season or two, the vision took shape: a building was erected, wines were made, a label designed, awards won, cases sold. Joel and his wife, Karen, ran the operation with seeming skill and grace, technically as employees of Snoqualmie's original owners, David and Priscilla Wyckoff (who also founded Coventry Vale), later in collaboration with CPA Robert Rohan and attorney Mike McCarthy.

Enter Wolfgang Langguth, the German entrepreneur whose own vision had led him to build a winery on the dusty Wahluke Slope. After four desultory years, Langguth finally recognized that he lacked the expertise necessary, not to grow and make wines, but to sell them in an unfamiliar American market, and he asked Klein for help.

Joel turned to his backers for funds, and the new investors helped Snoqualmie's holding company buy a controlling interest in Langguth. The first order of business was unpleasant: a technical bankruptcy to seek protection from Langguth's major creditor, the adjacent vineyard that supplied all of its grapes. In late summer of 1987, the investors hired Mike Januik to manage the Langguth facility. But the worst was still to come: although Joel was still president of Snoqualmie, the new owners dismissed him as winemaker and locked him out of the winery.

Suits and countersuits were filed; Joel has spent the last year preparing for a trial. Ironically, Joel used to say that he switched from chemical engineering to the wine business because he liked the people better. Karen Klein, in fact, is the daughter of the famous California enologist, Hod Berg.

"The biggest problem I had [as one of Washington's original winemakers]," Joel said to us recently, in a conversation about his career that avoided discussing the pending litigation, "was the lack of precedents. What's a Sauvignon Blanc supposed to taste like? Fortunately, I knew about more than California; I had worldwide experience, a broader perspective."

It all takes time, Joel points out. (He was talking about winemaking, but he could have been referring to his legal situation as well.) "If you don't have the patience, go make widgets."

But the patient, slow, and steady path has a downside, too. "You start small and get bigger, and finally, all you're doing is sitting at a desk and reading reports. It's not a question of *can* you do it, but do you *want to* do it?"

When it's over, there's a sense of relief. "Not because you *can't* handle it, but because you don't *enjoy* handling it."

SNOQUALMIE WINERY

1000 Winery Road
Snoqualmie, WA 98065
(206) 888-4000
(206) 392-4000 (toll-free from Seattle)

Owners: Snoqualmie Falls Holding Company
Winemaker: Mike Januik
Year established: 1984
Production capacity: 800,000 gallons
Vineyards: None
Touring region: Seattle [p. 30]

A bit of background. This winery, on a wooded hillside overlooking the Snoqualmie Valley and Cascade foothills, combines an unbeatable tourist attraction with modern winemaking technology. The opening of Snoqualmie Winery (pronounced Snow-QUAL-mee), just half an hour's drive from Seattle, was a watershed for the Northwest wine industry. This is a first-class tourist destination, just off Interstate 90, literally at the off-ramp to one of Washington's most visited attractions (Snoqualmie Falls, with 2 million visitors a year), and blessed with an incredible view.

The parent holding company also owns the F.W. Langguth winery in Mattawa; the combined production of its three labels (Snoqualmie, Langguth, and Saddle Mountain—sometimes referred to collectively as "Sno-guth Mountain") makes it the second-largest winery in the state.

A troubled legal history surrounds Snoqualmie and Langguth (see the profile of Joel Klein on page 156), and the winery's very size might lead snobs to belittle the wine. In fact, only 35,000 gallons of the Langguth facility's 1988 production was for the Snoqualmie label. More important, the quality has improved remarkably over the past two vintages, demonstrating clearly that Mike Januik, who took control after Joel Klein left, is one of Washington's most talented winemakers.

Visiting the winery ★★★☆. The site, half an hour's drive from downtown Seattle, presents a panorama ★★★★ that is nothing short of breathtaking. The mountainside on which the winery is located drops off steeply into the Snoqualmie Valley below; on the other side, so close you can almost touch it, looms Mount Si. The 137-acre hillside, leased from the town of Snoqualmie, has a natural population of deer and even bear.

Snoqualmie's "winery" building was meant to be an interim facility; the first wines were made at Coventry Vale. Now that Langguth's production facility turns out Snoqualmie wines as well, the current building will remain a visitor center with some remodeling scheduled for 1990. There's just enough winemaking to qualify as a bonded commercial facility; the spacious back room currently holds case goods and several barrels of Lemberger.

The visitor portion of the winery has attractive, professionally decorated tasting facilities, an open fireplace, cool gray carpeting, and stained glass. A deli case is stocked with picnic makings and nonalcoholic drinks; picnic tables are set out on the terraced lawn overlooking the valley.

Staff members exude enthusiasm, eager to share their knowledge and to suggest food combinations for the wines. Anna Murch, recruited from Covey Run, is in charge of all the visitor facilities and brings a sure touch to the tasting room, and Elizabeth Henson, a retired school teacher, turns a Sunday stop at the tasting counter into a delightful experience.

Tasting the wines ★★★☆. A former wine shop manager in Ashland who went on to take an enology degree in California, Mike Januik seems to have an intuitive skill. If a wine requires a hint of oak to round it out, he knows when to stop; he's a hands-on craftsman who avoids both bitterness and flabbiness in Gewurztraminer, yet retains the right note of bitterness in Riesling. As the winemaker for Stewart Vineyards, he made a small lot of Late Harvest Riesling that won the Seattle Enological Society's Grand Award; he now manages a million-gallon winery without losing his confidence or his modesty.

We think Snoqualmie's Fume Blanc and Semillon are two of Washington's best wines. The 1987 Semillon is particularly distinctive, with a bouquet of Anaheim peppers and juniper, round in the mouth with lush bell-pepper flavors and just the right twist of bitterness in the finish to make it a wonderful wine with food.

The 1987 Gewurztraminer had a lovely nose of dusty roses, quince, and grapefruit, with off-dry flavors of orange peel and nutmeg. The wine finishes off-dry, without any of the usual bitterness that makes so much Gewurz less than satisfying. On the other hand, the lush tropical flavors of the 1987 Riesling were highlighted by its slightly bitter finish. The next vintage of Chardonnay (made by Mike Januik) and Snoqualmie's new reds won't be released until later in 1989. A barrel sample of the Lemberger suggests it will be a clean, uncomplicated, cherry-like version of this variety.

Getting there. Eastbound, take Exit 27 from I-90, turn right up the hill, and left onto Winery Road.

Westbound, take Exit 31, follow the old highway through North Bend, turn left just before the freeway on-ramp.

Open daily from 10 to 4:30. No fee for groups.

Special events. A variety of summer events take place at the winery between May and August. There's an unspecified "special" event in late October, and a holiday gift show in November.

A word from the winery *"Come visit Snoqualmie Winery, browse in the gift shop, taste our commitment to producing fine wines. Picnicking is welcome, with a panoramic view of the Snoqualmie Valley and Cascade Mountains. Watch our development on site as we continue to grow to service your needs."*

1986 WASHINGTON STATE
SAUVIGNON BLANC

PRODUCED & BOTTLED BY STATON HILLS VINEYARD & WINERY
WAPATO, WA U.S.A.   ALCOHOL 12½ - BY VOL. FOR WA. 1986

STATON HILLS
71 Gangl Road
Wapato, WA 98951
(509) 877-2112

1910 Post Alley
Seattle, WA 98101
(206) 443-8084

Owners: David & Susanne Staton
Winemaker: Rob Stuart
Year established: 1984
Production capacity: 120,000 gallons
Vineyards: 16 acres
Touring regions:
    Yakima Valley [p. 14]
    Seattle [p. 30]

A bit of background The Statons have lived in the Yakima Valley since the early 1970s, growing apples and pears, and planning their winery. Florida-born and trained as a lawyer, Dave Staton worked as an attorney in the international division of Chase Manhattan Bank in New York and as a high-level executive for Trans World Airlines before moving to California, where he got interested in wine. The Statons looked at Napa

Valley property, found it overpriced, and moved to Yakima. But viticulture in eastern Washington was too uncertain back then, so they grew fruit. Dave was appointed to a couple of agricultural research boards along the way, and the Statons planted experimental plots of grapes near their orchards while proceeding with plans for the winery.

In terms of viticulture, Staton Hills today is one of the most innovative vineyards in the state. The 16-acre site, just 100 yards off the freeway, sits in a "banana belt" micro-climate that's usually five to eight degrees warmer than other spots in the Yakima Valley. It features three advanced types of trellising not often found in the Northwest: the Guyot trellis developed in the Bordeaux region of France, the gable trellis from South Africa, and the Tatura trellis developed in Australia. The viticulturists who pioneered these systems visited the vineyard to consult on the design and installation of the systems at Staton Hills. Some 144 miles of high-tension wires hold up the vines and expose the grape leaves to more sunlight, thereby producing faster growth in the young vines and, potentially, a larger crop.

Visiting the winery (Yakima Valley)★★★. You approach the winery through the state-of-the-art vineyards with their futuristic trellising. And what a winery it is! A handsome, 10,000-square-foot building sheathed in cedar, almost half of it devoted to visitor facilities. The tasting room features a great, two-story stone fireplace and cathedral ceilings, with Oriental carpets on the Swedish-finished oak floors.

Upstairs, there's a complete kitchen and a small banquet room that seats 40 people. From the deck, as from the wide porch downstairs, there's a spectacular view ★★★★ across the Yakima Valley of Mount Adams. Outside, terraced lawns, picnic tables, and a barbecue pit invite visitors to linger. The banquet room can be rented for private parties, and the tasting room stocks some deli supplies.

On the winemaking side, expansion of astounding proportions: 12,000 square feet more space, a second high-speed bottling line, another 20,000 gallons of French oak. A big financial commitment, which indicates that owners and bankers alike have confidence in the winery's progress.

Despite the many attractions of the fabulous setting and beautifully furnished facility, which merited the highest rating in our earlier edition, the tasting room staff has often seemed poorly trained and unfriendly. Our impressions have been confirmed in a number of reports from readers. To his credit, Dave Staton recognizes the problem and insists that "we have worked very hard to improve our customer relations."

Visiting the winery (Seattle)★★☆. The location, in the heart of the venerable Pike Place Market, of this mini-winery (for aging champagne and port) provides Staton Hills with a great marketing opportunity: access to thousands of shoppers. Regular visitor traffic makes it likely that the wines will be fresh and the staff more knowledgeable. There's not a lot to see here, any more than at Covey Run in Kirkland; champagne bottles and red wine barrels sit behind a glass partition. But all the Staton Hills wines can be tasted, and there's a good variety of wine-related gifts.

Tasting the wines★★★. Staton Hills enters competitions all over the country with an enthusiasm that rivals Chateau Ste. Michelle's. Adding up the medals, the *International Wine Review* ranked Staton Hills as the country's number six winery for 1987.

The winemaker is Rob Stuart, a genial young man who was assistant winemaker at Valley View Vineyards in Oregon. California guru Charles Ortman, a long-time friend of the Statons', acts as consulting winemaker.

Notes from our most recent tasting of Staton Hills wines, purchased at a Seattle chain store: we found the 1987 Sauvignon Blanc to be pleasantly floral, rather like a Sauvignon Blanc from Oregon; the 1986 Chardonnay was barrel-fermented, giving it a delightful butterscotch nose and smooth fruit flavors. Both wines were well balanced, although lacking in intensity. In the past, we've enjoyed the White Riesling, a dessert wine with overtones of quince. The Pink Riesling is another story altogether; see the page 163 for a separate comment.

Altogether, a wide array of well-made wines: Cabernet Sauvignon, Merlot, Pinot Noir, Chardonnay, Sauvignon Blanc, Semillon, Riesling, Gewurztraminer, and so on. In addition to all the standard varieties, there are two methode champenoise champagnes with 2• years on the yeast, and a port. Staton Hills recently contracted with Ted Gerber's Foris Vineyard in Cave Junction, Oregon, for Pinot Noir, which will put them into the select circle of Washington wineries buying Oregon grapes for this prestigious variety.

Getting there (Yakima Valley). The principal Staton Hills winery is less than 10 minutes from Yakima; take Exit 40 (Parker Rd) from I-82. Access to the winery is from Gangl Rd, just north of the interchange.

Open daily except Monday from 11 (winters from noon) to 5. Tour groups must make appointments; no fee.

Getting there (Seattle). The Seattle winery is in the Pike Place Market, on Post Alley (parallel to Pike Place) between Stewart and Virginia. Same hours.

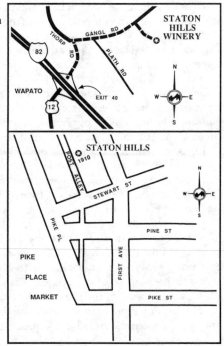

A word from the winery *"Fashioned like a French, country-style chateau, Staton Hills is surrounded by 14 acres of prime vineyard and manicured grounds which dominate a rolling hillside. Providing an oasis for tourists and travelers, the grounds offer picnic and barbecue areas for leisure visits. We are working hard at producing top quality wines and think our recent successes are worthy of note."*

RATING THE WINERY VISITS:

NR	Not rated: tasting room not open, no visiting
★	Don't bother
★★	Moderately interesting
★★★	Worth a detour
★★★★	Worth the trip

See the introduction (page 8) for additional information on the criteria used to rate winery visits.

PRETTY IN PINK RIESLING:
A success story?

Eastern Washington and southern Oregon turn out some of the best late-harvest, dessert-style Rieslings in the country. The Northwest generally leads the nation in the production of this variety, but not enough people buy Riesling (sweet or dry or in-between) to soak up the juice from its vast plantings. From enological success has come viticultural overabundance.

So here we are, sitting on thousands of acres of premium grapes, with an ill-defined and indifferent market. Never mind that Germany considers Riesling its most prestigious variety; American consumers want Chardonnay. Riesling is the Northwest's cheapest grape, frequently dropping below the cost of production.

Washington wineries have been making Riesling in an off-dry style, relegating these exquisite grapes (in our opinion) for the broader market of less sophisticated wine drinkers. While there are clearly some exceptions, we're saddened by the lack of attention paid to good, dry Riesling, arguably the best white wine to go with many foods, and by the lack of marketing for the Northwest's superb late-harvest Rieslings, which make an unrivaled after-dinner drink.

But there's still this lake of Riesling to deal with. Many "proprietary" white wines from Northwest wineries contain lots and lots of Riesling without saying so on the label. And one winery, Staton Hills, has had enormous success with a blush-colored Riesling blend actually called Pink Riesling.Chateau Ste. Michelle has paid it the ultimate compliment by releasing its own Blush Riesling.

Dave Staton says Pink Riesling is one of the fastest-selling Washington state labels in history, aiming for 100,000 cases in the first two years. (That's roughly a quarter-million gallons.) Demand has outstripped production capacity several times, once because the winery ran short of labels!

No doubt the thirst for "blush" wines helped propel Pink Riesling into prominence (it's even on the wine list at the Helmsley Palace in New York City). And there's certainly no requirement that every wine from the Northwest be "pure." We didn't much care for the 1986 vintage, but the 1987 is tasty, with a sweet, almost plummy flavor, and a clean finish.

We admire the wine's concept and marketing effort, but "Pink Riesling" is a misnomer; newcomers to wine, especially, could be misled into thinking that some Riesling grapes are red (just as some Zinfandel grapes are white, right?) Worst of all for us purists, Chateau Ste. Michelle's Blush Riesling (flavored with 28 percent Cabernet) became the winery's third-best-selling label within six months of its introduction.

CHARDONNAY
COLUMBIA VALLEY

STEWART
VINEYARDS

Produced and bottled by Stewart Vineyards
Granger, Washington Alcohol by volume 13.0%

STEWART VINEYARDS

1711 Cherry Hill Road
Granger, WA 98932

Mail: 1381 W. Riverside Avenue
Sunnyside, WA 98944
(509) 854-1882

Owners: George & Martha Stewart
Winemaker: Scott Benham
Year established: 1983
Production capacity: 30,000 gallons
Vineyards: 70 acres
Touring region: Yakima Valley [p14]

A bit of background George Stewart took a few semesters of agriculture at Mississippi State University but majored in chemistry and went on to earn an M.D. from Tulane University. He came west for his surgical residency in Portland at what is now the Oregon Health Sciences University and settled down to a practice in Sunnyside. In 1964 he bought a house on a 30-acre parcel of land that included four acres of Catawba grapes. That was enough to get him started.

Throughout the 1960s and '70s, Dr. Stewart practiced medicine in the Yakima Valley. His interest in farming, reinforced by an article in *Time* proclaiming the Columbia Basin as the new frontier of American agriculture, led him to Walter Clore, the man known affectionately as Washington's "Mr. Grape." Dr. Clore, who ran the viticulture program at the Irrigated Agricultural Research Extension Center in Prosser, took Stewart up to a spot on the Wahluke Slope, five miles southeast of Mattawa, and told him, "This is the place."

Stewart bought 160 acres and planted the first vines on the Wahluke Slope, where his plantings now take advantage of the sun, the slightly south-facing slope, and the air movement. He later expanded his acreage, explaining to us with his friendly Southern drawl, "They told me most of the good spots in the Yakima Valley were already taken."

When Stewart decided to make wine for himself, he moved quickly. Tom Campbell, then winemaker at Tucker Cellars, was engaged to handle the first crush, supervise the construction of the interim building, and manage the purchase and installation of the original winemaking equipment.

The following year saw the arrival of Mike Januik, a retail wine shop mananger from Ashland, Oregon, who had gone back to the University of California at Davis to earn a master's degree in enology. Januik demonstrated great skill making off-dry, highly drinkable whites. He was succeeded two years ago by his assistant, Seattle native (and UC-Davis graduate) Scott Benham.

Pictured on the Stewart Vineyards label is the native *Triteleia douglasii*, a delicate wildflower of the hyacinth family.

Visiting the winery★★★. The Stewart Vineyards winery sits atop a rise known as Cherry Hill, outside of Granger, at the west end of a promontory called Snipes Mountain. The building is surrounded by cherry trees and has an extensive view ★★★☆ of the surrounding valley. To get there, you need to leave the speedway that is Interstate 82 and zigzag your way along "real" roads where you can see and smell the vitality of the Yakima Valley. The winery itself has been considerably enlarged since it was built; there's now a grand, two-story cedar tasting room, complete with a walkway and balcony, attached to the original metal structure.

Picnic tables stand in the cherry orchard outside.

Tasting the wines★★★. Two Chardonnays lead the lineup; the regular 1987 is on the lighter side, but well balanced, while the Reserve bottling (which comes from the Wahluke Slope vineyard) is more flavorful. There's a White Riesling with delicate flavors of peaches, and a delightful Late Harvest White Riesling which hints of apricots and honey. The 1985 Late Harvest won a gold medal and the coveted Grand Prize at the Seattle Enological Society in 1986; we found an open half-bottle of it at the back of our refrigerator a year later and it was still wonderful!

The Gewurztraminer is spicy and fresh; the Muscat Canelli has overtones of orange blossoms. A Cabernet Sauvignon and a blush are the other wines currently made.

Getting there. Take Exit 58 from I-82 toward Granger, then follow Outlook Rd up the hill and continue as it becomes Cherry Hill Rd. The winery is at the top of the hill.

Open 10 to 5 Monday through Saturday, noon to 5 on Sunday. No tasting fee for tours, but the winery asks that groups call ahead.

Special events. A Cabernet and Chocolate tasting in February; Cherry Blossom Time in early April; the valley's Spring Barrel Tasting in late April; and fall releases on Thanksgiving weekend.

A word from the winery "*Enjoy our fine wines and the panoramic view of the lower Yakima Valley from our tasting room. Stewart Vineyards winery is built in a historical area known as Cherry Hill on the west end of Snipes Mountain. Stately cherry orchards and beautiful farmland surround the winery, which was chosen with optimum enjoyment in mind. We welcome visitors year-round; come and taste our premium varietal wines.*"

TAGARIS

5627 42nd Avenue S.W.
Seattle, WA 98136
(206) 937-4269

Owner: Michael Taggares
Winemaker: Peter Bos
Year established: 1987
Vineyards: 120 acres
Touring area: Seattle [p. 30]

A bit of background Mike Taggares, a big, broad-shouldered, genial and outgoing man, owns a large property atop Radar Hill in the Columbia Valley. Son of a prosperous farmer, he planned to live there, too, surrounded by vineyards and orchards, and to produce fine wine.

"We're not going to mimic French Chardonnay or California Cabernets," the winery promises. "We're going to try to make the best wines from Washington state in a style which is recognizably our own."

To handle the winemaking, Taggares enlisted Peter Bos, who had been the assistant winemaker at Columbia. They decided to return to the original spelling of Mike's family name for the winery label.

Visiting the winery (NR) There won't be a Tagaris winery (in the town of Snoqualmie) until 1990; the address above is an office at Peter Bos's home (his wife, Elizabeth, is the winery's business manager). In the interim, wines can be tasted at The Wine Rack in Woodinville.

Tasting the wines★★. The first vintage, made at the giant Langguth facility in Mattawa, came out mixed. The 1987 Riesling, with a delightful nose of apricots and cooked apples, took a gold medal at the Seattle Enological Society festival in 1988, and we enjoyed its flavors but felt the wine lacked acidity. A dry white called Arete, made mostly from Chenin Blanc, was devoid of varietal flavor and had a bitter finish. The 1987 Fume Blanc had a pleasant green pepper bouquet, and clean, vegetal flavors. The Pinot Noir, grown on the north-facing slope of the vineyard, had a faint, cherrylike nose but little flavor.

On a positive note, these wines are all clean, reasonably priced, and Peter Bos's record at Columbia suggests that the quality will improve.

Getting there. Tagaris will be located in downtown Snoqualmie. [**Map:** Snoqualmie Winery] The wines can currently be tasted at a shop called The Wine Rack in Woodinville; call (206) 486-9463 for details.

A word from the winery. *"Wine is a calming influence in a world of constant flux. It's one of the few beverages we sip and savor instead of gulping on the run. Making wine develops patience in the winemaker as well; in this business you have to wait for the fruits of your labor. Blending the old with the new is what making Tagaris wines is all about."*

PAUL THOMAS

1717 136th Place N.E.
Bellevue, WA 98005
(206) 747-1008

Owners: Paul & Judy Thomas
Consulting enologist: Brian Carter
Winemaker: Mark Cave
Production capacity: 60,000 gallons
Vineyards: None
Year established: 1979
Touring region: Seattle [p. 30]

A bit of background. It's hard to imagine Paul Thomas in the arid surroundings of his family's Ephrata homestead; he's too restless, too full of intellectual energy, to be tied to the land. Even now, as owner of one of Washington's best-known wineries, he has no vineyards of his own. He does devote endless hours to the promotion of the entire Washington wine industry (he was the first president of the Washington Wine Institute), to testifying before the state legislature, to arguing policies and procedures with the Liquor Control Board, and to overcoming the image of Paul Thomas as a "fruit winery."

He decided to "fire myself as winemaker" after the first year in order to devote more time to marketing, and hired Corvallis native Brian Carter, who had been with Montelena and Mount Eden, to take over winemaking duties. (Carter, once described by Paul Thomas as "the Northwest's most underrated winemaker," has since left full-time work at the winery to become a consultant; his considerable skills are already making a big difference around the Northwest.) Mark Cave, who had been cellarmaster, now holds the title of winemaker.

Paul Thomas was once something of a radical social science teacher at Seattle's elite Lakeside School, encouraging his students to become involved in the political process. Left over from those days, but no less pertinent to Paul's current activity, is a sign in the winery's reception room that quotes John Stuart Mill: "That so few dare to be eccentric marks the chief danger of our time."

Visiting the winery ★★★. The structure, next to a sporting goods warehouse, just blocks away from the jumble of Bellevue's shopping centers, could be another small manufacturing plant; it turns out to be one of Washington's larger wineries, meticulously clean, very compact, extremely efficient. The nontraditional tasting room shares space with the office, just off the winery floor; it includes a conference table, an old basket press, flower arrangements, a piano. Recent medals are draped across the chest of a large doll propped up in the corner.

Tasting the wines ★★★☆. Even before Paul Thomas winery, under Brian Carter's gifted winemaking, came to be recognized for its superlative Cabernet Sauvignon and Chardonnay, the winery established its reputation with a perfectly legitimate wine called Crimson, made from rhubarb. Rhubarb wine may not be to everyone's taste, but 95 percent of the wine-drinking public can't tell that this blush-colored wine isn't made from grapes; a supermarket tasting in California ranked the Crimson as the number one White Zinfandel! Made four times a year from frozen fruit, it accounts for almost half the winery's production. (Red wine production will double in coming years.) The Dry Bartlett Pear, made (without added sulfites) from fruit harvested in the Yakima Valley, goes particularly well with Asian and Creole cuisines and actually outsells the Crimson in California. Old Paul Thomas fans still ask why he no longer makes a dark, dry Bing Cherry wine or the fragrant Raspberry.

Varietal wines carry the Paul Thomas flag today. A Cabernet Sauvignon made in 1981 and released for the winery's fifth anniversary in 1984 won the Governor's Trophy as the state's best red wine; the 1983 vintage won the "Washington Wine of the Year" award from the Washington Wine Writers as the state's best food wine. Paul Thomas also became the first repeat "Wine of the Year" winner with its 1986 Chardonnay Private Reserve, a fabulous wine which also won a double gold medal at the San Francisco fair and the Grand Award at the Enological Society festival in Seattle.

Tasted recently, the "regular" 1987 Chardonnay had a subtle oaky, sea-coasty bouquet and flavors that hint of pears and anise with a tad of residual sugar in the finish. It's a clean, balanced wine readily available in Washington state for less than $10. The 1987 "Reserve" will be available later in 1989, and has more oaky, buttery characteristics; a barrel sample of the 1988 promises more high quality.

"When I pour the Cabernet in California, I can tell they're impressed," Paul Thomas says. "I just watch their eyebrows."

Getting there. From Hwy 520 eastbound, take Northup Wy to 136th Pl, turn right. From Bellevue, take Bel-Red Road, turn left on 132nd N.E., right on N.E. 16th, and left onto 136th Place. (Rumors circulate periodically that Paul Thomas is about to move—to an industrial park in Woodinville, to Bellingham, to Issaquah, etc.—

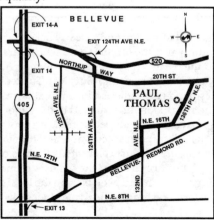

rumors that occasionally turn out to be accurate ... but so far, last-minute snags have always cropped up.

Open Friday and Saturday from noon to 5.

Special events. Paul Thomas is 10 years old in 1989 and will sponsor various activities throughout the year, including a celebration close to the August 4th anniversary date.

A word from the winery *"Paul Thomas and his winery continue to make bold statements in the wine industry. Look for more emphasis to the classic wine types of Cabernet Sauvignon, Merlot, and Chardonnay. Whereas Washington State's reputation was initially founded upon the high quality of its Riesling wines, Paul Thomas feels very strongly that Washington will be better known for its red wines than its whites in future years. Also, look for an increasing emphasis on the marriage of food and wine in our society. The winery is keenly interested in promoting the two together and will be staging events at the winery in future years."*

TUCKER CELLARS

70 Ray Road
Sunnyside, WA 98944
(509) 837-8701

Owners: Dean & Rose Tucker
Manager & winemaker
  Randy Tucker
Year established: 1981
Production capacity: 25,000 gallons
Vineyards: 60 acres
Touring region: Yakima Valley [p14]

A bit of background Dean Tucker has the air of a quiet English or Irish landowner, the sort of farmer who wears a jacket and tie when he goes out to the barns. (If you've ever watched *All Creatures Great and Small*, you know what we mean.) But Dean Tucker has lived in this valley all his life; his hands are calloused from real farm work. The Tucker family (all of them work on the farm and in the winery) has grown grapes, asparagus, spinach, and sugar beets on 400 acres of prime Yakima Valley land. Dean Tucker's father, in fact, was one of the earliest grape growers in the valley; the family has just celebrated 50 years of viticulture.

A big upheaval in the valley's economic stability came when U & I Sugar, which had been buying the local crop of sugar beets, pulled out of eastern Washington. Like the other growers, the Tucker family had to find something else to plant—something they wouldn't get stuck with. So the Tuckers built the produce market, and decided to build a winery as well in order to use their own grapes.

Dean Tucker has always employed a big crew, from spring to fall, to harvest his asparagus, spinach, corn, peaches, apples, and grapes. The winery allows him to keep most of them working all year. He designed the winery himself, too, and keeps its equipment running all year. After the grapes are crushed and out of the way in the bright stainless steel fermenters, he brings in apple culls from the packing house, puts them through the crusher, pumps the juice into empty tanks, and uses the winery's filters and bottling line to make the cider sold at the produce market.

Dean's son Randy, the current winery manager and winemaker, has also served terms as president of the Yakima Valley Winegrower's Association and as chairman of the Washington state regional tourism council for the Yakima Valley area. Among Washington winemakers, he's probably the most keenly attuned to the value of tourism to the wine industry.

Visiting the winery★★☆. It's impossible to travel along either of the Yakima Valley's main arteries, Interstate 82 or the Yakima Valley Highway (formerly called U.S. 12), without going past the Tucker fruit market with its displays of onions and apples out front and orchards of Elberta peaches and Rome Beauty apples out back. Half the building is devoted to the produce market; the other half contains the winery and a large open space that serves as tasting room and office.

The Tuckers' latest venture, marketing gourmet food items, is very much in evidence. The line includes honey, peaches, cherries, and popcorn in addition to wine. Designer Rick Eiber has developed a family of symbols for each product, such as a cluster of grapes for the wines, that appear on every label bearing the Tucker name.

Several picnic tables stand amidst young fruit trees in front of the winery. Plans for the summer include an RV park in the peach orchard out back, as well as construction of an 18-hole mini-golf course.

Tasting the wines★★. Estate-grown grapes are used in Tucker's Riesling, Chardonnay, Gewurztraminer, Chenin Blanc, Muscat, and Pinot Noir. There's also a Cabernet Sauvignon (which didn't find favor with our tasting panel). Best bet here would be the Muscat Canelli, whose attractive nose and residual sweetness make it a delightful sipping wine or aperitif.

Tucker wines are frequently featured with seafood at the Anthony's Homeport restaurants in the Seattle area.

Getting there. The winery is on the Yakima Valley Hwy at Ray Rd, halfway between Exit 69 and Exit 73 off I-82.

Open daily from 9 to 5. Tour groups are welcome, and there's no tasting fee.

A word from the winery *"The Tucker family has grown vinifera grapes in Washington state since 1938. Their Sunnyside farm expanded with orchards and vegetable crops, and today they invite you to visit the Tucker Cellars winery and their adjacent market of fresh fruit and produce."*

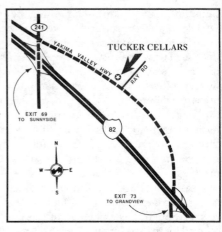

MANFRED VIERTHALER WINERY

17136 Highway 410 E.
Sumner, WA 98390
(206) 863-1633

Owners:
Manfred & Ingeborg Vierthaler
Winemaker: Manfred J. Vierthaler
Year established: 1976
Production capacity: 40,000 gallons
Vineyards: 0.5 acre
Touring region: Seattle [p. 30]

A bit of background In its own way, this is a success story, a classic tale of an immigrant who studied diligently and worked hard to achieve a position of prestige in his new country.

Manfred Vierthaler, born in Germany, came to Tacoma as a teenager, learned English at Lincoln High School, apprenticed in the restaurant business at his father's side (at Tacoma's popular Bavarian Restaurant), then studied winemaking during several summers at the University of California at Davis and at its German equivalent in Geisenheim.

Vierthaler eventually struck out on his own, building a spectacular chalet overlooking the Puyallup Valley. He encouraged the local growers to plant vinifera grapes in the Puyallup Valley, and was named Small Business Person of the Year by the U.S. Small Business Administration. He became the first person from the U.S. to join the Rheingauer Weinkonvent, and won a gold medal in Madrid from the International Alcoholic Beverage Producers.

Despite this record, we're not impressed. The bulk of the wine produced by the Vierthaler is just that: bulk wine of unknown provenance. (The winery holds 10 times the volume of his 1988 crush.) "Why pick on me?" Vierthaler asks. True, a lot of wineries buy bulk wine; Coventry Vale in Granger and several other processors supply ready-made wine to a number of smaller wineries. But the reputation of Northwest wineries should depend on the quality of Northwest grapes, not jug wine from California.

Visiting the winery★★☆. The chalet itself is impressive. It stands on El-Hi Road overlooking the Puyallup Valley; from the rooftop restaurant's expansive windows you can see Tacoma and Puget Sound. The restaurant offers a German menu with traditional Bavarian dishes and some exotic specialties like venison, wild boar, even hippopotamus ($24). The best visit is at dusk, to watch the sunset and see the lights of Tacoma come on.

Downstairs, the tasting room is lavishly decorated with all manner of Bavarian carvings. It's the kind of place some people find darling.

Tasting the wines★. You like what you like, and it's clear that somebody likes these wines. For our part, the only Vierthaler wine we've enjoyed was a Goldener Gutedel made from locally grown Chasselas grapes; you can keep the rest.

Principal varieties available at the tasting room are several vintages of Riesling, Muller Thurgau, and Cabernet Sauvignon. (The 1987 White Riesling, made from botrytis-affected Pierce County grapes, sold out at $100 a bottle.) Because Vierthaler wines are not in commercial distribution, you can only buy them at the winery. "Our wine sells itself by the people coming to our winery and sampling the wines," Vierthaler points out. "I don't have to enter them in contests to prove anything. Our customers like my wine, and we are still here when others aren't." *Chacun à son goût*.

Getting there. From I-5, take Exit 135 to Hwy 167, go south toward Puyallup, then east on Hwy 410 toward Bonney Lake. (From I-405, just take Hwy 167 southbound to Hwy 410.) The winery is 2 mi past Sumner.

Open daily from noon to 6.

A word from the winery *"We invite you to visit our winery tasting room and sample our fine wines for yourself. We offer many kinds and a wide selection is always available for free tastings. Groups are also welcome. Enjoy our*

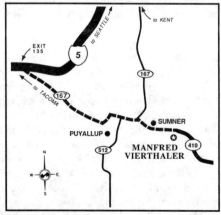

outstanding Roofgarden restaurant featuring Bavarian and American lunches and dinners, and enjoy our fine wines while overlooking our vineyard and the Puyallup River valley and spectacular sunsets."

BARREL FERMENTED
RESERVE
CHARDONNAY

1987

WASHINGTON STATE

Produced and Bottled by Waterbrook Winery
Lowden, Washington Alcohol 12.5% by Volume
CONTAINS SULFITES

WATERBROOK WINERY

McDonald Road
Route 1, Box 46
Lowden, WA 99360
(509) 522-1918

Owners: Janet & Eric Rindal
Winemaker: Eric Rindal
Year established: 1984
Production capacity: 25,000 gallons
Vineyards: None
Touring region: Walla Walla [p.22]

A bit of background This valley got its name Walla Walla from the Nez Perce Indians; it means "running water." Janet and Eric Rindal picked up on the historic designation at Waterbrook Winery, whose watercolor brushstroke on the label (designed by Sue Cummings) emphasizes the name and suggests that the theme of subtlety and balance will be reflected in the wines.

Eric Rindal worked in Alaska in the construction business before returning to the family farm nearby. Janet worked as a bookkeeper, but her degree is in marketing. The handsome young couple did a good deal of reading about viticulture, became impressed with the way that grapes fit in with their agricultural endeavors, and went off to attend seminars at the University of California at Davis on various aspects of winemaking.

The winery's rapid growth has put plans for their own vineyard on hold (you can't do everything at once), but the Rindals have found two of Washington's top suppliers, Moreman Vineyards near Pasco and Owings Vineyard on the Wahluke Slope. "We feel fortunate to be dealing with them, because they understand the pride of a family business and work hard with us to produce the finest wine possible," says Janet.

Visiting the winery★★☆. A plain metal building with a crushing pad out front has been put up in the rolling wheat and alfalfa country. Across the lush green fields you can see the Blue Mountains. (The alfalfa, by the way, is grown for seed.) There's a table on the lawn, but not a lot in the way of visitor amenities. "We are basically a production facility," the Rindals concede, "although we usually have kittens for the kids who visit."

Tasting the wines★★★. Waterbrook's first wines were lovely: a generic white made from Chardonnay and Chenin Blanc, and a gold-medal-winning Sauvignon Blanc. Expansion has been rapid. Waterbook crushed 16,000 gallons in 1987, 22,500 in 1988. Wines currently available include Cabernet Sauvignon, Merlot, Sauvignon Blanc, and Chardonnay. The regular Chardonnay is a delightful play of fruit and oak, well-balanced with rich, lingering flavor. The barrel-fermented Reserve Chardonnay, on the other hand, was dosed with so much sulfur dioxide that it was undrinkable. What happened to this wine in the barrels or bottling that required such drastic measures? It wasn't remotely recognizable as Chardonnay.

Getting there. From Lowden, go east on Hwy 12 about 1.5 mi to McDonald Rd; turn south and continue about 2.5 mi. The winery driveway is the first road on the right after you cross Frog Hollow Rd.

Usually **open** Wednesday through Sunday from 11 to 4, but call ahead to make sure.

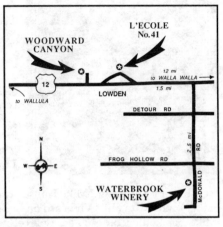

Special events. Spring releases in mid-May to coincide with the Walla Walla Hot Air Balloon Stampede. Fall releases on the weekend after Labor Day.

A word from the winery. *"What makes each grape-growing region unique is its own combination of soil, climate, and topography. What makes each winery different within that region is how that winery treats the grapes, juice, and wine. Waterbrook cannot claim to hold the secret technique for making the absolute best wine, but we can truthfully say we put forth an extra effort at each stage of the winemaking process to produce wine we feel stands apart from the rest."*

Washington State
JOHANNISBERG RIESLING
1986

Produced and bottled by Wenatchee
Valley Vintners. George, Washington
B.W. Permit Number 105.
11% Alcohol by Volume.

WENATCHEE VALLEY VINEYARDS

1111 Van Sickle Avenue
East Wenatchee, WA 98802
(509) 884-8235

Owners: Michael & Debbie Hansen
Winemaker: Mike Hansen
Year established: 1987
Production capacity: 50,000 gallons
Vineyards: 18 acres
Touring: Columbia Valley N. [p.19]

A bit of background Mike Hansen comes from a farming family; his father owns Roza Hills Vineyard on the Royal Slope north of Zillah, and Mike has settled on a 20-acre parcel near Wenatchee. A graduate of Central Washington University, Mike has worked for the past five years as a quality control technician for TreeTop, the apple juice cooperative, and as a consultant for J.E.T. (Juice Extraction Technology). He's also been taking classes at the University of California at Davis, preparing for the day when he'd put his chemistry background to use making wine.

The original proposal for a winery, to have been called Mission View, was formulated back in 1985. Then reality set in. "We need significant tourist exposure to make the profit side of a winery pencil out," the Hansens wrote; they decided to locate the winery in Leavenworth, visited by a million tourists a year. The Leavenworth plan never came off, so Mike and Debbie are making another run at a winery with Wenatchee Valley Vintners right on their home turf.

Visiting the winery (NR. The winery is built into the hillside with a picnic ground outside (six tables among the Cabernet vines, a landscaped path running between them). The Cascades make an impressive backdrop.

The Hansens have a terrific piece of property, a vineyard at 1,100 feet with gravelly soil and southeastern exposure. Something of a radical when it comes to viticulture, Mike planted 18 acres in the European style: on a three-by-six grid, instead of the six-by-10 customary in Washington. The dense European planting puts 2,400 vines on an acre, three times the more "tractor-friendly" American norm.

Does this make a difference? It should: per plant yields remain roughly constant, while per acre yields skyrocket. This increased production allows the vintner to press more gently, limiting himself to perhaps 100 gallons of juice per ton, rather than having to squeeze 150 or 165 gallons.

Tasting the wines (NR). Wenatchee Valley Vintners' first releases are inexpensive whites (Riesling, Chardonnay, and a blend of Riesling and Gewurztraminer called Valley Gold), all selling in the $4 to $4.50 range.

A line of sparkling wines called Maison Riviere Columbie (one made in the bulk Charmat process, one methode champenoise), is expected to follow shortly. There's a Reserve Cabernet available only at the winery, and Lemberger coming soon.

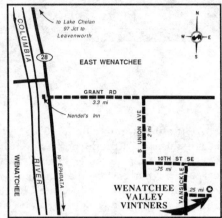

Getting there. Take Hwy 28 to East Wenatchee, turn east at the Nendels Four Seasons Inn and follow Grant Rd 4 mi towards the airport. Turn right on Union, go 2.75 mi, turn right on Van Sickle.

Open Friday, Saturday, and Sunday from noon to 6, except major holidays. The Hansens are usually available during the week for private tours; call ahead.

A word from the winery. *"Wenatchee's first and only premium estate winery. Established five years ago, our vineyards are producing some of the best wines in the Northwest. Family owned and operated, we are an estate winery in the truest European tradition. With premium oak-aged red wines and handmade methode champenoise sparkling wines to be released this next year, we will offer a select and special list of wines for the discerning wine drinker.*

"Stop in and taste our wines at our winery when you are in Wenatchee. Relax with a beautiful view of our vineyard and the lovely Cascade Mountains rolling upwards from the Columbia River."

WHIDBEYS GREENBANK FARM

Highway 525 at Wonn Road
P.O. Box AB
Greenbank, WA 98253
(206) 678-6702

Owner:
   Stimson Lane Wine & Spirits, Ltd.
Winemaker: Cheryl Barber
Year established: 1985
Production capacity: 134,000 gallons
Vineyards: 125 acres
Touring: Olympic Peninsula [p. 36]

A bit of background In the 1950s and '60s, American Wine Growers began shifting its production away from inexpensive, fortified berry wines sold under the Pomerelle and Nawico labels into European vinifera grapes grown in eastern Washington. Consumers appreciated the shift; American Wine Growers became Chateau Ste. Michelle (today part of Stimson Lane Wine & Spirits), and Washington state's modern wine industry was born.

But the original berry farm remained part of the company, even after the Pomerelle and Nawico labels were sold off. Now the property, Greenbank Farm (the country's single largest loganberry property) has been completely restored.

Visiting the winery★★★. The 125-acre farm drapes two sides of a gentle hill at the narrowest part of Whidbey Island. From the hilltop, you have views of the Cascades and the Olympics; you could watch the sun rise across Saratoga Passage and set over Admiralty Inlet. The rich soil is enhanced by a gentle mist, moderate rainfall, and stable year-round temperatures. The mature loganberry vines stand five feet tall, each plant yielding about six pounds of fruit for harvest in July.

The renovated red barn (with additions for tasting room, gift shop, and so on) stands at the bottom of the hill. A guided tour of the facility is hardly necessary; the barn itself contains a bottling line and a few tanks. Posters and panels describe the history of the facility and give visitors basic winemaking information. The barn's gift shop carries box lunches in summer and a few deli items all year. An inviting picnic area is set up on the tastefully landscaped grounds, surrounding a small pond.

Tasting the wines★★★. The newest and best product from Whidbeys is a delightful loganberry wine, only moderately alcoholic (12 percent—not enough to require all the additional folderol of being a spirit). It has a satisfying sweetness balanced with a slightly bitter finish; it might be even better with a bit more acid, but it's not a cloying "fruit wine" at all.

Whidbeys Port is essentially a "late harvest" Cabernet Sauvignon from the Cold Creek Vineyards in eastern Washington. Fermentation of the Cabernet grapes is stopped by adding brandy, well before the wine reaches dryness; the resulting fortified wine is then aged in old oak barrels. The 1985 vintage Port has distinctly oaky and cherry-like flavors, smooth in the mouth, with an off-dry finish. (About 10 percent sugar, 20 percent alcohol.) While we preferred the 1984, the current release is worth considering as an inexpensive alternative to "real" port, which easily costs two and three times as much.

The flagship product here is Whidbeys Liqueur, made from loganberries steeped in neutral grain spirits. Thanks to Washington state's archaic liquor laws, you can't sample the Whidbeys Liqueur in the tasting room; it's illegal to give away spirits, so you have to buy a miniature bottle (under $2) if you want to try it. And you can't even do that on Sundays. It's worth tasting, though: garnet-colored, with a nose of fresh berries, sweet but well balanced, Whidbeys is lower in alcohol than most liqueurs, quite refreshing as an after-dinner drink and wonderful on ice cream.

The enthusiastic tasting room staff normally pours the loganberry wine and the port, but will let you taste almost any of the current releases from Columbia Crest or Chateau Ste. Michelle as well. The entire family of products is for sale in the gift shop; the specials are often very attractively priced.

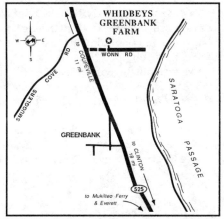

Getting there. The winery is just off Whidbey Island's main arterial, Hwy 525. It's 18 mi north of the Clinton ferry dock and 11 mi south of Coupeville.

Open 10 to 4:30 daily. No charge for regular visitors; special group tastings (with up to eight wines) cost $3 per person and must be arranged in advance.

Special events. An active roster of events; call the winery for a current schedule.

A word from the winery *"Whidbeys Greenbank Farm, located in a renovated turn-of-the-century barn, features a self-guided tour depicting the development of the island as well as the creation of its liqueur and port. Whidbeys Greenbank Farm is the perfect stop for those travelers seeking a unique combination of history, country charm, scenic beauty, and a selection of fine wines to taste."*

WHITTLESEY-MARK

5318 22nd Avenue N.W.
Seattle, WA 98107
(206) 789-6543

Owner &winemaker: Mark Newton
Year established: 1983
Production capacity: 20,000 bottles
Vineyards: None
Touring region: Seattle [p. 30]

A bit of background Mark Newton's concept is to use Oregon grapes for the noble purpose of making champagne. His first releases, quite successful sparkling wines from the 1984 and 1985 vintages, carried a Newton & Newton label; the name is being changed because of complaints from California's Newton Winery.

Visiting the winery (NR) Not open to the public. Mark Newton has long-term contracts with growers of Pinot Noir, Pinot Meunier, and Chardonnay in the Willamette Valley and makes arrangements to have the grapes crushed in Oregon. The juice is transported to a facility in Seattle's Ballard neighborhood for processing and aging.

Tasting the wines (NR) To be released later this year: two sparkling wines (a Brut blended from all three grapes and a Brut de Noir from Pinot Noir only) and one still wine (a Reserve Chardonnay that will carry the DiStefano label).

A word from the winery *"Newton & Newton Vintners, soon to be changed with the release of the 1987 vintage to Oregon Methode Champenoise, Inc., was established in 1983 by its owner and winemaker, Mark Newton, to be a sole producer of premium Oregon champagne. The 1987 release of Oregon champagne will be under the name Whittlesey-Mark. Both a Brut and a Brut de Noir will be released. A third wine is in the barrels to be released in 1990 as DiStefano Reserve Chardonnay, after Mark Newton's wife [Donna DiStefano]."*

WOODWARD CANYON WINERY

Route 1, Box 387
Lowden, WA 99360
(509) 525-4129

Owners: Rick & Darcey Small
Winemaker: Rick Small
Year established: 1981
Production capacity: 12,500 gallons
Vineyards: 10 acres
Touring region: Walla Walla [p 22]

A bit of background "I think I'm learning how to make Chardonnay," Woodward Canyon's Rick Small says modestly after his deep-flavored, oak-aged wine wins yet another gold medal. "I want it to taste like a Meursault," referring to the great white wine of Burgundy. His success with Chardonnay is only half the story. What brings him the most satisfaction is a new-found recognition for red wines from Washington— not just his own, either—in out-of-state competitions. His own Cabernet Sauvignon won a double gold in San Francisco, then went on to win the Governor's Trophy for best red wine produced in Washington.

Rick Small keeps fit by running 20 miles a week; he believes that a winemaker's personal conditioning—discipline, endurance—is reflected in his wines. Rick was studying to become an architect when his father asked him to take over the family's grain elevator business. He and his best friend, Gary Figgins, were drill sergeants in the Army Reserve together, and Gary had already established his own tiny commercial winery, Leonetti Cellar, while Rick was still making wine as an amateur.

The Small family has been involved in the agriculture of the Walla Walla Valley for half a century, raising livestock and wheat. And now grapes: Rick has planted a six-acre Chardonnay vineyard—and is planting four more—on a steep terrace where his yield is an almost pitiful half ton to the acre. But what an incredible wine it makes! The unusual climate of the Walla Walla Valley is the reason: limestone soil, lots of heat, and a 200-day growing season.

Even while they were devoting their energies to the vineyard and the winery, Rick and his wife, Darcey Fugman-Small, led the effort to establish the Walla Walla Valley as an Appellation of Origin. Their persistence (and Darcey's background as a land-use planner) paid off in the summer of 1984, when the Bureau of Alcohol, Tobacco and Firearms officially designated the valley as a premium winegrowing region. The appellation, which encompasses both Washington and Oregon vineyards, is one of only two in the country that cross state lines.

"A decade from now," Rick forecasts, "the Walla Walla Valley will have the reputation as the best in the state."

Visiting the winery ★★★. The highway cuts through the rolling wheat and alfalfa fields of the Palouse. Twelve miles from Walla Walla, you come upon a tall, thick cluster of grain elevators next to some railroad tracks beside the tree-lined highway. This is the agricultural center of Lowden, home of the Small family's million-bushel grain elevators. It's also the home of another Small family venture, the Woodward Canyon Winery, housed in an inconspicuous low building that was originally an agricultural shed, then a machine shop for the grain elevators across the highway. The 5,000-case winery is filled almost to the ceiling with French oak barrels. Woodward Canyon uses two small, hand-fed crushers (one for reds, one for whites) and a large basket press that doesn't squeeze the grapes too hard. Bottling, corking, and labeling are all done by hand, with the entire family participating.

Rick Small spends money on premium grapes, top-flight cooperage, and quality equipment, not on decor. But he's found a good assistant for the tasting room: Sharon Lintz, whose knowledge of wine and familiarity with the Woodward Canyon operation helps her convey a genuine sense of hospitality despite the unpretentious surroundings.

Tasting the wines★★★★. Basically, two wines: Cabernet Sauvignon (as deep and inky-black as they come) and Chardonnay (a green-gold wine, with good fruit and a lingering finish).

Woodward Canyon's Cabernet Sauvignon wins gold medals every year. The 1981 vintage took a gold at the 1984 Central Washington State Fair, plus the Consumer's Choice Award and the Winemaker's Award for best red wine at the Tri-Cities Festival.

The 1984 Cabernet did even better. Rick had bought grapes from five vineyards, and as the wine reached adolescence, he sounded like the parent of a difficult teenager. He'd had a hard time with the wine, he would tell people; he found it herbaceous, he was always amazed that people found it so pleasant.

"Pleasant" is too timid an adjective. Our notes over a two-year period contained nothing but superlatives; with a dish of lamb at the 1987 Wine of the Year dinner, it was nothing short of sensational. It won, of course.

We found the 1985 Cabernet over-oaked and over-extracted, but the 1986 Cab, now in the bottle, is much better. It has a complex nose of graphite, chocolate, bell pepper and blackberry; it gives clean, fresh flavors and a soft texture despite its high tannin.

In 1985, Woodward Canyon blended a wine called Charbonneau (named for its vineyard) from 70 percent Merlot and 30 percent Cabernet Sauvignon grapes. Although we've encountered a couple of bottles with obvious volatility, the one we sampled most recently didn't show any premature aging. Black-red in color, with a hint of rust on its fine, deep pink rim, it smells of cedar and black currants, with full fruit on the palate. It's such a big, beautiful wine we wished the finish were a bit longer, but overall, wow!

"It's good to get a vote of confidence," Rick admits when his wines wins top awards, but he remains modest (declining even to write "A word from the winery"). "It's my *job* to make good wine."

Getting there. Lowden is on Hwy 12 between Pasco and Walla Walla. The winery is at the east end of town, next to the landmark Lowden schoolhouse. [**Map**: Waterbrook]

Open in summer, Monday through Saturday from 10 to 5 and Sunday noon to 5. Winter, Monday through Saturday from 10 to 4, Sunday noon to 4. Closed on major holidays. Tour groups should call ahead; no fee. There's a shaded patio in back of the winery for picnics.

Special events. Woodward Canyon's spring releases usually coincide with Walla Walla's annual Hot Air Balloon Stampede, in mid-May.

WORDEN

(Worden's Washington Winery)
7217 W. 45th
Spokane, WA 99204
(509) 455-7835

Owners: Jack & Phyllis Worden
Winemaker: Brian Carter
Year established: 1979
Production capacity: 45,000 gallons
Vineyards: None
Touring region: Spokane [p. 24]

A bit of background Jack Worden, a former pharmaceuticals salesman, takes a generous view of the many inexpensive imported wines on supermarket shelves these days. "Get 'em started on French Rabbit," he says, believing that sooner or later the American wine buyer will go for a bottle of Worden's wine. In an industry which all too often puts marketing last, Jack Worden knows that promoting and selling really do come first. "A good salesman can sell a mediocre wine, but a good salesman with a good wine is good business," he says.

Jack himself got into the wine business in the early 1970s, after giving some thought to planting grapes in an apple orchard he owned near Lake

Chelan. But he soon discovered a shortage of grape buyers, so Grower Worden became Winemaker Worden instead. It wasn't necessary for the winery to be located where the grapes were grown (and these days, all of Worden's grapes are purchased from outside sources, many from the Moreman Vineyard, near Pasco), so Jack selected Spokane, the state's second-largest community and a city that had no wineries at the time. By now, Spokane is one of Washington's wine "capitals," with three first-class wineries.

Visiting the winery★★☆. Nestled among the tall evergreens that line the south side of Interstate 90 west of Spokane stands an A-frame cabin built of pine logs; it's the tasting room and office for the Worden winery. The log-cabin tasting room is cozy, with gift items spread along the walls. (The winemaking equipment is in another building out back.) Four picnic tables stand invitingly in the clearing.

Tasting the wines★★☆. Johannisberg Riesling is Worden's flagship wine; the other major variety is Chenin Blanc. The 1988 vintage Chenin has won several major awards, but the bottle we tried earlier this year was too spritzy to judge properly.

We had a good bottle of Gamay Beaujolais Rose from Worden's not long ago; it had a pleasant nose, some spritz in the mouth, and was nicely balanced. Another Worden wine we've enjoyed is the Cabernet-Merlot blend. Worden also puts out a line called Seafare, and does private labeling for stores, resorts, and large institutional buyers.

Brian Carter has taken over winemaking duties here on a consulting basis, which suggests that the wines will have more consistency in the vintages ahead.

Getting there. From I-90, west of Spokane, take Exit 276. South of the interchange, turn onto Fossen Rd, then Thorpe Rd, which curves into 45th.

Open daily from noon to 4. The winery is open for group tours and charges no fee.

Special events. Worden holds a wine festival and crowd-pleasing grape stomp on the first Saturday of October.

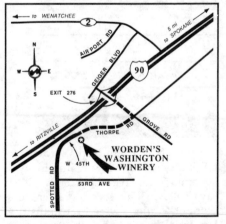

A word from the winery *"We offer tastings of our award-winning wines and a V.I.P. tour of our winery. We have lovely picnic grounds surrounding the winery as well. Maybe you'd like to bring a box lunch along!"*

YAKIMA RIVER WINERY

N. River Road
Route 1, Box 1657
Prosser, WA 99350
(509) 786-2805

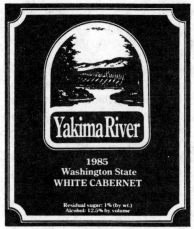

1985
Washington State
WHITE CABERNET

Residual sugar: 1% (by wt.)
Alcohol: 12.5% by volume

Owners: John & Louise Rauner
Winemaker: John Rauner
Year established: 1978
Production capacity: 30,000 gallons
Vineyards: None
Touring region: Yakima Valley [p15]

A bit of background John and Louise Rauner came to Washington from upstate New York after they tasted some distinctive Cabernet Sauvignon and Semillon wines from the now-defunct Boordy Vineyards in the Yakima Valley. Convinced that they, too, ought to make wines from Washington state grapes, the Rauners spent the following summer camping and working near Spokane, then moved west for good.

"There's a wonderful diversity here in the valley," John says, "with all the hops and mint and corn." And Louise Rauner, looking out her kitchen window at the velvety green slopes and purple sagebrush ridges of the Horse Heaven Hills, doesn't complain that there are no trees: "The mountains are so pretty."

A professional welder and steamfitter, John Rauner found work on the Hanford nuclear projects; he also took chemistry and microbiology courses at the nearby community college. When the Rauners bonded Yakima River Winery in 1978, it was one of a pioneering handful of wineries in the valley, after Hinzerling, Preston, and Chateau Ste. Michelle's Grandview plant.

Visiting the winery★★☆. The approach to the winery, along the north bank of the Yakima River, passes sweet-smelling apple orchards and a lush vineyard of Concord grapes before the house and winery appear at the end of the long driveway. The winery is in a big red barn, built to accommodate John Rauner's plans for growth; the tasting room is the former garage.

A vast expansion took place at Yakima River Winery when grower Don Toci installed a number of stainless steel tanks, anticipating a big overseas order for bulk Washington wine. Rauner crushed some 300,000 gallons for Toci in 1987, but the arrangement didn't last; Toci became a partner in Coventry Vale and moved his tanks there in 1988.

Rumors periodically surface that Yakima River is about to go out of business, to the point that "advertisements" for his equipment have appeared in various trade magazines. Stories like that don't help the winery's relationship with its distributors, and Rauner expends a lot of energy denying the rumors and trying to track down their source. "I just added 100 barrels," he told us late in 1988; not what you'd expect for someone supposedly on the brink of bankruptcy.

Tasting the wines★★. Among the whites, the best are probably dessert wines. A 1985 Dry Berry Selection White Riesling stands out in our notes, and there's an Ice Wine, too. The Fume Blanc has had a couple of good vintages; Rauner has given up on Chenin Blanc and Chardonnay.

Eighty-five percent of Yakima River's production is now on the red side. Cabernet Sauvignon and Merlot have been joined by a Pinot Noir made from Yakima Valley grapes. One favorite (years ago) was the 1982 Cabernet, produced from Mercer Ranch grapes, which showed zesty, complex flavors and plenty of tannin. We're concerned, though, about inappropriate aromas and flavors that occasionally turn up in Yakima River wines. The 1983 Cabernet was golden brown with a nose of ripe strawberries; it finished dead last in a blind tasting of nine 1983 Cabs. On the other hand, a pre-release sample of the 1984 Cabernet Sauvignon, blended with a touch of Merlot and Cabernet Franc, was delightful. Like a few other wineries whose owners spend more of their time on the road marketing the products, Yakima River needs the full-time attention of a competent cellarmaster.

Getting there. From I-82 at Prosser, take Exit 80 and follow Gap Rd toward town. Just before the bridge, turn right onto N. River Rd. The road does a sort of zigzag on Buena Vista Rd for about a block; keep heading along the river.

Open daily from 10 to 5. There's no fee for tour groups, but call ahead to let the winery know you're coming. Picnic tables are available on the lawn in front of the house.

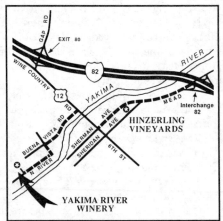

Special events. Yakima River Winery participates in the annual Yakima Valley Barrel Tasting during the last weekend in April. Traditionally, too, the Rauners hold an open house over the Fourth of July weekend to celebrate the release of their white wines, and again over Thanksgiving weekend to taste new reds.

A word from the winery. *"Plan a visit to our family-owned winery. Taste our well-known red wines and also sample our list of whites. You will always find the winemaker or his wife available to talk with you and to serve you the wines.*

"We are a family who owns Yakima River Winery, and we are professionals who take pride in our work."

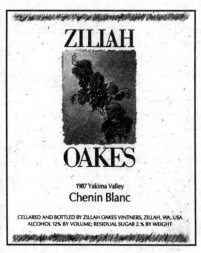

ZILLAH

OAKES

1987 Yakima Valley
Chenin Blanc

CELLARED AND BOTTLED BY ZILLAH OAKES VINTNERS, ZILLAH, WA, USA
ALCOHOL 12% BY VOLUME; RESIDUAL SUGAR 2.% BY WEIGHT

ZILLAH OAKES

P.O. Box 1729
Zillah, WA 98953
(509) 829-6990

Owner: Private partnership
Winemaker: Dave Crippen
Year established: 1987
Production capacity: 20,000 gallons
Vineyards: None
Touring region: Yakima Valley [p.14]

A bit of background Not surprisingly, vineyards around the state produce more grapes as they reach maturity. For independent growers, this healthy agricultural phenomenon produces a marketing quandary: how will they sell their bounty if there aren't enough wineries around willing to buy? Some growers have responded by starting their own wineries, others consign their grapes to large "custom-crushing" facilities and hope to sell the juice later on. But suppose you've already got a winery, a good one at that, but you lack the room for cost-effective expansion and don't want to compromise the reputation of your label just to take advantage of additional fruit. Suppose, in other words, that you are Covey Run, with your winery at the top of the Whiskey Canyon Vineyard snuggled up against the Roza Canal, and there's not a spare drop of tank capacity to ferment any extra grapes. What to do?

Covey Run's solution was to create an entirely new winery a few miles away, in the new industrial zone along the freeway. And to use the wine it produced in the new facility to attack another disturbing issue: the fact that less than 10 percent of the wine sold in the Northwest comes from grapes grown in the Northwest. (In other words, we're all drinking too much inexpensive "imported" wine.) Most California wine costs much less to produce simply because California wine grapes such as Thompson Seedless, grown at 20 tons to the acre in the Central Valley, are much cheaper than the premium varieties grown here at three or four tons to the acre. But when plenty of premium Riesling and Chardonnay becomes available at minimal cost, there's no reason we can't produce less expensive wines in the Northwest. And with the bountiful harvests of 1986 and 1987, that's just what wineries like Zillah Oakes and Columbia Crest set out to do.

Now, how did the winery get its name? Well, shortly after the turn of the century, when irrigation systems and railroads were getting started in the Yakima Valley, a surveyor by the name of Walter Granger became smitten with the teenage daughter (17-year-old Zillah Oakes) of the local railroad manager; he named the township he was surveying in her honor!

Visiting the winery★★. Zillah Oakes doesn't have the allure of most Yakima Valley wineries, many of which rise up amidst vineyards and open spaces. It's a freestanding building on a flat piece of land between Interstate 82 and a chalky bluff. You might wonder if the place resembles the rundown fruit and antique shops along other parts of the freeway, but the winery's attractive tasting room and friendly welcome will dispel your skepticism.

Tasting the wines★★. As you would expect, Zillah Oakes wines bear a strong resemblance to their sometimes more mature Covey Run cousins. One early and unexpected success came with a subtle, honeyed 1986 Late Harvest Riesling, which took best-of-show honors at the Tri-Cities festival in 1987, but samples we've tasted recently haven't been as impressive. The 1987 Riesling, for example, smells better (a pretty, floral nose) than it tastes (rather flat, with a bitter finish); it's an acceptable wine, but it's not memorable.

Still, Zillah Oakes wasn't designed for best-of-show awards; its avowed mission is to take market share away from California wines using Washington grapes and the talents of Covey Run's winemakers. No one complains if Gallo's so-called Rhine Riesling doesn't bowl over the critics, after all. And Zillah Oakes' Riesling, even with its faults, towers over the "imported" jug wines.

Getting there. From eastbound I-82, take Exit 52. The winery is in the industrial park at the base of the bluff. [**Map:** Covey Run]

Open daily from noon to 5.

Special events. Anniversary celebration in mid-May.

A word from the winery *"Welcome to Zillah Oakes, a new Yakima Valley winery and tasting room. Our wines have been produced from grapes grown along the southern slope of the Rattlesnake Mountains by experienced grape growers from Zillah to Prosser. Come and visit our new facility as you explore the wine country of the Yakima Valley."*

ORTHOGRAPHIC NOTE

It probably doesn't matter to more than half a dozen people, but here's the rationale behind our spelling of Pinot Noir, Cabernet Sauvignon, etc.

We have capitalized all words referring to wine varieties. (Note, by the way, that we don't call them varietals.) You wouldn't normally capitalize a variety of another species; for instance, you don't expect to see Red maple or Red Maple. But wine is different; the names of wines are still sufficiently new, like "Oleomargarine" a generation ago, that they have (temporarily, at least) assumed a sort of brand name status.

Our personal preference would be not to capitalize either word, but it doesn't "look" right, it doesn't "read" right.

A note from one of the winemakers informs us that "Pinot noir" and "Pinot gris" are the correct forms, as the words noir and gris are adjectives, not proper nouns. Indeed, this treatment has become routine at several newspapers. But even if they are mere adjectives, they're modifiers in a foreign language (French for "black" and "gray" respectively); as such, they could still legitimately be capitalized. One writes of the Khmer Rouge, the Cote d'Or, and the Cote d'Azur, for example. But more importantly, they're part of the wine's proper name. You wouldn't write david Lett or david Adelsheim or david Mielke.

David Lett, in fact, is one of the few winemakers who actually spells it "Pinot noir" on his label, upper and lower case. (Would he call it "Cabernet sauvignon" or "cabernet Sauvignon"? Which one's the adjective? What about Cabernet Franc or Sauvignon Blanc?) Our ampelography—dictionary of grape names—routinely capitalizes both words, as do many wineries. Most wine labels avoid the issue altogether by putting the whole thing in capital letters.

Our strictest sense is that one should capitalize the specific brand or label, as in "David Lett's 1986 Pinot Noir" but not the generic "Oregon pinot noir" or the entirely adjectival "pinot noir drinkers."

But the purpose of punctuation and capitalization is to give readers a sense of what you're writing about. Capitalizing the full names of wine grapes accomplishes that.

A peripheral note. Yes, Muller Thurgau (two words, no hyphen) has an umlaut on the "u" in Muller, and the proper spelling of Chateau has a circumflex on the "a," and so on. We left all that out in the interest of speedier composition and a more timely book. Next time.

OREGON'S
WINE TOURING REGIONS

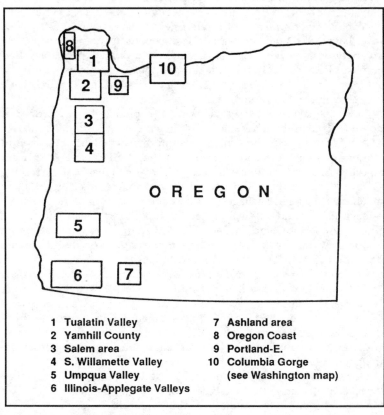

1 Tualatin Valley
2 Yamhill County
3 Salem area
4 S. Willamette Valley
5 Umpqua Valley
6 Illinois-Applegate Valleys
7 Ashland area
8 Oregon Coast
9 Portland-E.
10 Columbia Gorge
    (see Washington map)

WESTERN OREGON

Travelers who whip along the Willamette Valley on I-5 can only guess at the richness of the land. (It's pronounced Wil-LAM-it, by the way.) Fortunately, the valley is crisscrossed with scenic back roads and byways that wind around deep-shaded filbert orchards and through fields of tall-growing grass. From every village crossroad rises the abrupt silhouette of a silo, guarding a cache of filberts or walnuts or grain like a silent sentinel; the shape brings to mind the walls of a church that might dominate a wine village in Europe. But the wine country of Europe is often flat and uninteresting: rows upon rows of vineyards, unrelieved by trees or row crops. The vineyards of the Willamette Valley are but one element of a diverse economic and artistic patchwork.

Take the time to drive slowly along the back roads. Roll down the window and smell the dark, rich earth under the walnut groves. Look at the wildflowers growing up amidst the grassy weeds at the roadside, or at the hawks above a field of prancing lambs, or at the green of a nearby hillside as sunshine burns through the morning haze and washes over the land.

EASTERN OREGON

The climate and geography of the Pacific Northwest combine to make thousands of acres suitable for viticulture. And not just the Yakima Valley in Washington or the Willamette Valley of western Oregon. The Columbia Valley viticultural area holds the most promise. Most of it is in Washington but some lies in Oregon as well. The common characteristics don't stop at the political boundary: no native trees, little rainfall, no cloud cover during the growing season. From a satellite, this looks like North America's bald spot. It's a desert, with less natural rainfall than the Sahara.

Eastern Oregon includes 200,000 acres of farmland potentially suitable for grapes; all that's needed is an economic reason for farmers to convert their acreage. Easier said than done: it takes at least five years without a cash crop to convert a circle of alfalfa to bearing vineyards. Once established, wine grapes at $500 a ton, five tons to the acre, look pretty attractive. (Which assumes there will be wineries to buy the grapes.) More attractive than potatoes at $2,000 an acre, every other year at best. (Everyone wants french fries, though.) On the other hand, the impetus of new vineyards may go the way of other tax-sheltered investments under the revised tax code.

Right now, corporate farmers like Boardman Farms and Western Empire are leading the way. The biggest question isn't the productivity of the land, which no one questions, but the quality of the wine. The possibility exists, after all, that eastern Oregon could produce decent wine in large quantities, the long-awaited Northwest jug wine so many people seem to crave. Only time will tell.

More information about Oregon wines and wineries is available from the Oregon Winegrowers Association at 1359 W. Fifth, Eugene, OR 97402. Phone (503) 343-4078. Bill Nelson, a respected lobbyist and sought-after enology consultant, is the executive director; associate membership is $35 a year.

TUALATIN VALLEY

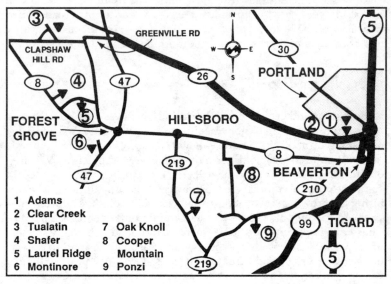

1 Adams
2 Clear Creek
3 Tualatin
4 Shafer
5 Laurel Ridge
6 Montinore
7 Oak Knoll
8 Cooper Mountain
9 Ponzi

The fertile soil of the Tualatin Valley extends westward from metropolitan Portland like a great green blanket, enriched centuries ago by the mineral deposits of lava flows from the Cascades and by prehistoric sand, clay, and silt. The Tualatin—its name means "lazy river" in the local Indian dialect—meanders across the valley floor toward the Willamette. Less than 200 years ago, the Twality Indians hunted deer, elk, bear, and geese along the shores of the river; within 50 years they had succumbed to smallpox epidemics brought by the white settlers of the Oregon Territory.

The timbered plains of the valley are no longer pristine, as housing developments and factories have marched westward from Portland. Yet the western half of Washington County, the jurisdiction encompassing most of the valley, has retained its agricultural character, and close to a dozen wineries now flourish among the farms and orchards.

The proximity of these wineries to metropolitan Portland allows for satisfying, uncomplicated wine touring; the wineries themselves have banded together as the Washington County Winery Association to encourage weekend and holiday touring by Portland residents and out-of-town visitors.

There's more to do in the region than visit vineyards. Antique hunting along the back roads is a popular pastime, as are the summer festivals in the small towns. You'll find an archetypal country store, Petrich's, along the highway in a community called Scholls. And some excellent wineries at the end of gravel driveways.

Tualatin Valley:
WINE COUNTRY MEALS & LODGING
Alphabetically by establishment

EMBASSY SUITES HOTEL
9000 S.W. Washington Square Rd
Tigard, OR 97223
(503) 644-4000
(800) 362-2779 (nationwide)

Cushy suites, pool, free breakfasts
on outskirts of Portland. Walk to
Washington Square shopping mall,
drive to wine country in minutes. A
comfortable way to combine wine
touring with proximity to a bigger
city.

THE GRAPERY
4190 S.W. Cedar Hills Blvd
Beaverton, OR 97007
(503) 646-1437

An oasis of gentility in high-tech
suburbia. Limited, eclectic menu
(veal shank, lamb curry, stuffed
pheasant, rib-eye steak) plus
homemade desserts. Well-stocked
wine shop; for $1 corkage you can
drink your selection with lunch or
dinner. Sunday brunch, too.

JAN'S FOOD MILL
1819 19th Ave
Forest Grove, OR 97116
(503) 357-6623

Moderately priced menu served in
a ranch atmosphere. Open every
day. Wine list gets good marks from
local vintners.

NENDELS
13455 Tualatin Valley Hwy
Beaverton OR 97005
(503) 643-9100 locally
(800) 452-0123 in Oregon
(800) 547-0106 nationwide

Consistent, dependable accommodations, reasonably priced.
Pool, cable TV, 24-hr coffee shop
next door.

Portland listings on following pages.

PORTLAND

The state's largest city, and its commercial heart, lies a short drive from the state's best wine country. This proximity is one reason that Oregonians have become fiercely chauvinistic about their wines. Over 30 percent of the wine consumed in Oregon is Oregon-made wine; in Washington, just across the Columbia, the comparable figure is under 10 percent. (Oregonians tend to be proud of whatever's homegrown, to support the home team; Washingtonians tend to be more pseudosophisticated, to feel that "imported" is better.) Oregonians also read more local wine news in their daily and weekly papers than their Washington counterparts.

There's one winery and the region's only distillery actually in Portland, but visitors and residents alike won't have a hard time finding half a dozen wineries to visit within half an hour's drive of town.

Portland:
WINE COUNTRY MEALS & LODGING
Alphabetically by establishment

ATWATER'S
111 S.W. Fifth Ave
Portland, OR 97204
(503) 220-3600

Impressive view from 30th floor of US Bancorp Tower, elegant surroundings, innovative menu, artistic presentations. Top-notch wine list (400 choices) designed by Mary Ross of The 95th in Chicago, currently under the eye of Art Fortuna, features many older Oregon vintages.

HEATHMAN HOTEL
1009 S.W. Broadway
Portland, OR 97205
(503) 241-4100
(800) 551-0011

Very elegant, completely restored downtown hotel (leather-bound rattan, brass, chintz). Impeccable service. Dining room under Chef Greg Higgins has won Oregon Winegrowers Association award as Restaurant of the Year. Innovative menu (example: Szechuan salmon with mustard, garlic, and peppercorns with a citrus beurre blanc), worldwide wine list with special emphasis on Oregon.

L'AUBERGE
2601 N.W. Vaughn St
Portland, OR 97210
(503) 223-3302

Blend of classic French and contemporary food preparation and presentation; fixed price, table d'hote dinners. Wine cellar carries 100 bottlings, half of them Oregon (including Eyrie's 1975 Pinot Noir).

Listings for establishments east of Portland appear on page 211.

YAMHILL COUNTY

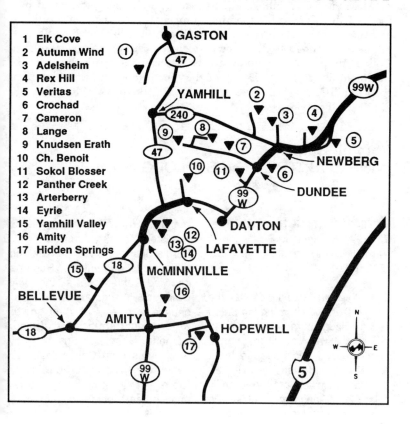

1 Elk Cove
2 Autumn Wind
3 Adelsheim
4 Rex Hill
5 Veritas
6 Crochad
7 Cameron
8 Lange
9 Knudsen Erath
10 Ch. Benoit
11 Sokol Blosser
12 Panther Creek
13 Arterberry
14 Eyrie
15 Yamhill Valley
16 Amity
17 Hidden Springs

Mornings in Yamhill County always seem to be overcast and cool. Not until noon, after the low gray clouds have burned away, does a strong, warm sunshine bathe the lowland fields and gently rolling hills with a pleasant, golden glow. The valley's rich harvest of fruits, nuts, and grain flourishes in this moderate climate, as do the hillside orchards and vineyards.

This is a county of small towns and prosperous farms, whose fertile soil gives root to crops as diverse as filberts, strawberries, cherries, pole beans, wheat, and rapeseed. It's also exceptionally good country for grapes: almost half of Oregon's wine grapes are grown in Yamhill County, as much for the soil as for the climate. The Jurassic clay in and around the famous Red Hills of Dundee is particularly beneficial for grapevines, though other soils in nearby areas have their proponents, too. When Oregon's winegrowing industry is as well established as Burgundy's, we may learn which vineyards produce Grand Cru and which vin ordinaire.

McMinnville, Yamhill's county seat, is a charming town that has escaped the roar of traffic zooming along Highway 18 between Portland and the ocean beaches. You easily get the feeling that McMinnville has retained a certain 1950s character: the picture-postcard campus of Linfield College, the peaceful shopping streets, the shaded city park, the spruced-up downtown buildings. Details on the wineries and their activities from the Yamhill County Wineries Association, P.O. Box 871, McMinnville, OR 97128. (503) 434-5814.

Yamhill County:
WINE COUNTRY MEALS & LODGING
Alphabetically by establishment

FLYING M RANCH
23029 N.W. Flying M Rd
Yamhill, OR 97148
(503) 662-3222

Conflagration didn't daunt the Mitchell family: when the log-sided Flying M lodge burned to the ground in 1983, it was rebuilt to original specifications two seasons later. As remote and rustic as ever, 28 spectacular miles into the foothills of the Coast Range from McMinnville on mostly gravel roads. Horseback riding, escorted trail rides, tennis, vast swimming hole. Lodging at campsites, in cabins, or motel units; no phones or TV. Restaurant in the lodge open daily; Sunday brunch draws the natives.

MATTEY HOUSE
10221 N.E. Mattey Ln
McMinnville, OR 97128
(503) 434-5058

Here's the best example yet of a wine country bed and breakfast. Start with a genuine Victorian mansion (now on the Historic Register). Plant grapes out front. Furnish the rooms with painstaking attention to authenticity. Become knowledgeable about all the local wineries. Offer some local wine and cheese to guests as they arrive. Keep menus from local restaurants on hand. Gene and Susan Irwin, transplants from California, have done everything right. Four lovely rooms, two luxurious baths, multicourse breakfasts, moderate prices.

NICK'S ITALIAN CAFE
521 E. Third St
McMinnville, OR 97128
(503) 434-4471

The ultimate wine country restaurant. A friendly, informal trattoria, Nick's is "headquarters": winemakers, politicians, journalists, wine collectors, and weekend tourists crowd in. Founder Nick Peirano (a refugee from California), dining room manager John West, and the rest of the small staff create a sense of welcome and well-being here that's unsurpassed. Wonderful Northern Italian food at moderate prices. Typical fixed price menu: an antipasto (steamed clams, or grilled asparagus, or prosciutto with melon), a tureen of minestrone, a fresh salad, an imaginative lasagna or ravioli (stuffed with pesto and pine nuts, perhaps, or seafood, or chicken), an entree (steak with caper sauce, or grilled trout), and a slice of chocolate brandy torte for dessert. You can skip the main course and still have plenty to eat.

As befits the "soul" of the Yamhill Valley, the wine list is extraordinary. Nick buys lots of good wine when it's released and doesn't overcharge when it's sold. (House wines, from Sokol Blosser, aren't great, but are inexpensive and drinkable.) You'd have to be crazy not to eat here at least once.

PINOT PETE'S
760 N. Hwy 99 W.
Dundee, OR 97115
(503) 538-6758
(800) 422-1186 (in Oregon)

Gourmet picnics to go (sandwiches, salads, entrees). Large selection of wines. Perfect for wine country picnics: call ahead, toll-free from Portland and pick up your lunch when you arrive. Open weekends, closed Monday and Tuesday.

ROGER'S
SEAFOOD RESTAURANT
2121 E. 27th St
McMinnville, OR 97128
(503) 472-0917

The specialty is fresh seafood in this cheerful, expanding restaurant behind the local fishmonger's. Pleasant setting, with expansive windows overlooking a brook and a stand of trees. Smoked game and poultry, too.

SIR HINKLEMAN
FUNNYDUFFER
421 E. Third St
McMinnville, OR 97128
(503) 472-1309

A cafe and wine shop that sells soups, salads, pizzas, quiche, homemade desserts, all available for take-out. Wine selection features Yamhill County bottles at reasonable prices; tastings available.

SAFARI MOTOR INN
345 N. Hwy 99 W.
McMinnville, OR 97128
(503) 472-5187

Well-run, moderately priced motel on the outskirts of town. Large rooms, spa, coffee shop.

YAMHILL COUNTY BED AND BREAKFAST
An association of half a dozen B&B homes in the wine country. Contact Mattey House or the Yamhill County Wineries Association for a brochure.

SALEM & EOLA HILLS

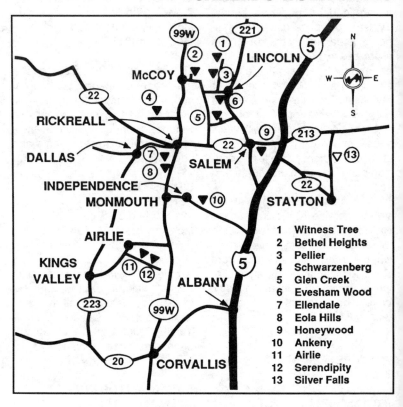

1 Witness Tree
2 Bethel Heights
3 Pellier
4 Schwarzenberg
5 Glen Creek
6 Evesham Wood
7 Ellendale
8 Eola Hills
9 Honeywood
10 Ankeny
11 Airlie
12 Serendipity
13 Silver Falls

Heading south from McMinnville, along Highway 99 W. (also called "99 Wine"), you come upon the Eola Hills, a 20-mile trail of knobs and knuckles quite heavily planted with vineyards. It's the up-and-coming wine region of Oregon, halfway between Portland and Eugene, with a soil of Jory clay loam.

Salem, Oregon's capital city, makes a fine home base for wine touring. Accommodations are plentiful, restaurants are numerous. But the principal attraction is still the land, the incredibly bountiful Willamette Valley. The settlers who arrived here a century ago found a land of plenty, and to celebrate their discovery they gave their towns and villages names from a biblical past to describe their joy: Sublimity, Bethel, Aurora, New Era, Damascus, Amity. Those ancient rhythms complement the Indian names that also mark the maps of the valley: Molalla, Chemeketa, Mehama, Waconda.

It's all in the imagination, of course, but the sky seems broader here, as the road traverses the softly rolling hills. It happens when you leave the freeway, with its flat, high-speed monotony. The roads go up and down the hills, and the changes in elevation, perhaps only a hundred feet, produce a new perspective, new vistas: an agglomeration of farm buildings, a combine cutting a wide swath through a field of fescue, a lone tree silhouetted against the horizon. And everywhere the broad, pastel expanse of sky.

Salem & Eola Hills:
WINE COUNTRY MEALS & LODGING
Alphabetically by establishment

EXECULODGE
200 Commercial St S.E.
Salem OR 97301
(503) 363-4123
(800) 452-7879 (reservations)

Large downtown motel within walking distance of the capitol building and shops. Free continental breakfast.

INN AT ORCHARD HEIGHTS
695 Orchard Heights Rd
Salem, OR 97304
(503) 378-1780

A 1937-vintage home with a contemporary face-lift: chrome, glass, mirrors. Continental menu, delicate sauces, fancy desserts from an in-house bakery. Wine list names 120 bottles, emphasizing Salem and Yamhill vintners. Dinner only.

SHILO INN
1855 Hawthorne N.E.
Salem, OR 97303
(503) 581-9410
(800) 222-2244 (nationwide reservations)

Predictably comfortable accommodations at reasonable prices. Free continental breakfast, movie channel, pool. Other locations in Portland suburbs, Eugene, Medford, Grant's Pass, Oregon Coast, Seattle area, Boise area.

STATE HOUSE
2146 State St
Salem, OR 97301
(503) 588-1340

B&B with four rooms, two baths. Red maples in landscaped garden, a gazebo, and hot tub provide refuge from the busy street. Co-owner Mike Winsett, a former butcher, provides hand-cut bacon (daily except Thursday) at breakfast.

VIA FLORENCIA
189 Liberty St N.E.
Salem, OR 97301
(503) 363-7578

Fresh pasta dishes to eat in or take out. Extensive salad bar. Sunday brunch. Moved from suburbs to downtown Reed Opera House.

Additional information: Salem Convention & Visitor Assoc., 1313 Mill St.. S.E., Salem, OR 97301. (800) 874-7012.

SOUTHERN WILLAMETTE VALLEY

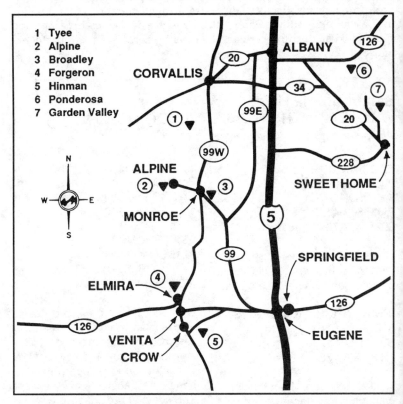

1 Tyee
2 Alpine
3 Broadley
4 Forgeron
5 Hinman
6 Ponderosa
7 Garden Valley

The Willamette Valley is Oregon's agricultural heartland, and viticulture has added its dimension to this countryside of historic covered bridges, old timber, orchards, seed grasses, and pastureland.

And here, at the southern end of the broad valley, visitors will be drawn to bosky byways along the river, the cultural advantages of Eugene, and the quality of the region's wineries.

Eugene, Oregon's second-largest city, is the seat of Lane County's "Emerald Empire," a region that extends from the ocean to the Cascades. The forested hillsides provide the timber on which much of the region's economy depends; the valley is covered with orchards and grassland, with stands of lichen-draped alder. As you travel the side roads, you see fields dotted with Christmas tree farms, intersections marked by fundamentalist churches.

Eugene itself, home of the University of Oregon, is prosperous and well educated, with 17,000 students, two public markets, and a 150-mile system of bike trails. Dozens of covered bridges await motorists who venture into the countryside, spanning assorted streams and tributaries of the Willamette River. Not long ago, these bridges played a vital role for wagons transporting hay, produce, and logs to market; many were built with roofs to protect the timbers below from Oregon's moist weather. A few are still in use today, but most have fallen under the watchful protection of local historical societies.

But if you can't drive across a covered bridge, you can still take a ferry ride across the Willamette. There's a handy crossing at Buena Vista (the locals pronounce it BYOO-na Vista), midway between Salem and Albany, that's been in operation for over a century. It holds only six cars; it's really just a barge, guided across the river by cables. But once the vessel starts to move, it has the same magic, restful effect that ferries always seem to have: life slows down, if only for a few minutes. The water view is calming, and as the shore recedes, you might even see a few wild geese overhead, heading for a touchdown at the Ankeny Wildlife Refuge.

Southern Willamette Valley:
WINE COUNTRY MEALS & LODGING
Alphabetically by establishment

LILLA'S
206 Seventh Ave S.W.
Albany, OR 97321
(503) 928-9437

B&B with three guest rooms, one bath. Full breakfast. Antique shop. The restaurant serves traditional fare, features wines from Alpine, Knudsen Erath, Amity.

MADISON INN
660 Madison
Corvallis, OR 97330
(503) 757-1264

Tudor-style home was first B&B in Corvallis. Seven rooms, two with private bath. Breakfast includes Dutch babies, fresh fruit. Popular with visitors to OSU. Opposite Central Park rose garden.

RUBE'S DELI
777 Ninth St
Corvallis, OR 97330
(503) 754-0100

Picnic foods, Oregon wines.

UMPQUA VALLEY

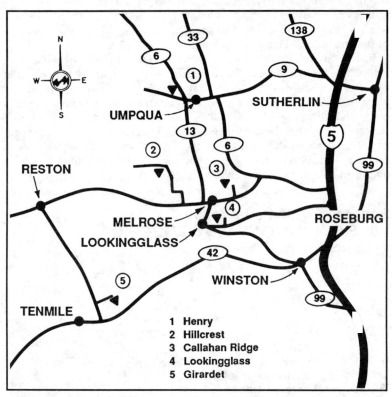

1 Henry
2 Hillcrest
3 Callahan Ridge
4 Lookingglass
5 Girardet

The Umpqua River has carved an impressive setting for this region. Its northern fork cascades over gleaming ledges, swirls around shallow rocks, languishes in deep, clear pools. Here, fly-fishermen stand up to their waists in the cold, swirling water, casting their lines with patient repetition, waiting for a strike. It's one of the very best fishing streams in the country, if not the world. When the spring Chinook or summer steelhead are running, the license plates of the cars parked along Highway 138 indicate how far their occupants have come for the thrill of fishing the Umpqua.

The wineries lie in the hills west of Interstate 5. Little brown creeks come rushing down creases in the sweeping mountainsides, between blankets of evergreen and lichen-draped deciduous trees. Barns, cows, sheep appear through the drifting mist that covers the valley floor. It's a cool climate, precisely what's recommended for the best grapes. Richard Sommer was the first to arrive with vinifera plantings in 1961; many growers have since followed, and all confirm one of viticulture's basic lessons: the more marginal the growing season, the longer the grapes take to ripen, the more difficult the conditions, the better the wine.

And so the region's wineries flourish. They're already having a positive influence on local tourism; the sunny Umpqua Valley, its golden hillsides laced with cool, clear streams and green vineyards, is becoming as famous for its wine as for its fly-fishing.

Umpqua Valley:
WINE COUNTRY MEALS & LODGING
Alphabetically by establishment

STEAMBOAT INN
Steamboat, OR 97447
(503) 498-2411
(503) 496-3495

Evenings begin with a glass of wine, sipped on the wide veranda. Guests (often fishing enthusiasts from around the world) share one large table. Fixed price dinner includes five courses and lots of conversation. Oregon wines. Reservations essential.

Accommodations a bit rustic, but the setting in the trees above the Umpqua is magnificent.

WINDMILL INN
1450 N.W. Mulholland Dr
Roseburg, OR 97470
(503) 673-0901 (local)
(800) 452-5315 (in Oregon)
(800) 547-4747 (nationwide)

Spacious rooms and suites, pool, sauna, cable TV. Pets okay.

ILLINOIS & APPLEGATE VALLEYS

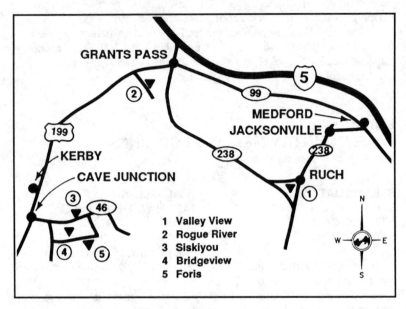

One-third of the tourists visiting Oregon spend some time in this part of the state to take advantage of the area's wide range of recreational and cultural opportunities. The Rogue River loops through the region in a 215-mile aquatic trail of roaring white water and smooth pools. Highway 199, the Redwood Highway, travels a majestic path through the cathedral-like canopies of towering trees as it crosses the Siskiyou Mountains, then levels out as it descends into the Illinois Valley, which has one of Oregon's best climates for growing vinifera grapes.

Medford, a lumber center, is the largest city in the region, but Ashland—a college town with a thriving professional theater company and a number of bed-and-breakfast homes—is the biggest tourist attraction. The Oregon Caves, a maze of corridors connecting spectacular marble caverns, also merit a visit.

JACKSONVILLE & ASHLAND AREA

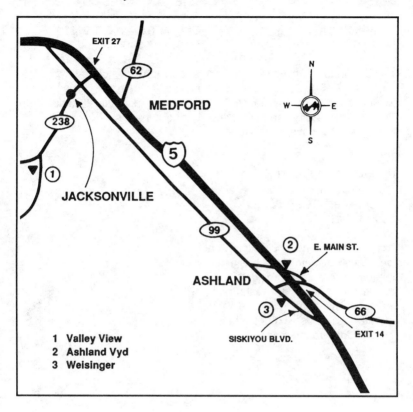

1 Valley View
2 Ashland Vyd
3 Weisinger

Southern Oregon:
WINE COUNTRY MEALS & LODGING
Alphabetically by establishment

ASHLAND BED AND BREAKFAST
(503) 488-0338

A clearing house and reservation service for all of Ashland's popular B&B establishments, including "B&B of the Year" Chanticleer.

ASHLAND HILLS INN
2525 Ashland St
Ashland OR 97520
(503) 482-8310
(800) 452-5315

Large, modern motel complex at I-5 Exit 14. Pool, tennis courts, putting green. Restaurant features Oregon wines. Shuttle service to Shakespeare Festival.

CHATA
1212 S. Pacific Hwy
Talent, OR 97540
(503) 535-2575

Cottage restaurant operated by a family of Polish immigrants with genuine hospitality, re-creating Old World flavors. Polish art covers the walls, wine list covers the world.

OREGON CAVES CHATEAU
Caves Toll Station No.1
Oregon Caves, OR 97523
(503) 592-3400

Comfortable, moderately priced cabins with great views of the Siskiyou mountains. Open only during summer.

JACKSONVILLE INN
175 E. California
Jacksonville, OR 97250
(503) 899-1900

Small hotel in a historic building on Jacksonville's main street has eight antique-decorated rooms, all with private bath. Basement restaurant serves classic prime rib. Wine shop upstairs carries 500 labels. Reservations recommended.

OREGON COAST

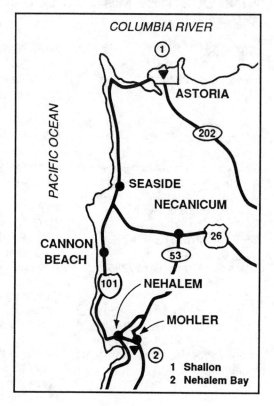

The magnificent scenery of the Oregon coast transcends the drab commercialism of several coastal towns. The coastline can't be kept pristine, of course; parts of it have always been associated with shipping, fishing, and logging. We're saddened by some of the raucous challenges to the beauty of the coast in the name of tourism; and heartened by the restoration of beachfront streets in places like Gearhart, and by resorts like Salishan that blend themselves into the natural surroundings. The great attractions of the coast, in addition to its wineries (!), are its natural wonders: Haystack Rock, the Devil's Punchbowl, and the expanse of beach itself, all in the public domain. Now, if there were only a way to keep cars off the beach!

Oregon Coast:
WINE COUNTRY MEALS & LODGING
Alphabetically by establishment

THE ARK
Sandrich Rd
Nahcotta, WA 98637
(206) 665-4133

A 15-minute foray across the Columbia River from Astoria to this famous restaurant. Owners Nancy Main and Jimella Lucas have written a popular cookbook, sponsor an annual garlic festival. Innovative cuisine, Northwest wine list.

CHEZ JEANETTE
7510 Old Hwy 101
Gleneden Beach, OR 97388
(503) 764-3434

A cozy roadhouse, just up the road from Salishan Lodge, with splendid fare and a good wine list. French country cooking with Northwest ingredients.

CRAB BROILER
Hwy 101 at Hwy 26
Cannon Beach, OR 97110
(503) 738-5313

A popular landmark with a good selection of Northwest wines. Fresh cracked crab is the specialty; the coleslaw is legendary.

INN AT OTTER CREST
P.O. Box 50
Otter Rock, OR 97369
(503) 765-2111

In the trees above Cape Foulweather. Cars park at top of bluff, guests and baggage descend by tramway. Units include kitchen, TV.

MO'S
1397 Sherman Ave
North Bend, OR 97459
(and other locations)
(503) 756-7536

A must-try. The best clam chowder on the coast, and nothing stronger to drink than milk

SALISHAN LODGE
Hwy 101
Gleneden Beach, OR 97388
(503) 764-2371 (local)
(800) 452-2300 (in Oregon)
(800) 547-6500 (nationwide)

Luxury resort in beautifully designed complex overlooking Siletz Bay. Handsomely appointed bedroom units overlook fairways of championship golf course. Fitness facility with pool, sauna, exercise equipment. Nature trails, beachfront access for guests.

The most impressive wine cellar in the Pacific Northwest (21,000 bottles) under Phil de Vito, serves the resort's restaurants and its retail wine shop.

(Gourmet Dining Room wine list is multiple winner of Grand Award from *Wine Spectator*) Private meals and tastings in the cellar by arrangement; tours on request.

SANCTUARY RESTAURANT
Hwy 101 at Hazel St
Chinook, WA 98614
(206) 777-8380

Moderately priced restaurant in former Methodist-Episcopal church (complete with stained glass windows and altar rail). Extensive wine list.

THE SHELBURNE INN
SHOALWATER RESTAURANT
Pacific Hwy at J St
Long Beach, WA 98644
(206) 642-2442

The restaurant blends French and Northwest cuisine, uses fresh ingredients. Co-owner Tony Kischner was dining room manager at Rosellini's Other Place before moving his family to the beach. Terrific wine list.

The inn is a historic home with intimate rooms and furnishings.

SWAFFORD'S
1630 N. Coast Hwy
Newport, OR 97365
(503) 265-3044

Fresh seafood is the ticket here. Buy your wine in the well-stocked retail shop, pay a modest corkage fee, and drink it with dinner.

WINDWARD INN
3757 Hwy 101 N.
Florence, OR 97439
(503) 997-8243

Old-fashioned, book-lined seafood and steak restaurant. More than 100 wine choices from adjacent shop.

PORTLAND (East) & MOUNT HOOD

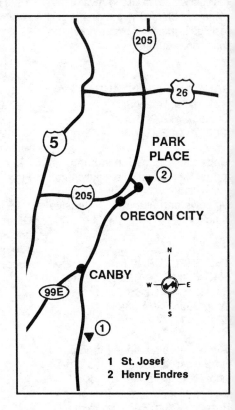

1 St. Josef
2 Henry Endres

As the Mount Hood Highway, Route 26, leaves Portland, heading east through pastures toward evergreen forests, you come first to the town of Sandy, which boasts one of the finest little wineries in the Northwest. There's a full-fledged resort complex at a place called Welches, then a succession of smaller trailer camps and motels. The highway climbs and winds through the tall firs and little towns; you pass a string of gas stations, general stores, and tourist cabins in Wemme, Brightwood, Zig Zag, Rhododendron. Finally, at the road's highest point, Government Camp, a wide range of ski slopes attracts day-skiers, while others may proceed up a winding spur to the impressive stone lodge at Timberline.

Followers of this mountainous wine trail will then head north, following a rushing stream toward the town of Hood River, right in the middle of the gorge carved by the Columbia River. Tourism entries for the Gorge area are in the Washington state section. (pages 27 to 29).

RIPPLING RIVER RESORT
68010 E. Fairway
Welches, OR 97067
(503) 224-7158 (from Portland)
(800) 452-4612 (in Oregon)
(800) 547-8054 (nationwide)

Resort built around modest mountainside golf course. Comfortable rooms; suites with kitchens, fireplaces. Two restaurants (one casual, one formal). Fishing nearby.

TIMBERLINE LODGE
Timberline, OR 97028
(503) 272-3311
(800) 547-1406 (nationwide)

National Historic Monument built during the Depression and decorated with carvings by WPA artists. Exterior resembles a European fortress, interior (decorated with carvings by WPA artists) resembles a medieval cathedral. Its beams, fireplace mantels, and stairwells are works of art. Crowded with skiers and day-trippers from Portland, but overnight guests have access to pool, sauna. Terrific view from dining room of surrounding mountains (best at breakfast or lunch).

Additional listings for the Portland area appear on page 194.

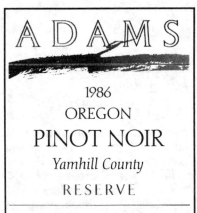

1986

OREGON

PINOT NOIR

Yamhill County

RESERVE

ADAMS VINEYARD WINERY

1922 N.W. Pettygrove
Portland, OR 97209
(503) 294-0606

Owners & winemakers:
  Peter & Carol Adams
Year established: 1985
Production capacity: 7,500 gallons
Vineyards: 12 acres
Touring region: Portland [p. 194]

A bit of background. The first "Peter F. Adams" wines were made in the romantic setting of the Adelsheim Vineyard in the Red Hills of Dundee rather than the industrial corner of northwest Portland. (Peter Adams and David Adelsheim attended Lincoln High School in Portland together in the early 1960s.) Peter and Carol Adams still have their vineyard there, planted with Pinot Noir and Chardonnay, but their non-wine business interests keep them in Portland. Peter and Carol had talked about moving to the country, to live where the grapes grow, but in the end they decided to build their winery in town.

Peter Adams' interest in wine began when he and his brother owned a wine shop; the store didn't last, but the fascination with wine did. He bought a vineyard property, took courses in winemaking at the University of California at Davis, and in 1981 began making wine. He runs the winery using his background as a management consultant.

Carol Adams, formerly a food columnist for a Portland newspaper supplement, is now winemaker. She is also a successful artist who designed the subtle, eye-catching label for the winery, with its silver lettering and delicate sumi wash of a vine tendril. Matt Kinne is the assistant winemaker.

Visiting the winery ★★. It's all bright colors around the Adams winery in northwest Portland: pink herringbone mosaic on the cupola of St. Michael's church on the nearby skyline; red, green, and silver lettering on the Consolidated Freightways trucks across the street. Carol Adams, attired in a yellow sweater, purple skirt, and shiny black pumps, watches the grapes arrive at the crushing pad, cuddling daughter Fanny, herself swathed in soft orange coveralls. Totes of dark blue grapes get dumped into the stemmer-crusher; all around stand golden oak barrels full of wine. There's no tasting room except for the lab counter, so visits must be by appointment.

Tasting the wine ★★★☆. Adams limits its production to Pinot Noir,

Chardonnay, and Sauvignon Blanc. The 1983 Pinot Noir continues to sport its vigor and multilayered richness. In 1984, a wet harvest produced a pleasant, meaty Pinot Noir but the flavors stop short. The 1985 vintage won a gold medal at the Oregon State Fair, and another at the American Wine Competition in New York. We've not tried its successor in recent months.

Half the Sauvignon Blanc was barrel-fermented, and all of it was oak-aged. It's a fine, fragrant wine.

Getting there. From I-405, take Exit 2-B (Everett St) and go east to 18th, then north on 18th to Pettygrove. Turn west, cross 19th, and the winery is on the left.

Open by appointment only.

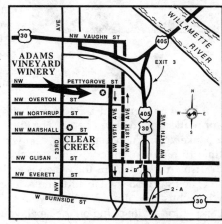

A word from the winery [in the form of a letter from Carol Adams]. *"Here is an update on the Adams winery. Carol and Peter are the winemakers. Carol oversees it all, cuz Peter has a full-time job crushing rock in Washington County. He is co-owner of Karban Rock. Yes, we get jokes about crushing grapes and rocks. Fanny is three and goes to child care. Portland [the older Adams daughter] is six and has a wine named after her, Portland's House Wine. She did the art on the label, a five-and-a-half-year-old rendition of her house. The label has been changed from Peter F. Adams to Adams, and Carol created the new look; the name change was because Carol is part of the project, too."*

ADELSHEIM VINEYARD

22150 N.E. Quarter Mile Lane
Newberg, OR 97132
(503) 538-3652

Owners: David & Virginia Adelsheim
Winemakers: David Adelsheim,
  Don Kautzner
Year established: 1978
Production capacity: 35,000 gallons
Vineyards: 18 acres
Touring region: Yamhill [p. 195]

A bit of background. David Adelsheim studied German in college and apprenticed with David Lett at The Eyrie Vineyards. He also worked as a banker, construction manager, and wine steward before devoting full time to his own winery. Ginny Adelsheim is an artist, sculptor, and draftsman who designs the winery's acclaimed labels and posters.

(The figure on the label for the Adelsheim Pinot Noir is Diana Lett, whose husband, David, makes wine at The Eyrie Vineyard. What's a competitor's wife doing on the label, you ask? You have to understand that most Oregon winemakers don't see themselves as competitors but as colleagues. The label simply recognizes the Letts' support for Adelsheim. On the label for Chardonnay is Barbara Setsu Pickett, an artist and chef who helped Ginny Adelsheim lay out the vineyard's original Chardonnay rows.)

The Adelsheims began planting their vineyard in 1972. "It was a romantic delusion," David now admits. But after a dozen years of planting, pruning, training, and weeding, David Adelsheim has become an authority on vineyard trellising systems; he wrote a 44-page paper on the subject for the *Oregon Grape Growers Guide*. He is also working with Oregon State University on a long-range program to import a broad range of clones from European test stations and study their differences, the first such research in the country.

Adelsheim, who is also fluent in French and had a sideline as a broker for French wine barrels, was instrumental in arranging for Burgundian shipper Robert Drouhin to purchase vineyard property in Dundee; he also helped set up Governor Neil Goldschmidt's trade mission to Burgundy. The Adelsheim home is a natural headquarters for winemakers from around the world who come to the annual International Pinot Noir Celebration in McMinnville every summer.

Visiting the winery (NR). Climb up Chehalem Drive, off the valley floor, and you'll share in the sense of excitement that attracts even the most jaded traveler to this part of the world. The Adelsheims' property—rows of carefully tended Pinot Noir, Chardonnay, and Riesling—slopes gently down toward the Willamette Valley. It's a magnificent vista that the winery's labels can only hint at.

David and Ginny and David's brother Michael have expanded the winery's production capacity greatly since the days when the entire operation was crammed into the basement of their home. Now, barrels and tanks have also been squeezed into an adjoining building. Fortunate visitors might be able to accompany David Adelsheim on a round of barrel tasting as he monitors the progress of wines whose only difference, for example, might be the type of oak used to make the barrel. Unfortunately, there is no tasting room, other than the crowded cellar or the Adelsheims' intimate living room; consequently, the winery is not open to casual visitors.

Tasting the wines ★★★★. David Adelsheim has learned to listen to the marketplace. No more Riesling, Sauvignon Blanc, or Semillon; they don't come up to the standard of his other wines. More concern with quality control to avoid bottle variation. The result is a much better, more consistent line of wines reaching the shelves in 1989.

The 1987 Willamette Valley Chardonnay, to mention just one, is a luscious, yielding mouthful of toasty oak and apple flavors, balanced by good acidity. The 1988 Pinot Gris is the most enjoyable of Oregon's malolactic-style Pinot Gris.

Pinot Noir from Adelsheim has always been very good; it's available in several designations.

The 1986 Oregon Pinot Noir underwent an evolution that can only be described as classically Oregon Pinot. It was slow to develop in the glass, passing from a generic cherry nose to mint and barnyard nuances. Then, a full day later, tobacco, plums, and pepper emerged. After another day, pure raspberries! What a delight! Of course, most people don't uncork their wines two days before a meal, but this schedule gave us a vision of the wine's future. Some initially alluring wines can lose their appeal, even develop offensive qualities, while others (like this Adelsheim Pinot) take wing.

The 1986 Yamhill County "Elizabeth's Reserve" Pinot Noir gives another picture of this grape as it expresses itself in Oregon. The high note in the nose is the green, sappy smell also prevalent in the Ponzi Reserve Pinot Noir; it easily balances the lovely, charred oak, and persists in the mouth to a long finish. It's soft-textured, well balanced, and satisfying.

Adelsheim wines are regularly offered to the public at the nearby Oregon Wine Tasting Room on Highway 28 outside of McMinnville.

Getting there. From New-berg, take Hwy 240 toward Yamhill. Just outside Newberg, turn right on Chehalem Dr. Cross North Valley Rd; turn left on Hillside Dr and con-tinue straight on Quarter Mile Ln when Hillside veers left. The winery is the first building on the left.

Open to the public only twice a year, for the Rain Revels in late June, and over Thanksgiv-ing weekend. To be sure of an invitation, write to the winery (or call), and ask to be put on the mailing list.

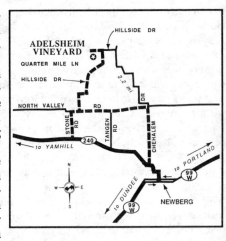

A word from the winery. *"Virtually all our capital investment goes into equipment that will actually improve the quality of our wines—the gentlest possible grape handling equipment and the best barrels—not into tourist facilities.*

"During the last 10 years we have carried out systematic research on many aspects of Pinot Noir production: barrels (coopers, oak origins, toast levels), fermentation techniques (must composition, temperatures, fermenter types, maceration), and fining (type and timing). Already we have refined many of our techniques—and our wines show it!

"Our focus has always been on the vineyard. We have compared training systems, clones of our principal varieties, moisture control programs, and pruning times. We are now looking more closely at site climates, soil depths and composition, and denser vine planting in order to create richer, more intense wines.

"In the first edition of this book, the Holdens indicated a concern about bottle variation between bottles of our wine. We feel the purchase of a new, small, fully automatic bottling line has gone a long way toward removing the potential for bottle variation. Not only are fill levels automatically controlled, but the headspace in each bottle is filled with inert gas.

"With 10 vintages behind us, we feel we have the combination of experience, international recognition, and the perfectionist spirit necessary to keep the name Adelsheim Vineyard synonymous with the best of Oregon wines."

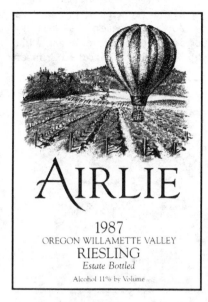

1987
OREGON WILLAMETTE VALLEY
RIESLING
Estate Bottled
Alcohol 11% by Volume

AIRLIE WINERY
15303 Dunn Forest Road
Monmouth, OR 97361
(503) 838-6013

Owners: Larry & Alice Preedy
Winemaker: Larry Preedy
Year established: 1986
Production capacity: 9,000 gallons
Vineyards: 15 acres
Touring region: Salem [p. 198]

A bit of background. Way back when, Airlie was the second-largest town in Oregon. Built as a stop on the stagecoach route between Salem and the coast, the community prospered with the advent of railroads. Flumes from the surrounding hills converged on local sawmills with fresh-cut logs, and puffing trains took away the timber. But the trains stopped running almost 60 years ago, the town faded away, and the forests have grown back.

A farming couple from Kansas, Larry and Alice Preedy, came out here a decade ago, bought a piece of property close to the Paul Dunn Forest, and started growing Christmas trees. Their neighbors down the hill started growing grapes, and their neighbors up the hill, Glen and Cheryl Longshore, started a winery. Before long, the Preedys were planting grapes, too. "We thought we could make a living just selling grapes, but we didn't want to look miles away for our market," Larry told us, "so we got into a new frontier." And started a winery.

Visiting the winery ★★☆. You couldn't find many spots more inviting than this hillside. Christmas trees cover about half the property, vineyards the rest. A picnic area overlooks a big pond. The modest winery is dug into the hillside. There's a stuffed owl in the corner of the tasting room that Larry Preedy thought might fool the robins in the vineyard. "It worked for half a day," he reports.

Tasting the wines ★★. We've particularly enjoyed Airlie's Muller Thurgau, made from estate-grown grapes, which has an appealing nose of honeysuckle and flavors of quince and oranges. The Gewurztraminer, slightly spritzy in the mouth, has an aroma of cinnamon and good flavors of ripe apples. The 1986 Pinot Noir went into French oak, but was still quite tannic when we tasted it last year. (An early release of the 1986 Pinot was called "Ceres" for the Roman goddess of agriculture; it tasted like peppery young cherries.) There's also a blush Pinot Noir called Crimson with an off-dry finish.

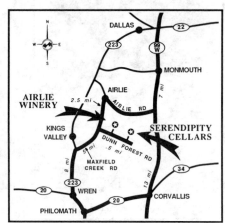

Getting there. From Corvallis, go 13 mi north on Hwy 99 W., then left on Airlie Rd 6 mi to old townsite of Airlie. Left 2.5 mi to Maxfield Creek Rd, left again 0.5 mi on Dunn Forest Rd.

Open weekends from noon to 5. Groups should call ahead.

Special events. There's a bluegrass festival over Memorial Day weekend.

WHAT THE RATINGS MEAN FOR QUALITY OF WINE:

NR	No rating: not tasted at all or not tasted recently; no releases
★	Barely drinkable
★☆	Occasionally acceptable
★★	Uneven
★★☆	Usually good
★★★	Good
★★★☆	Usually superior
★★★★	Consistently superior

ALPINE VINEYARDS

Estate Bottled
Willamette Valley

1985 WHITE RIESLING

ALPINE VINEYARDS

25904 Green Peak Road
Alpine, OR 97456
(503) 424-5851

Owners: Dan & Christine Jepsen
Winemaker: Dan Jepsen
Year established: 1980
Production capacity: 25,000 gallons
Vineyards: 20 acres
Touring: South Willamette [p. 200]

A bit of background. Here we have the first of several Northwest physician-winemakers who have made their medical practices subservient to the demands of time and energy required by a devotion to winemaking. Unlike Fred Benoit and Joe Campbell, however, who have since given up medicine entirely, Dan Jepsen continues to practice part-time at the University of Oregon's Student Health Center.

The choice between wine and medicine was not the first time Dan Jepsen has had to make a decision involving a career. He spent the summer of 1966, after graduating in chemistry from Carleton College, studying the cello in Graz, Austria. The question for him then was whether to pursue medicine or music. "The *great* musicians weren't bored," he remembers thinking, "but the others were *stuck*." So Dan Jepsen returned to the United States . . . and enrolled in medical school.

Before they built their brick home and winery in the verdant foothills of the Oregon Coast Range, the Jepsens spent two years in the Peace Corps in Africa. Their decision to move to Oregon was based largely on the availability of good vineyard land, Dan having discovered a passion for wine during his years at medical school in San Francisco.

Visiting the winery ★★★. The sun-drenched hillside is covered with 20 acres of Alpine Vineyards' Riesling, Cabernet Sauvignon, and Pinot Noir. Alpine uses its own grapes exclusively. "Eighty percent of the wine's quality is established in the vineyard," Dan Jepsen says. "The winemaker's job is to make sure nothing goes wrong after the grapes are harvested." So he insists on a long, cool fermentation process to prevent any undesirable oxidation, any darkening of the wine that would suggest loss of freshness. Dan is very sensitive to oxidation. "A golden Riesling is wrong as far as I'm concerned," he told one interviewer. "If it's golden, it's ruined."

The winery occupies the lower level of the house. The attractive tasting room and several picnic tables overlook the vineyard, where the Cabernet is ripened by the same sun that warms the Jepsens' home.

Tasting the wine ★★★. Alpine's wines are all estate-bottled—that is, made from grapes grown in their own vineyards. (Legally, the grapes could come from as far as five miles away.) Alpine's earliest success came with its Rieslings. The 1982 vintage (distinctly nongolden) was named best of show at the Tri-Cities Festival in 1983, and took a gold medal at the Enological Society in Seattle a month later. The most recent vintage had ripe, pineapple hints in the nose but offered no distinctive tastes.

There's a flavorful Chardonnay with a hint of oak that regularly wins gold medals at the Enological Society competition in Seattle. We recently tasted the 1987 vintage, which had a straightforward if faint bouquet, and pleasant, balanced flavors. There's Pinot Noir, too; we felt that the 1986 vintage had a deep, almost meaty bouquet but was overly tannic.

Their intense Cabernet Sauvignon may represent Oregon's northernmost commercial Cabernet. The Jepsens crushed 16 tons of Cabernet in 1985, a dry, warm season. "One year in 10," Dan says. "Every wine was the best we've seen." When we recently retasted the 85 Cab, it still showed its youthful color but had lost some of its early vigor.

Getting there. From the northern outskirts of Monroe, a community on Hwy 99 W. between Corvallis and Eugene, go west 4 mi toward Alsea to the village of Alpine. Continue 1.4 mi to Green Peak Rd, then wind for another 1.5 mi into the foothills of the Coast Range to the winery.

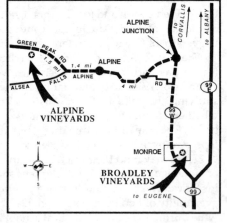

Open daily from noon to 5, mid-June through mid-September, weekends, noon to 5. The rest of the year, Saturday and Sunday afternoons only, except for annual closing, Christmas through January. Tour groups (over 10 people) should make an appointment and be prepared to pay $1 per person.

Alpine also operates a tasting room on the coast, at the Wood Gallery in Newport. It's open daily from noon to 5.

Special events. Two celebrations of new releases are scheduled each year, one in mid-June, the other in mid-September.

A word from the winery. *"Alpine Vineyards is committed to continue in its tradition, begun over a decade ago, of producing premium, hand-crafted estate-bottled wines. Please visit our winery and discover the magic of Alpine Vineyards."*

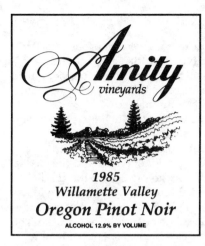

1985
Willamette Valley
Oregon Pinot Noir
ALCOHOL 12.9% BY VOLUME

AMITY VINEYARDS

18150 Amity Vineyards Road S.E.
Amity, OR 97101
(503) 835-2362

Owners: Myron Redford,
　Ione Redford, Janis Checchia
Winemaker: Myron Redford
Year established: 1976
Production capacity: 25,000 gallons
Vineyards: 15 acres
Touring region: Yamhill [p. 195]

A bit of background. From the beginning, Myron Redford was among the winemakers who took upon themselves the job of promoting Oregon wines to the entire nation, a task he has always performed with enormous enthusiasm and intellectual skill. A big, bushy sort of man with flecks of gray creeping into his beard, almost impossible not to like, he's always on the go, reminding some people of a bear on the prowl, others of a genial "mad scientist."

Actually, Redford began his career as a social science researcher at the University of Washington. He was recruited by Prof. Lloyd Woodburne to help out at the old Associated Vintners, and soon thereafter began looking for a vineyard property of his own. He ended up in the Yamhill Valley 10 years ago and hasn't looked back since. Today, Amity is one of Oregon's most successful "little" wineries, but it's been a struggle. Myron Redford has always been an innovator, a leader, a "winemaker's winemaker." He has confined himself to making relatively few varieties that are almost always ideal "food wines" because their dry style enhances the character of the grapes without overwhelming the food.

Visiting the winery ★★☆. The town of Amity, at the base of the Eola Hills, is the sort of place where the feed store stays open all day on Sunday. Turn left at the schoolhouse and head up the gravel road, into dense woods and through the vines, to reach the Amity Vineyards winery and an inspiring vista ★★★☆ of Willamette Valley farmland.

Amity's commitment to "public" tasting is more than fulfilled at the Oregon Wine Tasting Room on Highway 18, about seven miles to the east, where visitors can sample Amity products along with dozens of wines from "competing" wineries. Still, the winery is open to the public every afternoon, and sponsors several popular festivals throughout the year. Some visitors have found Amity's casual attitude toward visitors (combined with a very serious attitude toward winemaking and a most knowledgeable staff) to be refreshing; and the opportunity for a true vineyard picnic is enticing.

Tasting the wine ★★★★. Amity turns out several versions of its Pinot Noir, beginning with a Pinot Noir Nouveau that is released in mid-November after the traditional fermentation (by carbonic maceration, in an airtight tank). It's a simple wine, dry and balanced, with agreeable, cherrylike flavors, and goes well with autumnal fare.

The rest of the Pinot Noir is designated Willamette Valley, Estate, and Winemaker's Reserve, depending on quality and the amount of aging. The 1983 Winemaker's Reserve Pinot Noir was given Robert Parker's highest score in his rating of 1983 Oregon Pinot Noirs, and finished in second position in the "retaste" of the Oregon v. French Burgundies in New York in February 1986. Now available to the public, it is showing its evolution in the color, nose, and complexity. There is nothing more delightful than trying to pinpoint the subtle nuances of a fine wine. The warm strawberry, meaty qualities in this wine were at once identifiable but there were myriad others, like the bows on a kite's tail helping it to fly with more grace and style. The flavors are broadly placed and satisfying, the body a little light, and the texture a cushion. The 1986 Willamette Valley Pinot had a lively bouquet of strawberries and plums; in the mouth, it showed an earthy, barnyard character, with good balance and less than moderate tannins. We rate it among the top two or three 1986 Oregon Pinots.

Why would Amity—a small winery without huge reserves of cash—hold back a terrific wine from the 1983 vintage? The economics of wine selling means that consumers who don't have cellars almost never get to taste mature red wines. But by holding back a portion of the vintage, Amity makes it possible for even casual wine buyers to try a mature Pinot. "Our Reserve wines are our gift to consumers," Myron explained.

Amity's white wines include a blend called Solstice Blanc ("a perfect everyday wine" according to wine columnist Richard Paul Hinkle), a fine, dry White Riesling, a Gewurztraminer that David Lett calls the only Gewurz he's ever liked, and a Chardonnay. "We're moving toward the market," Redford explains of the 1988 Chardonnay; it's less austere, more forward, flavorful, and oaky than his previous Chardonnays.

Getting there. The town of Amity lies south of McMinnville on Hwy 99 W. At the northern end of town, turn east on Rice Ln. There's parking at the school

during festivals; a shuttle bus takes visitors up to the winery free of charge. At other times, private cars are allowed to make the climb to the hilltop winery.

Open daily from noon to 5, June through October. Weekends from noon to 5, November through May, except for the annual closing from the weekend before Christmas until the first weekend in February. $1 per person charge for tour groups over 10 people.

Amity also operates the Oregon Wine Tasting Room at the Lawrence Art Gallery on Hwy 18 in Bellevue; visitors can sample products of 35 Oregon wineries, including Amity wines, under the knowledgeable tutelage of Patrick McElligott. Open daily from 11:30 to 5:30. Phone (503) 843-3787.

Special events. Amity sponsors several popular festivals throughout the year. First there's "The Reds Are Coming," a county-wide celebration in May. Then comes the always-crowded Summer Solstice Festival on the third weekend in June. It's Oregon's oldest winery-sponsored wine festival, when Amity releases its new white wines (including, of course, the new Solstice Blanc); a souvenir wineglass is included with the modest admission charge.

Amity also sponsors a Pinot Noir festival in September, and participates in the Wine Country Thanksgiving in November.

A word from the winery. *"Come visit us! We offer some of the nation's best wines, and one of the Oregon wine country's best views. Our tasting room staff all work in the winery or vineyard and can make your visit a memorable one."*

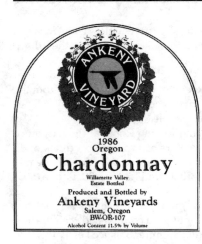

1986
Oregon
Chardonnay
Willamette Valley
Estate Bottled
Produced and Bottled by
Ankeny Vineyards
Salem, Oregon
BW-OR-107
Alcohol Content 11.5% by Volume

ANKENY VINEYARD
2565 Riverside Road S.
Salem, OR 97306
(503) 362-2508

Owners: Joe Olexa, Bob Harris, Jr.
Winemaker: Joe Olexa
Year established: 1985
Production capacity: 5,000 gallons
Vineyards: 15 acres
Touring region: Salem [p. 198]

A bit of background. The owners of this winery in the hills southwest of Salem are hardly newcomers to wine. Despite differing backgrounds, they have both been grape growers for a number of years.

Winemaker Joe Olexa, who holds a Ph.D. in political science and law from the University of Oregon, works at the Oregon Department of Justice. He's had his own vineyard since 1980. His partner, Bob Harris, is a third-generation farmer who views his vineyard, first planted in 1982, as a new challenge among the other crops on his 1,000-acre-plus farm.

Visiting the winery ★★☆. What a fine spot for a winery! If you take the freeway, Ankeny Vineyard is an easy and scenic 15-minute drive from Salem. You'll find yourself in an idyllic setting 300 feet above the Willamette River, with a panoramic view of the valley and the Coast Range. (Joe Olexa likes to suggest that the landscape reminds him of a Monet painting.) You might also see some of the waterfowl that glide into the adjacent Ankeny National Wildlife Refuge.

The winery stands on the pioneer homestead of Tom and Martha Cox, who were the first merchants in Salem. The original barn, built in 1848, stands next to the winery; the surrounding acreage has been farmed continuously since 1846. Cox Pioneer Cemetery, just up the hill, dates from 1849.

The tasting room, which takes up most of the ground floor of an old farmhouse, has picture windows overlooking the valley. Handsome decking outside provides additional seating.

Tasting the wines (NR). The current releases include White Table Wine, Pinot Noir Blanc, Riesling, Gewurztraminer, Chardonnay, Pinot Noir, and Cabernet Sauvignon.

Getting there. Take Exit 243 from I-5 and follow Ankeny Hill Rd 2 mi, then turn left on Buena Vista Rd. Go 1 mi and turn right onto Sidney Rd/ Riverside Rd 2 mi to the winery.

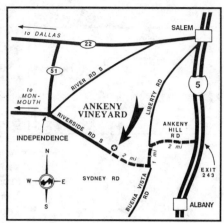

The wines can also be tasted at the Mission Mill Museum in Salem.

Open weekends from noon to 5, and by appointment. No fee is charged.

Special events. The year begins with a New Year's gathering. Then there's a summer festival, at the end of July, and a harvest festival, in mid-September.

A word from the winery. *"Our location and traditional methods of wine-making yield light, fruity, estate-bottled wines such as Pinot Gris and Gewurztraminer, made to be enjoyed young. Our primary focus, however, is the creation of full-bodied red wines like Pinot Noir and Cabernet Sauvignon, as well as Chardonnay, the queen of white wines. The expanded tasting room, with its large picture windows and decks front and rear, overlooks the slopes of the vineyard and the serene Ankeny National Wildlife Refuge, a view of the Willamette Valley which some have likened to a Monet painting. We invite you out to share our wines and our blending of old and new."*

ARTERBERRY WINERY

905-907 E. 10th Street
P.O. Box 772
McMinnville, OR 97128
(503) 472-1587, 244-0695

Owners:
Fred & Margaret Arterberry, Sr.
Winemaker: Fred Arterberry, Jr.
Year established: 1979
Production capacity: 15,000 gallons
Vineyards: None
Touring region: Yamhill [p. 195]

A bit of background. Arterberry is a family operation all the way, with Fred Sr. taking care of the business end of things, his wife, Margaret, in charge of the tasting room, brother Kelly doing the labels and promotion, and—at the heart of the winery—Fred Jr. making the wine. His education, at the University of California, Davis, trained him to be a winemaker, and he did in fact work for two other wineries in Oregon, but when Arterberry Winery started up, Fred Jr. chose to buy and ferment apples from nearby Sheridan to make a lightly sparkling, mildly alcoholic cider. The choice freed him from the rigorous schedule of an annual "everything-happens-in-one-frantic-month" grape crush, and allowed Arterberry to develop a reputation for an excellent product that was out of the ordinary. Arterberry has shifted almost exclusively into several grape varieties, and enlarged the winery itself so there's more room to riddle the bottles of sparkling wine.

Visiting the winery ★★. Arterberry is located in an industrial facility just down the block from The Eyrie Vineyards' winery. The newly enlarged tasting room in the front is spacious and cheerful. In back, the winery itself is kept on the cool side. We don't think we've ever seen Fred Jr. (bearded and bespectacled) without his purple ski cap, lumberman's shirt, and a vest—except when he put on a tuxedo in the spring of 1986 to receive the Commander's Award from the Oregon Knights of the Vine for his contribution to the Oregon wine industry: the first sparkling ciders in the state.

Tasting the wine ★★★☆. Cider is now made only for distribution in five-gallon cannisters to Portland-area pubs; Arterberry has become a true winery. Its principal varieties are Pinot Noir, Riesling (both still and sparkling), and Chardonnay.

The 1985 Pinot Noir, given a rating of 95 by Robert Parker, went to France for the Gault Millau "Olympics of the Wine World." We haven't tried it for about two years, but still remember its youthful vigor: fresh, elegant strawberries with a hint of earthiness to the nose, with lots of fruit and tannin in the mouth. The 1986 Pinot Noir, tasted recently, had a rich, sappy quality to the nose and smooth, satisfying flavors. There's also a Red Hills Blush made from Pinot Noir; it had delightful smells of strawberries and bananas.

Getting there. From Hwy 99 W. (as it enters McMinnville from the north) go south on Lafayette and turn right onto 10th. From E. Third (the principal restaurant and shopping street) go north on Johnson, which bears right into Lafayette; turn left into 10th. The Eyrie Vineyards' winery is in the same block.

Open Friday, Saturday, and Sunday from noon to 5. Closed in January. Tour groups are welcome by appointment, and are charged $1 per person; Arterberry will tap a keg of cider for large groups.

Special events. Arterberry sponsors an annual open house in late May, and a Friends of the Fish benefit in early September. The winery also participates in the Wine Country Thanksgiving sponsored by the Yamhill County wineries.

A word from the winery. "*Hospitality abounds at the family-owned and -operated Arterberry Winery. Large, cheerful tasting room with a friendly staff ready to answer questions. The family is available to chat with wine customers and taste champagnes or sparkling wines, let people see the tank room and barrel room, and observe the production of our Brut sparkling wines. We take our visitors very seriously; our pride is in our complete line of fine wines.*"

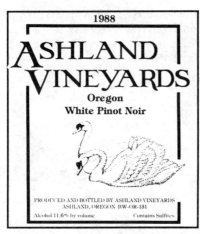

1988

ASHLAND VINEYARDS

Oregon
White Pinot Noir

PRODUCED AND BOTTLED BY ASHLAND VINEYARDS
ASHLAND, OREGON BW-OR-131

Alcohol 11.6% by volume   Contains Sulfites

ASHLAND VINEYARDS
2775 E. Main Street
Ashland, OR 97520
(503) 488-0088

Owners: Bill & Melba Knowles
Winemaker: John Eagle
Year established: 1988
Production capacity: 8,000 gallons
Vineyards: 8 acres
Touring region: Ashland [p. 205]

A bit of background. Both Bill Knowles and his son were international airline pilots who also farmed citrus in California. (Do you ever wonder where pilots get the energy for these extracurricular activities?) Now retired from Continental Airlines, but with the urge to grow crops as strong as ever, Bill Knowles has moved to southern Oregon and planted a small vineyard with Pinot Noir, Pinot Gris, Muller Thurgau, and Merlot. "Winemaking is a natural extension of the growing of the fruit," he tells us. "One would not be complete without the other."

Knowles studied and read extensively on the subject and knew enough to start by hiring a professional winemaker, John Eagle, formerly with Valley View Vineyards. His son Mark is the cellarmaster.

Visiting the winery ★★☆. Two spawning streams for steelhead and salmon, Emigrant Creek and Bear Creek, border the vineyards on the outskirts of Ashland. The winery itself, with stainless steel tanks, French oak barrels, and a fully equipped lab, is a handsome board-and-batten structure with a red gambrel roof. A cottage on the property is being converted to a tasting room in a turn-of-the-century motif with antique pine and oak furniture. Outside, picnic grounds with ponds and a mile-long jogging path around the vines are in the works.

Tasting the wines (NR). Ashland Vineyards released its first wines at its grand opening in the spring of 1989: a Muller Thurgau, a Chardonnay, and a White Pinot Noir. (Not tasted.)

Getting there. Take Exit 14 from I-5, go east on Hwy 66, then left 0.75 mi on E. Main St. From downtown Ashland, follow E. Main to the winery. [**Map:** Weisinger's]

Open Tuesday through Sunday, from 10 to 6. Groups are charged a $1 per person fee.

A word from the winery. *"On the banks of Bear Creek in the Valley of the Rogue River, we have planted our vineyard and built our winery. Each of our wines reflects the care and attention to detail that you will see as you tour the winery and taste the wines in our country cottage tasting room."*

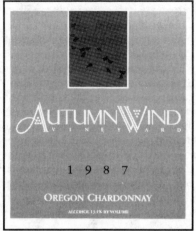

AUTUMN WIND VINEYARD

15225 North Valley Road
Gaston, OR 97119
P.O. Box 666
Newberg, OR 97132
(503) 538-6931

Owners & winemakers:
Tom & Wendy Kreutner
Year established: 1987
Production capacity: 10,000 gallons
Vineyards: 6 acres
Touring region: Yamhill [p. 195]

A bit of background. In the howling winds of Oregon's famous Columbus Day storm in 1962, a distraught cattleman near Newberg vowed that he would donate his property to God if he recovered from the loss of his herd. That land—92 acres on the hillside overlooking the Chehalem Valley—is now a nondenominational retreat center managed by George Fox College. Next door is a property purchased in 1982 by California refugees Tom and Wendy Kreutner, who rechristened it Autumn Wind.

The Kreutners' love of the outdoors (bicycling, backpacking) had prompted their escape from Los Angeles to the Northwest, and their careers as financial managers allowed them an upscale lifestyle. Their interest in wine (kindled by classes and tastings at Harris Wine Cellars in Portland) led them to look for wine-related business investments, a five-year search that ended with the purchase of the 52-acre farm and cherry orchard. Within a year, they had cleared away the cherries and planted the first 3.5 acres of grapes. (Next to Autumn Wind, by the way, is a vineyard owned by the brother-in-law of wine guru Robert Parker.) They're up to seven acres now and plan to add three or four more acres, mostly Pinot Noir, every year.

Wendy works as accounting manager for an industrial firm in Portland; Tom, a CPA, has just left his job as chief financial officer of the Oregon Bank. The Kreutners are serious, down-to-earth people, enthusiastic but perfectionists. "This is our retirement plan getting launched," they say.

Visiting the winery (NR). The Kreutners are enthusiastic about entertaining guests, and are keenly aware of the importance of tourism, but right now there's no tasting room other than the winery itself, so it might be a good idea to telephone ahead and make an appointment.

There's a picnic area at the top of the hill, shaded by tall oaks, where visitors to Autumn Wind will be able to enjoy barbecues. You can drive up, or walk from the parking area at the winery.

(One early sign of the caliber of visitors facilities we can expect here is the quality of Autumn Wind's very classy label.)

Tasting the wines ★★☆. The Kreutners will handle most of the winemaking duties themselves, with occasional advice from a consultant. First releases included Muller Thurgau and Pinot Noir Blanc under the Viento label (the name winemaking consultant Rich Cushman uses); they're wines designed to fit in with the countryside and picnics. But the Kreutners' intention is to make Autumn Wind into a winery known for Pinot Noir and Chardonnay. Eventually, they'll use their own grapes; for now, they're purchasing fruit from Courting Hill Vineyard near Banks.

The 1987 Pinot Noir we tasted before its release was superb, with a deep ruby color, a rich black cherry nose, good balance, and a long finish. A promising wine from a promising winery.

Getting there. From Newberg, follow Hwy 240 for 6 mi, go right on Ribbon Ridge Rd, then left on North Valley Rd. The winery is on the right.

Open weekends by appointment. Groups will be charged $1 per person, applicable to purchases.

Special events. The winery plans festivals in spring and at Thanksgiving.

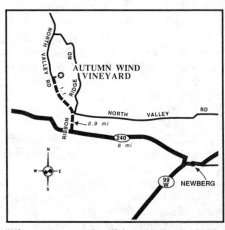

A word from the winery. *"The tasting room will be opening in 1989. Until then, we invite you to come and share the fun and excitement of a young winery in a more relaxed and casual way. With a little advance notice, arrangements can be made for parties, picnics, barbecues, vineyard and winery tours, and, of course, wine tasting. We are located only 7.5 miles west of Newberg and have a spectacular hillside view of the Chehalem Valley. We hope to meet you soon and have you enjoy our Pinot Noir, Chardonnay, and Muller Thurgau."*

BACHELOR COOLER

(S.C.S. Cellars)
514 Candy Lane
Roseburg, OR 97470
(503) 673-0419

Owners:
Sergio & Viviana Cervi-Skinner
Year established: 1985
Production capacity: 6,000 gallons
Vineyards: None
Touring: Umpqua Valley [p.202]

A bit of background. The recent success of coolers might lead us to think of them as quintessentially made-in-the-U.S.A. products, but drinks made with wine and soda water have been around a long time. Dr. Sergio Cervi-Skinner (an internist) and his wife, Viviana Cervi-Skinner (owner of an import business), remind us that in Argentina, at the afternoon meal, decanters of red wine are served along with club soda, lemon juice, and raw sugar cubes. Guests mix their own cooler, with as much of the strong wine flavors as individual tastes dictate.

The idea for an "Oregon" cooler similar to the South American one sprang from a quiet, sunny afternoon walk along a Costa Rican beach. Dr. Skinner and Viviana's father both felt that, given the popularity of coolers in North America, a cooler retaining the character of the wine would be popular. S.C.S. Cellars was founded in April 1985, and the first bottles were on the market by August.

Visiting the winery (NR). S.C.S. Cellars doesn't "produce" wine at all, but blends and bottles wine and other ingredients.

Not open to the public, although there's the possibility of a tasting room in the future.

Tasting the wine (NR). The first product, Bachelor Red Wine Cooler, consists of California-grown Pinot Noir purchased in bulk. Lemon extract, fresh water, corn sweetener, and preservatives are added; the mixture is then carbonated. The result is soft and fruity, not unlike a Sangria, but without the orange flavors that give Sangria its pleasant bitterness. It's sold in clear glass bottles, four to a pack, with a label depicting southern Oregon's highest peak, Mount Bachelor. Two other flavors are also made, promoted as coming from "the tropics of Oregon."

A word from the winery. *"S.C.S. Cellars invites you to experience our quality wine coolers produced in Oregon. We use only real juices and quality wines in the production of our three coolers: Fruity-Sangria, Kiwi-Pineapple, and Banana-Berry. You will find them to be a satisfying experience on a warm Oregon afternoon, or try our Fruity-Sangia served hot with spices and a cinnamon stick on a cold, rainy day. Either way, you will enjoy the light, fruity tastes of Bachelor Cooler."*

BETHEL HEIGHTS VINEYARD

OREGON PINOT NOIR

1986 WILLAMETTE VALLEY

GROWN, PRODUCED AND BOTTLED BY
BETHEL HEIGHTS VINEYARD, INC., SALEM, OREGON BW-OR-98
ALCOHOL 12.5% BY VOLUME. CONTAINS SULFITES.

BETHEL HEIGHTS VINEYARD

6060 Bethel Heights Road N.W.
Salem, OR 97304
(503) 581-2262

Owners: Pat Dudley & Ted Casteel,
Marilyn Webb & Terry Casteel
Winemaker: Terry Casteel
Year established: 1984
Production capacity: 15,000 gallons
Vineyards: 51 acres
Touring region: Salem [p. 198]

A bit of background. Ted and Terry Casteel, twin brothers, came to the winemaking business after a couple of detours. Ted and his wife, Pat Dudley, were graduate students in the south of France when they discovered the joys of wine. Terry and his wife, Marilyn Webb, were practicing psychologists in Seattle when they started drinking inexpensive Bordeaux. Reunited by their newfound interest in wine, the two families bought a 75-acre property northwest of Salem and, for the first few years, grew grapes for sale to others. The Eola Hills property on which the vineyards are planted was once intended to be part of a winery project called Stonewood. Even today, with the Bethel Heights winery underway, Gewurztraminer grapes from the vineyard go to Bonny Doon in California, and Pinot Noir to Adelsheim.

The entire Casteel clan is involved in the operation of Bethel Heights. Ted, considered an authority on viticulture, is responsible for the vineyard. Terry, after apprenticing at Sokol Blosser and winning several gold medals for amateur winemaking at the Oregon State Fair, handles enology for Bethel Heights. Marilyn served a term as chairman of the Oregon Wine Advisory Board and is the winery's business and sales manager; Pat serves as president of the winery and handles public relations.

Visiting the winery ★★★☆. It's a functional, red-roofed building at the entrance to the property, with a zigzag ramp that leads to the second-level tasting room; its windows overlook the winery floor inside and the 50 acres of vineyards outside.

Walking through the vineyards gives you the most interesting look at Bethel Heights. There's more Pinot Noir than anything else on these sloping, clay-loam hillsides, which eons ago formed part of a volcano. The gravel road leads you past high-trellised, double-curtain vines bearing Pinot and Chardonnay, past Ted and Pat's home, and through a stand of Little Red Ridinghood woods to Terry and Marilyn's house, where you're greeted not by Grandmother but by a grand vista of the Eola Hills. Take even a brief walk along this path in the company of Marilyn Webb; she's so articulate and enthusiastic about viticulture (as is her Washington state counterpart, Joan Wolverton at Salishan Vineyards) that you'll want to rush home and get busy in your own garden.

Tasting the wine ★★★. Among the whites, there's an off-dry Chenin Blanc, a Gewurztraminer with some residual sweetness, and a Chardonnay with a delicate, complex nose.

Bethel Heights has become one of Oregon's largest producers of Pinot Noir, shipping 2,400 cases in 1987. The vineyard includes two of the major Pinot clones, Pommard and Wadenswil, and Casteel blends the two to achieve a combination of delicacy and structure. The 1986 Pinot drew enthusiastic reviews from *The Wine Spectator* and *The Northwest Palate*. We've been sampling this wine at six-month intervals in blind tastings and find it steadily improving. A year ago, it had a reticent quality, hiding its fruit behind malolactic fermentation smells. Six months later, it was balanced but undistinguished. Most recently, it had begun to exhibit a rich, ripe berry bouquet and delicate cherry flavors, although it still needs time to develop core and body.

The Chardonnay is also a blend of two clones, called Wente and 108, one of which contributes tropical fruit aromas, the other lemon-vanilla. The Riesling is grown in the warmest pockets of the vineyard, and has an assertive ripe apricot bouquet that we found complex and satisfying.

Getting there. From Salem, cross the Willamette River on the Marion Street bridge; take the first right onto Wallace Rd and proceed north for 7 mi to the Lincoln Store. Turn left onto Zena Rd and go 4.3 mi to Bethel Heights Rd. Turn right and proceed 0.25 mi to the third driveway on the right.

Open Tuesday through Sunday from 11 to 5, March through September; closed New Year's Day, Christmas Day, and Thanksgiving Day, and all of January and February. Tour groups over five people are charged $1 each.

Special events. On Memorial Day weekend, Bethel Heights is one of the wineries on the Polk County Tastevin Tour.

A word from the winery. "*Bethel Heights wines offer a range of styles, with something sure to please every palate. Although we specialize in Pinot Noir and Chardonnay, we also make three popular off-dry wines in smaller quantities: Chenin Blanc, Riesling, and Gewurztraminer. The vineyard is situated in the Eola Hills, a rapidly developing viticultural area. The surrounding countryside has some of the oldest landmarks of Oregon's pioneer history, including the old*

Bethel Church and Bethel Cemetery. The heights above Bethel, from which our winery takes its name, offer one of the most spectacular vineyard views in the Willamette Valley. Visitors are invited to bring along a picnic and enjoy a glass of wine with the view."

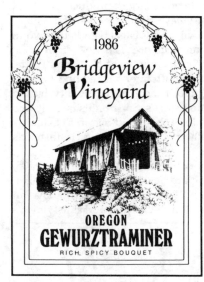

BRIDGEVIEW VINEYARDS

4210 Holland Loop Road
P.O. Box 609
Cave Junction, OR 97523
(503) 592-4688

Owners: Robert & Lelo Kerivan, Ernie Brodie
Winemaker: Laurent Montalieu
Year established: 1986
Production capacity: 100,000 gallons
Vineyards: 74 acres
Touring: Illinois Valley [p. 204]

A bit of background. Lelo Kerivan came to the United States from Germany in 1976 and instantly fell in love with Oregon's topography and climate, which reminded her of her Rhine River homeland. In 1980 she started planting a vineyard, and her enthusiasm prompted her husband, Robert, and a longtime friend, Ernie Brodie, to establish Bridgeview Vineyards.

Bridgeview's first winemaker, Dieter Hemberger, returned to work at his family's winery in Germany; he's been replaced by Laurent Montalieu, a German-born, French-educated enologist.

Visiting the winery ★★☆. You're only 10 miles from the California border here, at an elevation of 1,200 feet. The vineyards cover 74 acres of tightly spaced grapes (four feet apart in six-foot rows, triple the usual American planting). The winery building is enormous: 14,000 square feet, 100,000 gallons' worth of stainless steel tanks, a Seitz bottling line that can handle 1,000 cases a day. Production (including wines custom-crushed for Foris) has mounted from 5,000 cases in 1986 to a projected 40,000 cases in 1988.

Outside, pleasant meadows lead to mountain lakes where you can fish for trout, or just watch the swans and Canada geese glide past the snowcapped peaks.

Tasting the wines (NR). Our experience with these wines has been limited to quick tastings at large gatherings, so we'll limit ourselves to listing what's available: Pinot Noir, Chardonnay, Gewurztraminer (a silver medal at the Oregon State Fair in 1986), Muller Thurgau, and a snappy wine called Inspiration (available in red, white, and blush). Does it mean anything that Club Med buys Bridgeview wines for its vacation resorts in the Dominican Republic? How did they even find out?

Getting there. From Cave Junction, take Hwy 46 for 1.2 mi toward the Oregon Caves, turn right and go 2 mi on Holland Loop Rd. [**Map:** Siskiyou Vineyards]

Bridgeview also operates the rustic Oregon Wine Barrel tasting room and deli on Hwy 199 just north of Kerby.

Open by appointment only. Hours at the Oregon Wine Barrel tasting room are from noon to 5, May through September.

A word from the winery. *"Bridgeview Vineyards is nestled within a very special valley of the southern Oregon coastal mountains. Our vineyards are planted in the European way, with very close spacing so each plant provides fewer, but higher quality, grapes. Our winery is surrounded by 74 acres of vineyards. We produce Pinot Noir, Chardonnay, Riesling, Gewurztraminer, Muller Thurgau, and Pinot Gris. Our tasting room on Hwy 199 is open from May through September from 12 to 5, including the deli in our Oregon Wine Barrel."*

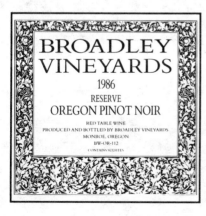

BROADLEY VINEYARDS
265 S. Fifth Street
Monroe, OR 97456

P.O. Box 10233
Eugene, OR 97440
(503) 847-5934

Owners: Broadley family
Winemaker: Craig Broadley
Year established: 1986
Production capacity: 7,000 gallons
Vineyards: 15 acres
Touring: South Willamette [p.200]

A bit of background. A dream from the 1960s: two young people (Craig and Claudia Broadley) working at the City Lights bookstore in San Francisco talk about having a little winery up in Oregon somewhere. They give up the California lifestyle and move to Eugene, take over a mail-order book distributorship, and buy a piece of land. Before they can plant any grapes, they have to build a road, dig a well, borrow money from his folks. "We didn't know it was going to be this much work," says Craig Broadley.

Over an eight-year period, the Broadleys planted 10 acres of Pinot Noir and five of Chardonnay.

Visiting the winery ★★. The familiar story comes to a happy conclusion with the opening of the Broadley Vineyards winery in a former car dealership on the highway in Monroe. The brick building has been refurbished as a tasting room; picnic tables in back overlook the Long Tom River. A deli will be added next season.

Tasting the wines ★★. Broadley's stated intention is to make Burgundian Pinot Noir and Chablis-style Chardonnay. The "regular" Pinot Noir we sampled tasted was as light and evanescent as a Nouveau: fresh, fruity, and forgettable. The intensely colored 1986 Reserve bottling, tasted in midsummer, started out with a rich, berry and cherry nose (again, like a Nouveau) but its tannin threatened to overwhelm the fruit flavors. (Others in our group admired this "rich and firm" character.) We found the 1986 Chardonnay over-oaked and unbalanced in the mouth, but one member of our tasting panel thought the oak and vanilla in the nose was reminiscent of "old Chablis." So maybe Craig Broadley's on to something after all.

Getting there. On Hwy 99W in Monroe. [**Map:** Alpine Vineyards]

Open weekends from 11 to 5. Closed January. Tour groups are welcome; no fee.

A word from the winery. *"Broadley Vineyards, on Highway 99 W in Monroe, specializing in Burgundian-style Pinot Noir and Chablis-style Chardonnays, is located in a 60-year-old brick building with the Long Tom River flowing along beside the parking and picnicking facilities. Our vineyards are established on the eastern slopes of the hills overlooking the town of Monroe. For tours, visits during off-hours, or to be on our mailing list, write or phone the winery."*

CALLAHAN RIDGE

Oregon Chardonnay 1987

DOERNER RANCH

Produced & Bottled by
Callahan Ridge Winery, Roseburg, Oregon (BW-OR-124)
Alcohol Content 13% by Volume

CALLAHAN RIDGE

340 Busenbark Lane
Roseburg, OR 97470
(503) 673-7901

Owners: Frank Guido,
    Mary Sykes-Guido,
    Richard Mansfield
Winemaker: Richard Mansfield
Year established: 1987
Production capacity: 13,000 gallons
Vineyards: None
Touring: Umpqua Valley [p. 202]

A bit of background. Musical wineries. Roseburg orchardist Frank Guido started out making fruit and berry wines, but his early efforts, under the names of DiMartini Wine Company and Guido Ranch, went sour. He found himself with an inventory of unsalable wine and a lot of expensive winemaking equipment, and was contemplating getting out of the wine business altogether when he received a call from Ray Higgins, a grape grower in the Willamette Valley: could Guido process his grapes? Higgins brought along Richard Mansfield, a young native of Newport, Oregon, who was studying for an advanced degree at the German Wine Institute in Geisenheim. Under the name of Garden Valley Winery, the venture lasted three or four years.

Since our last edition, Higgins has taken control of Garden Valley and moved the winery to Sweet Home, Mansfield has completed his degree in Germany, and Guido has started over again under the name Callahan Ridge. The cheerful Mansfield, this time with an equity interest in the operation, is back as winemaker, with complete control over management, production, and marketing.

Visiting the winery ★☆. The winery is nestled into a grove of trees a short drive east and south of Roseburg. The principal building—a dark, weather-beaten barn with hand-hewn floor joists—was built a century ago. Nearby stands a more modern prune dryer, a metal building that currently houses most of the winemaking equipment, including newly acquired French oak barrels.

An adjacent four-acre vineyard is planted with Cabernet Sauvignon and Chardonnay.

Tasting the wine ★☆. The standard repertory of Oregon wineries: Riesling, Chardonnay, Gewurztraminer, Pinot Noir (not yet released). There's also some locally grown White Zinfandel. At this point, the wines don't measure up to Mansfield's enthusiasm. The 1987 White Riesling was cloyingly sweet, low in acid; the 1987 Select Harvest Gewurztraminer was flat and bitter. The best of the group we tasted was the 1987 Chardonnay, not over-oaked, but without much character.

Getting there. Take Exit 125 from I-5 and go 2 mi west on Garden Valley Blvd. Turn left on Melrose and proceed 1.3 mi, turn right on Busenbark. [**Map:** HillCrest]

Open daily, 11:30 to 5:30, April through October. Groups should make arrangements with Richard Mansfield.

Special events. A jazz festival in the adjacent cherry orchard is planned for July.

A word from the winery. *"Increasingly the fan of Oregon wines is discovering that various subregions within Oregon exist. Each region puts its own distinctive trademark on the wines from that region. At Callahan Ridge we use only grapes from the Umpqua Valley—the cradle of the Oregon wine industry. Our wines are rich in aroma and full of flavor. I would like to invite you to come by and taste the wines we make—wines produced in the classic Oregon style."*

CAMERON WINERY
8200 Worden Hill Road
P.O. Box 27
Dundee, OR 97115
(502) 538-0336

Owners: John Paul, Teri Wadsworth,
    Eugenia Waterhouse,
    Bill & Julia Wayne,
    Marc Dochez, Shawna Archibald
Winemaker: John Paul
Year established: 1984
Production capacity: 9,000 gallons
Vineyards: 17 acres
Touring region: Yamhill [p. 195]

A bit of background. John Paul had a Ph.D. in marine microbiology when he succumbed to the romance of wine. In 1978 he gave up a research position in California and headed north to Oregon, where Bob McRitchie (another Ph.D. scientist) was sympathetic to his educational background and gave him a job . . . scrubbing Sokol Blosser's fermentation tanks. "It was some of the best training I ever got," he recalls.

Back in California, John Paul worked at Konocti and Carneros Creek. He and his wife, Teri Wadsworth (a chemist who has worked for Robert Mondavi and The Christian Brothers), also traveled to Burgundy, where they realized that great wines don't necessarily need fancy equipment, and to New Zealand, where they were impressed by the emphasis put on yeast cultures.

Returning to Oregon, John and Teri teamed up with vineyard growers

Bill and Julia Wayne, and builder Marc Dochez and his partner, Shawna Archibald (of Archibald Vineyards), to start a winery of their own, named for the Scottish Cameron clan.

Visiting the winery (NR). When Cameron Winery's owners wanted to move out of the manufacturing neighborhood where they began (across from Eyrie and Arterberry), they had to fight an ironic interpretation of the county's zoning: they had to show that the use of their semi-rural property on the outskirts of Dundee would be primarily agricultural, not industrial. Farms and vineyards, the neighbors seemed to be saying, were picturesque and desirable; winemaking would pollute the air, poison the water, and lower property values.

It took a couple of years, but Cameron convinced the recalcitrant neighbors that it wasn't an industrial giant like Gallo, and that its winery would fit in with the scale of its surroundings. The new winery sits back from Worden Hill Road like a neat, unassuming farmhouse, complete with front porch and parlor. Nobody lives here, though. Marc Dochez built the winery from scratch, and had the grace to make it look like a home instead of an impersonal processing facility. So the "parlor" is a tasting room for visitors, the "front bedroom" is John Paul's office, the working winery covers most of the ground level (out of sight), and the "basement" is the barrel cellar.

John and Teri's young daughter, Tawny, is Cameron's official assistant winemaker; her tiny work boots are neatly lined up at the top of the stairs, next to her trike, and it's her voice you hear on the answering machine.

Tasting the wines ★★★☆. What difference, you might ask, does it make if a winemaker ferments his must with this yeast or that? Who cares? Well, if you pay attention, if you set up an experiment where yeast is the only difference, then the choice of yeast makes all the difference; the only issue then is whether the difference is perceptible and significant.

John Paul thinks the yeast question is important, and he demonstrated why to one of our recent wine tours. In the crowded underground level of the winery, he drew barrel samples of two lots of 1988 Chardonnay, identical except for the yeasts used. The first, made with Montrachet yeast, had the classic, bready aroma of Chardonnay but was still austere in the mouth. The second, made with a yeast from Australia called 10A81, had less aroma but tasted softer, with more creamy viscosity in the mouth. He intended to blend the two lots to get the best characteristics of both.

Also tasted at the winery, the 1987 Chardonnay had a figgy bouquet and melon flavors. In a subsequent blind tasting, Cameron's 1987 Reserve Chardonnay showed particularly pleasant mouth feel (that Australian yeast!) and deep flavors.

Tasted at the winery early in 1989, the 1986 Pinot Noir Reserve had a whiff of cherries and strawberries, pepper and plums, and was still quite tannic, with austere flavors reminiscent of pie cherries.

Getting there. From Hwy 99 W in Dundee, turn up Ninth St., go 0.5 mi to the winery. [**Map**: Knudsen Erath]

Open by appointment only. $1.50-per-person charge for group tours.

Special events. The two annual events sponsored by the Yamhill County Wineries Association on May Day weekend and Thanksgiving weekend.

A word from the winery. " `Good things come from small packages.' How many times did I hear that as a child? And yet it is often true! Cameron is built on that premise because I have found that being small allows attention to many details. The result, I hope, will be consistently high-quality wines to choose from. Small production also necessarily means limited availability. Many releases, particularly the Reserve wines, are gone within a few weeks or months of their release. So if there is a particular wine that you seek from Cameron, we ask that you make your desire known at the time it is released!"*

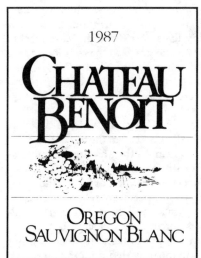

CHATEAU BENOIT

6580 N.E. Mineral Springs Road
Carlton, OR 97111
(503) 864-2991 and 864-3666

Owners: Fred & Mary Benoit,
   Bill Wittenberg
Winemaker: Gerard Rottiers
Year established: 1979
Production capacity: 70,000 gallons
Vineyards: 22 acres
Touring region: Yamhill [p. 195]

A bit of background. Fred Benoit, by his own description, is a physician who doesn't like golf. "So I took up winemaking," he explains. First as a hobby, then as a commercial venture. He and Mary planted a vineyard near Eugene (recently sold) with Pinot Noir and Chardonnay, then found a 60-acre parcel near McMinnville where Chateau Benoit (Ben-WAH) stands today. The Benoits hired a full-time winemaker, planted more grapes, built the beginnings of a huge winery, and moved both home and professional practice to the new site.

The current winemaker, a Frenchman named Gerard Rottiers, comes from Chablis, where he had his own winery, Domaine Rottiers.

Visiting the winery ★★★. From Mineral Springs Road, visitors can see the stark concrete winery atop a distant rise. A long, narrow road leads straight through a Riesling and Muller Thurgau vineyard to the hilltop. The crowded winery itself is the beginning of what will eventually be a Ushaped chateau; the Benoits hope to break ground for an expanded facility and a new tasting room within the coming year. In the meantime, wines are poured at a refectory table beside the barrels and stainless steel tanks.

There's a very pleasant arbor outside, along with eight picnic tables overlooking a magnificent panorama ★★★ of Yamhill County farmland.

Tasting the wines ★★. We're in real trouble here. The Benoits are unfailingly polite and cheerful, Gerard Rottiers an amusing and outgoing fellow; the wines they sent us to sample, however, were not up to snuff.

Best was the 1987 Sauvignon Blanc, which has a distinct nose of juniper, good fruit flavors, and a bitter finish that makes the wine improve with food. A nonvintage blend called Rainbow Gold has the honeyed nose of a Chenin Blanc and tastes off-dry, though it's not particularly lively.

Two other whites deserve a miss. The 1987 Muller Thurgau smelled skunky and rubbery; in the mouth, its slight spritz wasn't backed up with enough acid to hold the sugar. The 1987 Chardonnay had the "sour mash" nose we find typical of Oregon Chardonnay, overlaid with smells of burnt toast and a hint of oxidation; the flavors were short and unpleasant.

It doesn't get better with the reds. The 1987 Merlot was austere; it had good color and a restrained, oaky nose, but it totally lacked flavor. The 1987 Pinot Noir was showing bubbles in the glass and some peanutty-smelling oxidation; we hope it was just a bad bottle.

All this, sad to say, from a winery whose Oregon Brut sparkling wine was awarded the Best of Show ribbon at Tacoma's wine festival in 1985, whose 1983 sparkling Chardonnay took a gold medal there last year, and whose Sauvignon Blanc has long been one of our favorites. Let's hope winemaker Rottiers settles down quickly. (See the accompanying comment, "Fallible Gospel," for Mary Benoit's position on these critiques.)

Getting there. From Hwy 99 W, 4 mi northeast of McMinnville, turn north onto Mineral Springs Rd; the winery drive is on the right, 1.5 mi along.

Open weekends from noon to 5; weekdays from 11 to 5. There is a $1 per person tasting fee, refundable with wine purchase, for groups of 15 or more.

Special events. The most enjoyable of Chateau Benoit's festivals is their Bastille Day

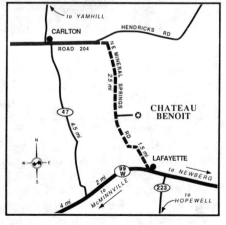

celebration, held on the weekend closest to July 14, the French national holiday. Chateau Benoit also participates in the Wine Country Thanksgiving organized by the Yamhill County wineries.

A word from the winery. *"From our scenic hillside in Yamhill County, picnickers enjoy the panorama and often stay to watch the sun set over the Coast Range mountains.*

"Though we have built our reputation on fragrant Sauvignon Blancs and hand-done sparkling wines, we and Gerard, our Burgundian winemaker, are now getting serious about full-bodied Pinot Noirs. We invite you to visit and enjoy!"

FALLIBLE GOSPEL

A comment from Mary Benoit, co-owner of Chateau Benoit in Yamhill County:

"Thank you for giving us a chance to correct and criticize. My criticism is meant to be constructive; you are doing a good job. Just be a little more gentle!

"I guess my main complaint [with the first edition of Northwest Wine Country*] is with the rating system. I feel that it is unfair, not just to us, but to many wineries. You and I know that this is your opinion and that you are not infallible, but to the consumer, you are the Gospel According to John! Quite a responsibility!"*

CLEAR CREEK DISTILLERY
1430 N.W. 23rd
Portland, OR 97210
(503) 248-9470

Owner & distiller:
  Stephen R. McCarthy
Year established: 1985
Production capacity:
  50,000 gal. mash, 2,000 gal. brandy
Vineyards: None
Touring region: Portland [p. 194]

A bit of background . Steve McCarthy, a Portland attorney, was running a company that manufactured equipment for duck and deer hunting ("Michael's of Oregon") when he realized that his family's orchards in the Hood River Valley had a lot of fruit going to waste. Having lived in Europe, he knew the attraction of clear fruit brandies (called *eau de vie* in French) such as Kirsch from cherries in Switzerland and Germany, Slivovitz from plums in Hungary, Grappa from grape pressings in Italy, Calvados from apples in Normandy, Poire from pears and Framboise from raspberries in Alsace. "They will be a major factor in the hospitality industry and the wine industry within a decade," McCarthy predicts. And he'll be ready. His market is building gradually, through word of mouth, with sales almost exclusively through Oregon State Liquor stores and in top Portland hotels and restaurants.

For the moment, the only domestic competition is a fruit distillery in California. (Whidbeys Loganberry Liqueur isn't a brandy but a cordial.) It's a very specific niche, but McCarthy is optimistic. By the turn of the century, he says, "we will have our own world class brandy and will be exporting all over the globe."

Visiting the winery ★★☆. The pears are picked as if for the "fresh" market, and are stored at the distillery until they're perfectly ripe. Then they're crushed and given a long, cool fermentation (as long as a month) in small tanks. Because the fruit contains only 13 to 14 percent sugar (compared with 20 to 24 percent for ripe grapes), the resulting pear mash has only 4 degrees of alcohol. (Apples start at 16 percent sugar and come out at 8 degrees of alcohol; it's like alcoholic applesauce.)

Then it's time for distillation. One batch, 60 gallons of the unfiltered, unstrained pear wine, goes into the pot still; an hour and a quarter later, one five-gallon carboy of pear brandy comes out. The distilling itself takes considerable skill; every run through the still is different. The trick is to get the right alcohol levels, retaining the fragrance of fresh fruit, and to discard the right amount of "heads" and "tails," the bitter and volatile products from the beginning and end of the run, which together make up a third of the distillate. It takes McCarthy two weeks to distill 10 tons of pears.

Clear Creek Distillery currently uses two pot stills, vessels that look like small wine tanks with tall copper chimneys. A low table holds the lab gear McCarthy uses to take measurements throughout each run of the still. The finished brandy is decanted into bottles in an adjacent kitchen. An Oriental rug covers the floor of the glass-walled office where visitors are received.

Tasting the wines ★★★★. Right now, the pear brandy (*eau de vie de poire William*) is the only product on the market, but there's a stash of over 1,500 gallons of apple brandy maturing in barrels. Only Bartlett pears are used for the Poire William, only Red or Golden Delicious apples for the Calvados. But the possibilities are limitless. Almost any fruit can be distilled, and Europeans have had great success with various berries, apricot, quince, even holly. McCarthy has experimented with plum brandy, cherries, a cognac-style brandy made from Chardonnay and Muscat grapes, and a rough brandy called marc, made from grape skins and seeds.

The fruit is more variable than you might think, pears especially. The 1987 season, for example, was too hot for pears but excellent for apples. The ideal growing season for the pears requires cold nights in August to concentrate the flavors. And it still takes 40 pounds of pears to produce a single bottle!

What a glorious spirit this is! The very essence of pear leaps out of the snifter, the result of careful fermentation. This is a totally dry, perfectly clear brandy; its greatest appeal for us is the sublime nose, as pure an expression of the fruit as we've ever found in the great *eaux de vie* of Alsace. It bears no relation at all to sugary "fruit brandies," such as peach or apricot brandy, or to the sweet berry cordials that consist of vodka with fruit flavorings. "This has to be the greatest way to sell fruit," McCarthy says.

Getting there. From the west end of the Fremont Bridge (I-405), take the St. Helens exit, go right on N.W. 23rd St and proceed four blocks to the winery. [**Map:** Adams]

Open weekdays during normal business hours. Visitors should call ahead. Saturdays by appointment.

A word from the winery. "*One of only two true eau de vie distilleries in North America, Clear Creek Distillery uses totally authentic European pot stills and techniques and the best fruit from family-owned orchards to produce an* eau de vie de Poire William *that has been very well received. An apple brandy, barrel-aged and resembling a Calvados, is being aged, but it is not ready for release yet.*"

COOPER MOUNTAIN
V I N E Y A R D S
1987 OREGON CHARDONNAY
WILLAMETTE VALLEY
ESTATE BOTTLED
Alcohol 12.9% by Volume

COOPER MOUNTAIN VINEYARDS

Grabhorn Road
Route 3, Box 1036
Beaverton, OR 97007
(503) 649-0027

Owners: Robert & Corrine Gross
Winemaking consultant:
  Rich Cushman
Year established: 1987
Production capacity: 3,500 gallons
Vineyards: 51 acres
Touring region: Tualatin Valley [p.192]

A bit of background. Bob Gross, a psychiatrist, and his wife Corrine, a social worker, have been amateur winemakers since 1973. They were living in Seattle and were part of a wine tasting group that included psychiatrist Hans Doerr, who later founded French Creek Cellars in Woodinville. When the Grosses moved to Oregon in 1978, they started growing grapes as well.

Visiting the winery ★★☆. Cooper Mountain itself is a volcanic formation overlooking the Tualatin Valley. Bob and Corrine Gross own the historic Cooper Estate, which dates back to 1854. The property encompasses 125 acres, with about 50 acres now under vine: Chardonnay, Pinot Noir, and Pinot Gris. (The balance of the land is forested or leased out.) The vineyard produces over 100 tons of grapes, making Cooper Mountain one of the largest independent growers in the state.

The decision to start a small winery, currently housed in the garage of the Grosses' home, stems from the desire to turn some of that fruit into a personal product. Near-term plans call for a new winery and tasting room.

Tasting the wines (NR). Two estate-bottled wines from the 1987 vintage have been released: a Chardonnay and a Pinot Noir. (Not tasted.)

Getting there. From Beaverton, take Hwy 10 (the Beaverton-Hillsdale Hwy) to Farmington. Turn left on Grabhorn Rd; go 1.1 mi to the winery.

From the Washington Square shopping center, follow Scholls Ferry Rd westbound past Ponzi Vineyards; turn right on Till Flat Rd, right again on Grabhorn Rd to the winery. [**Map:** Ponzi]

Open by appointment only. Jenkins Estate Park, a turn-of-the-century mansion surrounded by gardens and an arboretum, is at the foot of Grabhorn Rd; it's a lovely spot for a picnic.

A word from the winery. *"Cooper Mountain winery and vineyards are located on the southwest flank of an extinct volcano overlooking the Tualatin River. The original Cooper homestead stands near the winery site and was first settled in 1865. The vineyard, planted in 1978, supplies Pinot Noir, Chardonnay, and Pinot Gris grapes to wineries throughout the Northwest, New York, and Canada. Estate production will be limited to 2,000 cases of premium Pinot Noir and Chardonnay wines. Come enjoy wine from a well-established Oregon vineyard."*

CROCHAD

P.O. Box 280
Dundee, OR 97115
(503) 538-8520

Owners: Brian Croser &
   Robert Chadderdon
Winemaker: Rollin Soles
Year established: 1988
Production capacity: Unknown
Vineyards: None
Touring region: Yamhill [p. 195]

A bit of background. Brian Croser is one of Australia's most prominent winemakers, one of its finest talents with sparkling wines and Chardonnay. He studied at the University of California at Davis, then returned Down Under and made a name for himself as an innovative teacher and researcher. He founded a prosperous winery consulting business, and a few years ago he started a winery of his own, Petaluma (named for the town in California), on the outskirts of Adelaide; it ranks among the top half dozen in Australia.

For his first venture in the United States, Croser teamed up with New Jersey wine importer Robert Chadderdon to create a winery devoted to the production of sparkling wine. (Crochad comes from both men's names, but will not be the name of the label under which the wine is eventually marketed.) Not all of Oregon's Pinot Noir and Chardonnay grapes ripen completely every year, and these slightly green grapes (with their high acid levels) are well suited to champagne-style wines. So far, production of sparklers in Oregon has been limited to modest production at Chateau Benoit and Laurel Ridge; Whittlesey-Mark in Seattle also uses Oregon grapes for champagne. Now, rumor has it, Croser might release something like 10,000 cases of sparkling wine within the next year. If he does, and if it's as good as he obviously thinks, Oregon champagne could be as important a development in the 1990s as Oregon Pinot Noir was in the mid-1980s.

Visiting the winery (NR). Crochad has taken over a large complex on Dundee's main street (where the Filbert Farm used to be) and filled two buildings with presses, tanks, vats, and barrels. Rollin Soles, a former winemaker at Worden's and a consultant in Australia, manages the site.

Croser hasn't made up his mind yet what style of wine to release, what name to use on the label, or made any marketing plans that he would talk about. But he does realize that people have to know about his wines in order to buy them. He's personally very aware of the benefits of good public relations; the management at Petaluma and its associated Bridgewater Mill restaurant were very hospitable to us when we visited Australia in 1988. Unfortunately, though Croser personally assured us we would get cooperation from the staff at Crochad, we've had only one response to numerous requests for information (see below).

Tasting the wines (NR) . The 1985 vintage will be the first released, whenever that is. No decision has been made about which varieties to use. But Rollin Soles told a visitor, "We shouldn't rely on tradition to show us the way."

Getting there. The winery is on Hwy 99 W. in downtown Dundee. Not open to the public. [**Map**: Sokol Blosser]

A word from the winery (dated July, 1988). *"Please do not include Crochad in your publication. Crochad has no wine available, no label, and no name. There are no plans to release any wine until 1990. Thank you for your consideration and omission. Truly yours, Rollin Soles."* [Sorry to disappoint you; we can't ignore a bonded winery as big as Crochad. And 1990 is just around the corner.]

DOMAINE DROUHIN OREGON

P.O. Box 700
Dundee, OR 97115
(503) 538-7485

Owner: Robert Drouhin family
Winemaker: Veronique Drouhin
General manager: William Hatcher
Year established: 1988
Production capacity: 7,500 gallons
Vineyards: 8 acres
Touring region: Yamhill [p. 195]

A bit of background. A year and a half ago, a tall, white-haired, blue-eyed Frenchman, dapper in his light tan suit and speaking perfect English, stood in the bright September sunshine and made a startling announcement: he was buying about 100 acres of land in Yamhill County to start a vineyard. It's hard to overstate the impact of this modest real estate transaction. The buyer, Robert Drouhin, is the leading wine shipper in Burgundy, the man who staged his own retasting after an Oregon Pinot Noir (from The Eyrie Vineyards) bested some of the best French wines in Paris in 1979. Drouhin came to Oregon to meet Eyrie's owner and winemaker, David Lett, a year later, and has respected Oregon's potential as a winegrowing region ever since. He visited Oregon several times, and sent his daughter Veronique to live and work with Oregon winemaking families. He gave the keynote address at the first International Pinot Noir Celebration in McMinnville in 1987. But buying land? Some of the Champagne houses had bought land in California, there were some joint-venture operations between Bordeaux estates and famous producers in the Napa Valley, but no one from Burgundy had ever bought land in Oregon.

Suddenly a prime parcel of land suitable for planting a vineyard became available. As it happened, Lett was vacationing in Burgundy as Drouhin's house guest when he heard the news. Drouhin and his family quickly agreed to the purchase. Back in the U.S., winemaker David Adelsheim acted as Drouhin's agent and put the deal together. Within weeks, Robert Drouhin was in Oregon to sign the papers.

The press conference was held at Bethel Heights Vineyard near Salem, one of the places Veronique had worked. Oregon's governor, Neil Goldschmidt, a connoisseur of fine wines and an enthusiastic supporter of his state's wine industry, acted as master of ceremonies.

It began as passion, Drouhin told the cluster of reporters. And the passion (for Oregon) was followed by reason (the logic of expanding into new areas). We do not come as competitors, Drouhin said. He can experiment in the vineyard, with new clones, with spacing. He intends to make Domaine Drouhin Oregon a model, something for the long term, the next generation.

To demonstrate his commitment to the project, he named his daughter Veronique, a recent graduate of the enology school in Dijon, as Domaine Drouhin's winemaker.

A couple of months later, an adjacent parcel of 40 acres became available and was added to DDO's holdings. Though it's not all suitable for vineyards, the total acreage involved is significant. The Joseph Drouhin firm, which Robert Drouhin heads, now owns as much land in Oregon as in Burgundy!

The resident manager for DDO is William Hatcher, a Seattle-born management consultant with an MBA in finance who spent the first part of his career with Dayton Hudson stores.

Visiting the winery (NR). The 140-acre property is on the slopes of the famous Red Hills of Dundee, just up the road and around the corner from The Eyrie Vineyards and overlooking the Sokol Blosser winery. The beginnings of a vineyard are already visible, eight acres of Pinot Noir, but this isn't going to be a quick project. A winemaking facility and residence are also being established.

Tasting the wines (NR). Drouhin's 1988 crush, some 8,000 gallons, took place at the Veritas winery in Newberg. Tanks designed in Burgundy were shipped from France to Veritas in time for the crush. DDO bought grapes from half a dozen growers in the Dundee Hills and Eola Hills. "I want to know the country better before making a lot of wine," Drouhin told an interviewer.

There's no indication at this point when the wine might be released.

Neither the separate DDO facilities at Veritas nor the DDO vineyards are open to the public at this time.

LAFITE AT FIRST SIGHT?

Anyone can enjoy wine, but the more you know about it, the more you're able to enjoy it. Still, it takes a certain spirit of adventure to learn about wine in the first place, and a fair amount of sophistication to appreciate the qualities of the best wines.

It's possible, of course, to love Lafite at first sip, but chances are you'll have a greater appreciation of its allure if you've tasted many other wines, other Cabernets, other Bordeaux, other Premier Grand Crus, not to mention other red varieties, especially Pinot Noir. There's no substitute for experience, for tasting. And although the destination of total knowledge may be elusive, the journey itself is a source of endless pleasure.

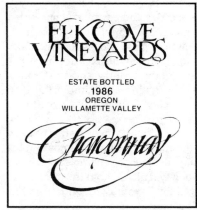

ESTATE BOTTLED
1986
OREGON
WILLAMETTE VALLEY

ELK COVE VINEYARDS

27751 N.W. Olson Road
Gaston, OR 97119
(503) 985-7760

Owners & winemakers:
Pat & Joe Campbell
Year established: 1977
Production capacity: 55,000 gallons
Vineyards: 45 acres
Touring region: Yamhill [p. 195]

A bit of background. It was a baptism by fire, typical of the tough start that marks the struggle to start a winery. For several years in the late 1970s, Harvard-trained Dr. Joe Campbell would commute from his new vineyard in the foothills of Oregon's Coast Range to Longview, Washington, and pull three shifts a week in the hospital emergency room. His wife, Pat, made and sold jewelry and raised three children while learning on the job to be a winemaker and vineyard manager.

The hard part, says Pat Campbell, isn't even making wine, it's coping with the deer, rabbits, and birds that nibble the vines. Robins and cedar waxwings roost in the trees just beyond the vineyards, waiting for those few days when the grapes reach the point of juicy perfection. Shooting the birds isn't allowed, and shooting *at* them doesn't have much of an effect; the Campbells put nets over the vines, an expensive, time-consuming job.

Visiting the winery ★★★★. For the sheer natural beauty of its setting, Elk Cove ranks with the top half-dozen in Oregon. The "cove" is a sheltered fold of trees nestled high in the hilltops that separate Yamhill and Washington counties. Visitors follow Olson Road through stands of evergreen, maple, and alder, as vistas ★★★★ of the Tualatin Valley give way to views over the Willamette Valley. The Campbells own 136 acres, 45 of them planted with Pinot Noir, Chardonnay, Gewurztraminer, Pinot Gris, and Riesling. Herds of Roosevelt elk migrate here every spring, visiting the site in the early morning hours, before the tourists arrive.

The splendid winery itself, combined with a large public tasting room, rises at the end of the drive; its circular, skylit tasting room overlooks the panorama. Six picnic tables stand on the lawn under the oak trees; it's also possible to sit in a shady grape arbor.

Tasting the wines ★★★☆. We've sampled a number of Elk Cove's wines over the past few months, and can report that most of them are equal to the best.

The "regular" Estate Bottled 1986 Pinot Noir had a pleasing strawberry nose and a generous spread of flavors in the mouth; it was a complex yet up-front wine, somewhat short in the finish. The 1986 Estate "reserve" was even better: a lovely blend of raspberries and earthy smells, with a broad, satisfying palate. The 1987 "Dundee Hills" Pinot Noir won best-of-show honors earlier this year at the Newport Wine and Seafood Festival; and Richard Olney, a noted American food writer who lives in France, has singled out Elk Cove's Pinot Noir as one of the country's best red wines. Elk Cove is also getting into Cabernet Sauvignon. We found the 1986 vintage to have a clean cherry nose and "meaty" flavors; it was a relatively simple, perfectly good wine.

On the white side, we liked the Pinot Gris (one of the very few Oregon Pinot Gris we actually enjoyed) and the slightly herbaceous nose on the Gewurztraminer. The 1987 Chardonnay displays the characteristic "sour mash" nose unique to Oregon Chardonnay fruit. Once in the mouth, the texture is smooth, the balance good, and the flavors sweet with fruit. The 1986 Chardonnay was clean and well balanced.

Getting there. Six mi south of Forest Grove, 20 mi north of McMinnville, on the southern fringe of Gaston, turn west from Hwy 47 onto Olson Rd and proceed just under 3 mi into the hills. The driveway to Elk Cove is a sharp right turn.

There's an Elk Cove tasting room on Hwy 99 W in Dundee, and another (featuring mid-Columbia wines, too) at Hood River Village Inn on the waterfront in Hood River.

Open daily from 11 to 5.

Special events. Elk Cove sponsors its own Riesling Festival in May and a Pinot Noir Picnic in September. Admission to each event runs about $5, which includes wine, a souvenir wineglass, music, and food, as well as additional discounts on case-lot purchases. Elk Cove also participates in the Wine Country Thanksgiving sponsored by the Yamhill County wineries.

A word from the winery. *"A visit to Elk Cove Vineyards winery and tasting room is a pleasant experience indeed. Nestled in a secluded valley, the view of the vineyards competes with the beauty of the Coast Range, from where the magnificent Roosevelt elk migrate. Visitors are welcome to picnic here under an arbor of Gewurztraminer or on the lawn.*

"The wines—Pinot Noir, Chardonnay, Cabernet Sauvignon, Pinot Gris, Gewurztraminer, Riesling (late harvest bottlings as well)—offer consistent quality every vintage and in good years are excellent. The tasting room has room for large groups, and the efficient and friendly staff are happy to help you learn more about the wines of Elk Cove Vineyards."

ELLENDALE VINEYARDS

1 Main Street
Rickreall, OR 97338
(503) 623-6835
winery:
300 Reuben Boise Road
Dallas, OR 97338
(503) 623-5617

Owners: Robert & Ella Mae Hudson
Winemaker: Robert Hudson
Year established: 1981
Production capacity: 10,000 gallons
Vineyards: 15 acres
Touring region: Salem [p. 198]

A bit of background. Robert Hudson says he's been making wine since he was 14, though not always with his father's approval. Toward the end of his Air Force career, he bought an 80-acre orchard and began clearing cherries, prunes, apples, and stumps to prepare the land for grapes. The first time he planted the vineyard, every vine was eaten by deer. After he retired in 1975, he tried again, with miles of deer-proof fence surrounding the property, and planted Pinot Noir, Riesling, Chardonnay, Cabernet Franc, Cabernet Sauvignon, and Aurora.

At first, the Hudsons purchased grapes from Washington for their varietal wines, and made their original reputation with fruit and berry wines. As the vineyard matured, Hudson shifted away from sweet berry wines, though he retains a proprietary wine called Woolly Booger (a blend of blackberries, loganberries, and cherries). Says Ella Mae, "It paid for our sparkling wine equipment."

Visiting the winery ★★. Ellendale is actually one of Oregon's original towns, founded in 1844, and today's Ellendale Vineyards was part of the original land grant. The pioneer community boasted the first gristmill, sawmill, boarding house, and general store in Polk County. And the present-day winery looks like it could have come from that era: it's like a movie set for a Western saloon, with a peaked roof and a covered veranda. Several acres of vineyards slope down toward the treeline; the 100-year-old Hudson home (guarded by a friendly, barking black Labrador) stands across the parking lot.

Most visitors won't see this, however. Instead, there's a new tasting room (and separately bonded winery) on the highway, in the heart of tiny Rickreall (itself named for the La Creole River, now called Rickreall Creek, which runs nearby). Outgoing Ella Mae Hudson will receive visitors here, with other staff helping out. There's a window at the back of the tasting room that looks into where Ellendale produces meads (honey wines), offered here in a range of sweetnesses from three different types of Polk County honey.

In addition to his winemaking, Robert Hudson is a self-taught landscape painter who produces detailed scenes from his own photographs. He and Ella Mae have traveled the length of the Oregon Trail, and Robert Hudson's paintings reflect this interest. Many of his canvases are displayed at the winery and are offered for sale at moderate prices.

Tasting the wines ★★. Ellendale currently produces vintage-dated, estate-bottled Pinot Noir, Pinot Noir Blanc, Chardonnay, Riesling, and Cabernet Franc. Since our last edition, a line of methode champenoise sparkling wines has been added. It's called Crystal Mist, a blend of two-thirds white Pinot Noir and one-third Chardonnay; it receives 18 months of cellaring on the yeast. The first release in 1987 was named best of its class at the International Eastern Wine Competition.

Ellendale's best wine in our recent tastings was the 1986 Rose of Cabernet blush, which had a lively bouquet of bell peppers, and off-dry flavors that were complex and well balanced; it was made from Cabernet Franc grapes. Another blush, the 1986 White Pinot Noir, smelled more like cream soda than strawberries but was well balanced, with earthy, berry flavors. We appreciated the rich plum tastes and smooth textures of the 1986 Pinot Noir, and the smooth texture of the 1985 Pinot. The 1985 Cabernet Franc tasted rather thin and simple, but at $6 it's not making pretensions of $20 grandeur.

We were less impressed with the whites. The 1986 Chardonnay had a bouquet of very ripe pineapples, with a bit of spritz in the taste and a slightly bitter finish. The slightly effervescent 1987 Gewurztraminer smelled and tasted of burned toffee; it must have been a bad bottle.

Getting there. From Hwy 22 westbound from Salem, turn left onto Hwy 99 W and proceed south 0.25 mi (to the caution light) to the new tasting room. The original winery is no longer open to the public.

Open from 10 to 6 daily, April through December. Slightly different hours January through March: 10 to 6 Monday through Saturday, noon to 5 on Sunday. A fee is charged only at festivals (see below) and to taste the Crystal Mist sparkling wine.

Special events. Ellendale participates in the Salem-area Tastevin Tour over Memorial Day weekend, and sponsors a Wine and Art Fair, held from Thanksgiving through the first week of December.

The actual vineyards, winery, and original tasting room can be visited by appointment.

A word from the winery. "*Although the tasting room for Ellendale Vineyards and Winery is located on Highway 99 W. in Rickreall, we will make every effort to insure that your visit is not the usual 'impersonal tasting room experience.' The showroom is the gallery for the beautiful landscape oil paintings of Robert. Ella Mae will be greeting folks personally at least half the time, and her able assistants will make you welcome the rest of the days. We have a nice picnic area under the arbor and feel that the convenience of the location on the highway and the longer hours we are open will overcome any disappointment for not visiting the vineyards.*"

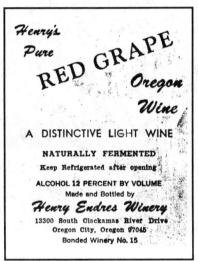

HENRY ENDRES WINERY

13300 S. Clackamas River Drive
Oregon City, OR 97045
(503) 656-7239

Owner & winemaker:
  Henry C. Endres
Year established: 1935
Production capacity: 15,000 gallons
Vineyards: None
Touring: Portland East [p. 209]

A bit of background. Three generations of the Endres family have built their lives around this modest winery, which began when Henry Endres, a German immigrant, established the business after Repeal. The favorite product then was loganberry wine, known in local taverns as Henry's Lowball. Henry Jr. was trained as a zoologist and public health officer, but took over the winery almost 35 years ago; his specialty was rhubarb wine. Henry III, known as Bucky, manages the day-to-day operations now, and he's looking at producing Riesling from the vineyard on his father's property. But the popularity of the fruit wines, especially for consumption in taverns, is likely to continue for a long time.

All the wines here are sold in 1.5-liter bottles with screw caps, and everything costs the same (under $10). It's what Henry Endres, Jr., calls "the Model T theory of marketing: any color you want, as long as it's black." Makes the bookwork easier, too.

Visiting the winery ★. The winery looks like an Italian hill town, a waterfall of little green houses cascading down a slope that runs alongside the Clackamas River. Most visitors just step inside a porch that's attached to the building called "Winery D" and stand up to a counter where they taste wine from tiny paper cups.

The vats and fermenting tanks in the winery buildings farther up the hill don't present much of an attraction to most visitors, who arrive in a steady stream of cars, pickups, and motorcycles; they come to buy wine, period. And buy they do: some 4,000 cases of 1.5-liter bottles every year.

Tasting the wines ★. A variety of fruit wines (apple, rhubarb, mead, elderberry, loganberry, rasperry, Concord grape, Niagara grape, plum), and a mead. Most of these are two years old, except for the cane-grown berry wines, which are from the previous year's crush.

You won't see these wines among the winners of tastings and competitions; Henry Endres doesn't enter them.

Getting there. Take Exit 10 (Park Place) from I-205 and follow the Clackamas River Rd northbound for 1 mi to the winery.

Open Monday through Saturday from 10 to 7, except for major holidays. Tours of the winery by appointment.

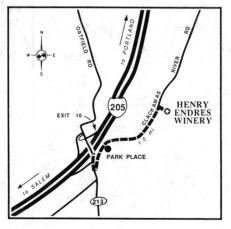

EOLA HILLS
WINE CELLARS

OREGON
PINOT NOIR BLANC
1987

Produced and bottled by
Eola Hills Wine Cellars, Rickreall, Oregon
Alcohol 11.0% by volume   Contains Sulfites

EOLA HILLS
WINE CELLARS
501 S. Pacific Highway W.
Rickreall, OR 97371
(503) 623-2405

General manager: Tom Huggins
Winemaker: Ken Wright
Year established: 1986
Production capacity: 25,000 gallons
Vineyards: 67 acres
Touring region: Salem [p. 198]

A bit of background. Tom Huggins, a business administration graduate of Oregon State University, has been the vineyard manager for Oak Grove vineyards since 1982, as well as an independent insurance agent. Oak Grove is the principal supplier of Pinot Noir to Ken Wright's Panther Creek Cellars in McMinnville. Ken also happens to be the winemaker for Tom's new winery in Rickreall, Eola Hills.

Visiting the winery ★★. This is a big facility, some 9,000 square feet of space; you can see the working winery from the tasting room without having to step over hoses or get your feet wet.

Tables, benches, and a gas barbecue stand at the ready outside; the inside can be rented for weddings, banquets, receptions, or private meetings.

Tasting the wines ★★☆. The best Eola Hills we tasted was the 1986 Pinot Noir, made by Ken Wright, with strawberry, raspberry, and leather accents in the nose, moderate fruit and tannin in the mouth. An interesting and satisfying wine. Wright also made the 1986 Chenin Blanc, which was distinctly spritzy and initially smelled like crushed raw almonds. It gradually took on a more varietal aroma of honeyed fruit, but the wine lacked the lively acid that would have balanced the natural bitterness of the grape. The Chardonnay from the same vintage had acceptable flavors but an aggressively acetic nose; the winery literature indicates this was made by Gerard Rottiers at Chateau Benoit.

Additional wines include a Sauvignon Blanc and a Cabernet Sauvignon. The 1987 vintage, Tom Huggins reports, was particularly good for these varieties. The Sauvignon Blanc won the Oregon State Fair award for best label design (by the winner of Eola Hills' own mini-contest among graphic design students).

Getting there. From Salem, go west on Hwy 22, turn left on Hwy 99 W. The winery is on the highway in the community of Rickreall. [**Map:** Ellendale]

Open daily in summer from noon to 5, on weekends and by appointment in winter. Groups are charged a $1 tasting fee.

Special events. The Tastevin Tour in May, a "steak-out" in July, the Eola Hills wine and jazz festival in August, and a holiday gift show on November and December weekends.

A word from the winery. *"Please come visit our tasting room, where you can enjoy the wines while viewing the entire winery operation. Experience our barbecue-picnic area, weather permitting. Or take in one of the many festive events happening at Eola Hills throughout the year, from jazz festivals to casino nights to charter buses to ballgames in Eugene and Corvallis. Check with the winery for a brochure and schedule of upcoming events."*

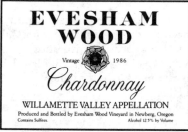

EVESHAM WOOD
2995 Michigan City Avenue N.W.
4035 Wallace Road N.W. (mail)
West Salem, OR 97034
(503) 371-8478

Owners: Russell & Mary Raney
Winemaker: Russ Raney
Year established: 1986
Production capacity: 3,000 gallons
Vineyards: 8 acres
Touring region: Salem [p. 198]

A bit of background. Russ Raney's father did some home winemaking, and Russ himself, a native of Arkansas, lived in Germany and France for a time. After graduating with a degree in German from Westminster College in Fulton, Missouri, he set off for the State Technical School of Enology and Viticulture in Bad Kreuznach, Germany, the only American in the class. He made wine in Germany, sold wine for four years in St. Louis, and ended up coming to Oregon to pursue the elusive elixir of Pinot Noir.

We first met Russ when he was knee-deep in grapes at Adams Vineyard Winery in northwest Portland. He left to start his own winery, Evesham Wood, and made the first wines at a temporary facility in Newberg: wine writer Judy Peterson-Nedry's garage.

Visiting the winery ★★. It took Russ two years to find the right spot for his winery and vineyard. He picked a spot on a low terrace of the Eola Hills' eastern face, just north of West Salem. The rocky soil will ensure the deliberately low crop yields Raney is seeking for his wines. The name Evesham Wood, by the way, is inspired by England's Evesham Vale, an important fruit-growing region of the Cotswolds that Russ and Mary Raney visited on their honeymoon.

Tasting the wines ★★. The unfiltered 1986 Pinot Noir scored 90 points with Robert Parker (higher than even Knudsen Erath's or Amity's 1986 Pinots), who commended its fragrance and richness. We can't say. What we did try was a sample of the barrel-fermented 1986 Chardonnay, which was far from brilliant. It looked about four years old, with some strange particles (not tartrates) floating in it; it didn't smell oaky so much as dirty. The flavors were balanced but with a short, alcoholic finish.

The 1987 vintage should be better. A tank sample last year showed the Chardonnay sweet with fruit. A barrel sample of the Pinot Noir from Freedom Hill vineyard (one of three lots, blended before release) was big, bright, and vigorous, tannic with a warm, toasty nose. The 1988 vintage, Raney reports, was well balanced, but won't have as much fruit as 1987.

Getting there. From Salem, cross the Willamette River on the Marion St bridge (Hwy 22), and immediately turn north on Wallace Rd (Hwy 221). Proceed 3.5 mi to Michigan City Ave, turn left and continue 0.5 mi to the winery. [**Map:** Bethel Heights]

Open by appointment only until a new tasting room is completed in November 1989.

Special events. New release tasting, May; open house, November.

A word from the winery: "*Evesham Wood's guiding thought would have to be the natural winemaking approach. Our limited production allows us to adhere to this principle as we can more easily exercise control over our whole operation from the vineyard to the bottle. In keeping with this, we can't accommodate a grandiose tour facility; however, you are cordially invited to visit us and sample our wines by appointment, while enjoying our idyllic pastoral setting and a fine view of the Willamette River.*"

THE EYRIE VINEYARDS

935 E. 10th
McMinnville, OR 97128
(503) 472-6315

P.O. Box 697
Dundee, OR 97115

Owners: David & Diana Lett
Winemaker: David Lett
Production capacity: 33,000 gallons
Vineyards: 26 acres
Year established: 1970
Touring region: Yamhill [p. 195]

A bit of background. David Lett, a very private man, is perhaps the best winemaker in Oregon and certainly the most famous. In person, he is intense and reserved, with shining eyes, a trim white beard, and a delightful habit of expressing his opinions about wine and winemaking in no uncertain terms. Were he a recent arrival, his iconoclastic ways might make him an outcast, but because he has been established in the Willamette Valley longer than anyone else, he has converted an entire generation of Oregon winemakers.

Two decades ago, abandoning a career in dentistry (of all things) and fresh out of the University of California at Davis, where he took a degree in viticulture, David Lett worked for a year at Souverain Cellars, traveled for a year in France, then set out in search of a climate where he could grow Pinot Noir—the great red grape of Burgundy. He found what he was looking for in the now-famous Red Hills of Dundee, and in 1966 began planting a 30-acre vineyard. To support his family, he sold textbooks; to support the vineyard, his wife, Diana, toiled among the vines.

The late 1960s were not good years to be pioneers. The newly transplanted Californians (not to mention the vines) found the weather miserable, and it would be years before winemaking colleagues appeared on the scene. But after a decade, the Letts' dedication paid off: the 1975 Pinot Noir from The Eyrie Vineyards was entered in two tastings in France, where it astounded the judges by coming within two-tenths of a point of beating a 1959 Chambolle Musigny. The sensational showing made headlines around the world, and brought an overnight reputation to Oregon wines.

That reputation continues. Robert Parker recently gave a 1981 Pinot Noir from The Eyrie Vineyards his top score among Oregon Pinots. And in a rematch of the now-famous 1983 Oregon v. 1983 Burgundies tasting in New York early in 1986, Eyrie's 1983 Pinot finished in a tie (with Knudsen Erath) for first place. David Lett himself is honored as Oregon's most illustrious winemaker, and even found himself named recently to a list of Who's Who in American Cooking.

What it's like to visit (NR). The 26 acres of The Eyrie Vineyards—pronouced EYE-rie, and named for the home of a family of hawks on the fringe of the property—are outside of Dundee, not far from Sokol Blosser. The winery building itself, in McMinnville's old industrial district, is one of the least imposing wineries in Oregon; it's a converted turkey processing plant near the railroad tracks. What is striking inside the plant, however, is the spare efficiency of the place, the stacks of French oak barrels used to age the Pinot Noir and Chardonnay. Stalking the aisles is Lett himself, frequently wearing a knit sailor's cap. "You sleep with Pinot Noir," he explains. "You get up every two hours to punch it down," referring to the "cap" of skins and stems that accumulates atop the fermenting wine.

There is no concession here to tourism, no tasting room, no picnic ground, barely an office. Except for pilgrims who make appointments, there are no visitors. But that's the way David Lett wants it. Alone among Oregon's winemakers, he can sell all the wine he wants to sell, has no interest in expanding, and has no need to welcome busloads of tourists in tennis shoes who want to try his (nonexistent) sweet Riesling.

Tasting the wine ★★★★. If David Lett had stopped making Pinot Noir with the 1983 vintage, he would be a living legend. But he's an artist as much as a winemaker, and artists don't retire, they create; they don't repeat themselves.

Speaking of the '83 Pinot, it made delightful drinking in mid-1988: raspberry, vanilla, and violets in the nose, and a most satisfying, crisp balance. The 1986 Pinot Noir is true to its Yamhill Valley origins: an elusive, agreeable bouquet of decomposition (barnyard and garbage come to mind), then white pepper, leathery smells, and tea. It has a silky mouth feel and true flavors, but lacks length.

The 1987 Chardonnay required several minutes to expel a yeasty, alcoholic aroma of pear brandy; this gave way to a pineapple and apple nose, and balanced flavors. The bottle states 12.5 degrees of alcohol, but the wine smelled and tasted hotter.

Eyrie also produces a dry Muscat Ottonel, best drunk young as an aperitif or as an accompaniment to curry.

Lett is putting increasing emphasis on Pinot Gris, a variety he pioneered in Oregon, even tearing out his Riesling vines in order to plant more. It's often described as the Northwest's perfect seafood wine.

Getting there. The best way to reach the winery is from Lafayette Ave, a north-south street accessible from Hwy 99W (as it approaches town from the north) or E. Third St (McMinnville's principal shopping and restaurant street). Tenth crosses Lafayette a block east of the winery. [**Map**: Arterberry]

Open once or twice a year to mailing list customers. The winery does not have regular hours because there is no permanent staff other than the Letts, the vineyard manager, Joel Myers, and a cellar assistant. But fans of David Lett's wines will not be turned away, provided they make arrangements in advance. Small groups of connoisseurs (i.e., people likely to buy more than a souvenir bottle) can make appointments, and the fees charged will depend on the cost of the wine poured.

Special events. Eyrie joins the Yamhill Valley wineries in an open house on Thanksgiving weekend to celebrate the release of the new wines.

SIXTEEN PINOTS

An unprecedented "vertical" tasting took place in the back room of Nick's Italian Cafe in McMinnville last summer: a retrospective of the first 16 vintages of Pinot Noir from The Eyrie Vineyards. Some 20 guests heard David Lett describe each wine's growing season, crush, and technical winemaking details from 1970 through 1985; and sampled the wines. Lett himself hadn't tried a number of them in years.

Our favorites included the oldest, a 1970 Pinot released as Oregon Spring Wine, still youthful; the 1975, with a wonderfully aromatic bouquet of fruit, tobacco, and pepper; the 1980, with tobacco and eucalyptus in the nose and cherry-raspberry flavors; and the violet-scented 1983, with a light, fresh taste of raspberries.

FLYNN VINEYARDS

2095 Cadle Rd
Rickreall, OR 97371
(503) 623-6505

Owner & winemaker: Wayne Flynn
Year established: 1984
Production capacity: None
Vineyards: 85 acres
Touring region: Salem [p. 198]

A bit of background. Flynn Vineyards has been around for a long time; the grapes are sold to several local wineries. Wayne Flynn is an airline pilot, frequently on the move, and hasn't devoted much time to matters enological recently.

Visiting the winery (NR). As Gertrude Stein once remarked about Oakland, "There's no *there* there." So it is with Flynn Vineyards.

Wayne Flynn has filed an application with Polk County for a permit to build a winery. Bureaucratic response: among the conditions imposed for the permit was that Flynn pave a section of county road. Not the access road to his projected winery, mind you, but a regular public road that happens to need paving. Your tax dollars at work . . . .

Tasting the wines (NR). The two current releases from Flynn Vineyards, made under contract by Yamhill Valley Vineyards, are a 1986 Pinot Noir and a 1987 Chardonnay. Very limited quantities are sold in Salem. Sparkling wine production is contemplated if the winery is ever built.

FORGERON VINEYARD

89697 Sheffler Road
Elmira, OR 97437
(503) 935-1117

Owners: Lee & Linda Smith
Winemaker: Lee Smith
Year established: 1978
Production capacity: 25,000 gallons
Vineyards: 23 acres
Touring: South. Willamette [p. 200]

A bit of background. Here's a winery with more than a touch of romance, a passion for flowers and art. The name itself, Forgeron, has an appropriately authentic French sound (it actually means "blacksmith" in French) and owner Lee Smith came to this peaceful setting by dint of methodical, disciplined work.

Smith has no formal training in enology, but he did travel a lot during the four years he was stationed in France and came to appreciate the value of wine in a civilized world. He worked as a salesman and driver for Royal Crown Cola before devoting full time to Forgeron Vineyards, which was first planted in 1971 on a wooded, 26-acre property below the Fern Ridge reservoir. From the start, Lee Smith has made wines (such as Cabernet Sauvignon) that require every bit of warmth and sunlight that the vineyard can soak up. He has put up three remote weather and climate stations on the property to take readings every quarter hour of the temperature, moisture, and radiation (sunlight); this data will be combined with a chemical analysis of the wines produced by grapes grown in these conditions, and with sensory evaluation of those wines. Smith predicts he'll soon have enough data to project crop and market value while the grapes are still in the field. "It's information that needs to be developed and understood if indeed Oregon is to be considered the premier wine-growing area in the world."

Along those same lines, Smith spearheaded one of the most important wine events ever held in the Northwest: an international conference on cool-climate viticulture that brought together experts in the technical aspects of winemaking with winemakers from Oregon, western Washington, and British Columbia.

Visiting the winery ★★★. You approach along a little road called Burgundy Lane that meanders through the woods to an 8,000-square-foot production facility set in spacious grounds. The adjacent garden, where Linda Smith plants thousands of flowers each spring, includes a fountain and picnic tables with umbrellas. There's a swing set for the kids, too.

The tasting room is part of the winery itself, along with a well-stocked gift shop and an upstairs gallery to display local art. Forgeron's souvenir wineglasses are particularly attractive: handblown lead crystal with the winery crest silk-screened in gold.

Tasting the wines ★★☆. Lee Smith makes Riesling, Chenin Blanc, Muller Thurgau and Pinot Gris, a blush wine, and two reds, Pinot Noir and Cabernet Sauvignon. The 1983 Pinot was a gold medal winner at the Seattle Enological Society Festival in 1986, quite an accomplishment the year after the big splash made by Oregon's 1983 Pinots. The 1985 Cabernet is still quite tannic but has a lively balance between fruit and oak. We've been fans of Forgeron's Chardonnays, with their delicate, nutlike flavors, but our most recent tasting (in early 1989) of the 1985 Chardonnay came too late. The wine was beyond redemption; surprisingly, we're told this was the Draper clone of Chardonnay, usually more austere.

Getting there. From Eugene, take W. 11th (Hwy 126) westbound toward Veneta, Elmira, and Florence. In Elmira, stay on Territorial Rd (Hwy 126 branches off) to Warthen Rd, turn left, and go 1.5 mi to Sheffler Rd, then 1.3 mi to the Forgeron mailbox.

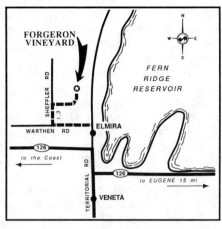

Open daily from noon to 5, June through September. The rest of the year, weekends only, from noon to 5. Closed January. Groups of over 15 should call ahead; there is a $2-per-person tasting fee.

Special events. Forgeron stages an immensely popular bluegrass festival on the third weekend in July, when the entire grounds fill up with people and the area in front of the winery itself becomes a bandstand.

A word from the winery. *"The fruits of our labors at Forgeron are the wines. But Forgeron is also a place—a beautiful place to spend an hour or an afternoon. The winery is nestled next to a protective wood of fir trees at the end of a long lane. Come out to the winery for a visit. Not only will you get a taste of Oregon when you try our selection of special wines, but you can also learn something about the tradition of winemaking. During the warm weather you can bring lunch and enjoy it at the picnic table under the fir trees or in the newly landscaped winery gardens."*

FORIS VINEYARDS
654 Kendall Rd
Cave Junction, OR 97523
(503) 592-3752

Owners: Merideth & Ted Gerber
Winemaker: Ted Gerber
Year established: 1987
Production capacity: 10,000 gallons
Vineyards: 20 acres
Touring: Illinois Valley [p. 204]

A bit of background. Ted Gerber has a degree in political science but has spent most of his adult life as a farmer. He's been a home winemaker since he turned 21, and has taught community college courses in wine-making. In 1986, he made wine commercially for the first time, using his own grapes and contracting with Bridgeview Winery down the road for production facilities.

Visiting the winery ★★. Foris is the Latin word for "outside" or "outdoors." The Gerbers actually have two ranches here, a total of almost 200 acres at an elevation of 1,500 feet on the "back terrace" of the Illinois River Valley. The vineyards, planted since 1975, are not irrigated.

The Gerbers grow grapes, hay, and seed for sugar beets; they also graze cattle. Democrat Creek runs in front of the winery, "but with a name like that we were concerned that Republicans might be leery of the wine," jokes Ted Gerber.

The Gerbers built a 4,000-square-foot addition to the winery in 1988 and will do more and more of the wine production on their own property from now on. The Illinois Valley still isn't a particularly well-known grape-growing area ("We thought of wearing Foris Vineyards sandwich boards while working in the vineyards," Ted wrote last year to retail customers), so wines from this region are relatively inexpensive.

Tasting the wines ★★. Grapes from Foris Vineyard have been showing up in a number of Northwest wines, from Amity's 1984 Pinot Noir and Gewurztraminer to Valley View's 1986 Chardonnay. Even Staton Hills in the Yakima Valley bought some bulk wine made with Foris grapes in 1986 and 1987. The Illinois Valley is sometimes called "the acid capital of Oregon." (Those acids pay off in firm, flavorful wines.) It gets hotter during the day and colder at night than in the Willamette Valley, though harvest dates are about the same.

The Foris wines we sampled were made at Bridgeview (described as "Chateau Vue du Pont" on the label). The 1987 Early Muscat had a lush nose of tropical fruit and a dry finish. The nonvintage Oregon Nectar, a blush wine with pale pink and orange tones, smelled like spring flowers and papaya, and tasted like sweet apricots. (Turns out it was made with Muscat, Pinot Noir, and sweet reserve.) Least satisfying of the Foris wines we've tried was the 1987 Gewurztraminer, with a nose of grapefruit but too bitter in the mouth.

Getting there. From Cave Junction, take Hwy 46 toward the Oregon Caves. Turn right onto Holland Loop Rd after 1.2 mi, right again onto Kendall Rd. (Or stay on Hwy 46 for 6 mi and turn right at the other end of Holland Loop Rd.) [**Map**: Siskiyou Vineyards]

Open by appointment.

A word from the winery. *"You've probably had our wine or grapes in someone else's bottle but you probably didn't know it. We are now retaining most of the vineyard for ourselves and bottling under our own name."*

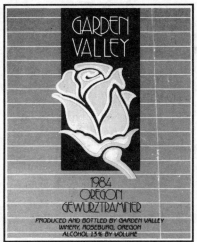

GARDEN VALLEY WINERY

29255 Berlin Road
P.O. Box 68
Sweet Home, OR 97386
(503) 367-6060

Owner & winemaker: Ray Higgins
Year established: 1984
Production capacity: Unknown
Vineyards: 25 acres
Touring: South. Willamette [p. 200]

A bit of background. Garden Valley began life in Roseburg, where it evolved from a series of companies controlled by Frank Guido. Ray Higgins of Markheim Vineyards in Sweet Home eventually became an investor in Garden Valley. He has now taken control of the Garden Valley name and moved the winery to his home in Sweet Home. Its future, to put it delicately, is uncertain.

Visiting the winery (NR). Under construction. The intention is to build a winery that takes advantage of the tourist traffic along Highway 20 en route to the popular Santiam Pass recreation areas (Hoodoo Bowl skiing area, Green Peter Dam, among others).

Tasting the wines (NR). There was no crush in 1988, so any Garden Valley wines currently on the market were made by Richard Mansfield at the former location in Roseburg.

Getting there. From I-5, take Exit 233 to Hwy 20 eastbound (the Santiam Highway) through Lebanon. Turn north on Pleasant Valley Rd, which becomes Berlin Rd. The winery is 3.6 mi from Hwy 20.

Open by appointment. There's a Garden Valley tasting room in Corvallis at Exit 228 from I-5.

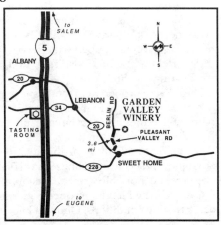

GIRARDET

CHARDONNAY
1987

PRODUCED AND BOTTLED BY GIRARDET WINE CELLARS
ROSEBURG, OREGON   BONDED WINERY OR-92

GIRARDET WINE CELLARS

895 Reston Road
Roseburg, OR 97470
(503) 679-7252

Owners: Philippe & Bonnie Girardet
Winemaker: Philippe Girardet
Year established: 1983
   (vineyard since 1972)
Production capacity: 10,000 gallons
Vineyards: 18 acres
Touring: Umpqua Valley [p. 202]

A bit of background. Swiss-born Philippe Girardet was designing technical instruments for the chemistry and astro-physics departments at the California Institute of Technology when he met Bonnie, a young teacher who had recently graduated from the University of California at Berkeley. After only one date they decided to get married; the following year they moved to a farm in Oregon. Bonnie Girardet says, "Neither Phil nor I had any experience in agriculture or winemaking, but we decided to take a gamble and start a vineyard."

They also began raising a family, now numbering five children, ages five to 16, who work in the vineyards with their parents. Bonnie teaches them all at home, too. "Jean-Paul, our oldest, has an excellent palate. His nose picks up defects right away. They all learn so much at the winery and in the vineyard," she says. "Unfortunately, most kids in this country have it too easy." Indeed, the entire Girardet family seems to have a remarkable inner peace, a spiritual calm that transcends the year-round pressures of the winemaking business.

Visiting the winery ★★★. The winery stands a short distance away from the Girardets' small home in the shadow of the Coast Range. The surrounding southern Oregon hills are golden brown with thick, dry grassland, in places topped with deep, green woods. The winery sports a bright, red-and-white Swiss flag, and there's a small picnic pergola overlooking the vineyards.

The 55-acre property currently supports 18 acres of grapes, including a unique collection of French cultivars (various vinifera crosses as well as hybrids) that the Girardets have planted over the years and blended into their Vin Rouge and Vin Blanc. (The Vin Rouge is about one-third Pinot Noir, the Blanc mostly Chardonnay.) Red cultivars include Chancellor, Baco Noir, and Foch; the whites Seyval Blanc, Aurora, and Verdelet. These are grapes not normally seen in Oregon, although they are quite prevalent in Canada. The blends produce better, more complex wines given the local growing conditions, Girardet believes.

Tasting the wines ★★★. The red and white blends are enjoyable and very well priced. The white varietal wines are Riesling, Gewurztraminer, and Chardonnay. There's a Pinot Noir and an upcoming release of Cabernet Sauvignon.

Girardet wines—whose labels sport the Girardet family crest—have had their greatest success close to home, at the annual Greatest of the Grape competition in Roseburg. In 1985, the Vin Rouge was named Best Red; one of the tasters said it was the equal of a fine Chateau Lafite and should be selling for $14 a bottle. In fact, all the Girardet wines are quite modestly priced; Matt Kramer, in *The Oregonian* last year, wrote that no southern Oregon winery has a better track record when it comes to value.

The Vin Rouge is 35 percent Pinot Noir, with the balance coming from Baco Noir and De Chaunac; it's a rich, spicy wine with a creamy taste that reminded us of a Cote du Rhone. Its white counterpart, Vin Blanc, is the house wine at Eugene's Excelsior Restaurant; it's 75 percent Chardonnay, with Verdelet and Aurora making up the rest.

We enjoyed the 1986 Chardonnay, which makes for good drinking now. We didn't find the 1986 Riesling particularly impressive, however, and the first bottle of 1986 Pinot Noir we tried was probably corky. What a pleasure to find another bottle in a subsequent tasting: this time it had a complex and beguiling nose of raspberries and leather, penetrating flavor, and a balanced finish.

Getting there. From I-5, take any of the three exits that lead to the town of Winston (113, 119, or 120). In Winston, turn onto Hwy 42 westbound and proceed 9 mi toward Coos Bay. Turn right on Reston Rd; the winery is 0.5 mi down the road.

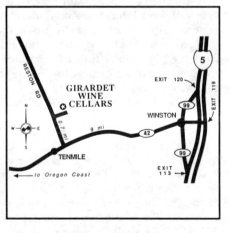

Open daily from noon to 5 from May through September. From October through April, open Saturday only from noon to 5, or by appointment. Closed January. Groups should call ahead; a fee of $1 per person is charged if no wine is purchased.

Special events. The winery holds its anniversary celebration in early June.

A word from the winery. *"When you visit our tasting room you will almost always be served by either Philippe or Bonnie. This personal touch will make it a memorable visit. Our wines reflect the European philosophy that wine should first of all be drinkable and enjoyable, for the accompaniment of food. For our family, wine is a way of life, a beverage of moderation, and a joy to drink, with food. We love making the wines and hope you enjoy drinking them."*

1·9·8·6
OREGON WHITE PINOT NOIR

GLEN CREEK
WINERY

PRODUCED AND BOTTLED BY GLEN CREEK WINERY, SALEM, OREGON
ALCOHOL 12.5% BY VOLUME   BW-OR-88

GLEN CREEK WINERY

6057 Orchard Heights Road N.W.
Salem, OR 97304
(503) 371-9463

Owners: Thomas & Sylvia Dumm
Winemaker: Thomas Dumm
Year established: 1982
Production capacity: 12,000 gallons
Vineyards: 20 acres
Touring region: Salem [p. 198]

A bit of background. The way Tom Dumm listens to you, not like the high-powered manufacturing executive he used to be, but like the quietly assured winemaker he has become, tells you he values your opinion. He really wants to know how you like his wine, what you think of his place. Years back, Dumm worked in Southern California, responsible for budgeting and production with a company that made steel valves, castings, and forgings. All numbers and metal; no romance, no people.

Tom's interest in wine was triggered when his wife, Sylvia, bought him a copy of Hugh Johnson's *World Atlas of Wine* Before long he had his own wine shop called Le Grand Cru, one of the first in Southern California to feature Northwest wines. To take advantage of a more relaxed lifestyle, he moved his family to the Salem area in the mid-1970s and started making wine in his garage. In 1982 he bonded the premises and began commercial operations.

Visiting the winery ★★★. Glen Creek is located in the rolling countryside 10 minutes west of Salem, at the southern end of the Eola Hills, which now encompass some 500 acres—arguably the greatest concentration of vineyards in Oregon.

Chardonnay and Gewurztraminer vines are planted along the road that leads toward the Dumm residence and adjacent winery, and an arbor with picnic tables stands invitingly at the end of the drive. There's a bandstand, too, for the musicians who play at the regular events and occasions like weddings. (A pickup truck whose license plate reads "CHRDNY" reveals Dumm's passion.) The fermenting tanks have been mounted on an outdoor slab, while a few steps away the aging cellar has been built into the hillside. Here the winery's tasting room shares space with the Nevers oak barrels used to age Glen Creek's Chardonnay.

Tasting the wines ★★. Glen Creek produces a "Whole Cluster Fermented" Pinot Noir, as dark as a young Cabernet and full of intense cherry and berry flavors. It's released very soon after the crush, as if it were a Beaujolais Nouveau, and it's the only Glen Creek wine we've tasted in some time.

Glen Creek had some success with Sauvignon Blanc a while back, perfumed like juniper or oregano, depending on the vintage; the first release won a gold medal in Seattle, back in 1983. The Chardonnays and Gewurztraminers have had their ups and downs.

Getting there. From Salem, take Hwy 22 westbound toward Dallas 5.8 mi; turn right on Oak Grove Rd. (From Hwy 99 W., take Hwy 22 eastbound toward Salem for 4 mi to Oak Grove Rd and turn left.) Go 2.4 mi on Oak Grove, then turn right on Orchard Heights Rd, and go 0.3 mi. The winery's driveway is on the left.

Open Tuesday through Sunday, from noon to 5. (Closed New Year's Day, Thanksgiving, Easter, and Christmas.) Tour groups by appointment.

Special events. Glen Creek has live bluegrass and Cajun music, and a variety of food items, on occasion; call the winery for a schedule.

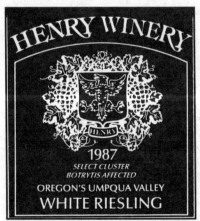

HENRY ESTATE WINERY

687 Hubbard Creek Road
P.O. Box 26
Umpqua, OR 97486
(503) 459-5120

Owners: Scott & Sylvia Henry
Winemaker: Scott Henry
Year established: 1978
Production capacity: 40,000 gallons
Vineyards: 31 acres
Touring: Umpqua Valley [p. 202]

A bit of background. Scott Henry, a carefully spoken, unassuming man, was working as a scientist for Aerojet General in Sacramento when one of his colleagues, the late Gino Zepponi, asked him for help with some design problems. (Zepponi was then starting a small Napa Valley winery called ZD; he later became general manager of Domaine Chandon.) Scott Henry's experience with the nuts and bolts of winery operations gave him the confidence to start his own winery when he returned to Oregon some years later to manage his family's property near Roseburg. As it happened, the land included some acreage on the banks of the Umpqua River, where the Henry Estate Winery is located today.

Visiting the winery ★★★. The drive from Sutherlin takes you through golden farmland and orchards, past patrician homes set among the trees. The winery itself sits modestly beside the north fork of the Umpqua. No razzle-dazzle show here, just good wines produced by the fertile soil and warm sun. Perhaps too fertile: the yield from Scott Henry's bottomland vines is easily twice that of most Oregon vineyards.

Scott Henry owns a total of 31 acres of Gewurztraminer, Chardonnay, and Pinot Noir, some of which are in the hills near his home. But there are plenty of vineyards at the winery itself, and there are picnic tables under the trees nearby. If you visit before bud break in April, you might also see some sheep grazing in the vineyard; Scott uses them to keep down weeds between the rows of vines. A second winery, with complete landscaping and more diversified visitor facilities, is planned sometime in 1990.

Tasting the wines ★★★. Henry Estate produces relatively few varieties, a healthy practice that allows the winemaker to concentrate on his best wines. Pinot Noir, Chardonnay, Gewurztraminer, and Riesling make up his repertoire. We were very fond of the early vintages from Henry Estate. The 1978 Pinot Noir was soft and complex with fruit and American oak, and the 1979 Pinot Noir smelled of the riverside earth and exploded in the mouth with the taste of dill! In our 1982 book on Oregon wineries, we called Henry's Pinot our favorite in the state.

The quality faded for a while but seems to be recovering. (As assistant winemaker Scott Henry IV points out, distinctive styles—such as American oak—tend to breed controversy.)

Currently available are a 1987 Early Harvest Pinot Noir—light cherry nose with no detectable oak, a fine spritz, and good balance—and the 1985 Pinot Noir aged in American oak. Although the oak dominates the fruit, the plum and strawberry influence are still apparent. It's a lively wine with good acidity and very welcoming to food.

The 1985 Reserve Chardonnay is sweet with oak and fruit; it has fine balance and a long finish. The regular bottling of 1986 Chardonnay is less distinguished by its fruit, and has pronounced but pleasant oak flavors. The 1986 dry Gewurztraminer has good spice and grapefruit flavors, and a wonderful smooth texture.

Much has been written about the luscious 1987 Select Cluster, Botrytis-Affected White Riesling, which took the Governor's Trophy at the Oregon State Fair in 1988. (Myron Redford at Amity calls it the quintessential Oregon dessert wine.) We were among those seduced by its honeyed, apricot quality, and can only suggest that you try to buy some.

Getting there. From I-5 north of Roseburg, take Exit 136 (Sutherlin) and go west on Hwy 138 toward the coast. Turn left on County Rd 9; proceed through Umpqua. Turn right on Rd 6 and cross the Umpqua River; the winery is on the right side just past the cement bridge.

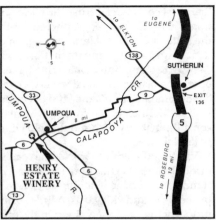

Open daily from 11 to 5, except major holidays.

Special events. There's a "Henry Goes Wine" festival on the third Saturday in August.

A word from the winery. *"Plan a special outing in the country . . . visit Henry Winery, home of Henry Estate wines. Tucked away in the picturesque Umpqua Valley west of Sutherlin, Henry Winery is a feast for the eyes. Surrounded by gently rolling hills, fertile wheat fields and farmland, and the beautiful Umpqua River, 31 acres of meticulously trellised vines annually produce about 30,000 gallons of exquisite wine. Timing poses a challenge to fine winemakers. Just as the delicate balance of Oregon nature determines prime harvest time, the master winemaker determines the prime time to release each wine. Henry wines are allowed to mellow to maturity, resulting in outstanding wines made from Chardonnay, Pinot Noir, Gewurztraminer, and Riesling grapes."*

HIDDEN SPRINGS

9360 S.E. Eola Hills Road
Route 1, Box 252 B
Amity, OR 97101
(503) 835-2782

Owners: Don & Carolyn Byard, Al & Jo Alexanderson
Winemakers: Don Byard & Al Alexanderson
Consultant: Bob McRitchie
Year established: 1980
Production capacity: 10,000 gallons
Vineyards: 20 acres
Touring region: Salem [p. 198]

A bit of background. Although the Byards and Alexandersons first planted their vineyards in 1972 (when they were both working in Salem), their first commercial crush didn't occur until 1980. Byard, whose education is in the field of geography, currently works as a highway planner for the state of Oregon; Alexanderson, an environmental attorney, is president of an energy company in Portland.

Byard, a long-time home winemaker, says he's still excited about the operation of a commercial winery, "even after the sweat-equity phase of development." That's the kind of commitment it takes, though.

Bob McRitchie, the former winemaker at Sokol Blosser, is now the consultant here, which should help Hidden Springs do more to realize its potential.

Visiting the winery ★★☆. The road from the valley climbs and winds through the Eola Hills until it reaches Hidden Springs, where the winery stands on the edge of a hillside covered with cherry trees, holly, Italian prune trees, and vineyards. A little spring bubbles up from a swale on the property line. The view ★★★ to the east is down the broad, fertile plain of the Willamette River, across to the snowcapped Cascades in the hazy distance; to the west, the productive Yamhill basin is rimmed by the Chehalem Mountains and the Coast Range.

Half the 50-acre Hidden Springs property is planted in grapes (Pinot Noir, Chardonnay, Riesling). Surrounding crops include Brooks prunes; not surprisingly, the winery itself is a converted prune-drying shed. (Brooks prunes are remarkably fat and flavorful; try poaching them gently in a sweet white wine for several minutes, then letting them cool in their juice. Serve with lightly whipped cream for a tasty dessert.)

Picnic tables overlooking the orchards are set up on the crushing pad behind the winery. You might think you're at a European country cafe, sitting at one of those picnic tables out back, with their view of the Cascades and the Willamette Valley!

Tasting the wines (NR). Hidden Springs' 1980 Pinot Noir, its first release, won the only gold medal awarded to a Pinot at the 1983 Enological Society festival in Seattle; the winery won additional awards with its 1981 Reserve Pinot and 1983 "regular" Pinot. The '83 version was still giving off a very pleasant strawberry-jam nose at our most recent sampling. The 1985 Pinot has light cherry flavors and won a high rating from the tasting panel at *The Wine Spectator*.

Hidden Springs makes two styles of Riesling, a Chardonnay aged in small oak barrels, and a flavorful, pretty blush called Pacific Sunset, made from Pinot Noir, Sauvignon Blanc, and Riesling.

Bob McRitchie has just signed on as consultant to this winery, and hopes to revitalize it by providing more professional supervision for the wines.

Getting there. From Hwy 99 W in Amity, go west toward Hopewell on the Bellevue-Hopewell Hwy over the Eola Hills. Turn right toward Hopewell on the Hopewell-Lafayette Hwy and right again 0.5 mi farther. The winery is about 2 mi up Eola Hills Rd, close to the top of the hill.

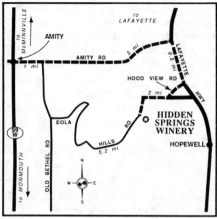

Open Wednesday through Sunday from noon to 5, and by appointment. Tour groups should make appointments; $1 per person fee.

Special events. Hidden Springs participates in the Wine Country Thanksgiving sponsored by the Yamhill County wineries and in the Memorial Day Tastevin Tour sponsored by the Salem-area wineries. Both are three-day events.

Hidden Springs wines can also be tasted at a store called Old Oregon Farms on Highway 18 in Valley Junction.

A word from the winery. *"All Hidden Springs wines are 100 percent grown in Oregon. Winemaking philosophy at Hidden Springs is simple and traditional. Select only the best grapes. Then do only what is necessary to allow and encourage the changes brought about by nature. Hidden Springs wines are matured in French oak barrels, then hand-finished under the personal care of the owners."*

HILLCREST VINEYARD

240 Vineyard Lane
Roseburg, OR 97470
(503) 673-3709

Owner: Richard H. Sommer
Winemaker: Patricia Green
Year established: 1963
Production capacity: 30,000
Vineyards: 35 acres
Touring: Umpqua Valley [p. 202]

A bit of background. Yes, 1963 is correct; HillCrest Vineyard was the first winery to grow European vinifera varieties in Oregon since Repeal. Richard Sommer is the pioneer, inspired by Prof. Maynard Amerine at the University of California at Davis to seek a cool climate. "Go north, young man," he might have said.

Sommer, a young graduate student at the time, rose to the challenge. A man of quixotic yet determined spirit, he planted a 35-acre vineyard whose influence is felt throughout the state. Without Sommer to show the way, Oregon might not have had David Lett, Dick Erath, or Dick Ponzi, or the generation of winegrowers who followed them.

Sommer's interest is viticulture, the hands-on business of growing grapes. He knows pruning, trellising, tractor work. When the would-be winemakers come to pay their respects, Sommer teaches them what grape growing in Oregon is all about. He leaves the enology to his winemaker, Patricia Green.

The Knights of the Vine elevated Sommer to the rank of Supreme Knight three years ago; he was the first person in Oregon to receive the distinction, which is reserved for individuals who have made a "monumental contribution" to wine in America.

Visiting the winery ★★☆. We've always enjoyed our visits to HillCrest, and regret that we can't come by more often. The vineyard and winery are on a secluded hillside relatively high above the Umpqua Valley floor. It's warm enough to avoid winter frosts yet cool enough for the "marginal" growing conditions that make Oregon vines struggle for quality.

The road approaches the winery past vines trained in the Geneva Double Curtain style, which allows the leaves to cascade down between the rows and absorb as much sunlight as possible. There's a tasting bar inside the winery; and upstairs, a room with picnic tables that opens onto a lovely terrace overlooking the vineyards.

Tasting the wines ★★☆. HillCrest markets many Oregon wines, but Riesling is clearly the mainstay of the operation (and the major portion of the vineyard). It's HillCrest's most consistent wine. When the growing season is long, HillCrest makes a Late Harvest of Select Harvest Riesling .(In 1978, conditions were right for an Ice Wine: ripe berries froze on the vine, and were picked and crushed while frozen. The result was a rich, sweet, and very expensive dessert wine.) The 1983 Riesling received a gold medal at the Seattle Enological Society festival in 1987; and in 1988, the 1985 Select Harvest Riesling received the Best of Show award at the Greatest of the Grape.

In addition to many other still varieties, including some of Oregon's oldest red wines, there's a line of sparkling wine sold as Oregon Mist.

Getting there. Take Exit 125 (Roseburg) from I-5 and go west on Garden Valley Rd. Take the Melrose turnoff, go through Melrose, bear right onto Doerner Rd and turn right on Elgarose Loop Rd. Follow Elgarose for 2.4 mi, then turn left into Vineyard Ln.

Open daily from 10 to 5. Closed on major holidays. Tour bus passengers are charged $1, refundable with purchase.

Special events. HillCrest's annual "Sommer Fest" is held in mid-June, around Father's Day.

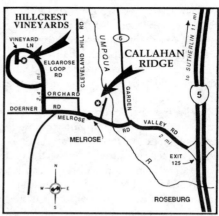

HINMAN VINEYARDS

27012 Briggs Hill Road
Eugene, OR 97405
(503) 345-1945

Owners: Doyle Hinman, David Smith
Winemaker: Doyle Hinman
Year established: 1979
Production capacity: 99,999 gallons
Vineyards: 27 acres
Touring: South. Willamette [p. 200]

A bit of background. Doyle Hinman, a high school teacher and television producer who studied winemaking at Geisenheim in Germany, has guided the fortunes of his winery with considerable acumen. He processes as many grapes here as any winery in Oregon (keeping just under 100,000 gallons, the point at which Oregon's taxes change). He has an arrangement with Boardman Farms (a 400-acre vineyard in eastern Washington) to process their fruit; in exchange, Boardman's parent company bought stock in the winery, allowing for needed expansion. Last year, he also crushed 250 tons of Chardonnay for Fetzer, a California winery that's buying a lot of Oregon and Washington grapes for its moderately priced "American" appellation wines. He supplies 18-liter boxes of varietal wines to restaurants around Oregon, and does private bottlings for a restaurant chain.

His partner in this venture, David Smith, lives in a farmhouse across the road; Doyle lives on the vineyard property, in a modern A-frame tucked into the trees.

Visiting the winery ★★★. A very scenic approach to the winery makes this a lovely excursion from Eugene (the post office says it's still in Eugene). The driveway meanders past rows of Gewurztraminer and Riesling, across a little bridge to the winery, which looks more and more like a small European castle with a squared-off tower, nestled into the side of a wooded hill. When we first visited Hinman Vineyards, we were quite taken with the beautiful setting and the handsome brick winery; now the building has been remodeled, and it's even more impressive.

Original artwork hangs in the winery, and there's a spacious, grassy amphitheater out front that makes a perfect spot for picnics, weddings, and concerts.

Tasting the wines ★★. Hinman makes a line of popular table wines (named Tior, the Old German word for deer) in addition to moderately priced premium varieties. There's also a sparkling White Pinot Noir; the sparkle was added in a custom Charmat process at a Portland facility.

"The Pinot Noir consumer is only one type of consumer," Doyle Hinman told a reporter last year. "We're reaching people who have never had the opportunity to drink Oregon wines" because they've been relatively expensive. Hinman's wines are affordable, usually $5 to $8 a bottle. Still more expensive than California jug wine, but (so the rationale goes) made with higher quality grapes.

Although this is Oregon's largest volume winery, we haven't tasted any Hinman wines for a couple of years, and won't comment on their quality.

Getting there. From Eugene, head west along W. 11th St (Hwy 126). Before you reach the intersection with Beltline (I-205), turn south on Bertlesen and go south 4.4 mi to Spencer Creek Rd. Turn right, go 3 mi to Briggs Hill Rd, then left 4 mi to the winery.

Coming from Elmira or Veneta, take Territorial Rd through Crow, and turn left at the foot of Briggs Hill Rd.

Open from noon to 5 daily. (Closed Christmas Day through New Year's Day.) No charge for groups.

Special events. Summer concert in July.

A word from the winery. *"All of us at Hinman Vineyards extend a warm welcome to visitors to come share a memorable experience at our newly remodeled winery. Wine tasting can now be enjoyed in our new visitors' reception room that overlooks the breathtaking view of the serene Briggs Hill Valley.*

"A glass of fine wine, a picnic, and a friend, and you too will be among the many who have shared a memorable moment with Hinman Vineyards."

HONEYWOOD WINERY

501 14th Street S.E.
Salem, OR 97301

P.O. Box 12278
Salem, OR 97308
(503) 362-4111

Owner: Paul Gallick
Winemaker: Bill Wrey
Year established: 1933
Production capacity: 150,000 gallons
Vineyards: None
Touring region: Salem [p. 198]

A bit of background. Paul Gallick is no doctor or engineer turned winemaker; he is, by profession, an entrepreneur and manager. He was president of the Franklin National Bank in Minneapolis when his involvement with Honeywood began, originally as a private investment. A few years later the winery came up for sale; Paul bought the 50-year-old facility, moved his family to Oregon, and took on the full-time job of managing Honeywood.

Visiting the winery ★★. A grand old warehouse, Honeywood was the first winery to be bonded in Oregon after Repeal. It made a variety of wines from the abundantly available Willamette Valley fruits and berries, and even (briefly) distilled brandy. Under Gallick's ownership, a second-story tasting room has been added; the gift shop alone is bigger than many of Oregon's vest-pocket wineries.

Honeywood is *huge*; current production levels use less than a third of the winery's capacity. The barrel room houses two dozen giant redwood vats, interconnected by a sturdy web of catwalks. The sight of these magnificent specimens reminded us of a French *négociant* warehouse, where similarly ancient casks are used to blend and age some of the great red wines of Burgundy.

Indoor picnic facilities are available at the winery; outdoor tables can be found at Mission Mill Village half a block away.

Tasting the wines ★★☆. A full line of varietal wines, a full line of fruit wines, and now more! In 1987 Honeywood added a Twin Harvest series (98 percent Riesling and 2 percent natural juices), the "twin" harvest of grapes and other fruits. These flavored Rieslings are available with peach, strawberry, raspberry, elderberry, and passion fruit.

We had a bottle of the Strawberry Twin Harvest in a blind tasting and found it clean, fruity, and appealing; strawberry lovers might find it very attractive, and it would make a lovely spritzer with soda or champagne.

Getting there. Take Exit 253 from I-5 and head toward Salem on Mission St. Bear right on Hwy 22, which becomes State St, and turn left on 14th. (NOTE: Honeywood will move to a new facility by September 1989 because the property has been purchased by Tokyo University for a satellite campus. The new location is expected to be on State St, east of Salem's city limits.)

Open Monday through Friday from 9 to 5; Saturday, 10 to 5; Sunday, 1 to 5.

Special events. Honeywood participates in the Salem Wine and Food Festival on the first weekend in November.

A word from the winery. *"Visit Honeywood Winery for the most complete and ambitious lineup of wines in the entire Northwest. Now producing a full line of varietal wines, Honeywood has produced premium fruit wines since 1934 and offers the most extensive list of fruit wines in the Northwest. Our Twin Harvest is a whole new category of wines, which is gaining in popularity. Come to this `Full Service and Historic' Oregon winery for a tour and tasting, and prepare to spend a little more time here than at other wineries."*

'REAL WINE'

Paul Gallick is an outspoken advocate for Oregon fruit wines:

"The public doesn't have a snob attitude about fruit wines," he says. "Fruit wine is real wine, too."

Do Honeywood's fruit wines vary from year to year? "What Mother Nature gives you this year, that's what we bottle. We hear it as a criticism, but we take it as a compliment."

What about complaints that his fruit wines are too sweet? "Our wines are getting less sweet as public tastes change. Besides, we're not trying to make raspberry that tastes like Chenin Blanc."

HOOD RIVER VINEYARDS

4693 Westwood Drive
Hood River, OR 97031
(503) 386-3772

Owners: Cliff & Eileen Blanchette
Winemaker: Cliff Blanchette
Year established: 1981
Production capacity: 7,000 gallons
Vineyards: 12 acres
Touring: Columbia Gorge [p. 27]

A bit of background. Cliff Blanchette's background, as owner of a small manufacturing business in Hood River, doesn't seem to be the ideal training ground for an enologist. It isn't until you learn that he's also an orchardist (of Alsatian heritage at that) that you get a sense of why he does so well: he knows how to make things grow; he has a sense of how things should taste.

As a winemaker, he got his start years ago using fruit from his Post Canyon Farms orchard that would have gone to waste. Even now, after nearly a decade of commercial winemaking, Cliff and Eileen personally pick the Bartlett pear orchard every autumn to ensure a good supply of fruit for their pear wine.

Visiting the winery ★★★. There's a feeling, at the end of the zigzagging road that leads to the winery, of being on top of the world. You're on a meadow overlooking the Columbia River, backed up against tall evergreens; the tip of Mount Hood is visible in the distance.

The winery itself once served as a lean-to where the fodder for livestock was put out (a cattle-loafing barn, it was called). Expansion has added extensive storage space, skylights, stained glass windows, and paneling. The Blanchetts' new home is just up the lane.

Tasting the wines (NR). A gamut of grape wines, including Pinot Noir, Cabernet Sauvignon, Zinfandel (from local grapes), Chardonnay, Gewurztraminer, and two fruit wines, a deliciously sweet raspberry and an off-dry pear.

Hood River wines have done very well in the past. The Chardonnay took gold medals two years in a row at the Oregon State Fair; wine judge Darrell Corti told the 1984 Tri-Cities Festival that the 1982 Riesling was the first wine to which he'd ever given a perfect score. We're in the awkward position of having to say that we haven't tasted Hood River's wines in quite some time, and that we've heard nothing from the winery (except for an update of 1988 production figures and 1989 tasting room hours) in over three years.

Getting there. Take Exit 62 from I-84 and follow Country Club Rd for 1.6 mi. Turn right on Post Canyon Dr, right again on Westwood. The winery is close to the end of the road, about 1 mi from the Post Canyon turnoff.

Open daily from 10 to 5.

Special events. The annual Blossom Festival in Hood River is a major attraction; it's held in mid-April.

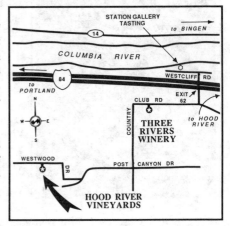

A WORD ABOUT OUR METHODS

To compile the individual winery entries, we relied on our own files, which contain tasting and touring notes on each winery (sometimes going back to the late 1970s); on letters and comments from readers; and, above all, on information supplied by the wineries themselves. We sent a detailed questionnaire to every new winery, and "update" questionnaires to existing wineries. We asked the established wineries to correct any errors in earlier editions. And we asked them to contribute a short item called "A word from the winery." We also asked the wineries to send us samples of any releases they wanted us to taste. The write-ups in this edition reflect these recent tastings, but the ratings take into consideration a winery's entire winemaking history. Predictability of good quality and consistency of execution are as important as success with a particular variety or vintage. Because the ability of individual winemakers makes a difference, personnel changes could also affect the ratings.

Not all the wineries sent us everything we asked for. Even after lots of phone calls and additional mailings, some wineries *still* didn't send updated production information, or maps, or labels; some didn't take advantage of "A word from the winery." Some didn't send wine.

We're well aware that small wineries don't have the resources to answer every questionnaire. Paperwork, we know, is the bane of entrepreneurs everywhere. But our resources are limited, too, and we can't afford to hold this book hostage to the inattention, procrastination, or lack of motivation of a few marginal wineries. That would be unfair to those who cared enough to send us their material and who *did* meet the deadlines.

HOUSTON VINEYARD
86187 Hoya Lane
Eugene, OR 97405
(503) 747-4681

Owners: Steve & Jewellee Houston
Year established: 1985
Vineyards: 5 acres
Production: 2,200 cases

A bit of background. The Houston family has been growing grapes in California's Central Valley for five generations, but land near Lodi was too costly when Steve Houston wanted to start his own vineyard. So he arranged a transfer to Oregon (he works for the Southern Pacific railroad), bought property on the flat riverland east of Eugene, and planted five acres of Chardonnay.

Came time to sell the grapes (five years ago) and the Houstons found no market. Their solution: send the fruit to Washington to be custom-crushed at Coventry Vale and put a Houston Vineyard label on it. To sell the wine back in Oregon, they obtained a bonded wholesaler's license. Jewellee Houston does the marketing, mostly in the Eugene area.

Tasting the wines (NR). Only Chardonnay is made; in 1987 (the most recent vintage released), 1,400 cases were produced, selling for about $6 a bottle at retail. Yields from the vineyard are in the six-tons-per-acre range because of the fertile bottomland. The style is described on the label as "semi-dry" and in the sales literature as "light . . . without the addition of processing-oriented flavors such as oak or yeast."

Open by appointment for vineyard tours.

NOTE: Separate ratings are given for the quality of Pinot Noir by Oregon wineries whose Pinot is significantly *better* than the rest of their wines.

VINTAGE SELECT
1985
OREGON
PINOT NOIR
YAMHILL COUNTY

PRODUCED AND BOTTLED BY
KNUDSEN ERATH WINERY, DUNDEE, OR, USA BW-OR-52
ALC 13% BY VOL

KNUDSEN ERATH
17000 N.E. Knudsen Lane
Dundee, OR 97115
(503) 538-3318

Owner & winemaker: Dick Erath
Year established: 1972
Production capacity: 100,000 gallons
Vineyards: 25 acres
Touring region: Yamhill [p. 195]

A bit of background. If we had to explain our passionate interest in Northwest wine, it would probably hinge on the appeal of a wine from Knudsen Erath. When we returned to Seattle after several years on the East Coast and in France, we bought a case of 1976 Knudsen Erath White Riesling, and with it discovered an entire world of "local" wine. Winemaker Dick Erath was already a formidable presence back then, and his reputation has soared with his nationally recognized Pinot Noirs.

It all began in 1969, when Dick, trained as an electronics engineer, came to Oregon to investigate a job possibility and was "converted" to full-time winemaking by an old acquaintance, Richard Sommer at Hillcrest Vineyards. Dick soon combined his vineyards with Cal Knudsen's property five miles away and formed a partnership with Knudsen to start the winery. (He bought out Knudsen's share last year.) Over the years, Knudsen Erath pulled ahead of Tualatin and Sokol Blosser as Oregon's largest winery.

It's no great trick, you might say (!), to turn out great Pinot Noir if your entire production consists of a few barrels. But Dick Erath makes a huge amount of wine by Oregon standards, and is the largest producer of Pinot Noir in the country: 16,000 cases in 1987. And he markets his wine with innovation and flair: proprietary labels, sparkling wine, special bottlings, a satellite tasting room on the Oregon Coast, low prices.

Visiting the winery ★★★. Worden Hill Road travels up and over the Red Hills of Dundee, the most famous patch of winegrowing acreage in Oregon. At Crabtree Park, turn sharply left and enter the Knudsen Erath estate: over 100 acres of Chardonnay, Pinot Noir, and Riesling vines stand in thick, red clay. The tasting room at the end of the driveway is attached to Erath's home; its patio overlooks a sea of vines, with views of the Willamette Valley and Mount Hood.

The winery itself stands below, in a clearing on the hillside.

Tasting the wines ★★★☆ (Pinot Noir: ★★★★). The 1986 "Vintage Select" Pinot Noir is as good as it gets in Oregon. Great quality (gold medals at the Oregon State Fair and at the Seattle Enological Society) and great price (as low as $12 at one point). Some 7,000 cases of this wine were made, so it may still be available. In our blind tastings, it has shown a generous bouquet of raspberries and strawberries, with undertones of mint, cinnamon, allspice, and pepper; its flavors were broad and intense, and it was just gorgeous with food. (Every once in a while a wine comes along that's so good you can't bring yourself to analyze it any more; you give in and enjoy it.) This on the heels of the 1985 Vintage Select (platinum medal at the American Wine Competition in New York) and the 1983 Vintage Select, which regularly comes out on top in blind tastings over the years.

The other wines from Knudsen Erath include Cabernet Sauvignon, regular and Vintage Select Chardonnay, estate-bottled Riesling, Gewurztraminer, and two blended wines, Pacific Mist (white) and Coastal Mist (blush). While the value is exceptionally good across the board, we've been disappointed by some of the lesser Knudsen Erath bottlings lately. And we regret the loss of the nonvintage Pinot Noir in magnums. Still, year in, year out, Knudsen Erath makes some of the best (and often the best) Pinot Noir in Oregon, produces a lot of it, and sells it at reasonable prices. Don't fight it.

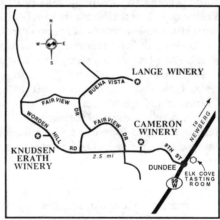

Getting there. From Hwy 99 W. in Dundee, turn west on Ninth, which becomes Worden Hill Rd. The driveway is 2.5 mi from the highway.

Open daily from 11 to 5; from 10:30 to 5:30 in summer (mid-May to mid-October).

Special events. An annual harvest party is held in late August; local restaurants participate with favorite dishes.

A word from the winery. *"Knudsen Erath was founded on the concept that great wines are made only from grapes grown in a climate that matches their needs. We found an area in Dundee whose warm summer days and gently cooling autumn allow the perfect ripening of the noble varieties, giving us the chance to make highly distinctive wines.*

"Modern technology is used to support and to complement time-honored and uncompromising practices of winemaking. We use the minimum amount of processing necessary to produce our wines. We feel that being an estate bottling winery allows us an intimate familiarity with our own grapes and a consistency of flavors and high quality from vintage to vintage.

"We welcome visitors to our tasting room daily."

LA CASA DE VIN
Laurel Lane
P.O. Box 428
Boardman, OR 97818
(503) 481-3151

Owner & winemaker: Ed Glenn
Year established: 1982
Production capacity: 1,000 gallons
Vineyards: 9 acres
Touring: Columbia Valley S. [p. 15]

A bit of background. Ed Glenn, a former attorney in Boardman, began his winemaking career with dandelions and rosehips, then graduated to grapes. By 1980 he had planted his own vineyard in the flat desert plains of eastern Oregon, and in 1983 he made the first commercial Riesling ever produced in eastern Oregon from local Morrow County grapes.

Glenn's tiny winery, La Casa de Vin, is the first in eastern Oregon and could presage major wine production on the Oregon side of the Columbia Valley appellation. One big grower, Boardman Farms, is already involved with Hinman Vineyards in the production of table wine.

Glenn publishes a newsletter called the *Winegrape Market Report*, part authoritative record of grape prices, part insider gossip, part industry ads.

What it's like to visit (NR). The seat of Morrow County, Boardman is a small town on the broad banks of the Columbia. The nearest big winery, Columbia Crest, is half an hour away by road, but only seven miles as the crow flies. But just outside of town you'll find La Casa de Vin's winery and tasting room, looking like a Spanish doll house at the edge of a 10-acre vineyard. It's probably Oregon's least-known winery and least accessible tasting room: no regular hours, no guarantee you'll find Ed Glenn on the premises. *Northwest Wine Country* is the only guide that even mentions the place. ("That's part of the charm," he muses.)

Wines to taste (NR). The 1988 crush produced an off-dry Riesling, some Sauvignon Blanc, a bit of Cabernet Sauvignon, and a blush called Desert Sunrise. Basically a hobby operation, La Casa de Vin bottles perhaps 40 cases at a time, using help from friends and neighbors and "lots of quality control," Glenn says.

Getting there. The winery is just off Exit 165 (Boardman's Industrial Park) from I-84. Or take the Boardman turnoff (Exit 164), go south on Main St, and east on Wilson Rd. A sign pointing to the winery is at Laurel Ln.

Open by invitation.

LANGE WINERY

18380 N.E. Buena Vista Road
Dundee, OR 97115
(503) 538-6476

Owners: Don & Wendy Lange
Winemaker: Don Lange
Year established: 1987
Production capacity: 5,000 gallons
Vineyards: 2 acres
Touring region: Yamhill [p. 195]

A bit of background. You wonder, as you meet Don Lange, if this might not be the way Shakespeare appeared to his contemporaries: a tall man with longish hair and an irrepressible, irreverent sense of humor. But would Shakespeare have been this calm and quiet? Don Lange is, in fact, a poet with a master's degree from the prestigious Writers Workshop at the University of Iowa. Until he got into the wine business, he earned his living as a songwriter, performer, and teacher. For her part, his wife, Wendy, has been a ballet dancer and taught English literature.

The Langes got their first tastes of wine in California's Santa Ynez Valley. Don soon found work in the valley's golden hills, first with Austin Cellars, then as assistant winemaker at Ballard Canyon and the Santa Barbara Winery. It was the caliber of the Oregon Pinot Noirs he tasted, from Knudsen Erath and Eyrie, that prompted him to move north in early 1987.

Visiting the winery (NR). The Langes bought a choice property in the Red Hills of Dundee. Enough room for a house and a small vineyard. Two of the hillside parcel's 27 acres have been planted with Pinot Noir; at an elevation of 900 feet, with exposure to the south-southeast, there's lots of potential.

For the moment (and the foreseeable future), you won't find a tasting room at the Lange Winery, though the wines themselves (with a terrific label by Santa Barbara designer Nancy Johnson) are available at a few specialty stores in Portland.

Tasting the wines (NR). Until their own vineyard matures, the Langes are buying their grapes from a couple of established growers. (One of them is Allan Holstein, vineyard manager for Crochad, among other things.) The only Lange Vineyards wines we've tasted so far were tank samples in early 1988. The 1987 Pinot Gris had a deep tarragon and anise nose, rather on the soft side with a slightly bitter finish. (We also tried one of Don's California reds, fermented in oak, big and rich and toasty.) The plan is to emphasize three varieties (Pinot Noir, Pinot Gris, and Chardonnay), but Don Lange made some Cabernet Sauvignon and Sauvignon Blanc in 1988.

Getting there. From Hwy 99W in Dundee, take Ninth St up the hill (toward Knudsen Erath, which becomes Worden Hill Rd. After 1 mi, turn onto Fairview Dr, and 1.5 mi later onto Buena Vista (private road). Bear right at the T and follow to the end. [**Map:** Knudsen Erath]

Open by appointment only. A $1 fee is charged.

A word from the winery: *"Tucked away in the Red Hills above Dundee, Lange Winery is a small, family-owned operation dedicated to the production of three premium varietals: Pinot Gris, Chardonnay, and Pinot Noir.*

"Our home is surveilled by red-tailed hawks and gray fox, and is nestled among towering fir trees. Wines and vines in the pines! Give us a call, come and taste the wines."

OREGON PINOT GRIS

Judging by the number of Oregon winemakers growing and bottling Pinot Gris, this variety must have found a toe-hold in the marketplace. Its billing as the perfect seafood wine no doubt piques the curiosity of many consumers.

The grape ripens earlier than White Riesling, Gewurztraminer, or Sauvignon Blanc (a boon in Oregon, where early rains regularly threaten to ruin the harvest), and it is prolific, another factor making it an economically sound choice in the vineyard. The wine in the bottle, however, resembles neither the seductively perfumed Pinot Gris of Alsace in the cooler years, nor the more vinous and consistent product from Italy. Oregon Pinot Gris comes in many guises: malolactic, non-malolactic, oaked, unoaked. People tend to love it or hate it.

The three original Oregon producers—Eyrie, Adelsheim, and Ponzi—opted for a uniform style, using a malolactic fermentation. This, they felt, would make the wine more predictable. One thing's for sure: malolactic fermentation reduces the wine's acidity. Too much so, in many cases.

Half a dozen more wineries have started making Pinot Gris, with less predictable results. Stick your nose in any glass of Pinot Gris, and you'll get an extraordinary range of odors! Still, it's early in this wine's stylistic evolution.

Will it ever be the perfect seafood wine? One day, someday, from some wineries, maybe.

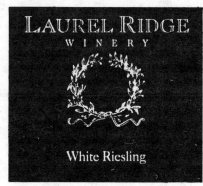

White Riesling

LAUREL RIDGE WINERY

Route 1, Box 255
P.O. Box 456
Forest Grove, OR 97116
(503) 359-5436

Owners: David & Susan Teppola,
  Michael & Kay Dowsett,
  Helmut & Lilo Wetzel
Winemaker: Rich Cushman
Year established: 1986
Production capacity: 22,000 gallons
Vineyards: 74 acres
Touring: Tualatin Valley [p. 192]

A bit of background. The history of this winery goes back over a century, to a German immigrant named Frank Reuter who declared that the Willamette Valley would become "the Rhineland of America." He built a home and planted vineyards on David Hill, near Forest Grove, and before he died he produced several noteworthy Rieslings. But the vines were torn out during Prohibition and subsequent attempts to recapture Reuter's dream failed. The Charles Coury Winery didn't make it, nor did a rescue attempt under the label of Reuter's Hill Vineyard.

Laurel Ridge is the latest winery on the site; it shows more promise than its predecessors and intends to make a serious run at sparkling wine production. Three families share an interest in the winery itself. Mike Dowsett, the city attorney for Beaverton, and his wife, Kay, have restored the grand old farmhouse and rehabilitated the original vineyard. Their partners include David and Susan Teppola, owners of the 250-acre Finn Hill Vineyard in Carlton, and a third couple, Helmut and Lilo Wetzel. The 24-acre vineyard at Laurel Ridge and the Finn Hill property (its 50 bearing acres just now coming into maturity) will provide all the grapes for the winery.

Rich Cushman is the winemaker. He has a biology degree from OSU, did two years of graduate work at U.C.-Davis, and spent time in Germany before returning to his native Oregon. He was working at Chateau Benoit, where he honed his skills in sparkling wine production, when he signed on with the Laurel Ridge group.

Visiting the winery ★★☆. The outskirts of Forest Grove have barely fallen away when you turn up the narrow road; from the ridgetop you see vineyards, mountains, the lush valley full of truck farms and gardens. Turn down the driveway and you're at Laurel Ridge Winery.

In addition to the white farmhouse, three structures occupy the hillside: the large winery itself, an adjacent pressing facility, and a separate storage building. (To process the grapes quickly and gently—essential for sparkling wine—Laurel Ridge has installed an enormous stainless steel press, one of the two biggest in Oregon, that can press and dejuice 15 to 20 tons in a single cycle.) A new tasting room has been added since our last visit; "We now have light and heat!" reports Susan Teppola. A picnic area is planned for 1989.

Eventually, more ambitious plans: caves, dug into the hillside, to store and age the best bottles of sparkling wine. And transforming the farm-house into a visitor center, with a tasting room and banquet space.

Tasting the wines ★★☆. We haven't tasted these wines regularly for a while, but reports on the most recent vintage are encouraging, particularly the 1987 Sauvignon Blanc. (We tasted the 1986 version, which was fine.) There's also a blend called Laurel Blanc (Sauvignon Blanc, Semillon, and Sylvaner) finished in a dry style, and priced under $5.

Laurel Ridge produces two "Oregon Sparkling Wines," one called Brut, made from Pinot Noir, which spends four months on the lees after fermentation, one called Cuvee Blanc, made from Riesling. Rich Cushman says sparkling wine represents 25 percent of the winery's output now, and might become half its production within a couple of years. The bottle of Brut we tasted had a nose of grass and hay, with eucalyptus flavors in the mouth and a pleasant aftertaste.

Unlike many wineries, which don't want to offend their retailers by offering special prices at the winery, Laurel Ridge offers good savings on many of its wines at the tasting room.

Getting there. From Forest Grove, head west on Hwy 8, turn right on Thatcher Rd for 1.5 mi, then left on David Hill Rd and go 1.5 mi to the winery. [**Map:** Tualatin]

Open from 12 to 5 on weekends and by appointment. Closed Christmas through January. Groups of 15 or more are charged $1 per person, refundable with a purchase.

Special events. A Fourth of July Barrel Tasting, a mid-July "anniversary special," a harvest party in early October, the Thanksgiving weekend wine tour (along with other Tualatin Valley wineries), and a December case sale.

A word from the winery. *"With a commanding view of the Tualatin Valley, Laurel Ridge Winery sits on a knoll just west of Forest Grove. Chosen in the 1800s by a German winemaking family, it is one of Oregon's oldest vineyard/winery sites. Although the original vineyard was lost during Prohibition, it was replanted in 1966. The house, built in 1883, still stands and is occupied by two of the principals, by whom it was lovingly restored.*

"From the vineyard at the winery and our other vineyard in Yamhill County come all the grapes for Laurel Ridge wines. Sparkling wines by the traditional méthode champenoise *and premium white varietal wines are the emphasis here. Please visit and sample our wines."*

LOOKINGGLASS WINERY

6561 Lookingglass Road
Roseburg, OR 97470
(503) 679-8198

Owners: Gerald & Margie Rizza
Winemaker: Gerald Rizza
Year established: 1988
Production capacity: 5,000 gallons
Vineyards: 4 acres
Touring: Umpqua Valley [p. 202]

A bit of background. Nuclear engineer Gerald Rizza has traveled all over the United States to build power plants, but the vivid memory of Sunday meals under the grape arbor with his grandfather and uncles has exerted the most powerful influence on the way he lives now. It's a transatlantic heritage, from the rocky hillsides of Syracusa, Sicily, to the golden green slopes of southern Oregon.

Visiting the winery (NR). The Rizzas originally planted their vineyard in 1974 and lost it to foraging animals ("Deer 1, Rizzas 0" is how Gerald described it). They're going to try again this year, putting in four acres of Pinot Noir on the 47-acre property.

The winery itself was dug 14 feet into the deep Josephine clay. It's made of "slumpstone" and covered with a blue tile roof. The large tasting room has a gift shop (jewelry, antiques); its windows include stained glass from a church in New York.

Tasting the wines (NR). The first crush was limited to about 1,000 gallons of White Riesling, made from botrytised, late-harvest grapes, and scheduled for release in April 1989.

The Rizzas expect to sell almost all their production at the tasting room. "You make the wine, and I'll sell it," Margie Rizza tells Gerald.

Getting there. From I-5, take Exit 124 to West Roseburg and proceed west on W. Harvard. Turn left onto Lookingglass Rd. After 4.5 mi turn right onto Cinbar Dr. The winery is the second driveway on the left.

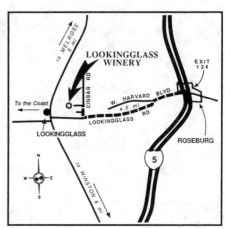

Open daily, noon to 5, April through December. Tour groups are welcome; $1 tasting fee refundable with purchase. Wheelchair accessible.

Special events. Mid-April barrel tasting; late October harvest party.

A word from the winery. *"We are a family-owned winery continuing a winemaking tradition that spans several generations. Our philosophy of winemaking emphasizes quality fruit, temperature control, and minimizing the use of antioxidants.*

"We look forward to sharing a part of our dream-come-true with the visitors to our tasting room. Barrel-tasting in the cellar is available for the obvious enophile."

MERIDIAN VINTNERS
(Springhill Cellars)
2920 Scenic Drive N.W.
Albany, OR 97312
(503) 928-1009

Owners: Michael & Karen McLain,
   Gary Budd, Mervin Anthony
Winemaker: Mike McLain
Year established: 1988
Production capacity: 1,500 gallons
Vineyards: 7 acres
Touring: South. Willamette [p. 200]

A bit of background. Mike McLain and his wife, Karen, planted their vineyard on Spring Hill, above Corvallis, 10 years ago, and Mike has regularly won awards for amateur winemaking at the Oregon State Fair. As a real estate broker specializing in vineyard property, he has traveled all over Oregon putting together deals for others; now, with Karen's father, Mervin Anthony, and a business associate, Gary Budd, he's started a winery of his own.

Visiting the winery (NR). Meridian Vintners buys its grapes from Mike McLain's vineyard and has its facility located on the Spring Hill property. The first wines produced were 1,200 gallons of Riesling, Pinot Noir, and White Pinot. Muller Thurgau and Chardonnay may be added in 1989. A tasting room may be open by summer; visitors should telephone the winery.

Getting there. From I-5 northbound, take Exit 233; from I-5 southbound, take Exit 234 to downtown Albany. Cross the Willamette on Hwy 20, going toward Corvallis. Take the second turn to the right after the bridge to reach Scenic Dr.

MONTINORE VINEYARDS

Dilley Road
P.O. Box 560
Forest Grove, OR 97116-0560
(503) 359-5012

Owners: Mr. & Mrs. Leo Graham
President & general manager:
  Jeff Lamy
Winemaker: Matt Hill
Year established: 1983 (vineyard),
  1987 (winery)
Production capacity: 300,000 gallons
  (planned)
Vineyards: 430 acres
Touring: Tualatin Valley [p. 192]

A bit of background. Keep this winery well in mind: though it's only been around since last summer, Montinore Vineyards is on its way to being the biggest winery in Oregon. With a production capacity of 300,000 gallons, it's going to be a dominant force in the Oregon wine industry. The winery's production will be large enough to appeal to out-of-state distributors; the wine will have the kind of marketing support (advertising, promotion) that wholesalers like to see. The winery intends to take the lead in staging its own wine promotions in distant markets, and the historic headquarters should do well in attracting tourists. (It's a little like watching a six-foot-six eighth grader shooting baskets on the playground: you know he's going to make the team on the basis of size alone, you just don't know how good he's going to be.)

The Grahams, whose investment is making Montinore Vineyards possible, are involved in several business ventures, including Stimson Lumber Company. The property's original owner, John Forbis, named the estate. An attorney for the Southern Pacific Railroad, he'd worked for Anaconda before moving west, and dubbed his new home Montinore (for "Montana-in-Oregon").

Jeff Lamy, who's been appointed president and general manager, is a Yale graduate and business consultant who had worked with several wineries and vineyards in Oregon. His enthusiasm for Montinore is based, as much as anything, on its site and its soils. The exposure for much of the property is east-facing, like the best vineyards of the Medoc, Sauternes, the Cote d'Or, and Alsace, and without the cloud cover that blankets the Napa Valley. The soils are ideal, five feet deep over deep marine sediments, with a "soil profile" similar to the vineyards of Burgundy, and in fact the same soils (Jory, Laurelwood, Cornelius) that produce award-winning wines for Tualatin, Shafer, and Eyrie.

Lamy points out that European wineries acknowledge the importance of the grower, of the site, while Americans tend to celebrate the skill of individual winemakers. To redirect the public's attention to the primacy of the vineyard, Lamy and Graham have instituted the "Montinore Vineyards Trophy," given each year to the grower (or two) whose vines produce the wine that wins the Governor's Sweepstakes Award at the Oregon State Fair. Up to two trophies will be given each year.

Visiting the winery ★★★☆. "Montinore will be Oregon's first great wine estate," Lamy promises. It's certainly an impressive place to visit.

You turn in from the public road and head up a driveway lined with statuesque bigleaf maples toward the old mansion; its manicured grounds overlook a pond and vineyards. It could easily be a wine domaine in France. Along with Chateau Ste. Michelle and Columbia Crest, Montinore conveys a sense of Old World permanence.

The estate consists of nearly 600 acres, of which 430 are already planted with vineyards (150 acres in Pinot Noir alone). The centerpiece, the fabulous 1905 mansion, will be converted to administrative uses, and the adjoining pool house will become the tasting room and visitor facility. Several picnic areas are planned.

For the moment, Montinore wines are being made in a rented building near Forest Grove. Three phases of construction are planned. To begin, a basic winery with underground champagne cellars. Next year, an additional building. Finally, in 1990, a 30,000-square-foot building for storage of case goods.

Tasting the wines ★★★. The first Montinore wine we tasted, the 1987 Pinot Gris, didn't bode well; though its off-dry style is legitimate for Pinot Grigio in northern Italy, it was far too sweet for our taste. (It looked for a moment as if that gangly kid wasn't even going to dribble the ball downcourt, let alone score a slamdunk.) So what do we know? The wine sold out in a flash.

We've recently tasted the 1987 Montinore Pinot Noir, produced from four-year-old vines, early in its evolution, a few months before release. It was a clean, robust wine with the oak and fruit competing for the limelight. Complex cherry and berry nose, licorice and earthy flavors in the mouth. The texture was smooth, tannins moderate, the finish long.

The 1987 Chardonnay needed more intense fruit to support the oak and alcohol. Perhaps that will emerge with more bottle age. A clean wine. The 1987 Oregon White Riesling was bright, balanced, tasty, and a little spritzy. Initially, the nose had some unexpected hay and menthol notes, but the flavors were pure Riesling.

Montinore named its winemaking team as we were going to press. Matt Hill, the longtime assistant to Bill Fuller at Tualatin, gets the lead spot, while Paul Gates, formerly at Veritas and Shafer, will be assistant winemaker. Lamy will continue his supervision of the sparkling wine production.

Getting there. From Forest Grove, travel 2.4 mi south on Hwy 47. At Dilley (an unincorporated community), turn west on Dudney Ave. One block later, turn north on Dilley Rd and continue 0.3 mi to the entrance.

Open weekends from noon to 5 and by appointment.

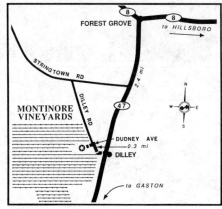

A word from the winery. *"Montinore embraces the European concept that great wines are made in the vineyard; design and intensive management maximize grape quality. Still and sparkling wines are handcrafted in small lots so as to realize the fruits' greatness."*

MT. HOOD WINERY
88510 E. Gov't Camp Loop Road
P.O. Box 99
Government Camp, OR 97028
(503) 272-0209

Owners: Doug Whitlock, Gary Hood
Winemaker: Doug Whitlock
Year established: 1974
Production capacity: 3,000 gallons
Vineyards: None
Touring region: Mount Hood [p.210]

A bit of background. Founded by Lester Martin 15 years ago in the community of Mount Hood, in the Hood River Valley, this winery produced a range of interesting wines from apples and berries, cherries and pears (the blueberry was best), and was just getting into coolers. But Martin, a retired chemical engineer, had intended to spend more time trout fishing than winemaking when he moved here from California, so he sold the winery last year to a Vancouver, Washington, attorney named Doug Whitlock.

Visiting the winery (NR). Whitlock moved the tasting room to Government Camp last year, where there's lots of tourist traffic: skiers in winter, hikers and nature lovers in summer. Government Camp, once a bustling place (with a European-style tramway running up to Timberline Lodge), shriveled to a two-block cluster of restaurants and shops after the highway bypassed the town; the tramway terminal was converted to condominiums. Mount Hood's building is a small, peaked-roof structure on the south side of the bypass highway, next to Charlie's restaurant.

If you're in the area, we recommend a quick trip up to the lodge, where you can enjoy a splendid view ★★★ and have a glass of grape wine as well.

Tasting the wines (NR). Five fruit and berry wines were made at the new facility in 1988: we haven't tasted them. Plans call for doubling the amount of fruit wine produced in 1989, as well as crushing some Gewurztraminer and Pinot Noir in anticipation of a new line of varietal grape wines in the near future.

Getting there. Hwy 26 from Portland now bypasses Government Camp, but the "Loop Rd" goes right through town.

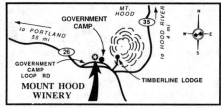

Hours will be flexible during the skiing season and in summer. Open Tuesday to Sunday, 10 to dark, is a possibility, with the winery closed weekdays during the off-season. Call ahead if you plan a visit.

NEHALEM BAY WINERY

34965 Highway 53
Nehalem, OR 97131
(503) 368-5300

Owner: Pat McCoy
General manager & winemaker:
  Jeff Daniels
Year established: 1973
Production capacity: 10,000 gallons
Vineyards: None
Touring: Oregon Coast [p. 207]

A bit of background. Oregon's coastline, which draws more tourists to the state than any other attraction, is a natural place to show off Oregon's wines. Pat McCoy, the owner of Nehalem Bay Winery, is an enthusiastic promoter of tourism. His winery has been in existence since 1973, first as a fruit and berry operation; grape wines were added in 1981, and the passion here is clearly for promotion, rather than winemaking.

McCoy is a former broadcaster with a flair for the theatrical. A few years ago, he transported a pack of young Yorkshire and Berkshire pigs to an island in the Columbia River, intending (he said) to harvest a regular crop of "wild boar" for gourmet restaurants and festivals at his winery. Looking for all the world like Orson Welles, McCoy solemnly assured the reporters and TV cameras who assembled for the first "hunt" that he would "kill no swine before its time."

Visiting the winery ★★☆. From its hillside overlooking the Nehalem River, the winery sits on a portion of the Oregon coast devoted to dairy farming and cheesemaking. The structure, formerly the Mohler Creamery, was abandoned when McCoy bought it in 1973, but he reasoned that a cheese factory, with its sound construction, constant inside temperature, and thriving cultures of helpful lactobacillus bacteria, would make a good winery. He remodeled the outside and installed a blackberry winery. With its half-timbered facade, its tasting room, and an upstairs art gallery, it presents an alluring attraction, just off Highway 101.

Tasting the wines ★. Two or three vinifera wines are offered; their provenance, formerly California, is now said to be Oregon. At last report, they included Chardonnay and Pinot Noir, in addition to red, white, and blush table wines. Other wines might include rhubarb, apple, or Niagara. The lineup varies, depending on the availability of fruit and grapes. Two versions of Tillamook blackberry wine were released in late 1988.

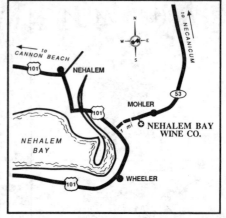

Getting there. From Hwy 101 (the Oregon Coast Hwy) between Wheeler and Nehalem, take Hwy 53 for 1 mi toward Mohler. The winery is on the right.

Open daily from 10 to 5. Tour groups are welcome without charge.

Special events. Not so much a festival as a tourist attraction, the Tillamook County Cheese, Food, and Wine Tour provides one of the few "tours" on the Oregon coast. It's a chain of loosely connected businesses that begins with the Nehalem Bay Winery at the northern end, hooks up with three attractions in Garibaldi (Phil & Joe's Crab Company, Smith's Pacific Shrimp Company, and the Bay Front Bakery), and ends 23 miles later in Tillamook at the Tillamook Cheese Company.

A word from the winery. *"Winemaker Jeff Daniels invites our guests to visit and experience the 1909 cheese factory which now serves as our winery in the plush, green Nehalem Bay area. We offer five premium, blush, unique-to-Oregon dessert wines, self-guided tours, picnic area, always free tastings, and advice on special sight-seeing."*

Oregon Montmorency
Cherry Wine

*Oak Grove Orchards
Winery*

ALCOHOL 12.5% BY VOLUME. CONTAINS SULFITES
PRODUCED & BOTTLED BY OAK GROVE ORCHARDS WINERY
6090 CROWLEY RD. RICKREALL, OR 97371

OAK GROVE ORCHARDS WINERY
(Stevens Cellars)
6090 Crowley Road
Rickreall, OR 97371
(503) 364-7052

Owners: Carl & Louise Stevens
Winemaker: Carl Stevens
Year established: 1987
Production capacity: 3,000 gallons
Touring region: Salem [p. 198]

A bit of background. Carl Stevens is a longtime amateur winemaker who has started to make wine commercially, using his own native American grapes and cherries. A structure from the Oregon National Guard's training facility at Camp Adair was moved to the Stevens property and renovated for use as a tasting room and picnic shelter.

Tasting the wines (NR). Stevens makes wine from Concord and Golden Muscat grapes and from Montmorency cherries. He reports that the 1988 vintage was exceptional for the Golden Muscat grapes.

The Montmorency (pie cherry) wine has a devoted local following.

Getting there. From Salem, take Hwy 22 westbound, turn north on Oak Grove Rd, jog left and right at Farmers Rd, continue north on Oak Grove and right on Crowley Rd. [Map: Glen Creek]

Open from noon to 5, Tuesday through Sunday (and holidays), from February through December.

Special events. The Salem Tastevin Tour on Memorial Day weekend. There's a $1 charge for food and entertainment.

A word from the winery. *"Come visit our winery, located on the west slope of the beautiful Eola Hills, overlooking a large expanse of agricultural land, consisting of cherry orchards, oak timber, and grain fields, with the Coast Range in the background. We have a large picnic area and seating capacity for 20 people in our tasting room."*

1985 VINTAGE SELECT
 OREGON PINOT NOIR

Willamette Valley Table Wine

PRODUCED & BOTTLED BY
OAK KNOLL WINERY, INC. HILLSBORO, OREGON

OAK KNOLL WINERY

Burkhalter Road
Route 6, Box 184
Hillsboro, OR 97123
(503) 648-8198

Owners: Ron & Marj Vuylsteke
Winemaker: Ron Vuylsteke
Year established: 1970
Production capacity: 95,000 gallons
Vineyards: None
Touring: Tualatin Valley [p. 192]

A bit of background. Ron Vuylsteke was an engineer for Tektronix when he and his wife, Marj, made a bumper crop of blackberries into wine. The hobby became an art, then a livelihood, and Oak Knoll was bonded in 1970. First known as a fruit winery, producing as much as a third of all Oregon wines a decade ago, Oak Knoll has since shifted 90 percent of its production to vinifera grapes.

"The heyday of fruit and berry wines in Oregon was in the late '70s," Steve Vuylsteke told an interviewer last year. Steve is barely 30, the youngest member of the large Vuylsteke family; his background as Oak Knoll's director of marketing made him the ideal choice for the winery's new president.

It's very much a family company. One brother runs the warehouse, another is assistant winemaker to his father. And Ron Vuylsteke still has the reputation of being one of the most knowledgeable chemists in the Oregon wine industry.

Because Oak Knoll doesn't own any vineyards, it can buy whatever amount of grapes it needs to make whatever amount of wine it can sell. This flexibility allows the winery to respond more readily to market conditions than competitors who are saddled with extensive vineyards.

Visiting the winery ★★☆. Oak Knoll looks like it ought to be a dairy farm, and in fact it once was. But inside the old cow barns, in stalls that heifers once occupied, stand stainless steel fermenting tanks and 200 French oak barrels (including a few from Chateau Lafite). A guided visit with a member of the Vuylsteke family (at some point, every member of the large family has worked for the winery) can be fascinating, especially if it includes tank sampling. A picnic under the oak trees is delightful.

Tasting the wines ★★☆ (Pinot Noir: ★★★). The best Oak Knoll wines are small lots of Pinot Noir labeled Vintage Select. And they can be remarkable. One example, from the 1983 Oregon State Fair: Andre Tchelistcheff, the Russian-born dean of American winemakers who was serving as senior wine judge, reportedly held high a glass of Pinot Noir and pleaded with the judging panel, "I am prepared to defend this wine with the last breath in my little body!" The wine was Oak Knoll's 1980 Vintage Select Pinot Noir; with Tchelistcheff's support it went on to win a gold medal and the Governor's Trophy for the best vinifera wine in the competition. As soon as the wine's identity was revealed, Tchelistcheff telephoned the Vuylstekes to offer his congratulations. "One of the greatest Pinot Noirs I have come across in 50 years of tasting," he said. That same year, Oak Knoll also won the Governor's Trophy for the best fruit wine with their raspberry.

Pinot Noir leads the list of the varietal wines available for tasting, followed by Chardonnay, Riesling, Gewurztraminer, and a blush wine.

Followers of Oak Knoll's popular Niagara (a native American grape) will be pleased that it's back again. And Oak Knoll continues its line of fruit wines: rhubarb, loganberry, raspberry, blackberry.

Disappointed by the results of several out-of-state judgings, Oak Knoll now enters its wines only at the Oregon State Fair. We regret that we've also been disappointed by recent Oak Knoll wines. The 1986 Vintage Select Pinot Noir had a lovely, silky mouth feel but a bitter finish; the regular bottling was lacking in flavor. (For close to $20 a bottle, we expect more.) The 1987 Chardonnay, better than the over-oaked 1986, impressed us as rather one-dimensional. Yes, Robert Parker loves these wines. Sorry, we can't muster the same enthusiasm.

Getting there. From Beaverton, take Hwy 10 past the community of Farmington; turn right on Rood Bridge Rd, left on Burkhalter Rd. From Hillsboro, go south toward Newberg on Hwy 219 for four mi; turn left on Burkhalter Rd. [**Map:** Ponzi]

Open Wednesday through Sunday from noon to 5. Saturday, 11 to 5. Other days by appointment. There's a $1 per person fee for tour groups.

Special events. The biggest festival sponsored by an Oregon winery is Oak Knoll's "Bacchus Goes Bluegrass," a two-day blast in the second half of May that gets as crowded as Woodstock.

A word from the winery. *"You can have the best winemaking equipment money can buy, the best grapes from the most ideal growing region, and the most talented winemaker in the world, but if the wine isn't what you, the consumer, likes to drink, the winemakers end up drinking a lot of their own wine. At Oak Knoll, we keep a pulse on the wine-drinking public to identify what wine qualities are most desirable. You might say I'm obsessed with finding out what it is in a glass of wine that excites you . . . and brings you back for more."*

MAKING WHAT THE CONSUMER WANTS:
Oak Knoll's Rebuttal

In the first edition of this book two years ago, we wrote: "The atmosphere in the tasting room [at Oak Knoll] . . . is a bit like dropping in at Baskin-Robbins after school." Oak Knoll's president Steve Vuylsteke responds.

"I sensed that this statement (which made the hair on the back of my neck stand on end) has something to do with the fact that we produce close to a dozen wines and that (except for reserve bottlings) we have all the wines available for tasting. I know that many wineries choose a few wines from their list and only pour what they want to pour. A customer comes in, asks to taste a wine not open, and is turned down—is this good for the winery image? My belief has always been that getting the wine into people's mouths is the best form of promotion.

"In regard to making 12 wines, I think if a winery proves itself successful, regardless of the number of wines it makes, that makes a `Baskin-Robbins' statement ridiculous. Unlike wineries and vineyard operations that grow their own grapes, we buy from many areas of the Willamette Valley. This gives us a broader understanding of micro-climate differences and a definite marketing advantage. We are a market-driven winery; we research what the consumer wants to drink and then make that type of wine. This gives us considerable flexibility in the marketplace and a greater opportunity to meet the ever-changing consumer taste preference. Many a winery, large and small, suffers from being production-driven, tied to the specific varieties they have in the ground. Of course they have to make these varieties (or sell the grapes) and in turn must form their marketing strategy to meet their production mix.

"The fact that we've been around 18 years and are a growing, viable, profitable operation able to change our product mix when demand warrants should say something about us. As our winery continues to mature (we've gone from 15 fruit and berry wines and eight varietals in 1980 to six varietals and four fruit/ berry), we will continue to put great emphasis on making wines the consumers ask for, in the style they want, and at a reasonable price. If the day comes when all the consumer wants is red or white, by golly we'll make red and white."

PANTHER CREEK

1501 E. 14th Street
McMinnville, OR 97128
(503) 472-8080

Owners: Ken & Corby Wright
Winemaker: Ken Wright
Year established: 1986
Production capacity: 3,500 gallons
Vineyards: None
Touring region: Yamhill [p. 195]

A bit of background. "There is no shortcut to wine production," says Ken Wright, with the certainty of a legal counselor advising a recalcitrant client.

Ken switched from a pre-law program at the University of Kentucky to pursue studies in winemaking and viticulture at UC Davis. He'd already worked as a bottling line supervisor for Brown Foreman distillers in Louisville, and waited on tables in restaurants. Once in California, he worked as winemaker for two Monterey County wineries, Ventana Vineyards and Robert Talbott Vineyards. Travel in Burgundy and Bordeaux confirmed his conviction that constant attention to detail is crucial: harvesting at the proper time, sorting grapes before crush, gentle racking, barrel management. In all, the concept of "least possible intervention."

The Wrights and their two young sons left California in 1985, attracted to Oregon by the potential of making Pinot Noir and the prospect of getting in on an industry that was (and is) still young. For a time after they moved to McMinnville, you could find Ken Wright waiting on tables at Roger's Seafood Restaurant. That was before Panther Creek got off the ground. These days, he's also a consultant to Eola Hills Winery.

Corby Wright spends most of her time as the only permanent staff member for the most successful community-based wine festival in Oregon, the International Pinot Noir Celebration; she also does public relations for the Yamhill County Wineries Association.

Visiting the winery (NR). Panther Creek's beige and brown winery is a modest Western-style building in one of McMinnville's industrialized neighborhoods; Eyrie and Arterberry are nearby. It's open only to people in the wine trade, who sell half the winery's production outside of Oregon; with only one product for sale, there wouldn't be much for tourists to taste.

Tasting the wines ★★★. The first release from Panther Creek was a blend of Cabernet Sauvignon, Merlot, and Cabernet Franc that was brought in barrel from California; it was a flavorful wine with nicely balanced fruit and oak.

Better established now, Panther Creek buys its grapes (exclusively Pinot Noir) from growers in the Eola and Dundee hills, limiting its

---

purchases to vineyards that keep the yield to three tons per acre. Ken and Corby Wright sort the grapes to remove all leaves, unripe fruit, and mold (very picky!). Ken uses up to five different strains of yeast to give the wine a greater complexity, ferments on the skins for up to three and a half weeks to extract more tannins for longer life and greater color. The wines are racked only once and bottled without filtering.

Ken Wright's Pinot Noirs are intense and tannic, vigorous wines that would benefit from an extra year or two of bottle age. We found white pepper and cherries in the nose of the 1986 Pinot, well balanced with lush fruit.

Panther Creek bottles are shipped lying on their sides, not "neck down," so the sediment won't collect behind the cork. Ken advises decanting the wines and letting them breathe; a full day isn't too long.

Getting away from the subject of Pinot Noir for just a moment: Ken Wright believes that better clones of Chardonnay will eventually be available in Oregon, and will radically change the quality of Chardonnay in Oregon. Hear, hear!

Getting there. Traveling south on Hwy 99W as you enter McMinnville, turn left on Lafayette Ave, then right on 14th. Panther Creek is the third building on the right. [**Map:** Arterberry]

Open to the trade, by appointment only.

A word from the winery. *"We are a small winery dedicated to the production of Pinot Noir only. All of the winemaking operations are performed by the owners, Ken & Corby Wright."*

NOTE: Separate ratings are given for the quality of Pinot Noir by Oregon wineries whose Pinot is significantly *better* than the rest of their wines.

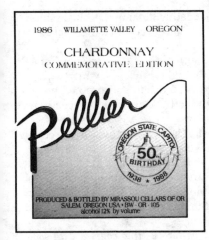

1986   WILLAMETTE VALLEY   OREGON

CHARDONNAY
COMMEMORATIVE EDITION

Pellier

OREGON STATE CAPITOL
50ᵗʰ
BIRTHDAY
1938 ★ 1988

PRODUCED & BOTTLED BY MIRASSOU CELLARS OF OR
SALEM, OREGON USA • BW • OR • 105
alcohol 12% by volume

PELLIER

(Mirassou Cellars of Oregon)
6785 Spring Valley Road N.W.
Salem, OR 97304
(503) 371-3001

Owners: Mitch & Beverly Mirassou
Winemaker: Mitch Mirassou
Year established: 1985
Production capacity: 35,000 gallons
Vineyards: 45 acres
Touring region: Salem [p. 198]

A bit of background. The story goes back to the 1880s, when Mitch Mirassou's great-grandmother Henrietta Pellier, daughter of a French-born vintner, married Pierre Mirassou. The Mirassou-Pellier dynasty survived the near-total destruction of California vines by the phylloxera root louse, as well as the rigors of Prohibition. Mirassou Cellars has emerged as one of California's best-known names, producing some of its best sparkling wine.

Mitch and Bev Mirassou, not in the direct line of succession to the California operation, moved to Oregon in 1981 and started a nursery business. They also began planting 45 acres of their own 90-acre property not far from Bethel Heights Vineyard. By 1985, they were ready to bond their winery, and decided to sell their wine under the name of Mitch's ancestors, the Pelliers.

The original label featured an ancestral-looking horse and wagon; the new label may be more stylish—it won a lithography competition for its printer—but it's somehow less distinctive.

Visiting the winery ★★★. Mirassou Cellars of Oregon has been open to the public since May 1986. It's a 4,000-square-foot building with a tasting room in front and a crushing pad out back. Young vines—45 acres planted, another 40 to be developed—are growing on the terraced hillsides around the winery. A covered deck with tables makes for a sheltered picnic spot; attractive landscaping completes the setting. On a clear day, you can see across the Willamette Valley to the peaks of Mount Hood, Mount St. Helens, and Mount Jefferson.

Tasting the wines ★★. Initial wines on the market include a very good Pinot Noir Blanc (with a lovely salmon color), a Gewurztraminer, and a Riesling. An estate-grown Pinot Noir did well in an East Coast competition.

The 1987 Riesling is Pellier's best wine, off-dry with pleasant apricot flavors. The 1985 Cabernet Sauvignon had a slightly vegetal nose with good cherry flavors, and was still loaded with tannin. A blush, the 1985 Pinot Noir Blanc, was oxidized at our most recent tasting; perhaps an irregular bottle.

Getting there. From Hwy 99 W. south of Amity, turn east on Zena Rd, go 3.3 mi to Spring Valley Rd, then 1.2 mi north to the winery.

From Salem, cross the bridge to West Salem and proceed north on Wallace Rd (Hwy 221) for 5.8 mi. Turn left at Lincoln and proceed 2 mi to Spring Valley Rd. [**Map:** Bethel Heights]

Open from 11 to 5 daily except Monday. Groups over 10 are charged $2.50 per person, which includes a wineglass.

Special events. Pellier joins the Salem-area wineries as a participant in the Tastevin Tour over Memorial Day weekend, and offers an October Harvest Moon festival on the full moon weekend closest to October 1. There are also concerts on the last Sunday of each month, May through September.

A word from the winery. *"Our pastoral setting coupled with some of Oregon's finest wines make us a winery not to miss on your next tour. In the spring, relax on our deck with a glass of award-winning Pinot Noir and "listen" to the grapes grow. In summer, enjoy a glass of light fruity White Riesling as you watch the hawks circling overhead and the flock of sheep grazing in the pasture below. Fall arrives and the view from the tasting room changes from brilliant greens to oranges, golds, and reds. A glass of rich Chardonnay fits this scene, and with the cooler evening breezes you move into the cozy tasting room. It's winter, and you relax in the tasting room with a glass of warming Cabernet Sauvignon and watch the rain showers move up and down the valley.*

"Every day is new and relaxing as Mother Nature paints another beautiful picture around our winery. Please come and relax with us and enjoy our fine wines on any day."

PONDEROSA VINEYARDS

39538 Griggs Drive
Lebanon, OR 97355
(503) 259-3845

Owners: William & Judy Looney
Winemaker: Bill Looney
Year established: 1987
Production capacity: 4,000 gallons
Vineyards: 16 acres
Touring: South. Willamette [p. 200]

A bit of background. Bill Looney, a technician for Hewlett-Packard, has worked in mining and manufacturing as well. He says his interest in wine was triggered by Bible studies, and he's been making wine since 1984.

The label tells a story: the covered wagon represents the Looney clan's journey across the Rockies in 1843 with the Applegate wagon train (they were the first white settlers in Jefferson, Oregon); the pine tree stands for the Ponderosa pines on the current property; the various figures represent members of the present-day Looney family (six boys, one girl), and the peacock is one of their pets.

Visiting the winery ★★. The first winery in Linn County, Ponderosa Vineyards is part of a 75-acre property that supports cows, sheep, and goats in addition to Pinot Noir, Chardonnay, and Sauvignon Blanc grapes. The vineyard's elevation is about 700 feet, on clay loam soil with southeastern exposure, all of which bodes well for the quality of the fruit.

A Sunday afternoon visit to Ponderosa might include a treat for youngsters: a hayride from the winery to the vineyard.

Tasting the wines (NR). Wines with a gimmick: no sulfites. Production has been modest so far (850 gallons in 1987, 1,100 gallons in 1988), and the consumer demand for "sulfite-free" has been strong enough for the first releases to sell out.

Getting there. From Albany (I-5 Exit 233) take Hwy 20 eastbound. Turn off on Hwy 226 past Crabtree toward Scio. Turn right on Brewster Rd, follow the red and white "Winery" signs to Ponderosa Vineyards.

Open Sundays, noon to 5.

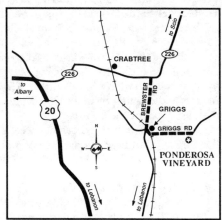

A word from the winery. "*Our wine is sulfite-free—contains no artificial chemical additives. Some people experience reactions after drinking wine that seem to be directly related to the wine itself. Headaches and other discomforts may be caused by sulfites in the wine. Ponderosa Vineyards wines are totally natural; nothing is added to produce the kind of reactions experienced by drinking many other wines. Our wine is a natural wine and may produce a small amount of sediment. This will improve the quality of our wine.*"

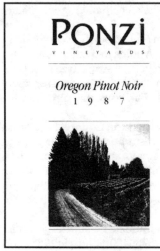

Oregon Pinot Noir
1 9 8 7

PONZI VINEYARDS

Vandermost Road
Route 1, Box 842
Beaverton, OR 97007
(503) 628-1227

Owners: Dick & Nancy Ponzi
Winemaker: Dick Ponzi
Year established: 1974
Production capacity: 15,000 gallons
Vineyards: 12 acres
Touring: Tualatin Valley [p. 192]

A bit of background. Dick Ponzi, son of Italian immigrants, earned a degree in mechanical engineering in Michigan and immediately moved west to seek his fortune in the then-booming aerospace industry. Instead, he found his wife, Nancy, (a Spanish-English major), a bungalow in the Santa Cruz foothills (rapidly filled with babies), and growing disillusion with the aerospace business. As his discontent with government contracts and policies grew, he discovered, in the bungalow's back yard, the vineyards of the Novitiate Winery. He changed jobs, from designing rockets to designing rides for Disneyland and Disney World, and started making wine for the family.

Ahh! Dick and Nancy became increasingly enamored of vines, wines, the earthy familiness of children stomping clusters of red grapes with their little feet, and the allure of Living Off The Land. They succumbed to the glories of Pinot Noir, and began a search for a suitable climate: Napa, Mendocino, the Okanagan Valley of British Columbia. Oregon's Willamette Valley proved "breathtakingly beautiful, theoretically perfect for the culture of Pinot Noir, and a great place for raising kids," Nancy recalls. The Disneyland folks gave them a highly skeptical farewell party, and the pioneer adventure began.

Visiting the winery ★★★☆. Except for Adams, which is right in Portland, Ponzi is the closest winery to the city center, just 10 minutes from Washington Square. And what a difference those 10 minutes make! You're in another world as you turn off Scholls Ferry Road and head down the driveway to the stone and timber winery, past Ponzi's carefully tended, 12-acre vineyard.

The tasting room—now managed by daughter-in-law Kelly Ponzi—has been remodeled to create more floor space, all tiled, with a viewing window into the barrel room; there's original art, sweatshirts painted by

Kelly's hand. No more weddings, receptions, or casual wine-tasting parties. Picnickers are always welcome on the oak-shaded lawn, and can buy wine by the glass.

(Not content merely to operate a winery, the Ponzi family has also started a pioneering microbrewery, Bridgeport, with its own brewpub,. at 1313 N.W. Marshall in Portland. And to keep himself busy, Dick Ponzi designed a new weathervane for Portland's Pioneer Courthouse Square; the giant sculpture plays the trumpet, sprays water, blinks its lights, and displays a dragon, a sun, or a heron depending on the day's weather.)

Tasting the wines ★★★★. "Ponzi's best wines are Rieslings," we wrote two years ago. For the past decade, that was the conventional wisdom. "Things have not stood still!" writes Nancy.

One example of change: the winery's new label. "Our original label was like wearing Nikes to the waltz in Vienna," the winery explained to its distributors. The updated concept, from Rickabaugh Design, has a striking black-and-white photograph of the Ponzi winery by Lawrence Hudetz.

The Ponzi Pinot Gris was the first wine to carry the new label; it sold out even before release. Their Pinot Noir gets especially high marks as well, in the very first rank of Oregon Pinot. The Chardonnay more than holds its own.

An important factor in the quality of Ponzi's current releases, unseen by visitors, is the addition of their oldest son, Michael, to the winery staff. Though his degree is in Italian and music (he's a talented jazz pianist), Michael has taken on the crucial, though hardly glamorous, issues of taxes, government relations, distributor liaisons, inventory. This frees Nancy to do more and even better public relations and leaves Dick to spend his time where he's happiest: in the winery itself.

The result is increasingly evident; Ponzi wines are now among the very best in Oregon. The Chardonnays are very representative of the way this grape expresses itself in the northern Willamette Valley, at their best lush with tropical fruit flavors (the 1985, for example). But the Pinot Noir . . . wow! It grows here, at Ponzi Vineyards, with unique characteristics: a nose that's sappy, with notes of leather and dill, lively flavors. The 1986 Reserve Pinot was elegant and lively, expanding beautifully in the glass with a follow-through in the flavors; the regular 1986 was very fine, with luscious and plummy fruit.

The fruit in the "signature" dry Riesling, at least in the 1987 vintage, was overwhelmed by the alcohol, but the balance was fine.

Robert Parker, whose newsletter has been giving unprecedented attention to Oregon wines, especially Pinot Noir, wrote last year that Ponzi "is emerging as Oregon's top winery." We don't disagree.

Getting there. From Washington Square, the big shopping center on Hwy 217 outside of Portland, take Scholls Ferry Rd (Hwy 210) toward Scholls for 4.5 mi; turn left on Vandermost Rd.

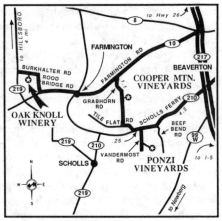

Open for tastings on weekends from noon to 5; wine sales during the week from 9 to 4. Groups of over 10 people are charged $1 per person for an informative tour of the vineyards and winery, often led by a member of the Ponzi family, with a wine (and sometimes cheese) tasting to follow.

Special events. A recent addition to Ponzi's roster of special events is a series of vineyard jazz concerts held on the last Sunday afternoon of each summer month (and postponed a week if it rains).

The Tualatin Valley wineries join forces for two events: the Fourth of July Barrel Tasting Tour (11 to 6) and the Thanksgiving Weekend Wine Tour.

A word from the winery. *"Ponzi Vineyards is the winery/vineyard closest to downtown Portland. With direct access to wine tour routes in both the Tualatin Valley and Yamhill County, the winery is perfectly located for beginning or ending a wine-touring visit. Best hours to visit are weekends from noon to 5 when all wines are open and an enthusiastic staff person is pouring and ready to discuss all aspects of wines. Ponzi specializes in Pinot Noir, Pinot Gris, Chardonnay, and Dry Riesling. A summer concert series, 'Vineyard Jazz,' presents top jazz artists in a casual vineyard setting. Contact the winery for other special events and group tour information."*

WINE AND THE NORMAL LIFE

Direct and enthusiastic, Nancy Ponzi used to work in the vineyards, teach wine-appreciation classes for women, write wine columns for the suburban newspapers, and take personal charge of special wine-tasting programs at the winery. (She was known to repeat an old German curse, "May you inherit a vineyard . . . .") With Ponzi's tasting room now in the capable hands of her daughter-in-law Kelly, Nancy remains a tireless apostle for the entire Oregon wine industry, but explains that times have changed.

"The good old personal days of Oregon wine touring have gone, to some extent. The Virginia Fullers, Nancy Ponzis, Diana Letts have exhausted their charming, imaginative answers to `How did you get into this business?' and `Gosh, I didn't know you could grow grapes in Oregon.' We no longer have to (want to, or can) do everything ourselves. It's not a matter of arrogance, it's that the nature of the business has changed so much . . . coupled with the overwhelming need to maintain sanity. We just can't warmly greet every visitor, answer every phone call, give every interview, answer the mountain of mail, cook those cute little gourmet dinners, do the laundry, remember our kids' birthdays, and sort of be normal . . . ."

REX HILL VINEYARDS

30835 N. Highway 99 W.
Newberg, OR 97132
(503) 538-0666

Owners: Paul C. Hart & Jan Jacobsen
Winemaker: Lynn Penner-Ash
Year established: 1983
Production capacity: 40,000 gallons
Vineyards: 22 acres
Touring region: Yamhill [p. 195]

A bit of background. No lack of ambition here. Says Paul Hart, a Portland investment adviser and actuarial consultant out to make the best Pinot Noir in Oregon, "I've probably had 25 bottles of great Burgundy in my life, and I remember them above everything." Hart's love for the wine made from Pinot Noir grapes explains why he and his wife, Jan Jacobsen, who describe themselves as "serious" wine drinkers and "romantic souls" by nature, started this grand winery. Their lofty standards require a lot of capital and a lot of patience. "Being an actuary is good training," Hart explains. "You take the long view and ignore the blips."

Before 1983, no Oregon Pinot had ever sold for more than $15 when it was released; Rex Hill's sold for $20. Paul Hart claims that the issue wasn't cost but market positioning. "How does the consumer know [which one is best] if all the prices are the same? A dollar's difference doesn't tell anybody anything. So we've tried to price our wines to say something about what we think the wine is worth, in terms of taste, staying power, and so on."

Lest anyone think he only wants to capture the sucker market, he points out that the weak 1984 Pinots sold for half the price of the 1983s. And the 1985s sold in the mid-teens, at prices comparable to many other Oregon wineries. "We have to educate the public away from California's claim that vintages don't make a difference. The Northwest will always have extreme variations."

A recent addition to the Rex Hill staff is winemaker Lynn Penner-Ash, a cheerful young woman who originally studied botany at UC-Davis before switching to viticulture and enology. After stints at Domaine Chandon and Chateau Ste. Jean, she spent four years as chief enologist at the prestigious Stag's Leap Cellars in California.

Visiting the winery ★★★★. Touches of class abound in this former nut-drying shed, which stands on a hillside overlooking Newberg: cool concrete tunnels filled with Nevers oak barrels to age the wines; formica paneling in the tank room; a handsome tasting room (undergoing extensive renovation in the spring of 1989). The classic fleur-de-lis motif, adapted to represent both a heart (Paul Hart) and a crown (Rex Hill), is everywhere.

The winery is easy to find, just off Highway 99 W., a mile outside Newberg. (Veritas Vineyard is across the highway.) Picnic tables stand in a grassy field outside the visitors' entrance, and you have a splendid view down the slopes of Rex Hill from the elegant tasting room upstairs. The laudable practice here is to offer samples of the better wines, including the top Pinots.

Remodeling has added a fireplace and a kitchen with banquet capacity. We expect that the second tasting counter will produce a more relaxed atmosphere, not only for visitors but for the staff as well, whose welcome can be rather perfunctory on crowded weekends.

Tasting the wines ★★★. Rex Hill follows the practice of releasing its best wines in vineyard-designated lots. For the 1983 Pinot Noirs, there were three such designations; the slow-maturing Maresh Vineyards (with deep berry and black cherry flavors) won best-of-class honors at the Grand National Wine Competition.

Our recent tastings suggest that the 1985 Pinots might have been released too early. The Archibald Vineyards Pinot in particular seemed unusually volatile and stemmy; the tannins in the Maresh Vineyards Pinot overwhelmed the fruit. The two lesser releases of 1985 Pinot are faring better, though the flavors of the generic 1985 Oregon Pinot Noir suffered from high alcohol levels. The Willamette Valley Pinot has an unusual gingery note in its nose, and its acetic quality overpowers the fruit.

Another important variety for Rex Hill is Pinot Gris; the 1987 vintage has the spicy, sour mash character that's distinctive in this variety. The Chardonnay we tasted recently had a flowery bouquet and a pleasing, unctuous mouth feel. There's also a moderately fragrant White Riesling, and, available only at the tasting room, an unusual wine called Symphony (a cross between Grenache Gris and Muscat), with a delightful perfume of peaches, but lacking the acidity to balance the natural bitterness of the grape.

Unlike some famous Oregon bottles, which sell out quickly, the best Rex Hill wines will be available in the future. Less than half the 1983 Pinot, for example, was sold in the first release; the balance was held back for re-release in years to come, a tactic that should find favor with consumers who can afford the (doubtlessly higher) price.

Getting there. From New-berg, go 3.5 mi toward Port-land on Hwy 99 W.; turn left at Ladd Hill Rd. From Portland, head south on 99 W.; the winery is 12 mi from the Hwy 217 beltway at Tigard.

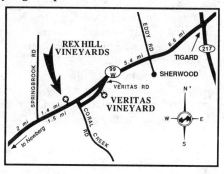

Open daily from 11 to 5, May through December. Open Friday, Saturday, Sunday, 11 to 5, February through April. Closed January. No fee for regular tastings, but tour groups are charged $1.25 per person.

A word from the winery. *"Rex Hill looks forward to welcoming you to taste its high-quality wines while enjoying the elegant atmosphere of its beautiful facility. The well-trained staff will guide you through your tasting of Pinot, Chardonnay, and Riesling, and answer your questions on the wines and winery. We practice traditional Burgundian winemaking, which includes extended cellar and bottle aging before release. Our goal at Rex Hill is to have every wine an excellent value for the money."*

ROGUE RIVER VINEYARDS

1985

CABERNET SAUVIGNON • BLANC

OREGON

CRUSHED, PRODUCED AND BOTTLED BY ROGUE RIVER VINEYARDS, LTD.
ALCOHOL 11% BY VOLUME, GRANTS PASS, OREGON

ROGUE RIVER VINEYARDS

3145 Helms Road
Grants Pass, OR 97527
(503) 476-1051

Owner: Albert Luongo
Winemaker: Bill Jiron
Year established: 1984
Production capacity: 20,000 gallons
Vineyards: 4 acres
Touring: Illinois Valley [p. 204]

A bit of background. The owner and winemaker of this fledgling winery in the southwestern corner of Oregon worked for large commercial wineries in northern California; they returned on weekends to their families, who share the five-acre property.

What it's like to visit ★. The Redwood Highway winds its way through the tall redwoods outside Grants Pass. Helms Road, which leads to the winery, is decidedly rural, with a view across dairy farms and mist-shrouded woods into the Siskiyou Mountains. Rogue River Vineyards consists of a small barn filled with winemaking equipment; a four-acre vineyard of Chardonnay is growing up behind it on the hillside. Several house trailers sit close to the road. There's an area with picnic facilities on a lawn planted with young trees.

The winery has opened additional tasting rooms in Ashland and Beaverton, but isn't strong in the paperwork department; we've had no response to our questionnaires for the past several years.

Tasting the wines (NR). The product line includes a nonvintage Chardonnay, several nonvintage table wines, and several coolers. Not tasted.

Getting there. From Grants Pass, go south for 7 mi on Hwy 199 (the Redwood Hwy). Helms Rd is on the left.

Open daily, 11 to 6.

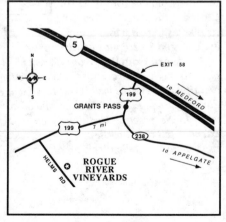

ST. JOSEF'S WEINKELLER

28836 S. Barlow Road
Canby, OR 97013
(503) 651-3190 or 651-2070

Owners: Josef & Lilli Fleischmann
Winemaker: Josef Fleischmann
Year established: 1983
Production capacity: 23,000 gallons
Vineyards: 11 acres
Touring: Portland-East [p. 210]

A bit of background. The baker's dough and the winemaker's wine are similarly "living" products, says retired baker Josef Fleischmann, who recognizes that the fermentation process for both depends "on time, temperature . . . and luck." Joe was born in Hungary and raised in Germany. After training as a baker, he and Lilli immigrated to Chicago, where he worked for Sara Lee; in 1970 they moved to Oregon and bought a bakery in Canby. For over a decade, Fleischmann's Bakery was without peer in Clackamas County.

When he began making wine, Joe Fleischmann was adamant that he would follow the example learned at his grandfather's knee: virtually no sulfur dioxide to control bacterial levels. (He eventually settled on a minute 30 parts per million for preservation purposes.) Fermentations is spontaneous, from naturally occurring yeasts, and meticulous filtration is used to produce stable commercial wines. "You'll never get a headache from one of my wines," Joe Fleischmann promises.

St. Josef (the German spelling of Joseph) is the patron saint of providers. Joe and Lilli Fleischmann checked with their parish priest before deciding to use the name; the good father was delighted to give his approval.

Visiting the winery ★★★★. The rustic scenery on the way to St. Josef's prepares you for the Old World experience that awaits. The road borders furrowed fields, plowed by a distant tractor; you pass grassy, sloping paddocks dotted with geese, cows, and horses, old barns, standing ponds, and gentle creeks. To your left, in the east, a backdrop of blue sky is accented by Mount Hood and Mount Adams.

The driveway between the Chardonnay and the Gewurztraminer takes you toward the lovingly restored farmhouse; out back, black calligraphy on the side of the old barn proclaims its function as St. Josef's Weinkeller. All this overlooks a carefully landscaped hillside, complete with a two-acre spring-fed lake and a dozen picnic tables, that is as inviting a spot as you could imagine for a summer afternoon. The tasting room, built by Lilli's father during a visit from Germany, looks like a European Weinstube, with oak floors, a beamed ceiling, even a *Stammtisch* (table for regulars).

Tasting the wines ★★☆ (Pinot Noir: ★★★). Two Gewurztraminers lead the lineup at St. Josef's: one is rather full-bodied; the other, named L'Esprit, is more delicate, with a hint of spritz and tart grapefruit flavors. The 1987 Riesling we recently tasted had an intriguing nose of old apples and flavors of citrus, a combination we rather enjoyed even if it wasn't typically varietal. The 1986 Pinot Noir had lovely fruit with a hint of leather; the taste was on the acidic side but will mellow. (The 1985 Pinot took a gold in New York a couple of seasons back.) St. Josef's Cabernet Sauvignon has also done well; the 1983 vintage won a silver medal at the Seattle Enological Society festival in 1986.

Finally, there's a Zinfandel, produced from California grapes.

Getting there. From Port-land, go south on Hwy 99 E. through Oregon City to Canby; or take the Canby ferry from the west side of the Willam-ette. From the Salem area, come north on Hwy 99 E. through Woodburn, Hubbard, and Aurora. At the southern fringe of Canby, turn southeast on S. Barlow Rd toward Monitor; the winery is exactly 4 mi on the left.

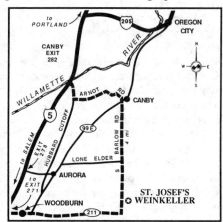

Open Thursday through Sunday, from 1 to 5.

Special events. There's a Grape Stomp on the last weekend in September, and—as one might expect—a spirited festival on St. Joseph's Day, March 19.

A word from the winery. *"We work hard to grow the grapes and make a fine wine. Each of our wines has been tended by hand and given personal attention through every stage of fermentation. The natural processes of grape growing and winemaking are timed perfectly, allowing us to provide the fullest and richest tastes. From vineyard to cellar to table, quality is our most important concern.*

"Come visit the winery; taste some of our award-winning wines, have a picnic or go for a walk on the hillside. Ask, and we would be happy to show you the winery's facilities."

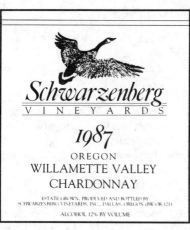

1987
OREGON
WILLAMETTE VALLEY
CHARDONNAY

ESTATE GROWN, PRODUCED AND BOTTLED BY
SCHWARZENBERG VINEYARDS, INC., DALLAS, OREGON (BW-OR-121)

ALCOHOL 12% BY VOLUME

SCHWARZENBERG VINEYARDS

11975 Smithfield Road
Dallas, OR 97338
(503) 623-6420

Owners: Helmut & Helga Schwarz
Winemaker: Norbert Fiebig
Year established: 1987
Production capacity: 20,000 gallons
Vineyards: 50 acres
Touring region: Salem [p. 198]

A bit of background. The Schwarz family of suburban Washington, D.C., has owned this property for a decade, carrying out a long-range business plan that called for planting vineyards first, then building a winery. Helmut Schwarz, a former executive with Volkswagen of America who now works for the Pentagon, and his wife, Helga, intend to resettle in Oregon as soon as the winery can support the move; meantime, their son Dirk handles the winery's on-site administration and marketing.

Visiting the winery ★★☆. The winery is located on a knoll overlooking the vineyards (Chardonnay and Pinot Noir) near the Baskett Slough Wildlife Preserve. The 140-acre, oak-covered site includes 40 acres of mature Chardonnay vines and 10 of Pinot Noir.

Tasting the wines ★☆. Winemaker and vineyard manager Norbert Fiebig trained for eight years in Heilbronn, Germany. His early releases were not promising; though low in alcohol, they showed little fruit. The 1987 Willamette Valley Chardonnay was very pale, smelled like candy, and tasted thin, sour, and bitter. The 1987 Pinot Noir smelled oxidized and had a thin, cherry flavor. Ironically, the winery's promotional literature quotes Robert Parker's praise of Willamette Valley wineries in general; it doesn't quote his reaction to the Schwarzenberg Chardonnays: "It is inexcusable to make wines in this style."

Getting there. From Salem, travel west on Hwy 22 towards Rickreall; then north 4.5 mi on Hwy 99 W. Left on Smithfield Rd; 2.5 mi to the winery. [Map: Ellendale]

Open Saturday and Sunday from noon to 5.

Special events. Memorial Day weekend. "Return of the Geese" celebration, beginning of October.

A word from the winery. *"Schwarzenberg Vineyards overlooks the beautiful Baskett Slough Wildlife Preserve, where migratory birds, including Canada geese, come to nest. As a symbol of our winery, we have adopted the magnificent `Wild Goose in Flight.' Our wines are delicate, crisp, fruity, and fun to drink. We invite you to visit and taste."*

Serendipity Cellars
1986 Oregon
Maréchal Foch

SERENDIPITY CELLARS WINERY

15275 Dunn Forest Road
Monmouth, OR 97361
(503) 838-4284

Owners: Glen & Cheryl Longshore
Winemaker: Glen Longshore
Year established: 1981
Production capacity: 5,000 gallons
Vineyards: 3 acres
Touring region: Salem [p. 198]

A bit of background. "Serendipity" means an aptitude for making fortunate discoveries more or less by accident. Glen and Cheryl Longshore, it would seem, have made one such discovery: a grape variety called Marechal Foch, well known in Europe and in Canada, as a source of red wine. At a time when Oregon's most widely planted red grape is Pinot Noir and everyone (including Longshore himself) has a cellar full of Pinot Noir, Glen Longshore complains that "very few winemakers are trying anything new."

Glen Longshore is a man whose daily life combines education and technology. He holds two master's degrees, and for the past dozen years has been a media specialist at Chemeketa Community College in Salem. (Cheryl, who manages the business side of the winery, has a master's degree in science.) What got Glen Longshore into the practical side of the winemaking business was a not-so-idle question during the crush to Myron Redford, owner of Amity Vineyards: "But where do you learn to do it?" Next morning, he was learning on the job, at Myron's side, up to his elbows in grapes.

Visiting the winery ★★☆. Once you turn off the highway and head west toward Serendipity Cellars, you feel a growing sense of peace and wonder. The soft, overlapping curves of the blue and green hills ripple down from the horizon like falling pillows. The Longshores are gentle people who have built their home, vineyard, and winery (the first in Polk County) on a 20-acre property surrounded by the tall firs of the Coast Range.

The winery is at the end of a narrow, single-lane road that winds its last quarter mile through trees. Picnic tables and a crushing pad stand outside the Longshore home, whose lower level is devoted to winemaking.

How unexpected, how serendipitous, for wine lovers to find in this peaceful pocket of forestland a man like Longshore, whose intense curiosity led him into winemaking in the first place and whose questioning of traditional styles and methods pushes him to creative experimentation.

Tasting the wines ★★☆. The Marechal Foch, for a start. Some people take to it instantly; it was the consumer favorite for two years running at the Greatest of the Grape festival. We're more recent converts to its considerable charms: deep red color; a rich, fruity nose; more forceful intense flavors (though less complexity) than Pinot Noir.

Speaking of Pinot, Serendipity's 1983 won a gold medal last year at the American Wine Competiton in New York, a feat many of Oregon's better-known wineries didn't manage. It's sold out by now, unfortunately.

We've also enjoyed the Chardonnay, which had a flinty nose and well-balanced, toasty flavors.

There's also Muller Thurgau, Chenin Blanc, and some Zinfandel. A Cabernet Sauvignon is coming. Some of the smaller lots are available only at the winery.

Getting there. Drive 7 mi south of Monmouth along Hwy 99 W., or 13 mi north of Corvallis, turn west on Airlie Rd. Six mi later, at Airlie, bear left on Maxfield Creek Rd. After 3 mi, turn left again on Dunn Forest Rd; the winery is at the end of the road.

The "back way" from Hwy 20, running from Corvallis to Newport, turns off at Wren; head toward Kings Valley, bear right on Maxfield Creek Rd and turn right 7 mi further on at Dunn Forest Rd. [**Map:** Airlie]

Open daily except Tuesday, May through November, from noon to 6. January through April, on weekends only. Group tours are welcome by appointment; $1 per person for groups over 12.

Special events. In early August, Serendipity puts on a Midsummer's Eve Festival (an evening spent stargazing and sipping wine, with limited admission). Over Thanksgiving weekend, there's a vertical tasting of Marechal Foch, beginning with the 1982 vintage; tasting fee varies.

A word from the winery. *"Winemaking is not just another business for me—it is in every sense an art form, and a very personal one at that. `Serendipity' occurs when a variety of variables, not all of which are controllable, come together to form a pleasing result. This describes my concept of winemaking perfectly—as something that is always a little different, always a little surprising, always having that spark of magic that separates dull sameness from unpredictable delight, and where the winemaker's skill plays an important part. I invite you to visit Serendipity Cellars to experience my wines firsthand and to perhaps come away from the experience with a little surprise and delight of your own."*

SHAFER VINEYARD CELLARS

Star Route, Box 269
Forest Grove, OR 97116
(503) 357-6604

Owners: Harvey & Miki Shafer
Winemaker: Harvey Shafer
Year established: 1981
Production capacity: 20,000 gallons
Vineyards: 20 acres
Touring: Tualatin Valley [p. 192]

A bit of background. A builder and farmer, Harvey Shafer got into the vineyard business because some of his neighbors—the fledgling wineries of the early 1970s—were willing to pay good money for wine grapes. For a few years, he was content "simply" to grow grapes (not that growing grapes well is all that simple). But even as he became known as one of the best growers in the Tualatin Valley, he increasingly felt that he was selling his children at birth, so he started his own winery. He knew firsthand what virtually all winemakers have come to accept: that three-quarters (or more) of the wine's ultimate quality comes from the vineyards, that the winemaker's job, in good years especially, is to avoid making mistakes with the wine. (In poor years, a good deal of technical wizardry may be necessary.)

Furthermore, he knew that to avoid the problems of spoilage and faulty equipment that plague many beginning winemakers, the first rule would be to keep the place spotless—a rule that's not followed as often as one might think. The winery that Shafer built may well be the cleanest place you'll ever encounter outside of an operating room.

Visiting the winery ★★★. The handsome, hand-carved sign at the base of the driveway is a good indication that you are in for a treat, a winery where the owners care about the effects of the smallest detail. Navigate the road up the hill, through 20 acres of Pinot Noir, Riesling, and Chardonnay grapes, to the winery itself, recently enlarged to accommodate additional case storage. There's a wide veranda out front and a spanking-clean tasting room inside. Eight redwood picnic tables and a covered gazebo await you in the grove of oak trees adjacent to the winery.

Tasting the wines ★★★. Shafer is known for Riesling and applauded for Chardonnay. We're also quite taken with the Sauvignon Blanc, a variety that seems to be on the wane in Oregon. Shafer's is grassy with overtones of oysters and the "seacoast" smells developed by French oak. We were less impressed by the Rieslings this year (one dry, one off-dry); they lacked breadth on the palate, perhaps the result of underripe fruit. The Shafer Chardonnay has always been a favorite with critics, who cite its Burgundian style. And there's Pinot Noir, of course; at last report, the 1985 vintage, estate-bottled, was still available.

Regardless of your preference, you can be assured that the winemaking will be meticulously clean and technically flawless.

Getting there. From Forest Grove, take Hwy 8 toward Tillamook. The winery is 4.5 mi out of Forest Grove; turn right and follow the driveway up the hill. [**Map:** Tualatin]

Open weekends, noon to 5. Closed in January. Tour groups should call ahead for appointments; the fee is $1 per person for groups of 10 or more.

Special events. Sunday afternoons in July and August you can taste new releases while listening to jazz artists; there's a modest admission charge.

The biggest festival in the region has nothing to do with wine. It's a sausage feed in nearby Verboort on the first weekend in November, attended every year by tens of thousands of visitors.

A word from the winery. *"Our goal is to produce flavorful, supple wines with characteristic style recognizable as Shafer. In the cellar, Nevers, Limousin and Allier oak barrels from France are used for the fermentation and aging of Chardonnay and Pinot Noir. Slow barrel aging contributes subtle, multidimensional flavors and adds richness and depth to the wines. The production of Pinot Noir Blanc and Riesling concentrates on capturing the natural, fruity flavors of the grape. This is accomplished by fermenting the wines slowly in temperature-controlled stainless steel tanks. This blend of tradition and technology is used to produce clean, natural wines which are attractive in their youth and continue to develop complexity with age.*

"The Shafer family cordially invites you to sample these fine wines at the winery tasting room overlooking the Gales Creek Valley. During the summer months visitors are welcome to relax under the large canopies of the old oak trees scattered throughout the picnic area and enjoy Sunday jazz performed by local artists."

RATING THE WINERY VISITS:

NR	Not rated: tasting room not open, no visiting
★	Don't bother
★★	Moderately interesting
★★★	Worth a detour
★★★★	Worth the trip

See the introduction (page 8) for additional information on the criteria used to rate winery visits.

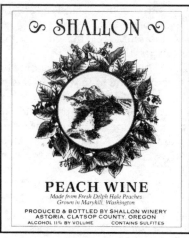

SHALLON
1598 Duane Street
Astoria, OR 97103
(503) 325-5978

Owner & winemaker:
Paul van der Veldt
Year established: 1978
Production capacity: 3,000 gallons
Vineyards: None
Touring: Oregon Coast [p. 207]

A bit of background. Paul van der Veldt—serious, white-haired, bearded, bespectacled—is Oregon's most unusual winemaker, a man whose intense passion is to make wine from a flowering evergreen shrub called *Gaultheria shallon*, commonly known as salal. (The black berries of the salal plant resemble large huckleberries and are edible, though they contain very little sugar.) The fact that no one has ever made salal wine doesn't deter van der Veldt, a one-time cook on a seagoing tugboat with a taste for classical music. (Some tugboat!) He managed the family's heavy construction business for 20 years, making wine as a hobby until he opened Shallon in downtown Astoria after his retirement in 1978.

Visiting the winery ★★★. Astoria itself is a community whose heritage of pioneer fishing days is readily apparent in its fortifications, monuments, museums, and historic homes. Many spots in the hillside town offer viewpoints to watch the traffic of oceangoing vessels as they cross the bar and head up the Columbia River. And the four-mile-long bridge from Astoria to Megler, Washington, is an attraction too.

Shallon itself is like no other winery you will ever see. The previous occupant was a freezer locker business, providing Shallon with space for a lab, an office, and corkboard-insulated storage. Van der Veldt added "improvements" such as bright pink plastic-epoxy paint to the walls (bright green for the floors) and trompe l'oeil murals depicting scenes from Astoria's past. He stresses sanitation, rigorous lab work, and wine that tastes like the earth, not syrup.

He also likes visitors; they're his only customers. So he paid the Highway Department to put up a Tourist-Oriented Directional Sign at the end of the Astoria-Megler bridge. He was soon overrun by hordes of rude, wine-guzzling freeloaders. (They were even worse, he reports, than the tourists who dropped in after eating at the fast-food joint next door, their palates deadened by frozen custard.) The official sign is gone again, but you shouldn't miss a visit.

Tasting the wines ★★. The best wine, we think, is the peach, but van der Veldt doesn't stop with the conventional. His Wild Evergreen Black-berry, a very pleasing wine from local fruit, ages like Cabernet Sauvignon; it might remind you of wet moss and dry leaves—a deliberate effect. His Cran du Lait, a unique wine made from cranberries and whey, bears little resemblance to any conventional wine we know. Then there's a concoction of lemon and whey that he proudly calls "Lemon Meringue Pie" and sells in a package with "crust" cookies. Van der Veldt is still experimenting with the salal . . . and with chocolate!

Getting there. The winery is at 16th and Duane streets in downtown Astoria, across from the Maritime Museum and half a block south of Hwy 30.

Open daily from noon to 6.

Special events. Although the winery doesn't sponsor any events on its own, the town of Astoria does: Maritime Week (May), the annual Scandinavian Midsummer Festival (June), the Astoria Regatta (August). For information, contact the Astoria Chamber of Commerce, Box 176, Astoria, OR 97103.

A word from the winery. *"Want to surprise your wine-snob friends who stick up their noses at fruit and berry wines? Confound your connoisseur friends with wild blackberry wine made like a Cabernet, and a dessert wine equivalent to Beerenauslese.*

"Grape wines make themselves. Connoisseurs are only quibbling about delicate nuances of flavor and quality. When you make fruit and berry wine, you have to know what you are doing. Come see my lab! The mystique of wine is part of my work (and the grist of wine writers), but I'm too old to be bothered with the snobbery. If you like it, drink it; if you like it a certain way, drink it that way, hot or cold; if you like it with certain foods, drink it with those foods.

"Try my peach wine with lobster! And maybe soon, Chocolate Mousse Pie wine for dessert!"

SILVER FALLS
WINERY
WILLAMETTE VALLEY • OREGON

CHARDONNAY
1983

PRODUCED & BOTTLED BY
Silver Falls Winery Inc. • Cascade Hwy. • Sublimity, Oregon
ALCOHOL 12% BY VOLUME

SILVER FALLS WINERY

4972 Cascade Highway S.E.
Sublimity, OR 97385
(503) 769-9463

Owners: John & Ralph Schmidt,
   Steve DeShaw, Jim Palmquist
Winemaker: Jim Palmquist
Year established: 1983
Production capacity: 20,000 gallons
Vineyards: None
Touring region: Salem [p. 198]

A bit of background. "We're mavericks here on the east side," Jim Palmquist used to say, referring to the wineries and vineyards on the east side of the Willamette Valley. Silver Falls was the first winery established on the east side, an area that Palmquist contends is more productive than the west. He speaks with the pride of a native, born and raised in the area around Silverton; he once worked on the property where Silver Falls Winery stands. Before he returned, he got a degree in food technology, worked as a research chemist and a quality control technician, and sold food processing equipment.

Silver Falls Winery produced wine in 1983 and 1984, but never got it bottled because of undercapitalization. A familiar story. Palmquist spent the next two years getting reorganized. John Schmidt (who owns a 10-acre vineyard), Ralph Schimdt, and Steve DeShaw (a doctor) became his partners and made it possible for Silver Falls to finish its building, purchase equipment, and make wine in 1987. The tasting room opened in March 1988, and saw 6,000 visitors by the end of the year.

Visiting the winery ★★☆. Most of the farmers in the central Willamette Valley produce grass seed. It's big business in these parts, with enormous acreages that grow the seed for lawns around the country; minimum size for a parcel here is in the 600-acre range, far too big for the intensive farming that a vineyard requires. You get the feeling that Palmquist's property, on the side of a modest knoll, wouldn't be big enough to turn around one of the combines.

The winery itself is a long, low farm building at the base of the little hill. Once used for farm animals and tractors, it now houses a tasting room, tanks, and barrels.

Visitors to the winery should go another seven miles or so to visit Silver

Falls State Park, one of the most attractive spots in Oregon. Whispering waterfalls and wooded canyons are accessible to everyone; there's a well-maintained trail connecting all of the falls, and parking areas for those who'd rather drive.

Tasting the wines (NR). Bob McRitchie, the former winemaker at Sokol Blosser, is consulting with Jim Palmquist on the current Silver Falls wines, which we haven't tasted. Silver Falls produced 9,000 gallons of Pinot Noir, Pinot Gris, Chardonnay, and Riesling in 1988, all from "east side" grapes.

Getting there. From Salem, go 12 mi east on State St to the Cascade Hwy, then south 2 mi to the winery. From I-5, take Exit 253 (Mission St) and go southeast on Hwy 22 toward Stayton and Sublimity. Bear left onto Hwy 214, then left again at the Cascade Hwy; 1 mi to the winery.

Open weekends from 10 to 6, or by appointment. Tour groups are welcome; no fees are charged for visits or tastings.

Special events. A summer festival the weekend following the Fourth of July, and a harvest festival the weekend following Labor Day. The latter coincides with the Sublimity Harvest Festival and Tractor Pull, held only four miles from the winery.

A word from the winery. *"Silver Falls Winery is located between Salem and Silver Falls State Park in the beautiful rolling foothills of the Cascade Mountains. Easy to find between Silverton and Stayton on the Cascade Highway, the winery is open for tasting on weekends from 10 till dusk or by appointment. Picnic facilities are offered for the enjoyment of visitors, or visit scenic Silver Falls State Park."*

SISKIYOU VINEYARDS

6220 Oregon Caves Highway
Cave Junction, OR 97523
(503) 592-3727

Owner: C.J. ("Suzi") David
Winemaker: Donna Devine
Year established: 1978
Production capacity: 15,000 gallons
Vineyards: 12 acres
Touring: Illinois Valley [p. 204]

A bit of background. The Illinois Valley, in the southwest corner of the state, has just the right micro-climate for grapes like Zinfandel and Cabernet Sauvignon. Chuck and Suzi David settled here after leaving California, and began planting a vineyard in 1974; by 1978, they had bonded Siskiyou Vineyards. When Chuck died in early 1983, Suzi could easily have chosen to sell Siskiyou Vineyards, but she was hardly the sort of person to give up on a business enterprise that had not yet realized its potential.

Instead, Suzi David went ahead with plans to expand production and build a new, two-story winery. She also gave a freer hand to her winemaker, Donna Devine, whose first visit to the winery had been as a reporter for the *Grants Pass Courier*. (In an industry historically dominated by men, Suzi David and Donna Devine became the first team of a woman owner and a woman winemaker—except for Joan Wolverton at Salishan—in the Northwest; furthermore, there is now an all-woman cellar crew in the winery itself.) The result is a steady improvement in the quality of the wine.

Visiting the winery ★★★. Siskiyou Winery, the southernmost winery in Oregon, lies six miles outside Cave Junction on the winding highway to the Oregon Caves. Tall fir trees surround the vineyards, which stretch across a clearing into green foothills of the Siskiyou Mountains. (There used to be a black sheep named Jonathan Lambington Sheep on the property; he would trot around behind Suzi like a faithful dog.)

Climb the stairs to the spacious tasting room and note that all the wood is hand-carved. It's the work of folk artist Faron Steele, who was also commissioned to construct entrance signs for the winery. A nature path lined with azaleas and ferns winds its way through the 100-acre property.

Tasting the wines ★★★. Red wines from southern Oregon don't always show the subtlety and softness of wines produced in the Willamette Valley; they tend to be more robust and less smooth in texture. Siskiyou produces fine Cabernet Sauvignon, deep, well-balanced wines that age well; the 1982 vintage was one of Oregon's best, the 1983 very good. The 1985 Cabernet evokes the Australian bush with its eucalypt, cedar nose; it is well-balanced, with deep and vigorous flavors. The 1987 Pinot Noir is a light-bodied, very drinkable wine, smooth-textured on the palate, with lingering notes of white pepper and that sweet, leather-and-garbage character the French call *"animal"* and English writers translate as "barnyard". (It's actually a very complimentary term.)

The 1986 Chardonnay has a light, clean, floral, apple nose, but lacks intensity of flavor. Siskiyou also makes a good Muller Thurgau with controlled aromas.

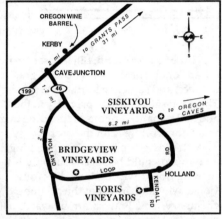

Getting there. From Cave Junction, take Hwy 46 (the Oregon Caves Hwy) for 6.2 mi; the winery is on the left. There's also a Siskiyou Vineyards tasting room in Ashland, at the Oregon Store.

Open daily from 11 to 5. Group tours are welcome, with appointments preferred.

Special events. The annual Spring Festival is held on the second weekend of June. Local artists and craftspeople set up their wares and equipment (looms, pottery wheels), musicians play, and a great variety of food (including traditional Greek dolmas) is served. There's also a Concert in the Vines, scheduled for September.

A word from the winery. *"Welcome! We hope you will visit our tasting room and winery facilities here in the scenic Illinois River Valley. Try our award-winning wines and meet our hospitable tasting room staff. Picnic grounds, nature trail. Enjoy the beauty of the Siskiyou Mounatins and relax."*

SB

Sokol Blosser

1985

Yamhill County
Oregon Pinot Noir

HYLAND VINEYARDS

A smooth, medium-bodied wine blended from selected barrels of Pinot Noir grapes grown by Hyland Vineyards in the hills near Sheridan.

PRODUCED AND BOTTLED BY
SOKOL BLOSSER WINERY, DUNDEE, OREGON (BW-OR-66)
Alcohol 13.0% by Volume

SOKOL BLOSSER WINERY

5000 N.E. Sokol Blosser Lane
P.O. Box 399
Dundee, OR 97115
(503) 864-2282

Owners: Bill Blosser, Susan Sokol, Durant Vyds., Hyland Vyds.
Winemakers: John Haw, Bill Blosser
Year established: 1977
Production capacity: 60,000 gallons
Vineyards: 125 acres
Touring region: Yamhill [p. 195]

A bit of background. Bill Blosser, an urban planner by profession, and Susan Sokol, a professor of history, graduated from Stanford, got master's degrees, and settled in Portland to pursue their careers and raise a family. They bought a 125-acre property in the Red Hills of Dundee back in 1971 and had romantic notions of spending their weekends planting a vineyard while the fruit trees on the property supplied a cash crop.

With Blosser's penchant for planning, it quickly became apparent that a vineyard could be successful only if he also built a winery. Knowing nothing about winemaking, he would have to hire a full-time, professional winemaker. (They hired Robert McRitchie, with a doctorate in chemistry, from Franciscan Vineyards in the Napa Valley.) Of course this meant that the winery would have to be big enough from the outset to pay the winemaker's salary, too.

Making a lot of wine meant selling a lot of wine, and selling meant exposing people to the concept of Oregon wine. This, in turn, required raising a good deal of capital to build a large winery and a genuine visitor facility that would attract people to the winery so they could taste the product. It also required prestige, the kind that comes from entering (and winning) international competitions.

Well, the Blossers did all these things pretty much as planned. Sokol Blosser today is one of the three biggest wineries in Oregon, and the quality of its best wines ranks at the very top. And if it all seems elementary today, bear in mind that they started long, long ago (as the history of Oregon's wine industry is measured), back when the very concept of Oregon wine was about as familiar as electric cars or vacations in space. The winery itself was designed and built by master craftsman Ken Haggard (who also did the wineries for Rex Hill and Elk Cove). The entire visitor center was the work of Portland architect John Storrs, who received a citation from the Knights of the Vine for outstanding service to the wine industry for the Sokol Blosser project.

In 1987, Hyland Vineyards and Durant Vineyards, which had been supplying grapes to Sokol Blosser since 1977, became shareholders in the winery, buying out the interest of members of the Sokol family. The owners' vineyards now supply virtually all the grapes used by the winery.

Visiting the winery ★★★. The 125-acre vineyard, planted primarily with Pinot Noir, Chardonnay, and Riesling, lies on the slopes of Oregon's most celebrated patch of soil, the famous Red Hills of Dundee. A private access road, Sokol Blosser Lane, leads visitors across acreage that was, until recently, covered with cherry orchards and walnut groves. (Bulldozers cleared the hillside and more vineyards were planted.) On a shaded knoll below the older vineyards stands the striking, angular shelter where visitors can picnic, taste wines, buy souvenirs, even hold club meetings. A new addition provides meeting space for groups of up to 50. Nine picnic tables await visitors in the landscaped area adjacent to the tasting room, and a few feet away, fitted into the hillside, is the cast-concrete winery, packed full with stainless steel fermentation tanks and huge oak barrels. Back in the tasting room, there are enchanting views into the vineyards. The room is lined with cases of wines for sale; you help yourself and pay at the counter.

Tours are conducted hourly. If anything, a visit here is almost too polished, the staff too mechanical.

Tasting the wines ★★☆. Said Bill Blosser after two of his 1983 Pinots swept a New York tasting, "We're learning to trust the grapes." And the grapes he trusts are those closest to home. He's even phasing out the admirable Sokol Blosser Sauvignon Blanc because he's committed to Yamhill County fruit, and there's not enough Sauvignon Blanc available.

Some of Sokol Blosser's wines have been quite fabulous, the 1983 Red Hills and 1985 Hyland Pinots specifically. But we find many of the current releases rather insipid and lacking in varietal character. Doubtless it's a hazard of large production, though we're not concerned here with the bulk wines. It's the 1987 Riesling that tastes like Gewurztraminer; the frankly oxidized 1986 Chardonnay; the cream soda nose and undistinguished flavors of the Pinot Noir Blanc. In recent blind tastings the 1986 Pinots have been particularly disappointing: the Yamhill County bottling was thin and tart; the Red Hills Pinot smelled like candy; its Hyland Vineyards counterpart simply had no depth. Bob McRitchie's departure as winemaker may be partly responsible, but something deeper seems to be awry.

Getting there. From Dundee, go south 2.5 mi on Hwy 99 W.; turn right on Sokol Blosser Ln. Coming from McMinnville, the winery entrance is 0.5 mi past the intersection of Hwy 99 and Hwy 18, opposite the fruit stand.

Open daily, 10:30 to 5:30 in summer (May to October), 11 to 5 in winter. No fees.

Special events. Sokol Blosser is a cornerstone of the Yamhill Valley Wineries' Thanksgiving Weekend. The winery releases its Pinot Noirs over the May Day weekend.

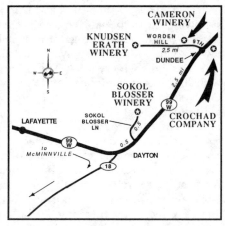

A word from the winery. *"Since our founding in 1977, Sokol Blosser has emphasized the importance of the grape in creating greatness in the wine. We purchase only the production of Oregon's oldest, most award-winning vineyards for our premium wines.*

"These vineyards (Hyland, Sokol Blosser, and Durant) are located in Yamhill County, recognized as the heart of Oregon's finest wine production. That recognition has extended far beyond Oregon, as shown by the decision of one of France's most prestigious wine houses, Joseph Drouhin, to plant vineyards adjacent to the Sokol Blosser and Durant properties . . . this underlining the fact that our region matches the classic qualities of soil and climate found in Burgundy, which for centuries has set world standards for Pinot Noir and Chardonnay.

"Sokol Blosser's striving for excellence from vine to wine has earned widespread attention and acclaim:

"Pinot Noir from our vineyards led all wines in the Oregon V. Best of Burgundy taste-off in New York in 1986 . . . . Hyland Vineyards (bottled under the Yamhill Valley label) earned first, Sokol Blosser `Red Hills' (a blend of Sokol Blosser and Durant vineyards) was second.

"The only Oregon winery placing in Wine Country *magazine's top 25 American wineries (selected from year-long tastings) the past two years.*

"Gold medals at such major competitions as London's International Wine and Spirits Competition, San Francisco Fair, West Coast Wine Competition, Grand National Wine Competition."

STRINGER'S ORCHARD

Box 191
New Pine Creek, OR 97635
(916) 946-4112

Owner & winemaker: John Stringer
Year established: 1984
Production capacity: 17,000 gallons
Vineyards: 18 acres

A bit of background. John Stringer, who trained as a civil engineering technologist in Arizona and worked briefly in Texas, moved to south-central Oregon about 10 years ago and started farming a 120-acre ranch. He's got 40 acres of alfalfa for hay and 14 acres of plum orchards. The plums, until recently, went exclusively into jams and jellies, but Stringer has also been a home winemaking enthusiast, and it was only a matter of time until he began turning some of his plum crop into wine as well. "The wild plums have long been prized for their distinct flavor," he tells us. "I believe that anyone who would try the wild plum wine will be equally delighted."

Visiting the winery (NR). About 50 miles east of Ashland you come to Klamath Falls (population 17,000, a lumber town); another 50 miles east, into the high mountain desert, and you come to Lakeview (population 3,000, county seat of Lake County). Wine tourists—unless they're hunting antelope, shooting waterfowl, or looking for unusual rocks, are unlikely to visit this part of the state.

Look closely at the telephone number for this winery. It's not an Oregon area code, you'll notice. Indeed, Stringer's Orchard has an Oregon post office address and for that reason we've included in this book; the federal Bureau of Alcohol, Tobacco, and Firearms considers this an Oregon winery though it's physically located just across the state line, in Modoc County, California.

South-central Oregon's climate is arid though not overly hot, with only five or six inches of natural rainfall a year; irrigation comes from the local flood control program. Stringer's Orchard, at an elevation of 5,000 feet, sits on benchland below Crane Mountain, highest peak of the Fremont National Forest. Goose Lake, a popular recreation area, is just across the highway. Stringer has put in a small tasting room and a couple of picnic tables for visitors, and he's building on to the back of the winery so he can process even more plums.

Tasting the wines (NR). Eight types of wine, from dry to sweet, all made from wild plums. It wins medals at the Los Angeles County Fair. You can buy Stringer's wild plum jams and jellies at Hickory Farm outlets in Portland; they make good ice cream toppings and garnishes for game.

Getting there. New Pine Creek is 14 mi south of Lakeview, the county seat. The winery is just 0.75 mi south of New Pine Creek, on the east side of Hwy 395, just across the California border.

Open Monday through Saturday from 10 to 5, Sunday from 1 to 5. No fee charged for groups.

A word from the winery. "*Our family-owned and-operated winery takes great pride in specializing in one type of wine, the wild plum. The unique fruit only grows wild in a limited part of northern California and southern Oregon. With such a unique fruit, we can boast of being the only wild plum winery in the world.*

"*We invite visitors to break away from the hustle and bustle and enjoy the friendly, laid-back atmosphere of the winery and tasting area. With breathtaking scenery, award-winning wines, and jams and jellies to offer, a stop at our winery will prove to be a memorable experience for the whole family to enjoy.*"

WHAT SHOULD YOU BUY?

Should you buy a wine because it's won a gold medal or a high rating? There are magazine and newsletters that assign numerical scores to wines; sometimes we agree with the numbers, sometimes we don't. But we don't buy a wine just because it's highly rated; we don't let someone else's palate rule our wallet, whether it's a magazine rating or a festival judge's medal.

The English wine importer Mark Savage, a judge at the Oregon State Fair in 1988, put it this way: "Our results aren't gospel."

Wineries that *didn't* win a medal shouldn't feel slighted, Savage continued. "It's always possible for good wines to slip through the net."

And possible, too, that *you* won't like the "winning" wines.

THREE RIVERS WINERY

275 Country Club Road
Hood River, OR 07031
(503) 386-5453

Owners: Bill & Ann Swain
Winemaker: Bill Swain
Year established: 1986
Production capacity: 7,500 gallons
Vineyards: 4.5 acres
Touring: Columbia Gorge [p.27]

A bit of background. Bill Swain was studying geology at the University of California at Davis when "wine classes seemed to click"; he switched to enology and got his degree in 1971. For the next nine years, he worked in the California wine industry, as assistant winemaker for Charles Krug and winemaster at Cresta Blanca. In 1981 he moved to the Northwest and began planting a small vineyard on the Washington side of the Columbia Gorge near the town of Underwood.

The vineyard, on the decomposed basalt soil that makes up the north side of the Gorge, is just now beginning to produce Pinot Noir and Riesling in commercial quantities. While waiting for the vineyard to mature and the winery project to get going (which it did in 1986), Swain worked in the grocery business and taught wine classes. He is certainly a patient man.

Visiting the winery ★★☆. It's called the Copper House, a charming, carpenter-crafted home just off the freeway west of Hood River. Here, flags flying, is where the Swains have set up the winery. The outside of the old house has been given a fresh coat of white paint with green trim, its living and dining areas polished up and converted into a bright, airy tasting room and gift shop.

The setting is charming. Though the road runs right past the winery's front door, there's a sense of distance from the bustle of traffic. The property drops off sharply toward a little stream; picnic tables stand in the shaded garden.

Tasting the wines ★★. Swain is starting off with purchased grapes; he's released three whites (Chardonnay, Gewurztraminer, Riesling), a red

(Pinot Noir, grown in The Dalles), and an attractive blush. Except for the Chardonnay, most of which comes from Washington, they all carry an Oregon appellation. He sells over half at the winery, the remainder in local restaurants and in Portland wine shops. We found all the wines technically sound, and particularly enjoyed the White Pinot Noir.

Getting there. Take Exit 62 off I-84 west of Hood River and go 0.5 mi on Country Club Rd, which runs along the south side of the freeway. [**Map:** Hood River Vineyards]

Open Monday through Saturday, 11 to 6, Sunday, 1 to 5, from April through December. From January through March, Friday and Saturday 11 to 5, Sunday 1 to 5. Tours up to 50 are welcome but should call ahead; groups over 12 are charged $1 per person, refunded with purchase.

A word from the winery. "In the heart of the Columbia Gorge three rivers converge. The White Salmon from the north and the Hood from the south empty their cool, glacial waters into the mighty Columbia. These rivers frame a distinctive viticultural region marked by unique soils and climate.

"Three Rivers wines are created from select Columbia Gorge vineyards. We invite you to visit our winery and tasting room, located in a charming, turn-of-the-century home with easy access and return from I-84."

TUALATIN VINEYARDS

Seavy Road
Route 1, Box 339
Forest Grove, OR 97116
(503) 357-5005

Owners: William Malkmus, William Fuller
Winemaker: William Fuller
Production capacity: 60,000 gallons
Vineyards: 83 acres
Year established: 1973
Touring: Tualatin Valley [p. 192]

A bit of background. Tualatin Vineyards was founded nearly 15 years ago on a long-established farm west of Portland by Bill Malkmus, a San Francisco-based investment adviser, and Bill Fuller, a winemaker with Louis Martini. From modest beginnings, Tualatin (pronounced TOO-ALL-a-tun) has grown to an 85-acre vineyard supplying all the grapes for one of Oregon's biggest brands. It's a 60,000-gallon winery with much of the quality you'd expect of a boutique winery one-tenth the size, a winery whose Chardonnay and Pinot Noir have won international recognition.

The spectacular accomplishment capping Tualatin's story came in London during 1984: two trophies, for best Chardonnay (their 1981 vintage) and best Pinot Noir (their 1980) from anywhere in the world, awarded at the International Wine and Spirits Competition. The trophies came only after the wines had first won regional gold medals; on the second round, they competed against the best from California and Europe. (The only other American winery to get a trophy was Jekel Vineyards of California, for its Cabernet Sauvignon.) With characteristic understatement, the British judges announced it was "interesting" that two trophies "were awarded to the same company in the relatively new wine-growing region of Oregon in the western United States."

Bill Fuller himself, should you encounter him on a visit, is a tireless advocate for all Oregon wines, not just his own, and for years has been showing the industry how to market Oregon wines out-of-state. "Oregon may be fifth in the country in per capita consumption of wine," he is fond of saying, "but there aren't that many `capitas' in Oregon!" So he takes his sample case in hand and climbs on a plane to Denver, New York, or Washington, D.C., to meet with distributors, retailers, restaurant owners.

Visiting the winery ★★★☆. The centerpiece of the vineyard is an elegant farmhouse, the Fullers' family home. There's an airy new tasting room with plenty of windows to take advantage of the lovely view and plenty of space to accommodate tour groups. The decor is rustic, with wood floors, and a wood stove in the corner. Visitors can move from the tasting room into the picnic area with ease (and it's an almost unbelievably lovely spot for a picnic, this hillside grove among the Riesling vines). No matter when you come, you're likely to meet Bill or Virginia personally taking charge of the tasting room, a rarity for such a big winery.

Tasting the wines ★★☆ (Pinot Noir: ★★★). Tualatin's history is filled with major awards, with gold medals from the mid-'70s at the Seattle Enological Society to the present day. We're troubled, though, by the fact that it's been five years since Tualatin has won a significant award. Lots of silvers, lots of bronzes, but no golds. Now, that doesn't mean Tualatin makes indifferent wines these days. In fact, Tualatin produces large volumes of commercially sound wine at very reasonable prices. The nonvintage white table wine, made mostly from Riesling and sold in magnums, has a particularly good reputation for value.

Our own recent favorite was the 1983 Chardonnay, a wine with intense tropical fruit flavors and classic balance. The 1984 wasn't up to its standard, though, and the 1985 sold out quickly; we haven't tasted the 1986. The 1985 Pinot Noir ("The best we've ever made," said then-assistant winemaker Matt Hill) had moderate tannins, a hint of earthiness, and a broad spectrum of cherry flavors. The Muller Thurgau had a nose of juniper, the Riesling a note of lime. Both Gewurztraminers (one dry, one off-dry) had enough acid to overcome the variety's inherent bitterness.

Getting there. Tualatin was one of the first wineries to take advantage of the law allowing wineries to put up highway signs, so it's not as hard to find as it used to be.

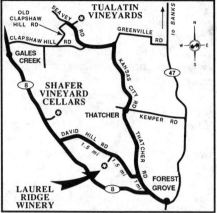

From Portland, take Hwy 26 toward the coast for 20 mi to the Hwy 6 turnoff; continue south toward Forest Grove on Hwy 47. Turn right on Greenville Rd and follow the signs to "Kansas City."

From Hillsboro, go west on Hwy 8, through Forest Grove toward Tillamook, and bear right on Thatcher Rd toward Kansas City. Travel north as far as the Kansas City Hall; turn left on Clapshaw Hill Rd, then bear right at Seavy Rd. The vineyards and winery are on the right.

Open weekdays from 10 to 4, weekends from noon to 5. Closed January and holidays. No tasting charge for drop-in visitors, but a $1 per person fee for tour groups.

Special events. Most fun: a Harvest Party that offers participants a chance to pick and process grapes, take hayrides, listen to music. Tualatin also hosts an annual art show over the Thanksgiving weekend in November, and participates in the Washington County Winery Association Barrel Tasting over the Fourth of July weekend. In late May there's a spring sale with significant discounts on wines and accessories.

A word from the winery. *"Tualatin Vineyards offers estate-bottled wines from grapes grown on its own 85-acre vineyard, established in 1973. Premium quality White Riesling, Gewurztraminer, Chardonnay, and Pinot Noir can be purchased at the winery. Enjoy a spectacular view of the vineyard and Tualatin Valley as you sip wine in the expansive new tasting room or picnic under the cherry trees. The tasting room is available for banquets, meetings, and weddings. Group tours of the winery by appointment. The winery is located an easy 30 miles west of Portland, on your way to the northern Oregon coast. Just follow the blue signs on Highway 26, then Highway 6.*

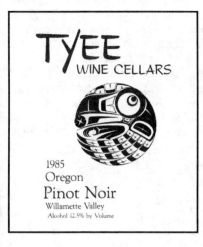

TYEE WINE CELLARS
26335 Greenberry Road
Corvallis, OR 97333
(503) 753-8754

Owners:
    Barney Watson & Nola Mosier,
    David & Margaret Buchanan
Winemaker: Barney Watson
Year established: 1985
Production capacity: 5,500 gallons
Vineyards: 7 acres
Touring: South Willamette [p. 200]

A bit of background. In the early 1970s, after a stint as a biochemist in Alaska, Barney Watson got a master's degree in enology at UC Davis, worked for a year in California, then moved to Corvallis and joined the Food Science and Technology Department at Oregon State University as winemaker and enologist for the state's (official) experimental winery. For the past 10 years, Barney Watson has been tireless in his devotion to Oregon wine: enology instructor and extension specialist to the wine industry, prolific contributor to scientific and trade journals, consultant to dozens of wineries and wine judgings, and enthusiastic home winemaker.

Watson's colleagues in his own commercial venture are his partner, Nola Mosier, a botanist at OSU, and the Buchanans, whom he has known since Alaska days. Dave Buchanan, who trained as a marine biologist at OSU, returned to Corvallis in the 1970s to manage the family farm—a 450-acre property near an ancient Indian encampment at the confluence of Beaver and Muddy creeks.

The four owners decided to name the winery Tyee because of its strong Northwest image. A "tyee" is a chinook salmon bigger than 35 pounds, or the "chief," biggest and best of a group.

Visiting the winery ★★☆. This is very much the sort of place Oregon wineries used to be: tiny, rural, charming, yet prepared to turn out the very highest quality wine. Some 30 acres of the Buchanans' spread are planted in filbert trees; a growing vineyard and rye grass (for the sheep) cover the rest of the ranch. To the west, there's a view of Marys Peak, highest in the Coast Range. Canada geese and whistling swans fly overhead, en route to the nearby Finley Wildlife Refuge.

A small covered picnic area is available near a 100-year-old Waxen apple tree adjacent to the winery. Hikes on the farm pass through the vineyards, the filbert orchards, and large stands of native Oregon oak, as well as the ancient Indian campgrounds near the two creeks.

Tasting the wines ★★☆. Best of the Tyees we've tasted so far was the 1985 Pinot Noir, which had an intense nose of raw red meat and strawberries with a hint of acetic acid; it had good flavors, too. The rest of the lineup was disappointing. The 1987 Pinot Gris had an uninteresting, hard candy smell, and a bitter finish. The Gewurztraminer was fragrant but bitter. The Pinot Noir Blanc was fine, with a pleasant, off-dry finish, and forgettable. The 1985 Chardonnay had the characteristics of Oregon Chardonnay: oak, vanilla, and tropical fruit in the nose, but was loaded with sulfur. Given the winemaker's talents, these should be better wines.

Getting there. Seven miles south of Corvallis on Hwy 99 W., turn west on Greenberry Rd. Afer 2.2 mi there's a small bridge; 150 yards later, turn right into the V. F. Buchanan Farm.

Open from noon to 5 on weekends from May to September, or by appointment.

Special events. New wines are released at two weekend festivals: Memorial Day and Thanksgiving.

A word from the winery. "*Tyee Wine Cellars is located on a family farm near Corvallis, nestled in the foothills of the Coast Range. Tyee to the early Indians meant 'the best' or 'chief.' It is used today to describe the largest of the chinook salmon. We specialize in limited production of the finest varietal wines, including Pinot Noir and Pinot Noir Blanc, Chardonnay, Pinot Gris, and Gewurztraminer. Our label, featuring a series of designs by Oregon artist James Jordan, emphasizes our commitment to and pride in the best of our Northwest heritage.*"

UMPQUA RIVER VINEYARDS

451 Hess Lane
Roseburg, OR 97470
(503) 673-1975

Owner & winemaker: G. S. DeNino
Year established: 1988
Production capacity: 3,000 gallons
Vineyards: 20 acres
Touring: Umpqua Valley [p. 202]

A bit of background. G. S. DeNino planted his vineyard in 1982 with Cabernet Sauvignon, Sauvignon Blanc, Cabernet Franc, and Chenin Blanc. He's now made his first wines, from the 1988 crush: Cabernet Sauvignon, Semillon, and a rose. Production will be limited to about 3,000 gallons a year.

Getting there. From Roseburg, follow Garden Valley Rd to the Melrose Rd turnoff, continue out Old Garden Valley Rd to Hess Ln.

Open weekends from 10 to 6.

Valley View Vineyard

1987 Oregon Chardonnay

PRODUCED AND BOTTLED BY VALLEY VIEW VINEYARD
JACKSONVILLE, OREGON BW - OR - 76
ALCOHOL 12% BY VOLUME CONTAINS SULFITES

VALLEY VIEW WINERY

1000 Applegate Road
1352 Applegate Road (mail)
Jacksonville, OR 97530
(503) 899-8468

Owners: Wisnovsky family
Winemaker: John Guerrero
Year established: 1978
Production capacity: 50,000 gallons
Vineyards: 26 acres
Touring: Ashland-Jacksonville
[p. 205]

A bit of background. Peter Britt, a pioneer photographer in southern Oregon, once planted orchards and grapevines in the Applegate Valley on a property he called Valley View. A century later the Wisnovsky family resurrected the name when it established a winery here. By the time Bob Wisnovsky graduated from Oregon State University a few years ago and stepped in as president of Valley View Winery, he'd had plenty of preparation: he'd watched his family plant the vineyards (26 acres of

Cabernet, Merlot, Chardonnay), and he'd worked every summer as the winery's marketing director. He pulled off quite a coup late in 1988 when Valley View wines were featured at a $5,000-per-person political fund-raiser hosted by Senator Robert Dole and attended by President Reagan. The only wines served were Valley View's 1983 Cabernet Sauvignon and 1987 Chardonnay.

Valley View's current winemaker, John Guerrero, comes from the University of California at Davis, and is steadily modernizing the winery's cooperage.

Visiting the winery ★★☆. A delightful drive through the woods south of Jacksonville, past the old Logtown Cemetery, brings you to Ruch. The view through the rows of Cabernet Sauvignon toward the hills on the opposite bank of the Applegate Valley is splendid. The tasting room is part of the barrel-filled winery itself, so you can enjoy the distinctive aroma and sounds of a working winery as you try the wines.

Tasting the wines ★★★. Valley View concentrates on slow-maturing red wines, and has large reserves of older reds: 1979, 1980, and 1982 Cabernet Sauvignon, for example, were all available in 1986. (For a European winery, this wouldn't be anything unusual, but it's less common here.) Also in the tasting room: Pinot Noir, Merlot, Chardonnay, and Gewurztraminer.

Scorn not the older vintages of Valley View's red wine! They are a refreshing, mature change from all those two- and three-year-old Cabs on the shelf. One of the wine writers in Houston was so impressed with Valley View that he snuck a bottle of their 1978 Cabernet into a blind tasting of world-class 1975 Bordeaux; it beat the Chateau Mouton-Rothschild!

Our sample of the 1987 Valley View Cabernet—very recently bottled—had a rich, woody smell and delicious fruit flavors that were marred by unexpectedly harsh tannins; we hope that the tannins will soften with a couple of years' aging. The 1982 Cabernet fared much better; it had a lovely cedar nose and pleasant, tart flavors. The 1983 Merlot was rich, with a good balance of oak and fruit, and a long finish.

Two 1987 Chardonnays are on the market. The regular bottling reflects the unmistakable fruit character of Oregon Chardonnay. The character of oak is more apparent (in the nose and mouth) in the Barrel Select; its texture is more viscous and the body bigger—a pleasant wine.

Success isn't universal, however. Last summer we tasted the 1986 barrel-fermented Chardonnay, which was prematurely oxidized. And a bottle of 1987 Cabernet Blush was simply spoiled, spritzy and smelling like nail polish remover.

Getting there. From Jacksonville, go south 7 mi on Hwy 238 to the town of Ruch; turn left on Applegate Rd and go south 1 mi.

Open daily, year-round, 11 to 5. Tour groups are welcome.

Two Valley View tasting rooms are located closer to tourist centers: the Oregon Wine Tasting Store at 52 E. Main in Ashland, and The Tasting Room at 690 N. Fifth in Jacksonville.

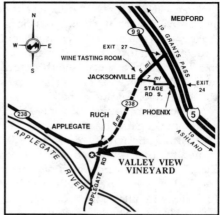

A word from the winery. *"Valley View Winery, owned and operated by the Wisnovsky family, is located in beautiful southern Oregon. The original Valley View was started in the 1870s by Peter Britt; the Wisnovsky family reestablished the name but moved the location eight miles southwest of Jacksonville. Our climate is quite warm and produces wines with unusual character and body not found anywhere else in the Northwest. Come taste the wines of the first name in the Northwest wine industry."*

VERITAS VINEYARD
31190 N.E. Veritas Lane
Newberg, OR 97132
(503) 538-1470

Owners: John & Diane Howieson
Winemaker: John Howieson
Year established: 1984
Production capacity: 17,000 gallons
Vineyards: 20 acres
Touring region: Yamhill [p. 195]

A bit of background. John Howieson, a professor of diagnostic radiology and associate professor of neurology at the Oregon Health Sciences University in Portland, has cultivated an interest in wine ever since he was sent to Austria by the U.S. Public Health Service in 1956. Since 1979 he has also been an increasingly enthusiastic amateur winemaker.

Howieson explains that the most significant aspect of his work is that it requires him to deal with pain and suffering. "After nearly 30 years of this, I want to be associated with a source of pleasure rather than pain," he says. "For me, winemaking is the perfect combination of agriculture, chemistry, biology, and esthetics."

No wonder he named the winery Veritas, from the Latin motto *In vino veritas*. In wine there is truth.

Visiting the winery ★★★. In 1984, Howieson's Chardonnay was named the best wine produced in Oregon by an amateur winemaker. Even before the award was announced, Howieson and his wife, Diane, had begun work on their 20-acre vineyard (Pinot Noir, Chardonnay, Riesling) on a hillside north of Newberg. In 1983 they crushed a modest 600 gallons at Sokol Blosser, but have since moved to their own winery.

The site, just across the highway from Rex Hill, is a splendid spot, and the facilities are attractive indeed. (Rex Hill's winery, to which Veritas will inevitably be compared, is a far grander one, and represents a much greater financial investment.) The Veritas tasting room is on the upper level, with a deck overlooking a corner of the vineyard and the valley beyond. A picnic site is planned for a viewpoint higher on the hill, overlooking the entire valley.

A second building was added to the winery in 1987, providing a new cellar set 15 feet into the ground, with storage space for more than 10,000 cases of wine and 200 barrels. Domaine Drouhin, without a facility of its own, has rented space here as well.

You can feel the well-merited sense of pride that the owners have in their wines and their winery.

Tasting the wines ★★★ (Pinot Noir: **★★★**). The first commercial release from Veritas included a remarkable 1983 Pinot Noir (part of the same lot as the first-place finisher entered by Yamhill Valley Vineyards at the famous taste-off of Oregon Pinots and French Burgundies in New York; it was made by Bob McRitchie at Sokol Blosser). Subsequent vintages of Pinot, from other vineyards, have been more than adequate. But it was for Chardonnay that Howieson had won the state amateur championship, and it was the 1985 Veritas Chardonnay that won the only gold medal at the Oregon State Fair. It had matured beautifully, with rich, complex, buttery flavors when we tasted it in late 1987.

The 1986 Chardonnay is aging in a less predictable manner. Bright yellow gold in color, it was emitted a moderately madeirized, rich raisiny nose more indicative of a brown muscat (grown in a warm climate) than a Willamette Valley Chardonnay. Flavors of raisins and nuts dominated. For all that, the balance was good, but the wine would be hard to recognize as Chardonnay.

The Veritas Pinot Noir from 1985 (a warm year in the Willamette Valley) is still very closed, giving off only a light loganberry perfume.

Does it have enough acid to sustain it until those enormous tannins resolve? Time will tell, obviously.

Getting there. On Hwy 99W, northeast of Newberg. From Portland, turn left on Corral Creek Rd 5.4 mi west of Sherwood. From Newberg, head toward Portland on Hwy 99 W; turn right 1.5 mi past Springbrook Rd. [**Map:** Rex Hill]

Open daily in summer from 11 to 5; weekends only in winter. Closed in January. Group tours by appointment; $1 fee during special events.

Special events. Veritas participates in the Yamhill County Wine Country Thanksgiving at the end of November. There's also a case-buyers' sale in late June, and a pre-harvest celebration in mid-September

A word from the winery. *"Veritas Vineyard strives to achieve the highest quality and the greatest expression of what is distinctive about Oregon wines. We agree that 'great wines are made in the vineyard' and we set our crop levels low to insure concentration and complexity. The finest quality imported oak barrels and meticulous care at every stage of the wine making are also vital. We would be pleased to have you as our guest at the winery to enjoy the beautiful countryside and a taste of Oregon."*

WHAT THE RATINGS MEAN FOR QUALITY OF WINE:

NR	No rating: not tasted at all or not tasted recently; no releases
★	Barely drinkable
★☆	Occasionally acceptable
★★	Uneven
★★☆	Usually good
★★★	Good
★★★☆	Usually superior
★★★★	Consistently superior

WILLAMETTE VALLEY

Pinot Noir

1984

WASSON

B R O T H E R S

Alcohol 11½% by Volume. Prepared and
Bottled by Wasson Brothers Winery
Sandy, Oregon   BW-OR-83

WASSON BROTHERS WINERY

41901 Highway 26
Sandy, OR 97055
(503) 668-3124

Owners: Jim & John Wasson
Winemaker: Jim Wasson
Year established: 1982
Production capacity: 10,000 gallons
Vineyards: 7 acres
Touring region: Mt. Hood [p. 210]

A bit of background. The record of this little winery (basically Jim Wasson's one-man operation) is an astonishing success story: five times winner of the Governor's Trophy at the Oregon State Fair in the past six years! And with three different wines at that: Pinot Noir, Chardonnay, and blackberry.

The story begins some years earlier, when Jim Wasson and his twin brother, John, were farming the family homestead outside Oregon City, in Clackamas County. Their sister gave them an auspicious present: a winemaking kit. (Same thing happened to Al Stratton at Mount Baker Vineyards, you may recall.) As luck would have it, the Wassons not only enjoyed winemaking, they were good at it. Before long, they were winning awards at the local fairs for their fruit wines. Encouraged by their success, they took the plunge and went professional in 1982. John, with a steady job as a project manager for the Army Corps of Engineers, helps at the winery on weekends; Jim, hardworking, modest, and kind, gave up his trade as a plumber to become the full-time operator of the winery. And by 1984 he had started his remarkable string of Governor's Trophies, with a bottle of his blackberry wine.

Visiting the winery ★★☆. You won't see the Wassons' seven-acre vineyard, planted with Pinot Noir, Chardonnay, Gamay, and Gewurztraminer, from the winery parking lot; it's at the family farm on the terraced hillside near Oregon City. Instead, you'll see a spanking new winery, right on the highway to Mount Hood, their second new facility in under three years. The first one, built on the west side of Sandy, was torn down just two years later to make room for a Safeway store; the new one, opened in early 1986, is on the east side of town. It's a broad-fronted building with a wide veranda, rather like an old-fashioned country store.

The bar in the tasting room is 28 feet long, and the walls are generously bedecked with ribbons and medals proclaiming the Wasson brothers' success as winemakers.

Tasting the wines ★★★★. The vinifera varieties available are Pinot Noir, Chardonnay, Riesling, Gewurztraminer, and an Early Muscat. Six fruit wines can be sampled: blackberry, raspberry, loganberry, strawberry, boysenberry, and rhubarb.

The 1987 Chardonnay fairly bursts with fruit, enhanced and balanced by a confident use of oak. The wine spreads generously in the mouth, and is succulent and balanced. We had little hesitation calling it the best Oregon Chardonnay in our recent tastings.

A pre-release tasting of the 1987 Pinot Noir revealed a restrained wine with a very quiet aroma that includes notes of dill and mint, rich underlying fruit, and moderate tannin.

The grapes for both wines came from the Wasson Brothers' 10-year-old vineyard outside Oregon City. "Clackamas County is a legitimate wine-growing area," says Jim Wasson, with misplaced defensiveness. Granted that he doesn't hang out with the Yamhill County cellar-rat pack, that he's not part of the Newberg-McMinnville axis, his record as one of Oregon's most accomplished winemakers speaks for itself.

Getting there. From Portland, take Hwy 26 toward Mount Hood through Sandy; the winery is just outside of town, next to Janz Berryland.

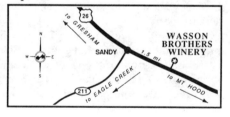

Open daily from 9 to 5. No charge for group tours.

Special events. None scheduled at the winery. The town holds a festival called Sandy Mountain Days in July.

A word from the winery. *"Why do you suppose a small, under-8,000-gallon-a-year winery can win five Best of Show awards, nine gold medals, plus eight silver awards and 10 bronze medals in only six years?*

"The Wasson Brothers invite you to come try their wines to see for yourself why no other winery can match such success. Pinot Noir, Chardonnay, blackberry, raspberry, and loganberry have all been gold medal winners."

WEISINGER'S ASHLAND VINEYARD

3150 Siskiyou
Ashland, OR 97520
(503) 488-5989

Owners: John & Sherita Weisinger
Winemaker: Donna Devine
  (consultant)
Year established: 1988
Production capacity: 6,000 gallons
Vineyards: 4.5 acres
Touring region: Ashland [p. 205]

A bit of background. John Weisinger grew up on a cattle ranch in Texas and earned a Master of Divinity degree before spending 20 years as a Presbyterian minister. He's been a teacher, consultant to employers, a family and marriage counselor, and director of several human service organizations. Winemaking has been a hobby for 30 years, so it was quite natural that Weisinger would meet up with Frank Wisnovsky, the founder of Valley View Vineyards, and start planting grapes on some of his 10-acre property.

Despite John's fondness for Italian wines (his favorite is Barolo), the original vineyard consisted entirely of Gewurztraminer. A year ago, he grafted over some of the vines to Nebbiolo. He plans to add Cabernet Franc in 1990. The vineyard is at an elevation of over 2,000 ft, on sandy loam and decomposed granite, and should hold heat very well. John believes more southern Oregon growers will move away from Pinot Noir toward Cabernet varieties and Italian grapes.

Visiting the winery ★★☆. John and Sherita Weisinger studied tasting room designs in Germany and Italy during an extensive trip in early 1988. What you see at Weisinger's today is the result of that research: a three-story structure, northern Italian in architecture, covered in white stucco. The cellar is below ground, the production area, tasting room and gift shop on the main level, and a banquet room with seating for 80 on the top.

The winery's grand opening came too late to be included in this edition, but Weisinger promises that visitors will be able to buy plates of coldcuts at the winery and take the food out the deck. The view, across the Rogue Valley to the Cascades, is splendid ★★★.

Tasting the wines (NR). Three wines (made mostly with grapes Weisinger purchased from various Jackson County growers) will be released in early May. 1988 Gewurztraminer and 1988 Cabernet Blanc are the two varietal bottles; the third is a blend called Mescolare. Donna Devine, the very capable winemaker from Siskiyou Vineyards, helped out with Weisinger's transition from hobbyist to commercial producer.

Getting there. Weisinger's is the southernmost Oregon winery (unless you count Stringer's Orchard in LaPine, Oregon, which is actually a quarter-mile inside California). Take Exit 11 from I-5 and head 1 mi toward Ashland on Siskiyou Blvd.

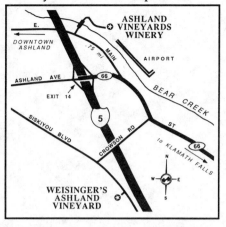

Open Wednesday to Sunday, 10 to 5. Tour groups welcome.

Special events. Two events (dates not set) are planned: a jazz weekend and a "Label Your Own Wine" weekend.

A word from the winery. *"Come visit our family-run winery, sit on our spacious deck or lawn, have a picnic, enjoy the view overlooking the Rogue Valley, admire the surrounding southern Oregon Cascades, ejoy the atmosphere and view of our Italian-style tasting room with its unique jams, jellies, sauces, honeys, and wine country gifts. Enjoy our varietal and Italian-style blends made from grapes grown in the surrounding Rogue Valley. Weisinger's boasts one of the only underground cellars in southern Oregon. Here wines are stored and aged at a constant temperature year-round.*

"Weisinger's is only one mile from I-5 and four miles from downtown Ashland with its many cultural and dining opportunities."

WILLAMETTE VALLEY VINEYARDS

8800 Enchanted Way S.E.
Turner, OR 97392
(503) 588-9463
(800) 344-9463

Owners: Jim Bernau & Don Voorhies
Winemaker: Bob McRitchie
Year established: 1990 (?)
Production capacity: 100,000 (?)
Vineyards: 15 acres
Touring region: Salem [p. 198]

A bit of background. What's this? A winery with an 800 number? Yes, indeed. That's so potential investors can make toll-free calls to order up shares (minimum order 1,000 shares at $1.70 each) in Oregon's first "publicly owned" winery. But first, Willamette Valley Vineyards has to raise about a million bucks in just eight months.

The driving force behind this venture is Jim Bernau, a lobbyist who heads the Oregon chapter of the National Federation of Independent Business, an association of over 10,000 small businesses in Oregon alone. Don Voorhies, his partner, is a retired General Electric sales executive who owns and manages Salem Hills Vineyard; for several years he served as superintendent of the wine division at the Oregon State Fair.

Visiting the winery. The intention is to build a winery that could produce up to 100,000 gallons of wine, and a tasting room big enough to accommodate hundreds of people at a time. A "destination," if you will.

Tasting the wines. No wines yet, but a few grapes in the ground: about seven acres of Pinot Noir and eight acres of Riesling so far. Mark Benoit, whose parents own Chateau Benoit, supervises the vineyard.

The company expects to plant more Pinot and some Chardonnay shortly. Until the winery starts up, the grapes are being sold (Pinot Noir to Knudsen Erath, for example). The soil, Bernau and Voorhies say, is similar to that found in Romanee-St. Vivant, one of the most highly prized Grand Cru vineyards of Burgundy.

To reach the envisioned level of production, Willamette Valley will also buy grapes, and is planning a long-term contract with Voorhies's Salem Hills Vineyard. Bob McRitchie, formerly with Sokol Blosser, could easily handle the production volume required for national distribution.

Getting there. The proposed winery will be 0.3 mi south of the Enchanted Forest tourist attraction at I-5 Exit 248.

Open sometime in 1990 . . . if Bernau and Voorhies get 700 or so investors to chip in by June 19, 1989.

WITNESS TREE VINEYARD

7111 Spring Valley Road N.W.
P.O. Box 5203
Salem, OR 97304
(503) 585-7874

Owner: Douglas Gentzkow
Winemaker: Rick Nunes
Year established: 1987
Production capacity: 10,000 gallons
Vineyards: 35 acres
Touring region: Salem [p. 198]

A bit of background. Doug Gentzkow, a retired Air Force meteorologist, is also an airline pilot. He's had a fine vineyard northwest of Salem for the last few years, and has now started a winery to make Pinot Noir and Chardonnay.

Rick Nunes, perhaps the least pretentious Ph.D. viticulturist in Oregon, is making the wines for Witness Tree. Nunes is the cellarmaster for Knudsen Erath, among other occupations. Gentzkow's no slouch himself: his amateur Chardonnays have won a fair share of blue ribbons.

Visiting the winery ★★. The nearly 100-acre property, dominated by an ancient oak tree (used as a reference point or "witness" by local surveyors), is planted with 35 acres of grapes. The 6,000-square-foot winery is at the south end of the vineyards.

Plans for the future include a tasting room, picnic area, nature trails, and riding paths.

Tasting the wines (NR). First releases were in late 1988; we've not tried them.

Getting there. From West Salem, go 5.6 mi north on Wallace Rd to Lincoln. Then left onto Zena Rd, 2.1 mi. Right onto Spring Valley, 1.5 mi (past Pellier) to Witness Tree. [**Map**: Bethel Heights]

Open by appointment.

A word from the winery. "*Witness Tree Vineyard was established in 1980 and its new winery in 1987. Located in the beautiful Eola Hills, nine miles northwest of Salem, Witness Tree takes its name from an ancient oak tree that stands like a sentinel overlooking the 100-acre vineyard. The oak is marked a historic 'witness tree,' used for decades by Willamette Valley surveyors. Douglas Gentzkow, owner of Witness Tree Vineyard, is committed to the production of limited bottlings of classic Burgundian-style Chardonnay and Pinot Noir. Visitors are welcome; contact the winery for an appointment. A tasting room, picnic facilities, and walking and riding trails are planned for this beautiful site.*"

1985 OREGON PINOT NOIR

PRODUCED AND BOTTLED BY
YAMHILL VALLEY VINEYARDS, McMINNVILLE, OREGON
Alcohol 13.2% by Volume

YAMHILL VALLEY VINEYARDS

16250 S.W. Oldsville Road
McMinnville, OR 97128
(503) 843-3100

Owners:
  Denis Burger & Elaine McCall,
  David & Terry Hinrichs
Winemaker: Denis Burger
Year established: 1985
Production capacity: 24,000 gallons
Vineyards: 50 acres
Touring region: Yamhill [p. 195]

A bit of background. Here's a scientist, Denis Burger, with a doctorate in microbiology and biochemistry, who's been working for the Oregon Health Sciences Center as a research professor in microbiology and immunology. (Why do some people get headaches from red wine? An immune response, says Burger.) With his wife and a couple of friends, he starts planting a vineyard with Pinot Noir, Chardonnay, Riesling, and Muller Thurgau at just the right time, 1983. From friends at Hyland Vineyards he buys 10 tons of Pinot Noir grapes; another friend, Bob McRitchie at Sokol Blosser, makes 1,600 gallons of wine from the grapes and puts it aside for Burger. Burger concentrates on building his winery, aiming for an opening in the fall of 1985. He doesn't make it; heavy equipment is still grading the hillside site in the winter snow. Meanwhile, he samples his slowly maturing Pinot. "Spectacular!" he thinks. A panel of experts, at a blind tasting in New York, agrees: Yamhill Valley Vineyards' Pinot Noir ranks first among two dozen 1983 Pinots from Oregon and Burgundy. Burger's got great luck: his first wine makes headlines even before the winery opens for business!

Visiting the winery ★★★★. Vineyards and fruit orchards share the 100-acre property, which unfolds across the gentle slopes outside McMinnville. Pinot Noir grapes dominate the plantings. You turn into the vineyard and drive up the first low rise, then dip down toward the elegant concrete winery, sheltered in a grove of white oak trees. Clerestory windows illuminate the winery's working area (filled with Allier oak barrels and cognac puncheons) as well as the cheerful tasting room. You walk out on the wraparound deck and hear the burble of a little stream; the trees, covered with milky green lichen and bright green moss, frame a view of the vineyards.

If you visit when Denis Burger or Dave Hinrichs happen to be around, they might be persuaded to take you down to the barrel room for samples.

Or ask for an invitation to the case-buyers party in late September, when you can buy Pinot Noir at pre-release prices: a fantastic deal if you can wait for a year or so to drink your bargain.

Tasting the wines ★★★☆. Burger's premise is indisputable: "It's up to the winemaker not to screw up good fruit." Unstated corollary: you need good fruit to start with. Yamhill Valley Vineyards crops its own vineyards at two tons to the acre.

We're not as excited as the winery folks about their Pinot Gris, which they make "in the Italian style"; we liked it better than most Oregon Pinot Gris, but thought it needed a lot more acid. Far more interesting was the 1986 Pinot Noir, a wine with complex aromas of raspberries and tobacco, nicely balanced in the mouth although quite tannic. Better still was a barrel sample of the 1988 Pinot, with intense blackberry aromas and flavors. Burger says it will be three years before this one is ready, but we'd be happy to take it tomorrow in comparison to many other Pinots.

Yamhill Valley's Chardonnays are getting better. (That's not to say they don't also turn out an $8 bottle of Chardonnay for restaurant "by-the-glass" programs along with the rest of them.) The 1987 vintage is the first that Burger believes to represent the winery's ultimate style: toasty, buttery flavors with good acids and a broad finish. We were even more impressed with a barrel sample of the 1988, which showed a lot of vanilla, lime, marmalade, and butterscotch flavors.

Let California wineries make White Zinfandel; Yamhill Valley Vineyards has something better: Elderblossom. It's 98 percent Riesling, perfumed with the extract of genuine elderblossom. Every May, a crew collects blossoms from a small stand of European elder trees near Salem (not the more common Oregon elder bush) and makes a hot-water extract that they save until the Riesling is bottled the following winter. "It's an old tradition in the Mosel and Rhine valleys," Burger points out. "We're after a unique segment of the market. It's a great wine to drink chilled at a picnic." And indeed the elder extract enhances the Riesling without compromising its classic flavors.

Getting there. From McMinnville, go southwest on Hwy 18 toward Lincoln City. Oldsville Rd branches off after 5 mi and rejoins the highway 4 mi later; it runs right past the winery.

Open daily from 11 to 5, April through December. Weekends only in March; closed Christmas through February. No fee for visits, a welcome holdout from the prevailing practice of Oregon wineries.

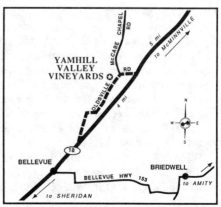

Special events. Yamhill Valley Vineyards will take part in both the Memorial Day weekend and Wine Country Thanksgiving events. In addition, there's an anniversary celebration in early May, an Elderblossom Harvest Festival in mid-June, and (best of all) a case sale and Pinot Noir pre-release at the end of September.

A word from the winery. *"We are dedicated to producing high quality wines in the emerging Oregon style, reminiscent of the finest Burgundian and Alsatian wines. Our Chardonnay ferments and ages in lightly toasted French oak barrels. Pinot Noir is fermented to achieve maximum color and fruit extraction while preserving the complex character of this wonderful grape. It is then aged in our temperature-controlled barrel room.*

"At Yamhill Valley Vineyards we strive to produce wines that receive the ultimate award, a place on your table."

DISCLAIMER

Ronald and Glenda Holden are solely responsible for the profiles, ratings, and recommendations in this book. We have no financial interest, direct or indirect, in any winery, in the importation of wine, the wholesale distribution of wine, or the retail sale of wine.

The ratings in this book were compiled independently over several seasons and vintages by the authors; no winery or distributor (or anyone else, for that matter) paid for or influenced any listing or rating.

Some of the wines tasted for review in this book were provided free of charge by the wineries. Such "tasting samples" are common in the wine trade and had no influence whatsoever on the ratings received by the wineries who furnished them.

Wine ratings are generally based on multiple tastings in a variety of settings, including winery visits, trade tastings hosted by distributors, formal judgings, and private blind tastings.

IDAHO'S WINE COUNTRY

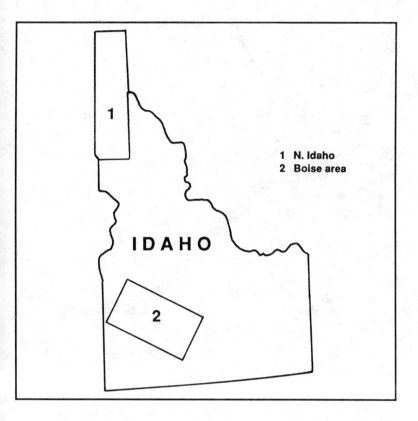

1 N. Idaho
2 Boise area

IDAHO

Admit it, all you Oregon and Washington natives who sputter furiously when visitors claim the only noteworthy product of the Northwest is rain clouds. You've got your own prejudice when it comes to Idaho: they grow potatoes, right?

True enough, but Idaho also turns out wine. Luscious Riesling, heady Chardonnay, complex Cabernet Sauvignon.

A visit to this remarkable region leaves the visitor with extraordinary images: a huge rock formation that looks like a 50-foot cobra balanced on

BOISE AREA

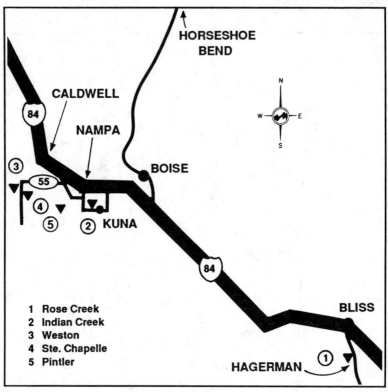

a pedestal no larger than a coffee table; a winery that resembles one of the most vibrant churches of France; a woodsy city; mountain lakes.

From the Snake River, 40 miles west of woodsy Boise, the long black rock outside the hamlet of Marsing looks like a giant lizard basking in the Idaho sun. This is Sunny Slope, Idaho's warmest and most fertile growing region, with row crops and orchards spreading across the valley floor and gently sloping uplands. In the dry, flat valley and on the irrigated bench land, farmers grow Idaho's famous potatoes, whose dark green leaves are dotted with white flowers in early August. (Locally, the potato crop is never called anything more than spuds.) Purple alfalfa fields adjoin the newly mown wheat fields, the chaff now baled like giant loaves of bread. Water for the flourishing sugar beets and onions is siphoned from irrigation ditches into furrows running through the fields. Across the river, in Oregon, you see the outline of the Owyhee Mountains.

Here on the Idaho side, on the gentle bench land slopes above the

NORTHERN IDAHO

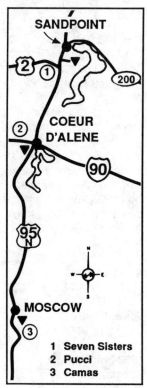

meandering Snake, dark Lambert cherries, tart Perfection apricots, and wild asparagus share the earth's nutrients with wine grapes. Hundreds of acres of Riesling and Chardonnay vines grow at the highest altitude in the Northwest, up to 3,500 feet.

The Idaho grapes benefit from the long, dry growing season and cool nights along Sunny Slope. As a result, the wines they produce have both the acidity and balance associated with Oregon's cool, moist climate, and the ripeness found in Washington's warmer vineyards.

NOTE:
Recommendations for Northern Idaho wine touring are grouped with Spokane (page 27).

Idaho (Boise area):
WINE COUNTRY FOOD & LODGING
Alphabetically by establishment

THE METRO
921 W. Jefferson
Boise, ID 83702
(208) 343-6436

A new deli, restaurant, specialty grocery store, and bakery in downtown Boise. Great selection of hot and cold dishes, local and imported wines (by the glass or from the grocery with $2 corkage). Open weekdays from 7 a.m. to 9 p.m., with brunch (and 2 p.m. closing time) on weekends.

NOODLES
PIZZA, PASTA & PIZAZZ
105 S. Sixth St
Boise, ID 83702
(208) 342-9399

1802 Franklin Blvd
Nampa, ID 83651
(208) 466-4400

The name says it all, except for the Idaho and other Northwest wines available. Large, fun establishments open daily 11:30 to midnight. No reservations.

OWYHEE PLAZA
1109 Main St
Boise, ID 83702
(208) 343-4611
(800) 223-4611 (toll-free)

Comfortable rooms in a Colonial - style brick motel complex. Pool.

Gamekeeper restaurant offers elk steaks.

RED LION INN RIVERSIDE
2900 Chinden Blvd
Boise, ID 83714
(208) 343-1871
(800) 547-8010 (toll-free)

Large, comfortable hotel on Boise's green-belt riverside. Weight room has sauna and Jacuzzi. Outdoor pool. Misty's restaurant serves Ste. Chapelle wines.

SANDBAR RIVER HOUSE
18 E. First
Marsing, ID 83639
(208) 896-4446

Steaks and seafood, prime rib on weekends; local wines. Open for lunch and dinner, except Monday evenings and Sundays in winter.

SOUPÇON
Leadville Ave
Ketchum, ID 83340
(208) 726-5034

Small, family-run establishment in a log cabin. Dinner only, with seatings at 6 and 8:30; reserve several weeks ahead. Inventive menu changes nightly. Open Labor Day to mid-October; Thanksgiving to mid-April. Not to be missed if you're in the area.

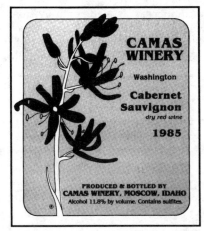

CAMAS WINERY
521 N. Moore Street
Moscow, ID 83843
(208) 882-0214

Owners: Stuart & Susan Scott
Winemaker: Stuart Scott
Year established: 1983
Production capacity: 3,000 gallons
Vineyards: None
Touring region: Northern Idaho

A bit of background. Stuart Scott, a gentle, scholarly man, lived for a time in Gilroy, California, where he planted a small vineyard and helped out at neighboring wineries as an unpaid apprentice. Professionally, he holds a master of arts degree in psychology, and works in Moscow as a federal probation officer.

The Camas lily, a wildflower native to the Palouse country of northern Idaho, once covered the terrain with a sea of blue flowers. (The Nez Perce Indians considered it a delicacy; members of the Lewis and Clark expedition ate it, too.) The rich soil of the Palouse has since been found ideal for cultivating wheat, peas, and lentils, and today the lily flourishes only in a few secret hollows.

Visiting the winery (NR). Because the winery is located in the basement of the Scott family home, in a residential neighborhood, zoning regulations forbid a tasting room. Scott has learned how to keep his costs down, buying good grapes at reasonable prices, reworking his cooperage, asking friends to help out with the crush and the bottling.

Production is stable at about 2,300 gallons. Stuart Scott says he intends to keep the winery at about that size "until I retire and expand."

Until then, Camas keeps going. "Finding our own special niche in the rapidly expanding world of wines and wineries is what has kept us in business since 1983," Sue Scott marvels.

Tasting the wine ★★. Have you ever tried—or thought of trying—a wine called Hog Heaven Red? Well, according to the label, early settlers in the Moscow area found their pigs going "hog wild" for the delicious taste of the wild blue camas bulbs. So the community got the nickname of Hog Heaven. The Camas Hog Heaven Red is a blend of Cabernet Sauvignon and Idaho cherry wine. In a blind tasting early this year, we enjoyed its bright nose, which resembled a young Pinot Noir; the surprise was that it tasted sweet! It might be good for people who want to start drinking red wine.

Its off-dry Hog Heaven White counterpart is made entirely from Gewurztraminer. Other varietal wines include Riesling, Chardonnay, Cabernet Sauvignon, and Sarah's Blush, named after the Scotts' fifth-grade daughter. We found both the Riesling and the Blush to have quite limited flavors.

Getting there. From Hwy 95 in Moscow, go east on D St, turn left on N. Moore.

Open by appointment.

Special events. None scheduled at the winery. The town of Moscow has several interesting events, however: a Mardi Gras parade at the end of February, a Renaissance Fair in early May, a theater festival sponsored by the University of Idaho throughout July, and an ice cream social at the McConnell Mansion at the end of July.

A book called *Daytripping in the Palouse* is recommended.

A word from the winery. "*Visitors to our winery leave feeling like one of the family. Since we are so small, we can accommodate comfortably six or so guests at once, so your tour will receive personal attention. You may even participate in, or observe, 'work in progress'! This is a unique opportunity to see a practical microbudget operation, where the money goes for quality grapes and you provide the ambiance!*

"*Discover our newest editions, a 100 per cent Gewurztraminer called Hog Heaven White, and our blush named Sarah's Blush under the theory that if you're shy about pronouncing or spelling it, you may never try it. We call it 'user friendly' labeling. If you're getting the impression that we'll only make wine as long as it's fun and the interaction with customers is enjoyable, you're on the right track! Please call first for an appointment so we don't miss out on your visit.*"

COVEY RISE

Symms Road
Route 4, Box 18835
Caldwell, ID 83605
(208) 336-2277

Owners: Steve & Leslie Robertson
Winemaker: Steve Robertson
Year established: 1985
Production capacity: 1,500 gallons
  (est)
Vineyards: 5 acres
Touring region: Boise [p. 352]

A bit of background. In the last half of 1988, several articles in the British press called attention to wines from Idaho. Not, as you might expect, Ste. Chapelle. (That was a couple of years ago; Ste. Chapelle is old news in London.) The new darlings are two wineries most Northwest wine fans haven't even heard of, Rose Creek and Covey Rise. Rose Creek is raising its profile at home as volume and quality increase. Covey Rise, on the other hand, is obscure to the point of phobia: they're so spooked by Covey Run, in the Yakima Valley, that they avoid virtually all marketing efforts and competitions lest the wine-buying public confuse the two Covey names. It helps, of course, that owners Steve and Leslie Robertson could sell every drop they make in England; the only domestic sales are at their seafood store, Mussels Fish Market in Boise.

Visiting the winery (NR). The vineyards, five acres out behind Ste. Chapelle's acreage, occupy one of the best sites in Idaho. The wines are made at Pintler's facility nearby because Robertson hasn't got a bond of his own.

Not open to the public.

Tasting the wines (NR). The British wine magazine *Decanter* staged a tasting of 85 of the world's best Chardonnays last year, and allowed the 1985 Covey Rise Chardonnay to be entered. That was Mark Savage's doing; he's a Master of Wine and a highly respected wine importer, and he'd discovered Covey Rise on one of his periodic trips to the Northwest.

Would you believe third place? "A shade too forward, but otherwise the fruit shows well, with a correct acid finish," went one commentary; another said, "Quite rich and open aroma and nice tight oaky flavour, flesh and finesse."

The London Sunday *Times* ran an article picking the top 20 "New World" wines, and Covey Rise's Chardonnay was in the group again. (So was Rose Creek's Cabernet and The Eyrie Vineyards' Pinot Noir.) Then the London Sunday *Express* did "Ten Newcomers." Guess which wines were picked.

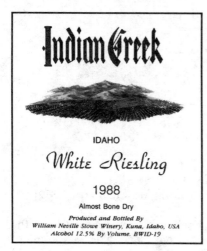

IDAHO

White Riesling

1988

Almost Bone Dry

Produced and Bottled By
William Neville Stowe Winery, Kuna, Idaho, USA
Alcohol 12.5% By Volume. BWID-19

INDIAN CREEK

(William Neville Stowe Winery)
Route 1, 1000 N. McDermott Road
Kuna, ID 83634
(208) 922-4791

Owners: William Stowe, Mike Stowe
 Rich Ostrogorsky, Bob Chapman
Winemaker: Bill Stowe
Year established: 1987
Production capacity: 12,500 gallons
Vineyards: 15 acres
Touring region: Boise [p. 352]

A bit of background. Bill Stowe spent 22 years in the U.S. Air Force, traveling the world, observing people closely. A zoologist with an M.B.A. degree, with duties as a military personnel officer, Stowe was particularly impressed by the Germans, who enjoyed both mental and physical challenges, who became increasingly satisfied by their work as they grew older. "Age was a positive factor," he concluded.

During the last three years of his service, he was chief of an alcohol and drug program on his own time, he took up farming. He'd been an enthusiastic home winemaker for a decade, and when he retired five years ago, he promptly won Idaho's Home Winemaker of the Year award.

Is it any surprise, then, that Bill Stowe would start a winery?

He found a willing supporter in his brother, Mike, and financial backing from two local businessmen. Mike is the co-winemaker by long distance; he lives in Davis, California, but visits Idaho regularly and has made wines with his brother for years. He has spent 25 years as a science teacher in the Davis school system. (He's also taken all the courses offered by the enology and viticulture department at the nearby University of California campus.) Says Mike: "I spend most of my winemaker duties hustling the California market and birddogging ideas that pertain to materiel procurement. Bill and I are on the phone constantly, as the phone company can attest."

Still, it's hard work: nothing like waking yourself up for filtering on a cold winter's day with six inches of snow on the ground, Bill says.

Visiting the winery (NR). The real Indian Creek runs through Kuna, but that's about all there is to see. Half the winery's production in 1987 was the custom-crush for Desert Sun (Pintler), an undertaking Stowe says was "too much for my physical capabilities and intentions." A tasting room where Stowe and his partners can welcome visitors (in compliance with local zoning laws) was scheduled to open in May 1989.

Two tourist attractions suggested by Bill Stowe that we'll pass along: the national "Birds of Prey" area near the Snake River, 20 minutes south of Meridian; and Givins Hot Springs, with a pool, hot baths, campground, and picnic area, 20 minutes south of the winery.

Tasting the wines ★★☆. Although Bill Stowe won a prize for his first Semillon (see details in the profile for Pintler), the wine we liked best of his initial releases was the White Pinot Noir. Very pretty with just a blush of pink, it blossomed with a bouquet of spicy tropical fruit. In the mouth, it tingled the tongue with slight spritziness and tasted of passionfruit. The Riesling was flabby and hollow, without discernable Riesling character, but an early sample of the 1987 Pinot Noir (from Kuna Butte Vineyards) was young, cherry-like, and straightforward. Also released: a Chardonnay and a late harvest Chenin Blanc. Stowe seems to be on the right track.

Getting there. Take Exit 64 (Meridian) from I-84; it's halfway between Boise and Nampa. Go 7 mi south on Meridian Rd, then 5 mi west on Kuna Rd. Turn north on McDermott, go 0.5 mi to the winery

Open from 11 to 6 on Friday, Saturday, and Sunday; other times by appointment.

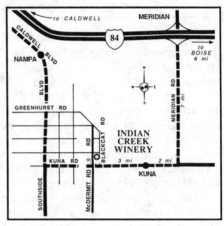

A word from the winery. *"We're situated midway between the mountains of the Boise front and the Owyhees on ground high enough to present a beautiful view. We also offer fine Idaho wine at the best price, and a tour of our small facility. At present, we are not zoned for tasting, but have plans for 1989, by summer. Weekend tasting, small picnic area, perhaps a small aviary. Don't forget to visit us."*

WHITE
RIESLING

1987

PINTLER WINERY

13750 Surrey Lane
Nampa, ID 83686
(208) 467-1200

Owners: Charles & Carol Pintler,
  Brad & Stacy Pintler
Winemaker: Brad Pintler
Year established: 1988
Production capacity: 11,000 gallons
Vineyards: 11 acres
Touring region: Boise [p. 352]

A bit of background. The time is 1987, the place, a farm southwest of Nampa operated by the Pintler family. The crop: Semillon grapes. The problem: their buyer refuses to take delivery. It's either eat lots of grapes or . . . ? The solution: take them over to Bill Stowe's place down the road, quick, and see if Bill will make them into wine. He says yes (whew!). The Pintlers and Stowe agree to split the wine; Stowe bottles his share as Indian Creek, the Pintlers go with the name Desert Sun.

Entered in competitions last summer, the identical wines won different prizes (Indian Creek a silver, Desert Sun a bronze)! Did the Pintlers decide that the Desert Sun name was bad luck? They bonded their own place this year as Pintler Winery.

Visiting the winery (NR). There's a real winery at Pintler Vineyard now, an impressive, two-story structure with a panoramic view over the 1,600-acre farm, the desert, and the black basalt canyons of the Snake River.

The Pintlers plan to add another five acres to the vineyard by 1989.

Tasting the wines (NR). Pintler used his own facility in 1988 to crush Semillon, Chardonnay, Chenin Blanc, and Riesling, plus small amounts of Pinot Noir, and Cabernet Sauvignon; 90 percent of the wine was from his own grapes

We didn't take notes on our first tastings of the early releases (under the Desert Sun label) at a crowded gathering in eastern Washington last summer.

Getting there. Take Exit 35 from I-84 and go south through Nampa. Proceed south 6 mi on 12th Ave S. Turn right onto Missouri Ave, go 4 mi, turn left on Sky Ranch Rd for 1.5 mi, then right onto Surrey Ln. The entrance to Pintler Winery is 0.7 mi ahead. Signs confirm the way from 12th.

Open from 11 to 5, Tuesday through Sunday.

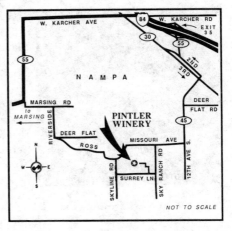

A word from the winery. *"Pintler Winery is located south of Nampa on the rim of Hidden Valley, overlooking the Pintler Vineyard with the Owyhee Mountains in the background.*

"Come on out, meet our family, and enjoy a glass of wine on the winery deck."

PUCCI WINERY

1055 Garfield Bay Road
Sandpoint, ID 83864
(208) 263-5807

Owner & winemaker:
  Eugene C. (Skip) Pucci
Year established: 1982
Production capacity: 6,000 gallons
Vineyards: None
Touring region:
  Northern Idaho [p. 353]

A bit of background. Skip Pucci, who works as a construction superintendent in Spokane and commutes to his home in the Bonner County mountains of Idaho, used to claim he'd seen only one vineyard in his life and had never visited a winery other than his own. His winemaking background comes instead from six generations of family tradition. The presses he uses are replicas of the hand-operated oak crushers used by his grandparents.

What's unusual about Pucci wines is that every wine is pressed, fermented, and aged in oak, even the Rieslings. The results are distinctive, to say the least.

Visiting the winery ★★. The Pucci family homestead is perched on Gold Mountain, high in the hills outside of Sandpoint, on a 10-acre site overlooking the Bitteroot, Cabinet, and Selkirk mountain ranges. You can look up the Clark Fork River into Montana, or down into Lake Pend Oreille, the second-deepest, second-largest natural lake west of the Mississippi. Nancy Pucci welcomes visitors to the winery; six picnic tables, a barbecue, and a horseshoe pit are available.

Tasting the wine ★☆. Pucci did not make wine in 1988. Left over from 1987 are Cabernet Sauvignon, Chardonnay, Chenin Blanc, and Riesling.

Getting there. From Sandpoint, go south 5.2 mi on Hwy 95 to the town of Sagle. Turn onto Garfield Bay Rd and continue east for 6.3 mi.

Open from May to September; hours not set at press time.

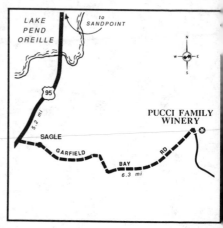

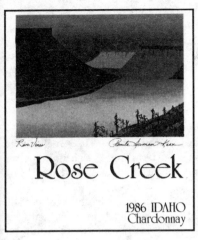

Rose Creek

1986 IDAHO
Chardonnay

ROSE CREEK VINEYARDS

(Valley Vintners, Inc.)
111 W. Hagerman Avenue
P.O. Box 356
Hagerman, ID 83332
(208) 837-4413

Owners: Jamie & Susan Lyn Martin
Winemaker: Jamie Martin
Year established: 1984
Production capacity: 6,000 gallons
Vineyards: 35 acres
Touring region: Boise [p. 352]

A bit of background. The Chamber of Commerce calls this part of Idaho "Magicland." And what magic it is! The Snake River carves a lazy path through this rich agricultural and sportsman's paradise. A. B. Guthrie, in his Pulitzer Prize-winning book *The Way West,* describes one fishing stream near Hagerman: "Ah, Salmon Falls Creek, where the Indians live in swallow-type birdhouses and the area literally reeked of rotting salmon." Nearby, at the southern end of the Hagerman Valley, just outside the town of Buhl, you'll come upon a stone formation that looks like a monstrous cobra ready to strike. It's a geological wonder, a 50-foot rock (as tall as a five-story building) precariously balancing on a pedestal no larger than a coffee table.

We always ask winemakers what triggered their interest in wine. It's usually family traditions or exposure to wine during travel overseas. But Jamie and Susan Martin first became involved with wine when they were given a wine shower before their wedding.

Jamie grew up on a farm in Idaho, where his family raised potatoes and wheat. Once bitten by wine, though, he turned his attention to viticulture. He began working for Ste. Chapelle, then for Weston. He developed vineyards for other growers, he traveled, he took winemaking courses at the Davis campus of the University of California. He began planting his 35-acre vineyard with Chardonnay and Riesling in 1980. Today, in addition to his own vineyard and winery activities, he works in landscape design.

Visiting the winery ★★★. Rose Creek Winery occupies a 100-year-old building of lava rock; it's a nice, shady spot, with wild roses growing around the winery. There's even a hitching post if you happen to arrive on horseback.

What's a winery doing way out here, anyway? Well, for a start, there's a lot of tourist traffic in these parts. The Hagerman Valley is famous for its scenic springs and hot-water baths. It attracts fishermen year-round, and summer tourists for its ripe fruit, especially melons. No surprise, then, that the Martins used to sell 80 percent of their production right at the winery, though that's changing as production increases and the winery's reputation spreads.

Tasting the wine ★★★. With his own grapes Martin has made Riesling, Chardonnay, and Cabernet Sauvignon. His Pinot Noir comes from Oregon fruit.

The 1985 Cabernet, made with grapes from Mercer Ranch in Washington, has stirred waves in England. The London Sunday *Times* included it in a list of 20 top wines from the New World, calling it "a stunning wine in a rich Bordeaux style." The London Sunday *Express* cited it among 10 "best newcomers."

We found it had a deep and lively nose of cedar, spice, and coffee, but (in March 1989) it was overwhelmed with oak (and puckery, feathery tannins) in the mouth; the color and bouquet suggested there would be more to taste. It has the potential to develop for many years to come.

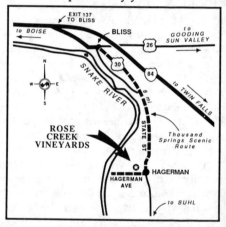

Getting there. Take Exit 137 (Bliss) from I-84 and go south on Hwy 30 to Hagerman. The winery is at the south end of town on State St, along the Thousand Springs Scenic Route, in the basement of the Idaho State Bank.

There's also a tasting room in downtown Boise in the Capital Plaza Terrace.

Open from 11:30 to 5:30 or by appointment.

A word from the winery. "*Our winery is located in a 101-year-old lav rock cellar in the small town of Hagerman. Our vineyards grow at the base steep, black basalt cliffs warmed by the sun that protect the vines during our c summer nights.*

"*The Snake River flowing through our valley gives us mild winter temper tures and endless summer fun. Boating, hot springs, marshes full of blue heror and wonderful trout fishing are some of Hagerman's offerings. Come visit o tasting room. We'll be your guides to the wines and sights of Idaho.*"

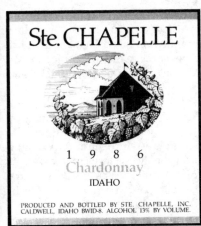

STE. CHAPELLE
Route 4, Box 775
Caldwell, ID 83605
(208) 459-7222

Owners: Symms family
Winemaker: Mimi Mook
General manager:
    Kathy Symms Mertz
Year established: 1976
Production capacity: 360,000 gallons
Vineyards: 180 acres
Touring region: Boise [p. 352]

A bit of background. The name of this place, an hour's drive west of Boise, is Sunny Slope; it's the warmest and most fertile micro-climate in the Treasure Valley, along the Snake River. Row crops and orchards spread across the valley floor and gently sloping uplands; so do hundreds of acres of premium wine grapes, grown at the highest elevations (between 2,500 and 3,000 feet) in the Northwest.

The winery was founded in 1976 by Bill and Penny Broich, and purchased by Symms Fruit Ranch two years later. The Symms family has been in the orchard business on Sunny Slope since the turn of the century; they had added vineyards in the early '70s. (One of the clan, Steve Symms, currently serves in the U.S. Senate.) Within a short time, the vineyard covered 200 acres of Sunny Slope's prime land, and construction of a winery was the logical next step.

Broich stayed on until 1985, when an investigation by the Bureau of Alcohol, Tobacco, and Firearms determined that he had been at the center of a bizarre "grape-laundering" operation, disguising the origins of purchased grapes and bulk wines in violation of federal regulations. Although Broich had since left the winery, and no financial motive could be determined, Ste. Chapelle paid a fine to settle the charges. The story is so byzantine that it would be an improbable plot even on *Falcon Crest.*

The current enologist is Mimi Mook, a friendly young woman from California's J. Lohr Winery, where she had been assistant winemaker.

Ste. Chapelle is the second-largest winery in the Northwest. The winery was originally designed to produce abut 25,000 gallons of wine a year; its sudden spurt of growth, well past the quarter-million-gallon mark, is the very conscious decision of the owners that the winery had reached a critical stage in its development. It would have to grow, to get a *lot* bigger, in order to prosper. Fortunately, the Symms family could manage the capital costs of such an expansion. Fortunately, too, Ste. Chapelle recognized what still seems so difficult for Northwest wineries:

that expert wine*making* is only the first half of a successful winery; more than anything, it needs expert wine *selling,* too. To sell Ste. Chapelle's wines, therefore, a totally separate organization called Chapelle USA has been formed, headed by experienced beverage marketing professionals. Chapelle USA already markets Ste. Chapelle wines in over 30 states and does a limited amount of exporting.

Visiting the winery ★★★☆. Inside the Palais de Justice in Paris is a small Gothic chapel, the La Sainte-Chapelle, built in the 13th century by King Louis IX to honor God and to house the relics of the Crusades. Its minutely detailed stained-glass windows glow with deep and vivid light. This marvel of art was the inspiration for the winery's name and its building. And though the purpose of the winery is clearly secular, the drive here from the freeway, across the valley and through the vineyards, is soul-satisfyng.

Manicured lawns and tall cottonwoods show off the winery's cream-colored exterior. Inside, the tasting room looks out over a patchwork of crops and vineyards to the distant Owyhee Mountains across the Oregon border. Through the pointed arches of the windows in the upstairs gallery, you can see the Snake River.

Tasting the wine ★★★. Ste. Chapelle wines have come up a dozen times in our tastings for this book. Our most enthusiastic notes concern the 1983 Cabernet Sauvignon, which was very aromatic, with a vegetal (peppers, mint, dill) rather than a berry bouquet and pleasing, balanced flavors.

We had no trouble telling which grapes the two blush wines were made from (Pinot Noir and Cabernet) even with their rather sweet finish, but we found the 1987 Gewurztraminer lacking in varietal character. The off-dry Riesling, on the other hand, had a true Riesling nose of apricots and honey.

The "regular" 1986 Chardonnay had the beguiling bouquet we've come to expect from Ste. Chapelle: light and delicate sea-coast and crab smells (suggesting a restrained use of oak), with a background of fruit (crisp apples). The flavors might be a bit deeper, but it's a fine wine nonetheless. The 1986 Reserve, from the Symms Family Vineyard, had a bouquet of oak and pears, and rather bland flavors; it didn't live up to the promise of a reserve bottling.

The sparkling wines produced by Ste. Chapelle are excellent values. The Sparkling Riesling is made entirely from Idaho-grown grapes and fermented by the bulk (Charmat) method, which is faster and much less expensive than the traditional methode champenoise.. It does require a large capital outlay for the equipment, however. But the Symms family believed that there was a big market for "affordable" sparkling wines, and that quality would be high if the grapes came from superior vineyards. The result was a slightly sweet, German-style *Sekt,* selling for under $7, but packaged to look three times as expensive. The Charmat-process Chardonnay sells for about $9, and a Blanc de Noir for about $8.

Getting there. Take Exit 35 (Hwy 55, Marsing) from I-84 and follow Hwy 55 west, then south for 11 mi. Turn left on Lowell Rd; drive through the orchards to reach the winery.

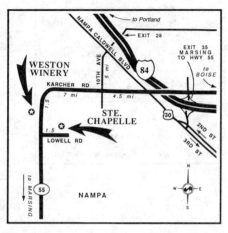

Open Monday through Saturday from 10 to 6. (In winter, the tasting room closes at 5.) Sunday from noon to 5.

There's also a tasting room in the Eighth Street Market Place in downtown Boise (phone 344-9074). Tour groups are welcome; no fees are charged at either location.

Special events. Ste. Chapelle sponsors monthly jazz concerts in the park below the winery on Sunday afternoons in summer. Occasional "celebrity" concerts as well; check with the winery for a schedule.

A word from the winery. *"Our goal at Ste. Chapelle is to emphasize the outstanding and unique fruit quality of our wines. While we treasure all of our awards, our first consideration in winemaking is a wine that is a delight to experience, for the novice as well as the experienced wine drinker.*

"We have free wine tastings at both our tasting rooms and free tours at the winery itself. The tasting rooms also have a selection of other Idaho gift products and a great many additional wine-related gift items. Our panoramic view is a never-ending pleasure to our staff, and, we hope, to you. But what we love most are the visitors!"

A lightly carbonated, hard apple cider made from 100% fresh squeezed apples. Best when served chilled.

Produced and Bottled By
THE SELKIRK CIDER COMPANY • BONNERS FERRY, IDAHO

SEVEN SISTERS
(Selkirk Cider Co.)
Highway 95 N.
at County Road 30A
Bonners Ferry, ID 83805

P.O. Box 2126
Sandpoint, ID 83864
(208) 267-7111

Owners: Kevin & Lisa Settles
Winemaker: Kevin Settles
Year established: 1987
Production capacity: 2,000 gallons
Vineyards: None
Touring region:
   Northern Idaho [p. 353]

A bit of background. Kevin Settles is not your ordinary ski bum. He did spend seven years as a full-time ski instructor, taking odd jobs in the off-season, waiting for the snows to return. But he attended Wenatchee Community College and got a degree in ski resort management. And he spent five summers working in various aspects of the apple business.

He'd always known about good wine, but not about hard (alcoholic) cider. Then he and his wife, Lisa, visited France, where Kevin's uncle introduced them to the great restaurants of Paris, the Bordeaux wine country, and the orchards of Normandy (home of Calvados, the most exquisite apple brandy) and Brittany (home of great ciders). "It really opened my eyes," Kevin reports. "I realized that this was something lacking in the U.S." He returned home determined to rectify matters.

Visiting the winery (NR). The tiny winery is located on property owned by the Kootenai Valley Juice Company, which furnishes the fresh apple juice. Visitors can come on Sundays to see the apples pressed. Kevin is planning an arrangement with the processor to set up a fruit and cider stand on the highway to take advantage of the tourist traffic.

Tasting the wines (NR). Settles uses a blend of apples (some sweet, some tart) to produce a well-balanced juice. In his first year, he used apples from Yakima and Wenatchee, and was hoping to use fruit grown closer to Spokane as well. People think cider is sweet, like apple juice, and they're surprised at the tartness of Seven Sisters (which we haven't tasted).

"I'm always fighting people's misconceptions because of what I call the TreeTop syndrome," Kevin says.

Getting there. From Sandpoint, go north 30 mi on Hwy 95 to Bonners Ferry, then 2 mi further to the intersection of Hwy 95 and County Rd 30A. The winery is on the left.

Open by appointment.

Special events. Sandpoint itself offers year-round attractions, including self-guided art tours, winter skiing and summer chair lift rides at nearby Schweitzer Mountain, a Waterfest in May, and a highly regarded music festival in July and August.

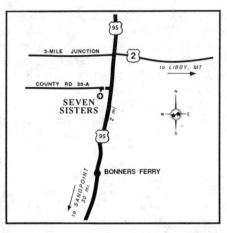

For details on tourism in this region, contact the Sandpoint Chamber of Commerce at P.O. Box 928, Sandpoint, ID 83864.

A word from the winery. *"Seven Sisters Hard Ciders are made from 100 percent fresh pressed apple juice. Using a blend of apples we can achieve an old-fashioned apple juice taste that sets us apart from all the other apple products. Great wines are not made from concentrate, and neither are great ciders. Give us a try. We think you'll be pleasantly surprised. There is nothing else like it!"*

Weston

"THE RIVER RUNNER"
1986
IDAHO
JOHANNISBERG RIESLING

WESTON WINERY
On Highway 55
Route 10, Box 257
Caldwell, ID 83605
(208) 454-1682

Owner & winemaker:
  Cheyne Weston
Year established: 1982
Production capacity: 10,000 gallons
Vineyards: 15 acres
Touring region: Boise [p. 352]

A bit of background. Cheyne Weston gave up a career as a documentary filmmaker (and good money, in season, as a river guide) to become a winemaker and settle down with his family. And he's still having fun.

Looking at us with sparkling blue eyes, he asks, "Do you know how to open a wine bottle without an opener? Follow me." We leave the little tasting room, crowded with tanks and barrels, and go out to the garden behind the winery. "You take the bottle firmly by the neck like this, you see," says Cheyne, "and thwomp its bottom solidly against a tree like *this* three or four times." Thwomp, thwomp, *thwomp!* The cork flies out, spraying Cheyne's woolly brown beard with Cabernet Blanc. "On the middle fork of the Salmon, you learn to make do." It's a demonstration Cheyne has done before; the tree has lots of thwomp marks.

Cheyne learned about winemaking as an apprentice at the old Charles Coury Winery in Oregon and as a sales manager for Sebastiani. He also worked during crush at Ste. Chapelle, just a mile down the road. Now he has vineyards of his own a few miles away, on a mesa above the valley floor. At 2,750 feet, they're among the highest in the Northwest.

Visiting the winery ★★☆. There's a monolithic black rock outside of Marsing (a community on the Snake River, not far from the Weston Winery) that looks like a giant reptile basking in the sun. It's known locally as Lizard Rock, and with a bit of creative perspective you can imagine it standing guard over the winery. The building is a straightforward, utilitarian structure, right on Highway 55. Cheyne's folksy welcome is genuine, and his pitch about "high-country winemaking" hits just the right note for many of his visitors. Picnic tables adjoin the winery and its garden.

Tasting the wine (NR). Riesling, Chardonnay, Gewurztraminer, and Pinot Noir, all from Idaho grapes, plus a Cabernet and some methode champenoise sparkling wine. There used to be an interesting wine called Syringa (named for the Idaho state flower), made entirely from Semillon. We haven't tasted Weston's offerings lately.

Cheyne Weston bottles his best wine every year as a "Salute to Idaho" with an original painting for the label. The labels feature a variety of Idaho scenes and sports, including hunting, fishing, river rafting, hang gliding, and native animals; they're the work of Cheyne's younger brother Jeff.

Getting there. From I-84 between Nampa and Caldwell, take Exit 35 and travel 13 mi south on Hwy 55. [Map: Ste. Chapelle]

Open Tuesday through Saturday from 11 to 5, Sunday from 1 to 5; closed Monday. No charge for tour groups.

Special events. In May, in conjunction with Marsing's "Flower of the Desert" celebration, Weston hosts the Idaho Home Winemakers Festival. Vineyard "dutch oven cookouts" are possible in summer months; contact the winery to make arrangements.

A word from the winery. *"A unique combination of climate, soil, and geographical position provides the foundation for Weston winemaking. Weston wines are Idaho's benchmark of quality and are regionally recognized for their affordable high-quality varietal flavor. Family owned, assisted by general manager Larry DeCoux, Weston wines are continually expanding and refining their vineyard and winery operations."*

REFLECTIONS ON THE PLEASURES OF WINE

An otherwise normal friend, more prone to exaggeration than to excesses of the flesh, argues that we grow up deprived in this country. Deprived not of food or shelter, not of formal book learning or health care or opportunity for advancement, but deprived of a sensual education. All too many of us, this friend contends, spend our days in a sensory prison, unable to appreciate the sensual pleasures of life.

It's not a question of carnality, you understand, but of training. From the beginning of school, teachers put us through the paces of mental and physical excercise. We learn how to read, how to spell, how to add, subtract, multiply. We race against flash cards. We memorize dates, do calisthenics, run laps. Education self-righteously focuses on our minds (and muscles) yet all but ignores our senses. Who teaches us how to smell, how to taste, how to see?

Schools to relegate sound and sight to the realm of artists. Musicians for the ear, painters and sculptors for the eye. The study of smell and taste is turned over to the processed food industry, to chemical engineers at Coca-Cola and Campbell Soup.

Why should this be? The average person takes 1.5 million breaths a year. Surely that's enough opportunity to distinguish how things smell. What's the smell of a newly mown lawn? Of a juniper bush? A tulip? A wet dog?

We eat a thousand meals a year, drink uncounted beverages. Can you smell the chlorine in the tap water? Does the coffee taste bitter? Do you add lemon or milk to your tea? Why aren't you paying attention?

The opportunities for smelling and tasting are all around us, but we must concentrate our mental faculties on what's going on in our nose and mouth. We can do that by tasting wine.

When we "taste" wine (smell it and taste it, that is), we have a unique opportunity to focus our sensory faculties. We enjoy wine not necessarily for its mild alcoholic content (indeed, professional wine tasters don't drink the wine at all; they invariably spit); what we appreciate is the interplay of the aromas, the complexities of its tastes. And when we taste wine with food, we add another dimension or two, because wine changes with food, improves it, enhances it.

So when people say they don't know anything about wine, beware! What they're really saying is that they haven't been paying attention, haven't been concentrating.

Wine talks, you know: it speaks the language of the senses. We have to learn to translate.

Oh yes, wine talks. It whispers the soft, seductive sounds of distant landscapes, of adventure and romance, of deep mysteries. It sings of far-off pleasures; it appeals to the vagabond in our soul.

We first heard the call as we drove down a French country road. *Dégustation Gratuite de Vin à 100 mètres* the sign read: Free Wine Tasting Ahead! The farmer steered his tractor toward the stone building to greet us, the wife emerged from a kitchen, holding a key. Inside the cool, dark cellar, the unforgettable smell of a winery: musty, fruity, with overtones of wooden barrels and of the earth itself.

In small towns all over France, that first year, the *dégustation* signs would draw us in, down quiet side streets, into corners of crowded groceries, alongside busy highways.

That was twenty years ago. We still visit wineries. Locally, regionally, overseas. We taste magnificent wines and indifferent bottles with the same curiosity (though we prefer drinking the better ones), and we haven't tired yet of tasting. We constantly find new smells, new tastes, new roads to travel.

The student of wine remains humble. No other subject expands so rapidly as you come to know it. Wine has its roots in agriculture; indeed the precise location of its viticultural origin is paramount. But the grapes are conditioned by weather—an unpredictable natural phenomenon—and only then transformed by human and industrial endeavor (and patience) into a beverage of strange excitement. No two bottles of wine are alike; even the most consistent wine changes minutely from day to day, let alone year to year.

Is it any wonder, then, that friends of wine from neophytes to connoisseurs should seek out the *source* of their pleasure? That wine country everywhere in the world attracts enthusiastic tourists? That winemakers stand ready to reward visitors with a glass offered in friendship?

Wine infuses its students with a fervor like that of pilgrims flocking to view an icon. And in the Northwest, with over 150 licensed and bonded wineries, there's no shortage of cathedrals for the faithful, or even the curious. But beware of the temptation to turn wine into a religion, with its own arcane tongue and a priesthood of snobbish sommeliers. Left alone, wine speaks the most democratic language imaginable.

What's wine *doing* in the Northwest? Why is there wine country *here*, exactly? Climate! A long, mild growing season (April to October). Warm days, cool nights, especially at the end of the growing season when the drop in temperature from daytime high to nighttime low keeps the grapes' essential acid levels high. The climate in turn is due to an accident of geography: The Northwest's wine country sits at precisely the right band of latitude (between 45 and 47 degrees). We get more sunlight here during the growing season than California does; some two hours a day more. And it's sunlight more than sunshine that makes plants grow. You don't need, don't *want* California's heat to grow great grapes.

Listen to the wines of the Northwest. Listen above all to Washington state's Cabernet Sauvignon! Its lusty voice will turn your head; its allure will reach out of the glass, draw you nigh, and make you swoon. At their best, these wines play a Beethoven symphony with your sense of smell. And keep your ears open for the clear bell notes of Washington's Late Harvest Rieslings, too.

Listen to Oregon's wine, to its Pinot Noir above all. A wine maddening ly difficulty to make well, but of great finesse and exquisite delicacy when climate and the winemaker's skill intersect, Pinot Noir seduces and conquers men and women from humble and exalted backgrounds alike. (A "below-the-neck-wine," says Jancis Robinson, the famous English wine writer.) If Washington's wines sound big, bold notes, Oregon's play chamber music. (You don't have to choose one for all time; a civilized person should enjoy both.) How will you know if it's love? The wine will tell you. "I don't deserve to stay forever in a musty cellar," it will whisper, and you'll know the moment won't come again. "Drink me! With this dish, tonight, in this company! *Now!*"

The pleasures of wine touring don't require long journeys; virtually every spot in Washington and Oregon is within an hour's driving distance of a winery. Scenic beauty, agricultural bounty, museums, history, and local festivals offer added attractions. You get off the freeways and smell the earth, you find that winemaking draws individuals from careers as diverse as law, medicine, engineering, and farming. We've always found that meeting the *people* was the most satisfying part of visiting wine country.

We do have a few practical suggestions to help newcomers get the most out of a tour, however brief.

• First, we recommend that you read up before setting out. The visit will be more interesting if you know something about the winery.

• Limit your visits. Two wineries in an afternoon is plenty. Racing from one to the next, trying to "do" or "hit" as many as possible is silly (and dangerous).

• If personal contact with the owner or winemaker is important, be sure to call ahead for an appointment. Otherwise you'll end up with a tasting room staffer and the luck of the draw; some are terrific, many are badly trained and don't care if you come or go.

• Try a bottle or two of the wines before you visit so you know the winery's style. No point (other than masochism) in visiting Big Foot Vineyards if your taste runs to Chateau Dainty.

• Wear a sturdy pair of shoes and a warm jacket. It gets cold inside wineries, and it's hard to be polite, let alone concentrate on what you're tasting, if you're worried about getting mud on your pumps or shivering in cold cellars.

• It's a compliment to the winemaker if you buy a bottle or two, but it's not required. If you don't like the wines enough to buy them, get a T-shirt or souvenir glass. Remember that wineries charge regular retail for their wines to cover tasting room overhead.

• When you're tasting wine, concentrate! Take notes, even. Think about the way the wine looks and smells, how it tastes, how you feel about it after you've swallowed (or spit out!) a mouthful.

In Oregon some wineries now charge a tasting fee of a dollar or so, sometimes refundable if you buy a bottle. That's if you arrive in a group, not a Buick. They say it covers the cost of running the tasting room and keeps away the non-serious wine-tasters. It seems to us those are the very folks you'd *want* in the tasting room, the innocent, potentially life-long customers. But more and more wineries are talking about charging, and you can't fight city hall; it's their winery, after all.

The do-gooders complain that wine touring is nothing more than an excuse to barrel down the road from one free sample of booze to the next. Winery owners have responded by limiting the number and size of tastes, a potential setback to serious wine tourists, who swirl, sniff, and *spit* their tastes. Tasting and drinking are two different things, after all. Still, only an idiot would imbibe and drive. Alternatives exist: formal wine tours like those we organize, or taking along a designated driver.

When to travel? There's no perfect season in the Northwest, so go anytime. There's beauty even during a downpour, and most of the wineries stay open year-round. You might see more during crush (that's wine talk for "harvest"), but the winemaking staff will be too busy to show you around; you'll have to make do with tasting room staff. Wines are bottled off and on throughout the year, with new releases coming out beginning in spring. Summer weekends get crowded, especially in Oregon, and some of the "festivals" are nothing short of madness. So go when you can, and enjoy yourself.

Which wineries? Follow our ratings or follow your hunches. All the wineries have something unique to offer: a road, a vineyard, a building; distinctive owners, perhaps, or unusual wines.

Just *go*. And *listen* to the wine.

YOUR TURN

We've told you what *we* think, what *we've* seen and tasted. What about you? Did you find wonderful wines, delightful restaurants, spectacular views? Were you disappointed or enchanted by one of our recommendations? We'd like to hear from you!

Please use this page to send your comments to Holden Pacific, 814-35th Avenue, Seattle, WA 98122. Telephone & fax (206) 325-4324. Cheers!

WINERY:

WINE(S):

MEALS:

LODGING:

ABOUT THE AUTHORS

Ronald Holden was born in Portland, Oregon, attended schools in Switzerland, and graduated from Yale University. He worked as a television reporter and news manager for King Broadcasting in Portland and Seattle, and for Westinghouse Broadcasting in Baltimore; as a public affairs manager for Weyerhaeuser Company; and as executive editor of *Seattle Weekly* before starting Holden Pacific in 1981. He contributes regularly to a variety of regional publications.

Fluent in French and German, he is a founding board member of the French-American Chamber of Commerce in Seattle, a founder of the Washington Wine Writers, and former director of Les Amis du Vin (Friends of Wine) in Seattle. He also originated the "Washington Wine of the Year" award.

Glenda Holden, a native of Australia and graduate of the University of Queensland, is a 20-year resident of the Northwest. She had a private practice as a physical therapist in Australia and served for several years on the staff of Group Health Hospital in Seattle; she now practices on a free-lance basis.

Glenda conducts much of the field research for Holden Pacific, especially for the Australia tours, and administers the wine-tasting programs for *Northwest Wine Country.* She is widely recognized for her "taste memory" as well as her ability to translate complex wine terminology into layman's terms. She served two terms as a director of the Enological Society of the Northwest (Seattle chapter), chairing a variety of educational programs.

The Holdens lived in a French village in the mid-1970s and have returned to France regularly ever since. They are the parents of three children and make their home in Seattle.

In 1985, Ronald and Glenda Holden received the Commander's Award from the Brotherhood of the Knights of the Vine for their contributions to the Oregon wine industry.

The Holdens have been designing and leading wine tours to destinations in the Pacific Northwest since 1981, to France since 1986, and Australia since 1988.

HOLDEN PACIFIC, Inc. was founded in 1981. Activities include publishing wine country guidebooks; educational programs for individuals and trade groups in the wine and hospitality industry; and the design, management, and marketing of wine tours.

MAILING LIST

We invite you to join Holden Pacific's mailing list. Please send in the **top coupon** on the next page to register your name. You'll receive a *free* quarterly newsletter from Ronald and Glenda Holden.

The other coupons on the next page entitle registered purchasers of this book to discounts on our tours. The *original* coupon should be presented when making a tour reservation.

Nick Gunderson photos